D1712913

GTON & LEE UNIVERSITY
LIBRARY
SEP 2 4 1986
GOVERNMENT
DEPOSITORY
#632
KINGTON, VA. 24450

CIVIL WAR MANUSCRIPTS

CIVIL WAR MANUSCRIPTS

A Guide to Collections
in the
Manuscript Division of the Library of Congress

Compiled by John R. Sellers

LIBRARY OF CONGRESS
WASHINGTON 1986

Rare
E
468
.L5
1986

Cover: Ulysses S. Grant

Title page: Benjamin F. Butler, Montgomery C. Meigs, Joseph Hooker, and David D. Porter

(Ref. Dept. M-FILM)
E
468
.L5
P4

Library of Congress Cataloging in Publication Data

Library of Congress. Manuscript Division.
  Civil War manuscripts.

  Includes index.
  Supt. of Docs. no.: LC 42:C49
    1. United States—History—Civil War, 1861-1865—
Manuscripts—Catalogs. 2. United States—History—
Civil War, 1861-1865—Sources—Bibliography—Catalogs.
3. Library of Congress. Manuscript Division—Catalogs.
I. Sellers, John R. II. Title.
Z1242.L48 1986 [E468]   016.9737   81-607105
ISBN 0-8444-0381-4

The portraits in this guide were reproduced from a photograph album in the James Wadsworth family papers, Manuscript Division, Library of Congress. The album contains nearly 200 original photographs (numbered sequentially at the top), most of which were autographed by their subjects. The photographs were collected by John Hay, an author and statesman who was Lincoln's private secretary from 1860 to 1865.

For sale by the Superintendent of Documents, U.S. Government Printing Office, Washington, D.C. 20402.

PREFACE

To Abraham Lincoln, the Civil War was essentially a people's contest over the maintenance of a government dedicated to the elevation of man and the right of every citizen to an unfettered start in the race of life. President Lincoln believed that most Americans understood this, for he liked to boast that while large numbers of Army and Navy officers had resigned their commissions to take up arms against the government, not one common soldier or sailor was known to have deserted his post to fight for the Confederacy. Unfortunately, secessionist leaders also believed that their cause was just, if not God ordained. Confederate apologists argued that in seceding from the Union the Southern States had only exercised their constitutional right to withdraw from a voluntary combination of states after the authorized government of those states demonstrated it was bent on a course destined to disrupt the South's established institutions. Any attempt to coerce the newly independent states back into the Union was both an act of aggression and a violation of individual liberty. This ideological impasse resulted in the bloodiest war ever fought by the American people.

Nowhere is the story of the Civil War better told than in the papers and records of the participants held by the Manuscript Division of the Library of Congress. But even the most talented researcher must have access to a specially prepared subject guide to survey effectively the Civil War manuscript holdings of a repository that contains over 40,000,000 original items in 10,000 separate collections.

Civil War Manuscripts evolved from a checklist prepared between 1965 and 1967 by Lloyd A. Dunlap, a specialist in American history in the Manuscript Division. After Mr. Dunlap's death in 1968, various individuals, including Gayle Thornbrough, Margherita E. Pryor, Frank J. Tusa, and Oliver H. Orr, expanded the checklist. Continuing public interest in the Civil War and the consequent demand for information about the Library's manuscript holdings suggested the production of a more comprehensive, annotated Civil War guide, using as a foundation the Dunlap manuscript, which was compiled largely from catalogs, finding aids, and other administrative tools.

v

Eventually, this task was placed in the hands of John R. Sellers, an expert in 18th- and 19th-century American military history who personally examined each collection, with the following results. It is hoped that with its expanded format the guide will satisfy the needs of present and future generations of Civil War scholars and contribute to a better understanding of the single most important challenge to our national form of government.

James H. Hutson
Chief, Manuscript Division

INTRODUCTION

On the morning of April 20, 1861, a large hydrogen-filled balloon drifted serenely over the South Carolina countryside, the tranquillity of its noiseless flight belying the boisterous calls to arms then echoing throughout the Palmetto State. In the gondola the pioneer aeronaut, Prof. Thaddeus S. C. Lowe, looking strangely out of place in a long Prince Albert coat and black silk top hat, was listening anxiously to trailing sounds of gunfire, slightly muffled by the sea of green below, as he searched for a place to land. Professor Lowe had been in free flight from Cincinnati, Ohio, since 3:30 a.m., in an attempt to test a theory that he could cross the Atlantic Ocean in a gas balloon by entering the steady eastward flow of air in the middle atmosphere. To prove that he actually had traveled in the jet stream, Lowe had made his ascent while the ground wind blew toward the west, and true to expectations, at an altitude of about 7,000 feet, he was wafted eastward on currents of air that followed the undulations of the land like an invisible highway in the sky.

Professor Lowe's flight was supposed to have ended somewhere along the New Jersey coast; unfortunately, when his rudderless craft cascaded down the eastern slope of the Appalachian Mountains, it was caught in a deep and fast-moving southerly flow of air and set adrift several hours later over South Carolina. Lacking enough buoyancy to sail back over the mountains and unprepared for an ocean crossing, Lowe was forced to the ground, ironically, in Union County, S.C., near the town of Unionville. The scenes that followed are worthy of a tale by Charles Dickens or Samuel Clemens, for it taxed the imagination of local officials and dignitaries to convince the thousands of suspicious secessionists who poured into the county seat to witness a Yankee hanging that the young scientist was not a spy or saboteur. The whole experience so exasperated Lowe that within a few weeks of his return to the free states he was again sailing over the southern landscape, this time as the chief aeronaut of the Army of the Potomac.

The military career of Professor Lowe, the manufacture and use of aerial reconnaissance balloons, and the organization and function of the U.S. Aeronautic Corps, which was first established as a branch of the Army's Department of Topographical Engineers, are all possible subjects of Civil War research in the American Institute of Aeronautics and Astronautics collection in the Manuscript Division of the Library of Congress. Interesting as such studies may seem, however, they constitute only a fraction of the research opportunities on the Civil War in 1,064 separately identifiable collections in the Manuscript Division's holdings. For example, the collections provide an abundance of information on the basic motivations and political attitudes of early volunteer soldiers on both sides of the war, Union and Confederate military and political organization and reorganizations, war finance, inflation, and diplomacy. Civil War scholars can also study the organization and service of philanthropic societies such as the United States Christian Commission, the United States Sanitary Commission, and the National Freedmen's Relief Association; follow hundreds of soldiers to their respective enlistment centers, training camps, bivouacs, battlefields, and graves; examine the performance and service records of companies, regiments, brigades, and divisions; trace the changing attitudes of Union soldiers toward noncombatants and "contrabands" in the South; assess the ability and contributions of individual political and military leaders; investigate the relationship between Union and Confederate soldiers both as prisoners of war and during their occasional peaceful encounters in the field; cringe at 19th-century medical practices; inquire into the role of women in the war; and refight a seemingly endless array of battles and skirmishes.

Also represented in the collections are the often baleful effects of Federal, State, and local bounty systems. Sometimes devoted family men such as Corp. John C. Arnold sought to avoid financial ruin by obtaining a bounty for joining the U.S. Army. Corporal Arnold, a laborer from Snyder County, Pa., enlisted in the 49th Pennsylvania Regiment for the support of his wife Mary and their three children. Arnold demonstrated his love for his family in regular letters of encouragement and instruction, which he occasionally closed with a careful drawing of his and Mary's joined hands. But Arnold's dreams of a better future ended at the Battle of Sayler's Creek, the last major engagement of the war. Less conspicuous in the competition for enlistment bounties were the bounty agents who pocketed thousands of dollars intended for soldiers, presumably for worthwhile services, and enterprising clerks like Orra Bailey, who was able to forward a considerable amount of money home to his wife in Hartford, Conn., through his association with the office of the provost marshal and the Board of Enrollment in the District of Columbia.

Many documents in the collections of the Manuscript Division highlight the early enthusiasm for war, North and South. Both military and civilian observers commented on the flood of volunteers, the growth of enlistment centers and musters, and the establishment of new training camps. Some observers also noted, albeit shamefacedly, the cooling effect on this war fever of casualty reports and the sight of sick and wounded soldiers. In addition, scholars can study the adoption of and reaction to conscription and perhaps uncover fresh examples of the extreme methods adopted by a few officers to fill their ranks. One Confederate officer was not above immediately forcing into line any eligible young man who strolled to the roadside to watch his unit march past. Somewhat surprising are the large number of letters from commissioned and noncommissioned Union officers to northern Congressmen and officials soliciting higher rank in a black regiment.

The contribution of Confederate women to the war effort is another well-documented subject in the collections. Most references of this type concern the traditional role women played as seamstresses, nurses, and hostesses, but careful and imaginative researchers will find numerous comments on the emotional or psychological support Confederate women gave their soldiers. Military and civilian observers described the women of the South as the heart and soul of the Confederacy. One Kentucky cavalryman, writing just after the war, was so impressed with the determined spirit of his female acquaintances that he was persuaded the South would have won the war had there been a metamorphosis of the sexes. Paradoxically, many plantation mistresses powdered two faces, so to speak, one gray and the other blue, for they seemed unable to deny enemy officers the hospitality of their homes and tables. Doubtless in most instances their invitations were designed, at least in part, to guarantee the protection of property, but all too often the visits appear to have been mutually agreeable. Although the parties debated the issues of secession and States rights, they obviously enjoyed the argument. In any event, the feigned friendliness of true Yankee haters was easily detected by their already suspicious guests, who would not tarry long at hostile tables or trouble themselves unduly about the depredations of their troops. Similarly, quite a few southern belles attended Federal military balls during the war, rationalizing their blatant unfaithfulness to their own soldiers by dancing only cotillions, firmly refusing the more intimate contact of the waltz.

Other facets in the behavior of Confederate women puzzled soldiers on both sides. For example, the gaiety of a group of well dressed ladies who climbed Kennesaw Mountain during the peak of the battle to enjoy the carnage between the armies of Gen. William T. Sherman and Gen. Joseph E. Johnston surprised and dismayed the participants, some of whom were within easy rifle shot of the women. Then there was the abrupt about-face in the conduct of more than a few Confederate women at or near the end of the war. In Charleston, S.C., female socialites somehow managed to transfer much of the anger they harbored toward the U.S. Navy, which had blockaded the harbor and bombarded the city and its outlying defenses for four years, to the Union Army, whose presence had scarcely been felt. Union naval officers expressed amazement at the welcome they received at important social functions in Charleston after the capitulation, particularly with the all-absolving remark as they were introduced, "He's navy." Nor can the enthusiastic response of the women of Savannah, Ga., to General Sherman's conquering army, oft reported in the correspondence of his soldiers, be ignored.

Materials relating to the contributions of northern women to the war effort portray many of the same sacrifices made by their counterparts in the South, especially in the reactions to the death or crippling of fathers, brothers, husbands, and sons. But Confederate women could not duplicate the elaborate fairs and expositions sponsored by benevolent societies in the North for the benefit of soldiers. Nor could they provide the same comforts and services available to Federal soldiers enroute to the war zone at strategically located soldiers' homes. The services of many northern women as nurses, teachers, missionaries, and agents, and occasionally as disguised or unofficial soldiers, are also represented in the collections; however, the records are surprisingly silent about the ever-present horde of camp followers and prostitutes on both sides.

Many Civil War soldiers felt compelled to recount their experiences as prisoners of war through letters, diaries, memoirs, and reminiscences. Most such records in the Manuscript Division concern Union soldiers, perhaps because of their higher numbers and better writing skills. Whatever the reason, the result is a wealth of information on Confederate military prisons (particularly Richmond's famous "Libby Hotel" and Belle Isle, and the notorious stockade prison at Andersonville, Ga.), prison escapes and attempted escapes, cartels for the exchange of prisoners, and the morale, diet, diseases, sufferings, and deaths of prisoners.

The manuscript collections also provide an opportunity for scholars to reexamine the performance of individual soldiers and military units in the war. For example, the widespread belief in an almost universal dread of Col. John S. Mosby's Partisan Rangers among Union soldiers stationed in northern Virginia is called into question by the comments of a Federal cavalryman who likened the nocturnal chases after Mosby's raiders to coon hunts. The exercise appears to have involved little danger and is presented as a welcome intrusion into the camp routine. Perhaps another unfounded belief concerns the discipline and prowess of Gen. John C. Frémont's famous "Pathfinders." After observing the actions of General Frémont's troops during their march into the Shenandoah Valley in the spring of 1862, one disgusted Federal officer remarked that these German soldiers marched off the road most of the way; the paths they followed led chiefly from one farm to the next, which they plundered in turn.

In the area of religion, extensive reading in the collections seems to lead to the conclusion that, at least during the height of the war, the militant Christian was a contradiction in terms. Moreover, if comments in the collections about professional men of faith who entered the army can be trusted, chaplains seem often to have failed in their mission. Occasionally, a particularly devout recruit would gather a half dozen followers for evening prayers and Bible study, but the sessions did not continue long and excited little interest among the rank and file. Delegates of the U.S. Christian Commission and Sanitary Commission visiting Federal troops in the war zone were greeted eagerly if they had food and clothing to distribute, but piety was at a discount. Some observers testified that the men fought mechanically, without malice, just as they would sift grain or saw wood. They might be moved greatly by jealousy of each other or become enraged at some petty encroachment by a comrade, a deficiency in their rations, or some insult or unfairness on the part of an officer, but of God and his worship— nothing at all. This regression in religious interest and observance is neatly outlined in the postwar remarks of William McDonald, a surgeon with the Army of the Potomac: "The chaplains were often called upon to hold Service on Sundays regularly during the winter of 1861 and 1862, not at all during the Peninsular Campaign, now and then during the winter of 1862 and 1863, and never after as far as my knowledge and observation went."

Few aspects of the war are better represented in the collections than its effects upon southern blacks. The hopes and achievements, the disappointments and sufferings of freedmen, appear in diverse and sundry ways: in the unlearned scrawl of a grateful black recruit, in the sharp rebuttal of a black officer defending the performance of his troops, in the compassionate observations of missionaries and volunteer teachers, in the casual but telltale remarks of officers and soldiers, and in the recollections of escaped Federal prisoners of war. The backdrops against which the lives of freedmen were acted out range from the newly established schools and freedmen's camps to ravaged towns and plantations, from smoking battlefields to long winter encampments, from plowed fields to massive earthworks, from coaches to military supply wagons, and from loading docks to the decks of northern ships of war. Many Union soldiers had never been in contact with blacks, free or slave, before they entered the South, and their unacclimated eyes caught nuances of black life and culture often overlooked by more experienced observers. It was also difficult to predict the reactions of individual white soldiers to blacks. Among officers, adverse feelings toward blacks sometimes outweighed the responsibility of their position, while common soldiers like Joseph Lester, an artisan with the 6th Wisconsin Battery, displayed a statesmanlike understanding of racial and political problems.

In the field of Civil War medicine, the Manuscript Division holds the correspondence and papers of Frederick Law Olmsted, general secretary of the United States Sanitary Commission; Ninian Pinkney, fleet surgeon and medical adviser for the Mississippi Squadron (USN); Daniel B. Conrad, chief surgeon at the Brock House Hospital in Richmond, Va., and later fleet surgeon attached to the C.S.S. *Tennessee*; and various field surgeons, medical assistants, regular and volunteer nurses, and sick and wounded soldiers. There is even a collection of original letters and photographs from a national postwar left-handed penmanship contest that was designed to boost the morale and employability of disabled Union veterans. The kind of information available in medically oriented collections concerns the contraction and treatment of diseases among combat troops and prisoners of war, treatable and untreatable wounds, the distribution of convalescents among hospitals throughout the northeast, medical facilities (surgical tents, emergency field hospitals, and departmental hospitals), medical conveyances (field ambulances, deep water transports, and hospital ships), hospital diets, and the attitude of soldiers toward doctors. Particularly diligent researchers may occasionally glimpse the frustrations of Civil War doctors whose medicine chests were pilfered by alcoholics and drug addicts, who were obliged to stand helplessly by while politically connected, though well intentioned, humanitarians like Clara Barton distributed apples to soldiers with serious stomach and intestinal wounds, or who were deserted by medical impostors they entrusted to seal the wounds of new amputees.

Researchers can pursue the design and construction of Civil War vessels (monitors, ironclads, rams, gunboats, mortar boats, torpedo boats, transports, hospital ships, and submarines) and ordnance (floating, submarine, and on-board torpedoes, and improved Dahlgren, Columbiad, and Parrott cannons) in the massive Naval Historical Foundation collection. Scholars interested in military intelligence, particularly during the early part of the war, will find the papers of the Pinkerton National Detective Agency and the papers of John C. Babcock, who was one of Pinkerton's operatives during the Peninsular and Antietam campaigns, extremely useful. And anyone studying the military postal service, the military telegraph, and military engineering and mapmaking will be rewarded by a careful perusal of the collections herein described. In fact, the list of possible research topics can be expanded in so many directions that the number of new or creditable studies on the war is limited largely by the searcher's own imagination.

The most noticeable weakness in the Manuscript Division's Civil War holdings is the imbalance in materials from the opposing sides, the ratio being at least three or four to one in favor of the North. The reasons that this situation exists cannot all be addressed here, but the larger number of Union soldiers, the higher literacy rate among northerners, and the survival of personal and public papers in a region relatively untouched by the war are obvious factors. At least Civil War scholars can be thankful that most secessionists accepted defeat more gracefully than one southern statesman who so hated the thought of a forced reunion with the North that on his deathbed late in the war he extracted a promise from his daughter to have a plow run over his grave if the South were subjugated.

John R. Sellers

HOW TO USE THIS GUIDE

Library of Congress manuscript collections consist largely of the personal papers of prominent Americans, as opposed to official government records, which are held by the National Archives and Records Administration. *Civil War Manuscripts* is a guide to the collections of the Manuscript Division that are made up of materials—either whole or in part—relating directly to the Civil War. The guide does not cover original materials in the Rare Book and Special Collections Division, the Prints and Photographs Division, the Music Division, the Geography and Map Division, or the general collections. Although it is focused on the period of the war, it does include a few significant postwar items, such as materials concerning the assassination of President Lincoln, the trial of the Lincoln conspirators, and the Fitz-John Porter and Henry Wirz trials. No attempt has been made to survey collections concerning prewar politics and the secession controversy. Also, it is not a guide to entire collections unless those collections are composed wholly of materials relating to the war, which is why *National Union Catalog of Manuscript Collections (NUCMC)* numbers have not been included. Users will not necessarily be led to all of the material on any one subject; however, if they possess a good knowledge of the war and basic research skills, they can be reasonably certain of having been directed to most of the relevant items. In no case are all the papers of or about a single campaign, battle, individual, place, or topic contained in the Library of Congress. It is indeed rare when additional information on any subject cannot be found in other major libraries and archives.

The entries in the guide are arranged alphabetically by collection title. Collections entered under personal names include the individual's birth and death dates, if known, and a brief statement of identification emphasizing occupation or profession, rank, and military unit or command. General officers of whatever grade are identified only as "Gen., USA" or "CSA." No effort has been made to cite each rank held by individual soldiers; rather, in most instances the rank mentioned will have been the highest attained during the war or the rank held during the period of service herein described.

Only an individual's war-related activities and career are discussed. The term "Volunteer" as applied to regiments and companies is used rather indiscriminately, but apparent discrepancies are usually the result of reorganizations and consolidations, temporary reassignments, and misunderstandings.

The second line in each entry contains a brief statement on the nature of the collection, such as personal or family papers, letters, diaries, and memoirs, which is followed by the inclusive dates and approximate size of the collection. The figures on collection size are for the collection as a whole and not for that portion relating to the war. Next is a statement on the kind or kinds of material involved other than originals, i.e., facsimiles, transcripts, photocopies, and microfilm. This in turn is followed by a description of the collection or pertinent items in the collection and an alphabetical list of the principal correspondents where applicable. The final line for many entries contains information on available finding aids, indexes, guides, and microfilm copies. The figure on the number of reels of microfilm refers to everything in the collection that has been filmed, not just the items from the period of the Civil War. In instances where the Library has purchased the collection on microfilm, the final line of the entry identifies the institution holding the original materials. Almost all materials on microfilm are available on interlibrary loan. No effort has been made to identify published items, though occasionally such references appear.

The Naval Historical Foundation, which is the source of 75 of the collections in the guide, is a nonprofit organization which was chartered in the District of Columbia in 1926. The purpose of the Foundation is to promote the study of the U.S. Navy through the collection and preservation of private documents, papers, and artifacts of naval historical interest. So successful in its endeavors that it soon was forced to seek larger facilities, the Foundation reached an agreement, in 1949, with the Library of Congress to place its materials on deposit in the Manuscript Division. These collections subsequently were cataloged and indexed with the support of the Foundation. Its deposits now number about 357,000 items in 267 separate collections, which are maintained as a unit.

Most of the abbreviations in the guide, including obsolete military ranks, are self-explanatory, but "USA," "USN" and "CSA," "CSN" refer to the respective armies and navies and not to the countries involved. Duplicate names for individual battles have been avoided, and the most commonly recognized names have been employed. Hence the Battle of 1st Cold Harbor or Chickahominy is consistently referred to as Gaines Mill, and the Battles of 1st and 2d Bull Run are called by their northern names of 1st and 2d Manassas.

Many of the collections listed in the guide came to the Library in the first half of the 20th century, roughly between 1900 and 1940, either as purchases or gifts. Occasionally, a collection will have been placed in the Library on deposit at some early date and subsequently converted to a gift. The collections continue to grow and readers are encouraged to inquire about any recent acquisitions. The papers of Gen. Nathaniel Banks, for example, were not acquired until 1964; those of Frederick Douglass, which contain a few significant Civil War items, came to the Library in 1972; and those of Orlando M. Poe and Francis P. Blair, Jr., arrived in 1982.

The index is primarily a name index; however, it includes a generous number of subjects. Essentially, the index reflects the collection descriptions. It is keyed to entry numbers rather than pages, and boldfaced numbers identify main entries. All volunteer regiments are listed under their respective states, but readers are advised that considerable additional information is available on military units in the accounts of the battles and campaigns in which they participated. Also, a researcher's study of a particular battle or skirmish should take into account the campaign in which the action took place.

CIVIL WAR MANUSCRIPTS

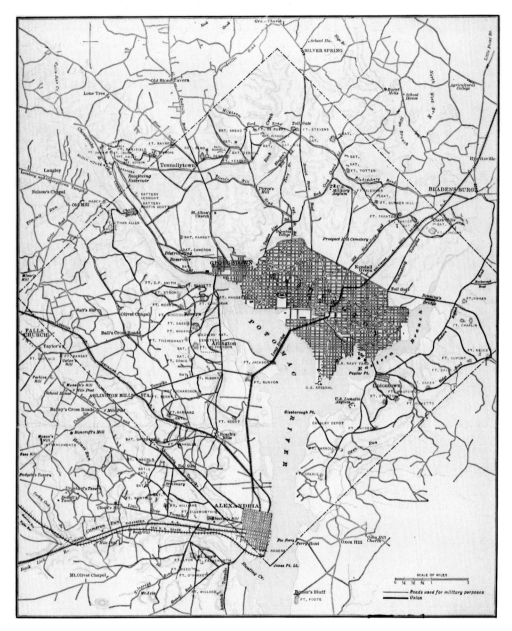

Defenses of Washington, 1865.

Geography and Map Division, Library of Congress

1
Abbe, Cleveland (1938–1916)   Meteorologist, U.S.
                                           Coast Survey
    Papers, 1850–1916. ca. 9,500 items.
    Contains four letters to Abbe from Albert S. Bickmore,
44th Massachusetts Volunteers, written while on special duty
as a nurse at Beaufort, N.C., Mar. 4–May 25, 1863.
    Finding aid available.

2
Abbott, Asa Townsend
(1841–1923)   2d Lt., U.S. Signal Corps
    Reminiscences, 1915–23.
    Microfilm, 1 reel, and enlargements prints, 69 p.
    Describes Abbott's service in northern Virginia with the
Army of the Potomac. Also includes an account of his military
service (4 p.) by Col. B. F. Fisher, chief signal officer, and two
undated letters describing an incident in July 1864 in which
President Lincoln came under fire at Fort Stevens during Gen.
Jubal Early's Washington raid.

3
Abbott, Samuel Warren (1837–1904)   Asst. Surg., USN
    Letterbook, 1861–80. 1 v.
    Medical correspondence, reports, requisitions, and lists of
sick and wounded sailors sent by Abbott to fleet surgeons George
Clymer and William Johnson, U.S.S. *Catskill*, South Atlantic
Blockading Squadron, Feb.–Oct. 1863; observations on sani-
tary conditions aboard ironclads; inventory of medical supplies
received aboard the U.S.S. *Niagara* while outfitting in New
York Harbor, Feb.–May 1864; postwar descriptions of 40 Massachusetts veterans examined by Abbott for disability; and miscellaneous medical notes. Additional recipients are John A.
Dahlgren, Samuel F. Du Pont, George W. Rodgers, Gideon
Welles, and William Whelan.

4
Abert, Charles   Lawyer, Montgomery County, Md.
    Diary, 1861–63.
    Microfilm, 1 reel.
    Covers the period May 20, 1861–July 8, 1863. Concerns
claims by Abert's clients for transporting Federal troops from
Fort Sumter, S.C., to New York, and the movements of Gen. J.
E. B. Stuart in Maryland during the Gettysburg Campaign.

5
Adams Family
    Papers, 1776–1914. ca. 225 items.
    In part, photocopies.

Includes a copy of the draft of William H. Seward's instructions to Charles Francis Adams (1807–1886), May 21, 1861, as Minister to the Court of St. James; and a copy of an unfinished and unsigned letter describing the position of British trade unions on the American Civil War, London, Mar. 26, 1863.

6
———

Papers, 1639–1889.
Microfilm, 608 reels.
Contains the papers of Charles Francis Adams (1807–1886), Minister to the Court of St. James during the Civil War.
Published finding aid available.
Originals in the Massachusetts Historical Society.

7
Adee Family
Papers, 1825–1953. ca. 300 items.
Includes a few clippings on the career of Maj. Gen. George L. Hartsuff (1830–1874), a postwar photograph of Hartsuff, and copies of general orders issued by Hartsuff at Danville, Ky. (1863), and Petersburg, Va. (1865).

8
Aldrich, Nelson Wilmarth
(1841–1915)   Sgt., 10th Rhode Island Volunteers
Papers, 1777–1930. ca. 42,500 items.
In part, photocopies.
Relates chiefly to Senator Aldrich's later career, but includes a "Company Roll Book" (1863); minutes of the Senate Finance Committee, Dec. 1863–June 1864; and copies of letters concerning Harris Hoyt's efforts to obtain information on military affairs in Texas.
Published index and microfilm copy (73 reels) available.

9
Alexander, Edward Porter (1835–1910)   Gen., CSA
Papers, 1854–65. 15 items.
In part, transcripts.
Copy of Alexander's "Personal Recollections of Knoxville Campaign," notes exchanged with General Longstreet during the Battle of Gettysburg, copies of notes from Alexander to General Pickett at Gettysburg, and part of Gen. R. E. Lee's pocket map showing an area along the lower James River.

10
Allen, Henry Watkins (1820–1866)   Gov., Louisiana
Letter, 1865. 1 item.
Letter from Allen to Col. John T. Sprague, May 16, 1865, Shreveport, La., concerning negotiations for peace.

11
Allen, Isaac Jackson (b. 1814)   Editor; U.S.
                                            Consul in China
    Autobiography, 1904. 1 item.
    Contains remarks on President Lincoln at Gettysburg (Nov.
1863) and on an interview with Lincoln in 1864 in which the
President expounded on the state of the war and the problems
he anticipated in disbanding the Army.

12
Allen, Samuel E.   Pvt., USA
    Letters, 1862. 2 items.
    Letters from Allen to his cousin, Sallie Rettew, July 19
and 29, 1862, describing the Battle of Mechanicsville and hospital care at Jamestown and Fort Monroe, Va., and Annapolis,
Md.

13
Allen, William A. H.   Asst. Eng., USN
    Diary, 1863—84. 14 v.
    Entries for Mar. 21, 1863—May 31, 1864, describe Allen's
voyage aboard the U.S.S. *Circassian* from New York to New
Orleans and subsequent service aboard the U.S.S. *Cayuga*, West
Gulf Blockading Squadron. Also includes an account of goods
and vessels seized along the coast of Texas, and a detailed plan
of Fort Jackson, La.

14
Allen Family
    Papers, 1865—1965. ca. 300 items.
    Includes personal reminiscences and autobiographical writ-
ings of Lt. Charles Julius Allen (1840—1915) describing life at
the U.S. Military Academy, West Point, during the war, troop
travel on the Mississippi River, conditions in New Orleans,
La., under the military governorship of Gen. Edward Canby,
the capture of Fort Gaines, Ala., the Siege of Mobile, particularly the attack on Spanish Fort, and an expedition to Texas
after the surrender of Gen. R. E. Lee's army. Also contains a
few maps and sketches.

15
Alston Family
    Papers, 1735—1957. 50 items.
    Includes an autobiographical letter by Jacob Motte Alston
(1821—1886?) containing reminiscences about the war in South
Carolina, particularly depredations by Federal troops and
"Tories" during General Sherman's march to the sea and the
burning of Columbia, S.C.

16

Alvord, Augustus V. (1834–1904)   Chaplain, 1st Connecticut
                                                              Heavy Artillery
    Letter, 1864. 1 item.
    Letter from Alvord to his brother, June 25, 1864, describing the repulse of a Confederate counterattack during the Siege of Petersburg and the devastation of the Virginia countryside.

17

Alvord, Jabez   2d Lt., 28th Connecticut Volunteers
    Diary, 1862–63. 1 item.
    Records the service of the 28th Connecticut from Nov. 15, 1862, to Aug. 28, 1863. Includes a detailed account of operations against Port Hudson, La., May 26–June 9, 1863, and descriptions of voyages, marches, and camp life at Fort Barrancas, Fla., Ship Island, Miss., and Brashear City (Morgan City) and Carrollton, La.

18

American Institute of Aeronautics and Astronautics
    Aeronautical archives, 1783–1962. ca. 30,000 items.
    In part, photocopies.
    Material from the former Institute of the Aerospace Sciences. Includes the papers of Thaddeus S. C. Lowe (1832–1913), "Chief Aeronaut of the Army of the Potomac," which comprise a memoir, "My Balloons in Peace and War," a diary, Apr. 30–May 5, 1863, correspondence, photographs, military orders, telegrams, newspaper clippings, and miscellaneous items. Contains information on the establishment of the Aeronautic Corps, the design and operation of balloons, reconnaissance flights, the defense of Washington, D.C., the Peninsular, Fredericksburg, and Chancellorsville campaigns, Confederate morale at the beginning of the war, and Confederate reaction to the use of balloons. Also includes sketches showing Confederate troop positions at Bailey's Crossroads, Va., Aug. 27, 1861, and fortifications around Richmond, Va., June 14, 1862. Diary entries consist largely of notes made during reconnaissance flights and figures on pay for noncombatants in the Aeronautic Corps. Principal correspondents include Joseph Hooker, Andrew A. Humphreys, George B. McClellan, George G. Meade, Fitz-John Porter, and Edwin M. Stanton.
    Finding aid available.

19

Anderson, Frank Maloy (1871–1961)   Historian
    Papers, 1899–1954. ca. 40,000 items.
    Includes research notes assembled by Anderson over a 20-year period for an unwritten history of the secession crisis.

Anderson's thesis and proposed organization of the work are explained in a draft introduction.

Finding aid available.

20

Anderson, John Emerson   Sgt., 2d Massachusetts Infantry

Memoir, 1861–65. 1 item.

Photocopy.

Detailed account of Anderson's service with the 2d Massachusetts Infantry in the Shenandoah Valley Campaign of 1862, the Chancellorsville, Gettysburg, Atlanta, Savannah, and Carolinas campaigns, and in operations against guerrillas and renegades in east Tennessee in the winter of 1863–64. Includes information on recruitment, training, marches, discipline, camp life, morale, depredations, foraging expeditions, the treatment of prisoners of war, military paroles, disease, hospital care, Federal spies, enlistment bounties, Union sentiment in the South, the attitude of noncombatants, and crime in the U.S. Army.

21

Anderson, Robert (1805–1871)   Gen., USA

Papers, 1819–1919. ca. 5,000 items.

Contains numerous personal and official letters received by Anderson and copies of his outgoing letters during his commands at Fort Moultrie and Fort Sumter, S.C., the Department of Kentucky, and the Department of the Cumberland. Also includes plans of forts and batteries, newspaper clippings concerning Anderson and the Fort Sumter affair, and presentation copies of the following books: R. Anderson, *Within Fort Sumter by One of the Company* (1861), T. M. Anderson, *The Political Conspiracies Preceding the Rebellion or the True Stories of Sumter and Pickens* (1882), and E. A. Lawton, *Major Robert Anderson and Fort Sumter, 1861* (1911). Principal wartime correspondents are P. G. T. Beauregard, Simon Cameron, Samuel Cooper, Richard B. Duane, W. W. Harlee, L. M. Hatch, David F. Jamison, Abraham Lincoln, Andrew G. Magrath, Francis W. Pickens, Winfield Scott, William T. Sherman, Edwin M. Stanton, Charles Sumner, Lorenzo Thomas, and George L. Willard.

Finding aid and index available.

22

Anderson—Moler Families

Papers, 1854–1931. ca. 140 items.

Includes about 30 letters written during the Civil War by Nelia Moler of Columbus, Ohio, and relatives in Anderson County, Kans., containing remarks on enlistments, training camps, and acquaintances in the Union Army.

Robert Anderson

23

Anglin, John S.   Pvt., Iredell Blues; 4th
                                        North Carolina Regiment, CSA
    Letters, 1861–64. 17 items.
    In part, transcripts.
    Letters from Anglin to his family written from Fort
Caswell, N.C., and from various camps in Virginia concerning
casualties in the 4th North Carolina in the Battle of Seven
Pines, efforts by Confederate soldiers to avoid infantry duty by
volunteering for service in the Confederate Navy, and camp
life, morale, disease, troop movements, diet, supplies, and deaths
during the Manassas and Peninsular campaigns and the Shenandoah Valley Campaign of 1864. Also includes comments on
inflation and the contribution of women in Virginia to the war
effort.

24

Anonymous
    Memoranda, 1864–86. 8 v.
    Commentary on events in Jacksonville, Fla., and vicinity
by an ardent secessionist. Provides information on the movement of troops and supplies, ship arrivals and departures,
skirmishes, prisoners of war, and the behavior of black soldiers.

25

Arnold, John Carvel (1833–1865)   Cpl., 49th Pennsylvania
                                                    Volunteers
    Papers, 1856–1937. 192 items.
    Includes about 40 letters from Arnold to his wife, Mar.
1864–Apr. 1865, concerning the Wilderness, Spotsylvania,
Petersburg, and Appomattox campaigns, Sheridan's Shenandoah Valley Campaign, and the movement of Federal troops
during Gen. Jubal Early's Washington raid. Provides detailed
accounts of the Battle of Cold Harbor (1864), the Battle of
Winchester (Sept. 1864), and the Battle of Hatcher's Run (Oct.
1864). Also contains letters by Sgt. W. Harman, John W. Snoke
(83d Pennsylvania Volunteers), and H. C. Shaffer.

26

Arthur, Chester Alan (1830–1886), Pres., U.S.
    Papers, 1843–1938. ca. 4,400 items.
    Contains the commissions of C. A. Arthur as inspector
general, New York State Militia, 1862, and Maj. William
Arthur, 4th New York Artillery, and two letters by C. A. Arthur
as quartermaster general in the State of New York, 1862.
    Published index and microfilm copy (3 reels) available.

27

Asbill, J. J.   Pvt., 19th South Carolina Volunteers
    Correspondence, 1861–62. 8 items.
    Letters from Asbill to his wife, Dec. 29, 1861–Aug. 11,
1862, written from camps in South Carolina, Mississippi, and
Tennessee concerning skirmishes, the election of officers, military organization, camp life, morale, and supplies. Also includes
a letter from J. L. Morris to Asbill, Apr. 16, 1862, concerning
the movement of Confederate troops between Atlanta and
Chattanooga.

28

Associated Survivors of the Sixth U.S. Army Corps
    Records, 1883–1930. 250 items.
    Includes a list of members of the "District of Columbia
Association of Ex–Union Prisoners of War," compiled in 1883.

29

Association of Acting Assistant Surgeons
    Records, 1888–98. 250 items.
    Contains lists of members for the period 1888–98.

30

Aston, Ralph (1841–1904)   Asst. Eng., USN
    Papers, 1861–1902. 8 v.
    In part, transcripts.
    Orders, notes and recollections, and the steam log of the
U.S.S. *Cayuga*, Mar. 1–July 1, 1863. Contains information on
the capture of New Orleans and routine naval affairs in the
West Gulf Blockading Squadron.

31

Averill, C. K.
    Scrapbooks, 1863, 1874. 2 v.
    Volume entitled "War Statistics" contains clippings from
various newspapers and magazines concerning military events
in November 1863.
    Indexed.

32

Ayers, George R.   Merchant, New Orleans, La.
    Letter, 1863. 1 item.
    Photocopy.
    Copy of a letter from Ayres to Isaac S. Waterman, Mar. 19,
1863, concerning the movement of Federal troops under Gen.
N. P. Banks up the Mississippi River, operations against Port
Hudson, La., and economic conditions in Louisiana.

33
Babcock, John C. (b. 1836)   Secret Service, USA
     Papers, 1855–1913. ca. 60 items.
     Letters from Babcock to relatives in Illinois, 1861–64, con-
cern his work as a confidential agent in the provost marshal's
office in Washington, D.C., the incarceration of female prisoners at "Prison Greenhough" in Washington, reaction to the
Trent affair, secessionist sentiment in Alexandria, Va., the
gathering of intelligence and mapmaking in the service of E. J.
Allen during the Peninsular and Antietam campaigns, and
Babcock's personal ideas on blacks and slavery. Letters from
Gens. George G. Meade, Andrew A. Humphreys, and Winfield
S. Hancock concern intelligence gathered from prisoners and
deserters and mapping of enemy positions during the Peters-
burg Campaign. Also includes a record of Babcock's service in
the Sturges Rifles (McClellan's bodyguard) and as a confiden-
tial agent for Gens. Daniel Butterfield, George G. Meade, and
Ulysses S. Grant, and an outline of the organization of the
Army of Northern Virginia.

34
Bache, Alexander Dallas (1806–1867)   Superintendent,
                                             U.S. Coast Survey
     Papers, 1828–63. ca. 2,000 items.
     Contains letters to Bache from Adms. John A. Dahlgren
and Charles H. Davis concerning the southern blockade, from
Gen. Isaac I. Stevens concerning military affairs in South Carolina and Georgia, and official policy toward blacks, and from
Maj. W. R. Palmer concerning the Peninsular Campaign. Additional correspondents are Lt. Comdr. Henry Preble and Col.
George E. Waring. Miscellaneous items include a list of regiments in the Missouri Cavalry, a plan for the defense of
Philadelphia, Pa. (1863), and proposals for the conduct of the
war by Gen. I. I. Stevens.
     Finding aid, partial index, and microfilm copy (5 reels)
available.

35
Badger, Alfred Mason (1808–1868)   Merchant–Contractor,
                                             Rochester, N.Y.
     Papers, 1830–68. 3 v.
     In part, transcripts.
     Includes copies of letters from Badger's son, Frank Apple-
ton Badger (1842–1864), 140th New York Volunteers, and
nephew, Hamlet F. Richardson (1842–1911), 108th New York
Volunteers, Dec. 1862–Feb. 1863, concerning campaigns in
Maryland and Virginia.

36
Bailey, Orra B.   7th Connecticut Volunteers;
                                                    Invalid Corps
    Papers, 1862—64. ca. 70 items.
    Letters from Bailey to his wife from camps in Florida and
South Carolina discussing camp life, morale, disease, desertions,
the treatment of prisoners of war, economic conditions in the
South, and land purchases by Federal soldiers. Includes a
detailed account of the siege and capture of Fort Wagner, S.C.
Letters from Bailey to his wife written from Washington, D.C.,
in 1864 concern profiteering from the draft.

37
Baird, Samuel John (1817—1893)   Presbyterian Clergyman,
                                                    Woodbury, N.J.
    Papers, 1834—92. ca. 650 items.
    Contains a few letters concerning Baird's efforts to estab-
lish an evangelistic ministry for soldiers and to assist wounded
soldiers and prisoners of war.

38
Baldwin, John Brown (1820—1873)   C.S. Representative,
                                                    Virginia
    Papers, 1863, 1865. 2 items.
    Letter from Baldwin to William Crawford, Apr. 24, 1863,
denying reports that he had voted in favor of flogging soldiers
as a means of discipline and expressing his opposition to an
increase in military pay; pardon signed by President Johnson
and William H. Seward, Sept. 28, 1865.

39
Ballou Family of Virginia
    Papers, 1736—1889. ca. 30 items.
    Microfilm, 1 reel.
    Contains three letters from soldiers in the 13th Missis-
sippi Volunteers written from Leesburg, Va., Oct. 1861, concerning the health of the regiment and the death of James E.
Ballou in the Battle of 1st Manassas; and four letters from
Rebecca Ballou to her mother, 1863—64, Jackson, Tenn.,
describing the occupation and evacuation of Jackson, depredations by Federal soldiers, skirmishes in the area, and the suffering and problems of blacks.

40
Bancroft, George (1800—1891)   Historian; Diplomat
    Papers, 1811—1961.
    Microfilm, 7 reels.
    Contains a few letters from Bancroft to his wife written

from Washington, D.C., during the war. Includes remarks on interviews with President Lincoln, a visit to the Freedmen's village and the encampment of black troops, Mary Todd Lincoln's influence over her husband, and the generalship of George B. McClellan, Winfield Scott, and Samuel P. Heintzelman.

Finding aid available.

Originals at Cornell University.

41
Bancroft—Bliss Families
Papers, 1788–1928. ca. 5,800 items.
In part, microfilm, transcripts, and photocopies.

Includes official and personal correspondence of Lt. Col. Alexander Bliss (1827–1896), quartermaster of Volunteers and assistant quartermaster, U.S. Army, concerning the procurement, transportation, and distribution of supplies, and problems relating to promotions, pay, and rank. About 15 letters from Bliss to his mother, 1864–65, describe conditions in New Orleans, La., under Gen. Edward Canby, the movement of troops and supplies on the Mississippi River, and expeditions to Arkansas and Fort Gaines, Ala. Also includes a "Narrative" (16 p.) of scenes in the Peninsular, Fredericksburg, Chancellorsville, and Gettysburg campaigns, an undated report on the "Organization and Strength of the Army of the Potomac, and other troops in Department of Virginia," "Claims for hire & value of Western Rivers Steamboats & Barges," and miscellaneous quartermaster reports and accounts. Correspondents include Nicholas Bowen, DeWitt Clinton, Louis Delafield, Charles Griffin, James A. Hamilton, William Hamlet, Samuel Hooper, Rufus Ingalls, William Le Duc, George B. McClellan, George G. Meade, Montgomery C. Meigs, Winfield Scott, William Smith, and Francis Walker.

Finding aid and partial index available.

42
Banks, Nathaniel Prentice (1816–1894)   Gen., USA
Papers, 1841–1911. ca. 50,000 items.

Official and personal correspondence, letterbooks, orders, reports, sketches, courts-martial records, commissions, discharges, muster rolls, intelligence reports, returns, clippings, scrapbooks, and miscellaneous items relating chiefly to the Shenandoah Valley Campaign of 1862, the 2d Manassas Campaign—particularly the Battle of Cedar Mountain—and the Red River campaigns of 1863 and 1864. Correspondents include John C. Frémont, Ulysses S. Grant, Henry W. Halleck, George B. McClellan, David D. Porter, William H. Seward, William T. Sherman, Franz Sigel, Edwin M. Stanton, and Lorenzo Thomas.

Finding aid available.

Nathaniel Prentice Banks

43

Barbee, James Dodson (1832–1904) and
David Rankin (1874–1958)

    Papers, 1784–1951. ca. 5,000 items.

    In part, transcripts and photocopies.

    Includes research notes of historian David R. Barbee on the capture of Jefferson Davis, and the postwar correspondence of Rev. James D. Barbee concerning restitution for Methodist properties confiscated during the war. Miscellaneous items include an anonymous memorandum on the possible involvement of Andrew Johnson in the assassination of President Lincoln; a letter by Robert E. Lee, May 5, 1861, discussing his sentiments on the war; a letter by Cornelia Grinnaw, Sept. 12, 1863, on depredations in Virginia; a letter from Albert Bledsoe to Jefferson Davis, Sept. 21, 1864, describing friends of the Confederacy in England; Bledsoe's manuscript apology of the South; and an essay by Col. Fred A. Olds, "How Sherman's Army Entered Raleigh," 1865.

    Finding aid available.

44

Barbour, Lucian (1811–1880)   Lawyer

    Papers, 1838–1939. ca. 1,000 items.

    Contains six letters from Sgt. J. V. Hadley to Mary Alice Barbour, 1862–63 concerning his service with the 7th Indiana Volunteers during the 2d Manassas and Chancellorsville campaigns; three letters from John P. Avery to Miss Barbour, 1862–63, written from camps in Tennessee, Arkansas, and Mississippi; and a letter from John T. Jackson to Miss Barbour, Oct. 16, 1861, describing operations in western Virginia. Includes comments on the attitude of noncombatants in the South, black life, Confederate morale, and hospital care.

    Finding aid available.

45

Barnes, James (1801–1869)   Gen., USA

    Letter, 1865. 1 item.

    Letter from Barnes to Maj. Adam E. King, Feb. 2, 1865, Point Lookout, Md., reporting the location of a suspected Confederate blockade runner.

46

Barnes, Samuel Denham
(1839–1916)   Capt., 72d Illinois Volunteers

    Papers, 1791–1867. 7 items.

    Diary (4 v.), 1860–67, relating in part to Barnes' service in the 72d Illinois Volunteers, the 7th Louisiana Volunteers of African Descent, and the 64th U.S. Colored Infantry. Describes campaigns in Kentucky, Tennessee, Mississippi, and Arkansas. Also includes a record of Barnes' correspondence.

47

Barnwell, Robert Woodward
(1801–1882)   C.S. Senator, South Carolina
      Letter, 1863. 1 item.
      Letter from Barnwell to W. Thompson, Mar. 28, 1863, Richmond Va., on proposed legislation against profiteering.

48

Barritt, Jasper N.   76th Illinois Volunteers
      Papers, 1862–65. 21 items.
      Chiefly letters from Barritt to his family written during campaigns in Arkansas, Kentucky, Tennessee, Mississippi, and Louisiana.

49

Barron, Wesley   Musician, 160th New York Volunteers
      Document, 1865. 1 item.
      Discharge, Nov. 1, 1865, signed by Capt. Henry S. Wood and Lt. John W. Pritchard.

50

Barstow, Wilson (1830–1869)   Capt., USV
      Papers, 1861–69. 53 items.
      Includes letters from Barstow to his sister written from Fort McHenry, Md., and Fort Monroe, Va., concerning the transportation of paroled prisoners of war, the fall of Norfolk, and a visit by President Lincoln to Fort Monroe.

51

Bartlett, Joseph Jackson (ca. 1834–1893)   Gen., USV
      Letter, 1863. 1 item.
      Letter from Bartlett to Capt. W. W. Winthrop, Aug. 12, 1863, criticizing Federal strategy during the Gettysburg Campaign.

52

Bartlett Family
      Papers, 1710–1931. ca. 10,000 items.
      Includes several letters and a diary by Ezra Bartlett (1832–1886) written on board the U.S.S. *Kearsarge*, 1862–63, and the U.S.S. *Spiria*[?], 1865; and a few letters by Ezra Bartlett (1811–1892), concerning his work as a physician (USA) in hospitals in Washington, D.C., and Memphis, Tenn., and at various places in Mississippi, Alabama, and Georgia, 1863–64.
      Finding aid and microfilm copy (17 reels) available.

53

Barton, Chauncey E.   Pvt., 17th Illinois Volunteers
    Letter, 1864. 1 item.
    Letter from Barton to Miss Jennie M. Fell, Apr, 14, 1864, describing the abuse of the civilian population after the fall of Vicksburg, Miss.

54

Barton, Clara Harlowe (1821–1912)   Nurse, USA
    Papers, 1834–1918. ca. 70,000 items.
    Correspondence, diary, lectures, newspaper clippings, and miscellaneous items relating, in part, to Miss Barton's work with sick and wounded soldiers. Also includes postwar correspondence with the families of missing prisoners of war and a list of Union soldiers buried at Andersonville, Ga.
    Finding aid available.

55

Barton—Jenifer Families
    Papers, 1663–1876. ca. 120 items.
    Includes accounts of the Confederacy with the Mobile and Girard Railroad, 1864, and recommendations for the promotion of Lt. Col. Seth M. Barton to brigadier general, signed by Gens. Henry R. Jackson and Thomas J. Jackson.

56

Batchelder, John Davis (1872–1958)   Collector
    Autograph collection, 1400–1960. ca. 1,500 items.
    Includes a letter by Maj. Gen. Abner Doubleday, June 16, 1864, opposing compromise with the Confederacy.
    Finding aid available.

57

Bateman, Francis Marion
(1843–1924)   Pvt., 78th Ohio Volunteers
    Letter, 1862. 1 item.
    Letter from Bateman to his parents, Feb. 23, 1861 [1862], concerning fortifications, casualties, and prisoners of war at Fort Donelson, Tenn.

58

Bates, Edward (1793–1869)   U.S. Attorney General
    Papers, 1859–66. 70 items.
    Diary (5 v.), notes, newspaper clippings, and memoranda. Includes remarks on the secession crisis, Cabinet meetings, events in Washington, and the progress of the war.

59
Battle of Aquia Creek, Va.
   Reports, 1861. 84 p.
   Transcripts.
   Copies of reports of skirmishes at Aquia Creek, May
31–June 2, 1861, by Comdr. James H. Ward, U.S.S. *Thomas
Freeborn*, Comdr. Stephen C. Rowan, U.S.S. *Pawnee*, Col. William R. Bate, and M. McCluskey.

60
Battle of Cedar Creek, Va.
   Poem, undated. 1 item.
   Poem honoring the Federal victory in the Battle of Cedar
Creek, Oct. 19, 1864.

61
Battle of Thompson's Station, Tenn.
   Letter, 1863. 1 item.
   Photocopy.
   Letter from an unidentified officer (surgeon?) in the 9th
Pennsylvania Cavalry to his wife, Mar. 13, 1863, Franklin,
Tenn., describing the Battle of Spring Hill or Thompson's
Station, skirmishes in the aftermath of the battle, depredations
by Union soldiers, and marches and camp life. Also notes the
presence of Indian soldiers from Arkansas in the battle of
Mar. 4.

62
Bayard, Thomas Francis
(1828–1898)   Lawyer, Wilmington, Del.
   Papers, 1780–1899. ca. 60,000 items.
   Contains material relating to the Fitz-John Porter court-
martial.
   Finding aid available.

63
Beard, Daniel Carter (1850–1941)
   Family papers, 1798–1941. ca. 72,000 items.
   Includes about 30 letters from Capt. Harry Beard, 30th
Missouri Infantry, to his mother, 1862–65, concerning the
Vicksburg and Mobile campaigns, operations along the Missis-
sippi River, the Arkansas Post (Fort Hindman) expedition, and
the occupation of Galveston, Tex., in June 1865. Provides infor-
mation on the organization and performance of black troops,
attitudes toward black soldiers, camp life, morale, marches,
discipline, foraging expeditions, diet, casualties, generalship,
Confederate deserters, the appearance and treatment of prison-

ers of war, and the treatment of noncombatants at Vidalia, La., New Orleans, La., Vicksburg, Miss., Mobile, Ala., and Galveston, Tex. Also contains details on skirmishes with Gen. Wirt Adams (CSA) in Mississippi, and Gen. Henry W. Slocum's expedition toward Jackson, Miss., July 3–9, 1864.

Finding aid available.

64
Beard, Richard (1799–1880)   Capt., 5th Infantry
                                                      Regiment, CSA
Letter, 1875. 1 item.
Transcript.
Letter from Beard to the editor of the Nashville (Tenn.) *Union and American*, June 27, 1875, defending himself against accusations concerning the death of Gen. James B. McPherson in the Atlanta Campaign.

65
Beardslee, Lester Anthony (1836–1903)   Lt. Comdr., USN
Papers, 1855–1900. 128 items.
Orders, 1861–65, and official correspondence, 1863–65, relating to Beardslee's service aboard the U.S.S. *Saratoga*, U.S.S. *Nantucket*, and U.S.S. *Wachusett*. Also, a diary, 1864, describing his service on the *Wachusett* with the South Atlantic Blockading Squadron, particularly his role in the capture of the C.S.S. *Florida* at Bahia Harbor, Brazil, Oct. 7, 1864.

Naval Historical Foundation collection.

66
Beauregard, Pierre Gustave Toutant
(1818–1893)   Gen., CSA
Papers, 1844–83. ca. 6,500 items.
Chiefly official correspondence, letterbooks, telegrams, orders, endorsement books, and newspaper clippings relating to the Fort Sumter affair, the 1st Manassas, Shiloh, and Corinth campaigns, the defense of Charleston, S.C., and the Siege of Petersburg, and the consolidation of Confederate forces after the Battle of Atlanta. Also includes Beauregard's autograph manuscript "Reminiscences," which was the basis for Alfred Romans' *The Military Operations of General Beauregard* (1884). Principal correspondents include Milledge Luke Bonham, Braxton Bragg, Howell Cobb, Samuel Cooper, Jefferson Davis, Wade Hampton, William J. Hardee, Daniel H. Hill, John Bell Hood, Joseph E. Johnston, Thomas Jordan, Robert E. Lee, James Longstreet, Francis W. Pickens, Leonidas Polk, Roswell S. Ripley, Earl Van Dorn, and Leroy P. Walker.

Finding aid available.

Pierre Gustave Toutant Beauregard

67

Beckwith, W. W.   Capt., USA

   Correspondence, 1864. 3 items.

   Letters to Beckwith of Feb. 3 and Apr. 3, 1864, from J. H. Devereaux, superintendent of military railroads, and assistant superintendent M. J. McCriekett, and a letter from Beckwith to Devereaux, Feb. 8, 1864, concerning fares charged on military lines.

68

Bedford, Wimer (1835–1905)   Capt., 48th
                                                     Illinois Volunteers

   Papers, 1864–65. 3 items.
   In part, transcripts.
   Diary (2 v.), Jan. 1, 1864–July 9, 1865, concerning Sherman's march to the sea, and a copy of Bedford's memoir, "Real Life in the Civil War." Contains details on the battles of Corinth, Port Gibson, Jackson, and Vicksburg, Miss., and Sherman's Savannah Campaign.

69

Beedle, William H. (1846–1893)   2d Main Battery;
                                      Veteran Reserve Corps

   Diary, 1865–66. 1 v.
   Diary kept by Beedle while on duty at the Douglas and Harewood Hospitals in Washington, D.C., Jan. 1, 1865–Jan. 1, 1866. Contains information on hospital care and the arrival of sick and wounded soldiers.

70

Beetham, Asa   USN

   Letters, 1861–65. 16 items.
   In part, photocopies.
   Letters from Beetham to his sister and relatives in New York City written while on blockade duty aboard the U.S.S. *Potomac* and U.S.S. *Pontoosuc*. Contains accounts of minor engagements in Mobile Bay and Southwest Pass (La.), and detailed descriptions of attacks on Fort Fisher and Fort Caswell, N.C. Also includes a brief note on Burton N. Harrison, private secretary to Jefferson Davis, as a prisoner in Washington, D.C.

71

Belknap, George Eugene (1832–1903)   USN

   Papers, 1857–1903. ca. 1,400 items.
   Includes a few miscellaneous writings on the Civil War, i.e., Gen. Ambrose E. Burnside's expedition to North Carolina, the service of Stephen Clegg Rowan, the construction and per-

formance of the U.S.S. *New Ironsides*, and the battle between the U.S.S. *Kearsarge* and C.S.S. *Alabama*.

Finding aid available.

Naval Historical Foundation collection.

72

Bell, George (d. 1907)   USA
     Papers, 1853–66. ca. 120 items.
     Correspondence, orders, circulars, and forms. Relates largely to the acquisition and distribution of military supplies. Also includes lists of officers in the Subsistence Department, 1864–65.

73

Bell, Henry Haywood (1808–1868)   Capt., USN
     Letter, 1862. 1 item.
     Report written from the U.S.S. *Hartford* off New Orleans, La., Apr. 26, 1862. Describes how gunboats commanded by Bell ran the Confederate batteries at Forts St. Philip and Jackson.

74

Bellows, Henry Whitney   Chairman, U.S. Sanitary
(1814–1882)   Commission
     Letters, 1861, 1866. 2 items.
     Letter from Bellows to "Cousin Harry," June 17, 1861, discussing commission affairs; letter from Bellows to Senator Morgan of New York, May 28, 1866, introducing the former Union surgeon, Horatio Stone.

75

Belmont, August (1816–1890)   Banker, New York
     Letters, 1861–72. 5 items.
     In part, transcripts.
     Contains copies of four letters to Salmon P. Chase, July–Dec. 1861, concerning public reaction to the American Civil War in England and France, the effect of the Federal blockade, the need for cotton in Europe, and reaction to the *Trent* affair.

76

Benham—McNeil Families
     Papers, 1772–1907. 145 items.
     Includes two letters from Gen. George B. McClellan to Capt. Henry W. Benham (1813–1884), May 16 and 21, 1861, concerning fortifications at Cairo, Ill.

77
Benjamin, Judah Philip
(1811–1884)   C.S. Secretary of State
     Papers, 1827–71. 7 items.
     In part, transcripts and photocopies.
     Includes an undated letter from Benjamin to Christopher
G. Memminger requesting the release of funds to be sent to
Mexico, and three postwar letters from Benjamin to James M.
Mason, London, England, concerning Benjamin's financial
recovery and the situation of former Confederate leaders.

78
Bennett, James Gordon
(1795–1872)   Editor, *New York Herald*
     Papers, 1845–1934. ca. 225 items.
     In part, photocopies.
     Chiefly letters to Bennett and his business manager, Fred-
eric Hudson, from war correspondents, military officers, and
informants in Washington, D.C., and in the field, 1861-64.
Includes information on the efforts of radical politicians to
remove General McClellan, McClellan's plan for the conduct of
the war, public reaction to Lincoln's Emancipation Proclamation, and campaigns in Maryland, Virginia, North Carolina,
South Carolina, Tennessee, Mississippi, and Louisiana. Also
includes remarks on the attitude of officers in the field toward
war correspondents, disputes between officers, military security and censorship of dispatches, problems of correspondents
in protecting their sources of information, difficulties in obtaining military passes, and the high cost of living in the South.
Principal correspondents include Finley Anderson, Nathaniel
P. Banks, James G. Bennett, Jr., Sylvanus Cadwallader, Hiram
Calkins, S. M. Carpenter, Thomas M. Cash, T. M. Cook, J. C.
Fitzpatrick, Henry M. Flint, Samuel R. Glen, James Hale,
Charles G. Halpine, S. R. Hanscone, Alfred C. Hills, Malcolm
Ives, Thomas W. Knox, George G. Meade, Daniel E. Sickles,
William H. Stiner, and L. A. Whiteley.

79
Beveridge, Albert Jeremiah
(1862–1927)   Historian; Author
     Papers, 1888–1927. ca. 98,000 items.
     Includes correspondence, notes, and drafts relating to
Beveridge's biography of Abraham Lincoln.
     Finding aid available.

80

Bickerdyke, Mary Ann Ball (1817–1901)   Nurse
    Papers, 1856–1905. ca. 1,800 items.
    In part, transcripts.
    Includes correspondence with medical and field officers,
officials of the U.S. Christian Commission, the Soldiers Aid
Society, the Western Sanitary Commission, and convalescent
soldiers concerning hospital care and management, supplies,
disease, diet, and the care of blacks. Provides a few details on
the battles of Lookout Mountain and Missionary Ridge, and
the Atlanta and Savannah campaigns.
    Finding aid available.

81

Biddle Family
    Papers, 1733–1886.
    Microfilm, 1 reel.
    Miscellaneous letters, 1861–65, concerning aid to prison-
ers of war, military appointments and promotions, black
citizenship, and routine affairs. Correspondents include Nathaniel P. Banks, John Gibbon, Henry W. Halleck, Joseph Hooker,
George B. McClellan, George G. Meade, Robert Patterson, Winfield Scott, William Smith, Roy Stone, and Isaac J. Wistar.

82

Bigelow, John (1854–1936)   Historian
    Papers, 1866–1936. ca. 25,000 items.
    In part, transcripts and photocopies.
    Contains correspondence and reports on military opera-
tions in Virginia, Tennessee, Mississippi, and Louisiana,
1861–64; research notes on the Chancellorsville Campaign;
and notes on an unpublished study of Robert E. Lee and the
secession movement. Also, an autograph collection of Civil War
letters with telegrams by Gens. Ulysses S. Grant, Leroy Pope
Walker, and P. G. T. Beauregard.
    Finding aid available.

83

Biklé, Philip Melanchton (b. 1844)   Professor,
                                               Pennsylvania College
    Reminiscence, 1930. 1 item.
    Transcript.
    Contains a few personal observations on Lincoln's Gettys-
burg Address.

84
Billings, Luther Guiteau (1842–1922)   Paymaster, USN
  Collection, 1865–1900. 12 items.
  In part, transcripts.
  Contains a memoir recounting Billings' service as an agent for Adams Express with Gen. Ambrose Burnside's army in North Carolina, as paymaster aboard the U.S.S. *Water Witch* operating between Port Royal, S.C., and Jacksonville, Fla., and his treatment as a prisoner of war at Savannah and Macon, Ga., Charleston, S.C., and Richmond, Va. Includes information on Burnside's attack on Confederate forces near Washington, N.C., problems with counterfeit money, the bombardment of Fort McAllister and the sinking of the C.S.S. *Nashville*, attacks on Fort Wagner and Fort Sumter, the capture of the C.S.S. *Atlanta*, the enlistment and performance of black troops, efforts by blacks to assist Federal prisoners of war, slavery and slave hunters, attitudes of noncombatants in the South, and escapes by Federal prisoners.
  Naval Historical Foundation collection.

85
Binckley, John Milton   Journalist, Virginia
  Papers, 1816–1943. 85 items.
  Two letters from Samuel Brooke (CSA) to his sister, Aug. 12, 1863, and July 3, 1864, discuss camp life, morale, and the progress of the war. Includes a sketch of the Siege of Petersburg, Va. Also contains two letters to Binckley from Confederate prisoners of war T. F. Mitchell and William M. Mitchell, 1865, and drafts and clippings of articles on the war and its aftermath in Virginia.

86
Black History Miscellany
  Collection, 1706–1944. ca. 500 items.
  In part, transcripts and photocopies.
  Includes documents concerning compensation for slaves impressed to work on Confederate fortifications, certificates of enlistment for several black soldiers, a letter by Robert Wright, Sept. 16, 1861, Livingston, Ala., accusing southern aristocrats of promoting war for their own ends, a copy of Lt. F. W. Browne's "My Service in the 1st U.S. Colored Cavalry," lists of officers and men in the 2d U.S. Colored Infantry, and a report by Col. Thomas J. Morgan on the service of the 14th U.S. Colored Infantry, Oct. 31, 1864, Decatur, Ga.

Francis Preston Blair

87
Black, Jeremiah Sullivan   U.S. Attorney General;
(1810–1883)   Secretary of State
    Papers, 1813–1904. ca. 10,000 items.
    Contains material relating to John Brown's raid on Harpers Ferry, President Buchanan's defense of his actions regarding Fort Moultrie and Fort Sumter, and notes from Cabinet meetings concerning Maj. Robert Anderson's removal to Fort Sumter.
    Finding aid and microfilm copy (36 reels) available.

88
Blackman, John P.
    Family papers, 1807–65. 51 items.
    Contains the commission of 1st Lt. Lack Weems, 15th Alabama Regiment, Oct. 4, 1861; Confederate bonds and certificates issued to Homer Blackman; and Homer Blackman's oath of allegiance, July 21, 1865.

89
Blaine, James Gillespie
(1830–1893)   U.S. Representative, Maine
    Family papers, 1777–1945. ca. 7,000 items.
    Includes a letter from Gen. Oliver O. Howard to Blaine, Aug. 24, 1864; a copy of a letter from Gen. William T. Sherman to Gen. Oliver O. Howard, Dec. 18, 1863; and a report on the system of discipline at the U.S. Military Academy.
    Finding aid available.

90
Blair, Francis Preston (1821–1875)   Statesman; Gen., USV
    Family papers, 1861.
    Microfilm, 1 reel.
    Contains two clippings from the London *Illustrated Times*, May 25, 1861, showing sketches of the members of Lincoln's Cabinet and of Robert Barnwell Rhett.

91
Blair Family
    Papers, 1755–1940. ca. 12,000 items.
    Contains correspondence, reports, and miscellaneous papers of Francis P. Blair (1791–1876), Maj. Gen. Francis P. Blair, Jr. (1821–1875), and U.S. Postmaster General Montgomery Blair (1813–1883). The papers of General Blair relate to campaigns in Mississippi, Louisiana, and Missouri, particularly the problems of obtaining recruits, establishing discipline, and solving rank disputes. Includes a report on the Battle of Chickasaw Bluffs, Dec. 31, 1862, and various orders and documents con-

cerning the Siege of Vicksburg. Montgomery Blair's wartime correspondence relates to politics and appointments in the Lincoln administration. Principal correspondents include John Albion Andrew, Thomas Hart Benton, Jr., Benjamin F. Butler, William E. Chandler, Charles A. Dana, Edward Everett, Gustavus V. Fox, John C. Frémont, Fitz-John Porter, Whitelaw Reid, William T. Sherman, Gideon Welles, and William Wood.

Finding aid available.

92
Blake, Charles Follen (1841–1879)   USN
    Diary, 1862–64. 1 item.
    Account of Blake's service in European waters aboard the U.S.S. *Constellation*, 1862–63; with the South Atlantic Blockading Squadron aboard the U.S.S. *Wabash* and U.S.S. *Lehigh*, 1863–64; and in the Battle of Mobile Bay aboard the U.S.S. *Brooklyn*, 1864. Includes information on Federal ship arrivals and departures along the coast of South Carolina, and the blockade of Charleston and Port Royal, S.C.
    Naval Historical Foundation collection.

93
Blood, Henry Boyden   Asst. Q.M., USA
    Diary, 1863. 1 item.
    Concerns the movement and issue of supplies during the Gettysburg Campaign and the retrieval of government property after the battle.

94
Bloomfield, Alpheus S.   Pvt., 1st Ohio
                                                   Light Artillery, USV
    Papers, 1861–93. ca. 160 items.
    Photocopies.
    Chiefly letters from Bloomfield to his family written during the Shiloh, Corinth, Chattanooga, Atlanta, and Franklin and Nashville campaigns. Describes enlistments, training, discipline, camp life, troop movements, equipment and supplies, the design and use of artillery, depredations, and economic conditions in the South. Includes a few sketches of encampments.
    Microfilm copy (1 reel) available.

95
Booth, Junius Brutus (1796–1852), and Family
    Collection, 1823–1953. 70 items.
    In part, transcripts, photocopies, and photographs.
    Excerpts from the diary of John Wilkes Booth, Apr. 14–21, 1865, relate to Booth's flight from Federal authorities after the assassination of President Lincoln.

96
Booth, Mrs. Lionel F.
    Collection, 1864, 1867. 2 items.
    Letter from President Lincoln to Charles Sumner, May 19, 1864, concerning Mrs. Booth, widow of Maj. Lionel F. Booth, who was killed at Fort Pillow, and her plea in behalf of the widows and children of black soldiers.

97
Bourland, James A.   Col., CSA
    Papers, 1841–96. ca. 200 items.
    Includes correspondence, orders, muster rolls, commissions, and miscellaneous items relating to Texas State troops, particularly the 21st brigade or Border Regiment, in the Red River Valley and along the Cherokee Nation frontier.
    Microfilm copy (3 reels) available.

98
Bourne, William Oland   Clergyman–Journalist,
(1819–1901)   New York
    Papers, 1856–84. ca. 1,500 items.
    Postwar letters of disabled veterans submitted in a contest for the "Exhibition of Left-Hand Penmanship," sponsored by Bourne, editor of *The Soldier's Friend*. Contributors generally describe their service in the war. Also includes numerous photographs of contributors and three autograph books signed by convalescents at Central Park Hospital in New York City, where Bourne served as chaplain.

99
Boyce, Charles H.   28th New York Volunteers
    Papers, 1861–1932. 10 items.
    Chiefly a manuscript history of the 28th New York Volunteers, May 1861–Sept. 1862. Describes the Shenandoah Valley Campaign of 1862 and the 2d Manassas Campaign, particularly the Battle of Cedar Mountain. Also contains remarks on a skirmish at Falling Waters, W. Va., July 3, 1861, Unionists in Virginia, camp life, marches, training, military organization, the occupation of Charles Town, W. Va., reconnaissance expeditions, discipline, casualties, morale, and the generalship of Samuel W. Crawford, John C. Frémont, George B. McClellan, Irvin McDowell, John Pope, and Franz Sigel.

100
Boyce, James Petigru   Clergyman–Educator,
(1827–1888)   South Carolina
    Papers, 1854–1907. 20 items.
    Several letters from Christopher G. Memminger to Boyce,

Dec. 10, 1862—Mar. 31, 1864, concern interest on Confederate notes and bonds. Also includes a table of "War Tax Assessments under the Act Aug. 19, 1861 so far as reported to date—Mch. 14, 1863."

101
Boyd, Crosby Noyes (1903–   )   Collector
    Autograph collection, 1791–1908. 146 items.
    Includes letters by John M. Botts, Belle Boyd, John P. Brophy, William G. Brownlow, Dorothea Dix, Col. Erasmus D. Keyes, President Lincoln, and Gen. John E. Wool, 1861–64, and photographs of the execution of the Lincoln conspirators.

102
Boyle, William   4th South Carolina Regiment
    Letters, 1864. 2 items.
    Letters from Boyle to his mother, Nov. 17 and 23, 1864, Dinwiddie Courthouse, Va.

103
Bradbury, William H.
(1829–1900)   129th Illinois Volunteers
    Papers, 1862–1900. 102 items.
    Chiefly letters from Bradbury to his wife, 1862–65, written from camps in Tennessee, Kentucky, and Georgia while serving as a clerk on the headquarters staffs of Gens. William Thomas Ward and Daniel Butterfield and in the office of the Judge Advocate General. Contains comments on Bradbury's unauthorized letters to the editors of the *Chicago Tribune* and the *Manchester Guardian*, camp life, entertainment, marches, depredations, morale, guerrilla warfare, peculation in the U.S. Army, the treatment of blacks, prisoners of war, and diet. Also contains some information on the Atlanta Campaign.

104
Bradford, Joshua Taylor   Surg., USA
    Diary, 1862. 1 item.
    Diary, Jan. 1–May 27, 1862, kept during the Shiloh Campaign and Gen. Henry Halleck's advance on Corinth, Miss.

105
Bragg, Braxton (1817–1876)   Gen., CSA
    Papers, 1861–63. 22 items.
    Photocopies.
    Letters from Bragg to his wife concerning the seizure of the Federal arsenal at Baton Rouge, La., defenses along the gulf coast between Pensacola and Mobile, and the Shiloh, Corinth, Tullahoma, and Chattanooga campaigns. Includes a

detailed report on the battles of Lookout Mountain and Missionary Ridge by Gen. Edward C. Walthall.

106
Brannigan, Felix (1843–1907)   Orderly Sgt.,
                                                   74th New York Volunteers
    Papers, 1861–64. 28 items.
    Letters from Brannigan to his sister concerning recruitment, training, and the Peninsular and Gettysburg campaigns. Includes information on camp life, troop movements, the Siege of Yorktown, and the battles of Williamsburg and Gettysburg.

107
Brayman, Mason (1813–1895)   Gen., USA
    Letter, 1863. 1 item.
    Transcript.
    Copy of a letter from Brayman to E. A. Parker, Sept. 3, 1863, Camp Dennison, Ohio, advocating vigorous prosecution of the war and the unconditional surrender of the Confederacy.

108
Breckinridge Family
    Papers, 1752–1965. ca. 200,000 items.
    Contains numerous letters from family members relating to the war. Of particular interest are the papers of Col. William Campbell Preston Breckinridge (1837–1904), 9th Kentucky Cavalry, CSA, which consist of an order book, Dec. 1862– Mar. 1864, and letters to his wife; also, the diary, 1864–65, and letters of Lt. Joseph Cabell Breckinridge (1842–1920), 2d Artillery Battalion, USA, written chiefly at Fort Barrancas and Fort Pickens, Fla.
    Finding aid available.

109
Brent, Joseph Lancaster (1826–1905)   Maj., CSA
    Collection, 1863. 2 items.
    Letter from Brent to Gen. Carter L. Stevenson, Feb. 24, 1863, concerning the capture of the U.S.S. *Indianola* and repairs to the C.S.S. *Beatty*. Also a steel engraving of Brent.
    Naval Historical Foundation collection.

110
Brewer, David L.
    Poem, 1865. 1 item.
    Transcript.
    Poem eulogizing the Confederacy copied from the back of a Confederate dollar.

111
Briggs, E. B. USA
   Document, 1862. 1 item.
   Pass issued to H. B. Barnes, Dec. 29, 1862, Fredericksburg,
Va.

112
Brincklé, John Rumsey
(1839−1910) Lt., 5th U.S. Artillery
   Papers, 1859−1936. ca. 275 items.
   Letters from Brincklé to his family, 1861−63, concerning
the recruiting service in Vermont, Connecticut, and Pennsylvania, and garrison duty at Fort Hamilton, N.Y. Letters
written by Brincklé from Virginia, 1864−65, relate to the
Wilderness, Spotsylvania, Petersburg, and Appomattox campaigns, and the Battle of Cold Harbor. Also includes a few
details on the Battle of Sayler's Creek. A diary, Feb. 3−Sept.
20, 1865, contains sketches of Federal batteries and shelters at
the Siege of Petersburg.

113
Bristow, Benjamin Helm
(1832−1896) Lt. Col., 25th Kentucky Volunteers
   Papers, 1839−1932. ca. 16,000 items.
   In part, photocopies.
   Letters from Bristow to his wife, Feb.−Apr. 1862, concerning the Fort Donelson, Fort Henry, and Shiloh campaigns. Also,
letters from Bristow to his wife, Col. L. D Bruce, and Gen.
Jeremiah T. Boyle, Oct.−Nov. 1862, concerning Bristow's service in the 8th Kentucky Cavalry. Includes an official report on
the participation of the 25th Kentucky Volunteers in the Battle of Shiloh.
   Finding aid and partial index available.

114
Bromwell, Henry Pelham Holmes U.S. Representative,
(1823−1903) Illinois
   Scrapbooks, 1817−1929. 31 v.
   Includes a letter from Maj. James A. Connolly to Bromwell,
Nov. 1864, concerning Sherman's march to the sea, and a let-
ter from M. Leroy Cook to Bromwell, July 30, 1862, on mili-
tary activities near Moscow, Ky., and rank disputes and morale
in the 54th Illinois Volunteers.
   Indexed.

115
Bronson, Theodore B. Capt., USA
   Letterbook, 1863−65. 1 v.

Contains about 250 letters written by Bronson as provost marshal of the 6th Military District of New York concerning recruits, enlistment bounties, desertions, and discharges.

Indexed.

116

Brooks, William Elizabeth (b. 1875)

Collection, 1862–1946.

Microfilm, 1 reel.

Letters of Maj. Charles H. Howard (USA) to his family, 1862–64, concerning the 2d Manassas, Fredericksburg, Chancellorsville, Chattanooga, and Atlanta campaigns; diary of Chaplain Marcus B. DeWitt, 8th Tennessee Regiment, Mar. 7–May 17, 1863, concerning campaigns in Mississippi, Georgia, and North Carolina; and diary of Alexander R. Boteler, aide-de-camp to Gen. J. E. B. Stuart, May 1864, concerning the Wilderness Campaign and the effect of Stuart's death on the Army of Northern Virginia.

117

Brown, Edgar F.

Letter, 1862. 1 item.

Letter from Brown to his wife, July 27, 1862, describing a conversation with President Lincoln concerning new recruits for the Army and the appointment of Gen. Henry Halleck as military adviser to the President and General in Chief.

118

Brown, Joseph Emerson (1821–1894)   Gov., Georgia

Letters, 1861–64. 3 items.

Letter from Brown to Gov. John Letcher of Virginia, May 14, 1861, requesting the loan of cannons for Georgia's coastal defense; and two letters from Brown to Gov. Zebulon B. Vance of North Carolina, Sept. 26, 1862, and Mar. 23, 1864, concerning efforts to prevent the manufacture of liquor, and State import and export duties.

119

Brown, Lewis Kirk (1843–1926)   USA

Collection, 1863. 5 items.

Three letters from Walt Whitman to Brown, Aug. 1863, Washington, D.C., concerning patients, deaths, and hospital care at Judiciary Square Hospital in Washington, and the progress of the war. Also a memorandum on the life and service of Brown, undated.

120

Brown, Thomas J. (1845–ca. 1915)   U.S. Government Clerk
  Papers, 1861–1909. ca. 1,000 items.
  Chiefly correspondence, notes, photographs, clippings,
drafts of articles, and printed matter concerning vital statistics
of the war and veterans' pensions.

121

Browne, George W.   Lt., USN
  Diary, 1860–69. 1 v.
  Diary kept in the form of a ship's log aboard the U.S.
Transport *Empire City*, Apr.–May 1861, during voyages
between New York and Virginia, and aboard the U.S.S.
Fernandina, Nov. 27, 1861–Apr. 14, 1862, while Browne was
on blockade duty along the Virginia and North Carolina coasts.
Describes ship sightings, skirmishes with Confederate batter-
ies along the James River, and the effect of the blockade on
Wilmington, N.C.

122

Browne, John Mills (1831–1894)   Surg., USN
  Papers, 1853–78. 10 items.
  In part, photocopies.
  Commission, June 19, 1861.
  Naval Historical Foundation collection.

123

Browning, Silas W.
(1820–1888)   Pvt., 53d Massachusetts Volunteers
  Papers, 1779–1890. 59 items.
  Chiefly letters from Browning to his wife and family con-
cerning his duties as a hospital steward, military discipline,
the health and diet of soldiers in the 53d Massachusetts
Regiment, the Port Hudson Campaign, and conditions in the
South. Most of Browning's letters were written in camps near
New Orleans and Baton Rouge, La.; a few came from camps in
Mississippi, Georgia, and Florida.

124

Brownlow, William Gannaway
(1805–1877)   Clergyman–Journalist, Tennessee
  Papers, 1862–68. 6 items.
  Includes two letters by Brownlow, Aug. 7 and Oct. 2, 1862,
concerning new recruits and the response to the "President's
draft" in New York and Michigan, and an article written for
the *New York Weekly*, June 28, 1862, containing remarks on
Union officers.

125
Brownson, Orestes Augustus
(1803–1876)   Philosopher; Author
     Papers, 1822–94.
     Microfilm, 19 reels.
     Contains a few letters to Brownson from officers and civilians in the South concerning politics, secession, slavery, and military activities.
     Finding aid available.
     Originals at the University of Notre Dame.

126
Bryan, Thomas Barbour
(1828–1906)   Businessman, Chicago, Ill.
     Papers, 1863. 2 items.
     Includes a letter from Bryan to Henry W. Bellows, Dec. 31, 1863, on the sale of Lincoln's original autograph of the Emancipation Proclamation for the benefit of the Chicago Soldiers Home.

127
Bryan, Wilhelmus Bogart
(1854–1938)   Historian; Author
     Notes, 1789–1888. ca. 3,500 items.
     Chiefly extracts from newspapers. Includes some information on the Civil War.

128
Buford, Charles (1797–1866)   Maj., CSA
     Papers, 1842–65. 38 items.
     Includes 13 letters written during the war concerning the battles of Shiloh and Perryville (Chaplin Hills), guerrilla activity in Kentucky and Missouri, runaway slaves in Missouri, efforts by Union officers to quell civil disorder in Kentucky, and prison life at Camp Douglas and Rock Island, Ill. Correspondents include James F. Buckner, W. N. Budd, Louis M. Buford, James W. Duke, J. F. Henry, William K. Poston, and George S. Williams.

129
Bulloch, Irvine S.   Acting Master, CSN
     Logbook, 1864–65.
     Microfilm, 1 reel.
     Logbook of the C.S.S. *Shenandoah,* Oct. 20, 1864–July 22, 1865. Contains a list of officers aboard the *Shenandoah,* the names and value of about 25 prize vessels, and information on tactics used to approach enemy vessels and the treatment of prisoners of war.

130

Burbank–Van Voorhis Family
    Collection, 1814–1913. 50 items.
    Includes the diary of U.S. Army Gen. Sidney Burbank (d. 1882), July 22, 1861–Oct. 20, 1880. Describes marches and skirmishes of General Burbank's brigade in the Chancellorsville, Gettysburg, and Mine Run campaigns. Provides a detailed account of the participation of the brigade in the Battle of Gettysburg.

131

Burch, Samuel   Lawyer
    Papers, 1775–1865. ca. 1,200 items.
    In part, transcripts.
    Includes copies of letters, 1862–65, describing depredations in Tennessee and reaction to the Lincoln assassination.

132

Burlingame, Anson (1820–1870) and Edward L.
(1848–1922)
    Papers, 1810–1937. ca. 550 items.
    In part, transcripts.
    Chiefly the correspondence and papers of Anson Burlingame, U.S. Minister to Austria and China. Includes three letters of instruction from William H. Seward to Burlingame, Apr.–May 1861, concerning the Federal blockade and contraband trade; a letter from John C. Frémont to Burlingame, June 4, 1861, on the purchase of arms for the United States; a photograph of General Frémont; and an unsigned manuscript entitled "Convention upon the subject of the rights of belligerents and neutrals in time of war, between the United States . . . and Austria," 1861.
    Finding aid available.

133

Burt, Elizabeth Johnston Reynolds (1838–1926)
    Papers, 1797–1917. ca. 125 items.
    In part, photocopies and transcripts.
    Transcript of Elizabeth Burt's autobiography, "An Army Wife's Forty Years in the Service, 1862–1902." Chiefly concerns war-related activities in Cincinnati and camp life during the Atlanta Campaign in company with her husband, Capt. Andrew Sheridan Burt, 18th Ohio Volunteers. Published in part in Merrill J. Mattes, *Indians, Infants, and Infantry; Andrew and Elizabeth Burt on the Frontier* (1960). Also includes a letter from Captain Burt to his father, Feb. 5, 1864, Chattanooga, Tenn., describing camp life and problems with drunk soldiers.
    Microfilm copy (1 reel) available.

134
Burwell, William MacCreary
(1809–1888)   Poet, Baltimore, Md.
    Papers, 1851–63. 14 items.
    Includes two letters from Robert A. Toombs to Burwell,
June 10 and Aug. 29, 1863, expressing dissatisfaction with the
Confederate Government, and a letter from B. J. Sage to the
Virginia House of Delegates, Sept. 30, 1863, on the subject of
State aid to schemes of private warfare sanctioned by the Con-
federate Government. Also a poem by Burwell, "Breckenridge
& Union."

135
Butler, Benjamin Franklin (1818–1893)   Gen., USV
    Papers, 1831–96. ca. 190,000 items.
    Personal and official correspondence, letterbooks, order
books, reports, notebooks, maps and charts, newspaper clippings, and miscellaneous items concerning Butler's commands
in Maryland, Louisiana, Virginia, and North Carolina. Includes
details on the capture of Forts Hatteras and Clark, Butler's
service as military governor of New Orleans, the Petersburg
Campaign, and the Fort Fisher expedition. Also contains letters from French and Spanish consuls in New Orleans.
    Finding aid and index available.

136
Butler, Charles
(1802–1897)   Businessman, New York City
    Papers, 1819–1905. ca. 2,100 items.
    Includes a letter from Butler to his wife, Dec. 19, 1861,
concerning the military atmosphere in St. Louis, Mo., and a
letter from Butler to his daughter, July 18, 1863, describing
the anti-draft riots in New York City. The letterhead on
Butler's letter from St. Louis has an engraved view of Camp
Benton.
    Finding aid and microfilm copy (4 reels) available.

137
Butler, Robert Ormond (1832–1874)   Surg., CSA
    Collection, 1862. 1 item.
    Photocopy.
    Letter from Butler to his sister, Sept. 22, 1862, Thibodeaux,
La., describing skirmishes at Boutté Station and Bayou Des
Allemands, La.

Benjamin Franklin Butler

138
Butler, W. P. (b. 1815) Merchant – Planter,
South Carolina
Papers, 1809 – 82. 5 items.
Includes a certificate of exemption from military service
for H. M. Drury, Henry County, Va., and a "Certificate of
Appraisement" for two horses owned by W. P. Butler acquired
by Wade Hampton's cavalry.

139
Butterfield, Daniel (1831 – 1901) Gen., USV
Collection, 1895. 1 item.
Galley proofs of Butterfield's address on Gen. Joseph
Hooker delivered at Chattanooga, Tenn., Sept. 18, 1895.

140
Cadwallader, Sylvanus
(1825? – 1905) War Correspondent, *New York Herald*
Papers, 1818 – 1904. ca. 250 items.
Contains a letter from Cadwallader to his daughter, Nov.
13, 1862, La Grange, Tenn., concerning camp life, foraging expeditions, and the treatment of free blacks and noncombatants
in the South; telegrams and documents concerning Cadwallader's draft notice and the securing of a substitute; letters
between Elihu B. Washburne and Gen. U. S. Grant, Dec. 1863,
concerning an official letter of gratitude from the U.S. Congress
for Grant's military service; letters from Grant and members of
his staff (1864) commending Cadwallader on his reporting of the
war; and a letter from James H. Wilson, Dec. 12, 1863, concerning the gift of a horse (Egypt) to General Grant. Also
includes a sketch of the McLean house at Appomattox, Va., a
list of officers who served on Grant's staff during the war, and
military passes.
Finding aid available.

141
Cameron, Simon (1799 – 1889) U.S. Secretary of War
Papers, 1738 – 1889. ca. 7,600 items.
Includes letters, 1861, relating to Cameron's appointment
as Secretary of War, various military appointments, and the
administration of the War Department.
Finding aid and microfilm copy (22 reels) available.

142
———
Papers, 1824 – 92.
Microfilm, 10 reels.
Contains numerous solicitations for military appointments,

Daniel Butterfield

1861. Correspondents are listed in the *Guide to the Microfilm of the Simon Cameron Papers at the Historical Society of Dauphin County* (1971).

143

Campbell, George Washington (1769–1848)
    Papers, 1793–1886. ca. 400 items.
    Photocopies.
    Contains four letters from Gen. Robert E. Lee or his Assistant Adjutant General to Gen. Richard S. Ewell, Aug. 1863–Mar. 1865, concerning military organization, desertions in the Confederate Army, the defense of Richmond, and the use of blacks in the army; a letter from Isham Harris to Mrs. Ewell, Mar. 7, 1864, Dalton, Ga., concerning military strategy, the progress of the war in Tennessee, the generalship of Braxton Bragg, the Battle of Chickamauga, and morale in the Army of the Tennessee; two postwar letters from Jefferson Davis to Maj. Campbell Brown on the use of blacks in the Confederate Army and an order Davis issued to General Ewell during the 1st Manassas Campaign; miscellaneous letters by Gens. P. G. T. Beauregard, Joseph E. Johnston, and U. S. Grant; and a "Map of the Battle Ground of Manassas From Actual Surveys by an Officer of Genl. Beauregard's Staff . . ." (1862).

144

Campbell, Given   Capt., CSA
    Diary, 1865. 1 item.
    Photocopy of a transcript.
    Describes the flight of Jefferson Davis from Greensboro, N.C., to Irwinville, Ga., Apr. 15–May 10, 1865.
    Microfilm copy (1 reel) available.

145

Cannon, William R. (1804–1858)   Mississippi
    Papers, 1849–63. 15 items.
    Letter from Jefferson Davis to Mrs. E. G. Cannon, July 18, 1863, acknowledging the gift of a Bible and expounding on the southern cause.

146

Capron, Horace
(1804–1885)   Col., 14th Illinois Cavalry, USV
    Papers, 1834–1961. ca. 1,800 items.
    Contains military correspondence, orders, reconnaissance reports, returns, muster rolls, commissions, and reports on battles and skirmishes. Includes detailed accounts of Gen. George Stoneman's raid to Macon, Ga., during the Atlanta Campaign, the capture of Capron with most of his command, and Gen.

Ambrose Burnside's campaign in east Tennessee. Also includes a letter to Capron reporting the death of his oldest son, Lt. Horace Capron, Jr., in Tennessee (1863), a letter to Capron's wife from a Confederate prisoner of war, Apr. 22, 1865, on the capture of her son, Lt. Albert B. Capron, a diary entitled "History of Marches &c. of fourteenth Regiment of Illinois Cavalry Volunteers from time of leaving Camp Peoria March 28th 1863," "Lloyd's Official Map of the State of Tennessee" (1862) with annotations showing the marches of the 14th Illinois Cavalry in Kentucky and Tennessee, and articles and biographical notes of Capron and his sons Horace, Albert, and Osmond, all three of whom served under his command.

Finding aid available.

147
Cardwell, Charles W.   20th Virginia Heavy Artillery
    Letter, 1942. 1 item.
    Photocopy.
    Letter from Cardwell to Melvin Scott, Aug. 18, 1942, reminiscing about his service in the Civil War, particularly his capture at the Battle of Sayler's Creek, Va.

148
Carlton, Caleb Henry
(1836–1923)   Col., 89th Ohio Volunteers
    Papers, 1831–1954. ca. 2,500 items.
    Letters from Carlton to his wife concerning the battles of Mechanicsville and Malvern Hill, the Chickamauga Campaign, and the battles of Kennesaw Mountain, Marietta, and Jonesboro in the Atlanta Campaign. Includes information on camp life, discipline, economic conditions in the South, the treatment of blacks and noncombatants, and life at Libby Prison in Richmond, Va. Also contains military commissions, orders, awards, audits, receipts, and furloughs; a map of the Battle of 2d Manassas; sketches of troop positions in the Chickamauga Campaign; a biographical essay, "Caleb Henry Carlton, Brigadier General, United tates Army," by his daughter, Mabel Carlton Horner; and miscellaneous items. Correspondents include William T. Sherman and Thomas J. Wood.

Finding aid available.

149
Carman, Ezra Ayers
(1834–1909)   Col., 13th New Jersey Volunteers
    Manuscript, 1861–63. 23 boxes.
    Unfinished history of the Civil War. Includes newspaper clippings and personal notes.

150

Carnegie, Andrew (1835–1919)   Industrialist
    Papers, 1830–1935. 67,000 items.
    Contains information on the transportation of military equipment and supplies and the organization of the military telegraph.
    Finding aid available.

151

Carrington—McDowell Families
    Papers, 1780–1897. ca. 300 items.
    Contains two dispatches from Capt. Benjamin L. Farinholt to Gen. Robert E. Lee, June 25 and 27, 1864, Staunton River Bridge [Va.], concerning preparations for and the repulse of a Federal raiding party.

152

Carruthers, George North (ca. 1840–1906)   USA
    Papers, 1864–69. 5 items.
    List of officers (field, staff, and line) in the 51st U.S. Colored Infantry, formerly the 1st Regiment, Mississippi Volunteers of African Descent; monthly reports, June 1864–Aug. 1865; account of the service of the 51st U.S. Colored Infantry in Louisiana, Mississippi, Alabama, and Florida; personal information on numerous recruits; and a photograph of 28 officers. Includes some information on an engagement at Millikens Bend, La., and the Mobile Campaign.

153

Carson, Christopher
(1809–1868)   Col., 1st New Mexico Volunteers
    Papers, 1842–69. ca. 70 items.
    In part, photocopies.
    Contains the headquarters letterbook for Carson's Navajo expedition, July 11, 1863–May 17, 1864. Describes military organization, strategy, routes of march, skirmishes, and casualties.

154

Carter, John C.   Comdr., USN
    Document, 1864. 1 item.
    Record of examination of Carter's fitness for promotion, 1864, with supporting letters from E. P. Door, David G. Farragut, and Gideon Welles.

155
Carter, Samuel Powhatan (1819–1891)   Gen., USV
      Manuscript, 1882. 1 item.
      Manuscript biography, "A Sketch of the Military Services
of Sam. P. Carter, Brig. Genl. & Brevt. Maj. Genl. of U.S. Vols.
during the Rebellion of the Southern States, 1861–5." Describes
Carter's efforts to organize and train loyalist volunteers from
east Tennessee (1st and 2d East Tennessee Volunteers), marches,
morale, reconnaissance expeditions, plans for the capture and
fortification of Cumberland Gap, the battles of Logan's Cross
Roads, Ky., and Kinston, N.C., and Carter's service as provost
marshal general in East Tennessee.
      Microfilm copy (1 reel) available.
      Naval Historical Foundation collection.

156
Cartter Family
      Papers, 1836–93. ca. 800 items.
      Contains letters from 1st Lt. William Cartter, U.S. Marine
Corps, to his mother, July 1861–Feb. 1865, concerning the
Battle of 1st Manassas and his service aboard the U.S.S.
Minnesota at Hampton Roads, Va., Pensacola, Fla., and off the
coast of North Carolina. Includes Cartter's eyewitness account
of the battle between the *Monitor* and *Merrimac* and informa-
tion concerning the transportation of prisoners of war from
North Carolina to New York. Also contains a few letters of 2d
Lt. David Kellogg Cartter, Jr. (d. 1862), 2d Ohio Cavalry, concerning the impact of the war in Missouri, Kansas, and Arkansas, and problems with western Indians.

157
Cary, Clarence (b. 1846)   Midshipman, CSN
      Report, 1905, 1926. 1 item.
      Report prepared by Cary in 1905 for the State Depart-
ment Library as a supplement to the diary he kept during his
service aboard the C.S.S. *Chickamauga*, 1863–65. Contains
additional information on tactics employed by blockade runners,
prize vessels, deserters, prisoners of war, and Gen. B. F. Butler's Fort Fisher expedition. Cary's diary was used by the State
Department in the discussion of the *Alabama* claims.
      Naval Historical Foundation collection.

158
Casey, Silas (1841–1913)   Lt. Comdr., USN
      Papers, 1771–1941. ca. 300 items.
      In part, transcripts.
      Includes correspondence between Capt. Edwin W. Suther-
land (USN), Lt. Col. Samuel W. Ferguson (CSA), Gen. John C.

Pemberton, and Gen. Franklin Gardner, Feb.– Mar. 1863, concerning Sutherland's planned defection and his attempt to sell a Federal gunboat (U.S.S. *Essex*) to the Confederacy. Also, a logbook kept by Casey, on the U.S.S. *Niagara* during blockade duty off Charleston Harbor, S.C., and in the Gulf of Mexico, Apr.– Aug. 1861; and miscellaneous orders relating to Casey's service on the U.S.S. *Niagara*, U.S.S. *Unadilla*, U.S.S. *Wissahickon*, and U.S.S. *Quaker City*.

Finding aid available.
Naval Historical Foundation collection.

159
Cater, Douglas J. and Rufus W.   19th Louisiana
                                                   Volunteers, CSA
    Papers, 1859–65. 60 items.
    Letters of Lt. Rufus W. Cater (d. 1863), Sept. 1859–July 1863, and his brother, musician Douglas J. Cater, Dec. 1862– May 1865, to their cousin, Fannie S. Cater, concerning camp life, marches, equipment and supplies, desertion, casualties, and morale during the evacuation of Corinth and in the Vicksburg, Tullahoma, Atlanta, and Franklin and Nashville campaigns. Includes information on the patriotism of southern women, the use of blacks as soldiers, conditions in the Confederate Army in late 1864, and feelings expressed by Confederate soldiers over General Lee's surrender at Appomattox, Va.

160
Cattell, James McKeen (1860–1944)
    Papers, 1835–1948. ca. 83,000 items.
    Contains a letter written by Calvin Ferriday to W. C. Cattell, Nov 14, 1862, from a camp near Fayetteville, Va.
    Finding aid available.

161
Causten, James H., and John T. and Theodore Pickett
    Papers, 1765–1916. ca. 33,000 items.
    Contains a few letters in the personal papers of John Thomas Pickett concerning relief for soldiers, a proposal for a shipping line to be partly owned by the Confederacy, military passes, and John T. Pickett's parole, Apr. 27, 1865.
    Finding aid available.

162
Chamberlain, Joshua Lawrence (1828–1914)   Gen., USV
    Papers, 1862–1910. ca. 1,000 items.
    Reports, orders, musters, returns, invoices, maps, and official correspondence relating to Chamberlain's service as lt. colonel and colonel of the 20th Maine Volunteers. Includes

detailed accounts of the Gettysburg, Petersburg, and Appomattox campaigns, and skirmishes at Aldie and Middleburg, Va. Manuscript and engraved maps in the collection show fortifications and troop positions at Gettysburg, Pa., and Yorktown, Groveton, Petersburg, and Five Forks, Va. Also includes a map of the area from Gettysburg to Appomattox Courthouse annotated to show the marches and battles of the 118th Pennsylvania Volunteers. Notes, regimental indexes, and lists of officers and battles in the collection were used in Frederick H. Dyers' *Compendium of the War of the Rebellion* (1909).

Finding aid available.

163

Chambers, Washington Irving (1856–1934)
Papers, 1871–1943. ca. 12,000 items.
In part, transcripts.
Includes notes on Confederate torpedoes and the use of torpedoes during the Civil War.
Finding aid available.
Naval Historical Foundation collection.

164

Chambrun, Charles Adolphe de Pineton, marquis de (1831–1891) Judicial Counselor to the French Embassy, Washington, D.C.

Letters, 1865.
Microfilm, 1 reel.
Letters of Chambrun, in French, to his wife, Jan. 13–June 30, 1865, concerning President Lincoln, American social life, and the Civil War. Source material for his *Impressions of Lincoln and the Civil War, A Foreigner's Account* (1952).

165

Chandler, Arthur Chelton CSA
Papers, 1862–1923. 16 items.
Includes a letter from Lt. C.W. Taylor, 60th Georgia Volunteers, to Mrs. Inman(?), July 30, 1862, Green Springs, Va.

166

Chandler, William Eaton
(1835–1917) Judge Adv. Gen., USN
Papers, 1863–1917. ca 25,000 items.
In part, transcripts.
Includes copies of six letters from Adm. David G. Farragut to William H. Shock, fleet engineer at New Orleans, La., Feb.–Oct. 1864, concerning ship repairs and modifications.
Finding aid available.

167

Chandler, Zachariah (1813–1879)   U.S. Senator, Michigan
     Papers, 1854–99. ca. 1,100 items.
     Includes a few letters from volunteer officers concerning
military commissions and supplies. Principal wartime correspondents are Nathaniel P. Banks, James G. Blaine, Simon
Cameron, Horace Greeley, Abraham Lincoln, Edwin M. Stanton, and Benjamin F. Wade.
     Finding aid, partial index, and microfilm copy (4 reels)
available.

168

Chase, Cornelius
(1780–1868)   Farmer; Educator; Clergyman
     Family papers, 1815–1947. ca. 3,000 items.
     Includes the papers of Cornelius Thruston Chase (1819–
1870), which comprise reports on Confederate hospitals in Virginia and South Carolina, medical contracts with private physicians in Richmond, Va., provision returns, circulars and special orders relating to the Medical Department, CSA, lists of
deserters, quartermaster reports, reports on prisoners of war,
and reports on sick and wounded soldiers. Also contains correspondence with slave traders (Browning, Moore and Company,
E. H. Stokes) operating in Virginia during the war, and a sketch
of Richmond, Va.
     Finding aid available.

169

Chase, Salmon Portland (1808–1873)   U.S. Secretary
                                             of the Treasury
     Papers, 1755–1898. ca. 12,500 items.
     Diaries kept by Chase during the war contain accounts of
Cabinet meetings, and private meetings with President Lincoln,
William Seward, Edwin M. Stanton, Henry Halleck, George B.
McClellan, and various other political and military leaders.
Subjects discussed include the evaluation, selection, and assignment of generals, military strategy, the disposition of troops,
the use of black troops, the draft, war finance, and the Emancipation Proclamation. Also includes correspondence with George
S. Denison, Chase's official and personal representative in New
Orleans, La., June 1862–Mar. 1865, and reports from officers
and Treasury agents in the South on the progress of the war,
conditions in the South and in the Confederate Army, and the
disposition and strength of Federal forces.
     Finding aid, index, and microfilm copy (38 reels) available.

170
Chesley, James A.   Master's Mate, USN
     Letter, 1862. 1 item.
     Serial letter to "All the Good People" in Wakefield, Mass.,
Feb. 6−7, 1862, describing the U.S.S. *Lancaster* and life on a
warship en route to San Francisco, Calif.

171
Chesnut, James (1815−1885)   Gen., CSA
     Papers, 1862. 23 items.
     Letterbook, Jan. 20−Nov. 24, 1862, maintained by Chesnut
as chief of the Military Department of South Carolina. Contains numerous orders from the Governor and council concerning enlistments, drafts, the selection of officers, the disposition
of troops, and the procurement of supplies. Also, miscellaneous
letters relating to the South Carolina militia, a list of draftees
from the 30th South Carolina Militia Regiment, and letters to
President Davis concerning the defense of Charleston, S.C.

172
Choate, Joseph Hodges   Lawyer, New York City
(1832−1917)
     Papers, 1745−1927. ca. 11,000 items.
     Includes a letter from Capt. James T. Sterling, 7th Ohio
Volunteers, to his wife, July 29, 1861, Camp Sutton, Va., concerning FFV's—"Fleet Footed Virginians."
     Finding aid available.

173
Church, William Conant (1836−1917)   Editor; Journalist
     Papers, 1862−1924. ca. 350 items.
     Contains responses by several Union officers to articles on
the war published in Church's *United States Army and Navy
Journal*. Includes Adm. Samuel F. Du Pont's defense of his
actions in the abortive attack on Charleston, S.C., in 1863, and
accounts of Sheridan's Shenandoah Valley Campaign (particularly the Battle of Cedar Creek) and General Terry's expedition against Fort Fisher, N.C., by Gen. Joseph R. Hawley. Other
correspondents are Samuel W. Crawford, John A. Dahlgren,
George B. McClellan, and Ormsby M. Mitchell.

174
Claiborne, John Francis Hamtramck
(1809−1884)   Planter−Editor, Mississippi
     Papers, 1818−85. ca. 600 items.
     Contains a letter from Claiborne's son, Capt. Willis H.
Claiborne (d. 1869) to his sister, Sept. 22, 1861, concerning the
Battle of 1st Manassas and the death of Gen. Barnard E. Bee;

correspondence between Captain Claiborne and Gen. Alexander W. Reynolds; orders and returns for Reynolds' brigade in the Chattanooga and Atlanta campaigns; and a letter to Captain Claiborne, Oct. 16, 1862, describing conditions in southwest Mississippi and the treatment of noncombatants by Union foraging parties. Also contains the diary (Mar. 25–June 5, 1861) and memoir of Claiborne's nephew, Henry A. Garrett, a courier for J. E. B. Stuart, concerning volunteer companies in Mississippi at the beginning of the war, campaigns in Virginia, 1861–63, and the Gettysburg, Wilderness, and Atlanta campaigns.

Finding aid available.

175
Clark, Mrs. Douglas W.
    Collection, 1861–64.
    Microfilm, 1 reel.
    Autograph book containing names, units, and home addresses of numerous Confederate officers held at Johnson's Island Military Prison; autograph book containing names, units, and home addresses of numerous Federal officers held at Libby Prison during the winter of 1863–64; telegraph book, Department of the Ohio, May 28–30, 1861, concerning the movement of troops and supplies in West Virginia; and diary of Capt. R. B. Beck, 30th Maryland Volunteers, Nov. 2, 1862–Jan. 12, 1863, concerning troop movements along the Mississippi River, the Vicksburg Campaign, and the Fort Hindman expedition. Diary entries include remarks on blacks, devastation along the Mississippi, looting of plantations, deaths, desertions, and morale in the 30th Maryland, and reconnaissance expeditions. Also provides a detailed account of the Battle of Chickasaw Bluffs and the names of 108 vessels in the Federal transport fleet.

176
Clay Family
    Papers, 1782–1865. ca. 100 items.
    Includes papers of Cassius Marcellus Clay (1810–1903), abolitionist from Kentucky. Correspondence and petitions concern the parole or release of Confederate prisoners of war. Also includes military passes, certificates of seizure, and affidavits by Mary A. Newman and Christopher I. Field of Bolivar County, Miss., concerning slave seizures and depredations by Federal gunboats.

177
Cleveland, Grover (1837–1908), Pres., U.S.
    Papers, 1859–1945. ca. 100,000 items.

Includes a copy of a letter from Gen. John F. Hartranft to Gov. Horatio Seymour, Dec. 17, 1864, concerning the promotion of Lt. Col. Walter C. Newberry (24th New York Cavalry) to the colonelcy of the 2d New York Mounted Rifles; and a copy of a letter from Adm. David D. Porter to Gideon Welles, Jan. 17, 1865, U.S.S. *Malvern*, on the transfer of Lt. Comdr. James Parker from the command of the U.S.S. *Maumee*.

Finding aid and microfilm copy (164 reels) available.

178

Clowry, Robert Charles (1838–1925)   Capt., USA
    Papers, 1862–78. ca. 75 items.
    A letterbook (Dept. of Missouri, v. 39), Mar. 3, 1864–Aug. 15, 1865, contains circulars and cipher records relating to Clowry's service as assistant quartermaster and assistant superintendent of U.S. Military Telegraph Lines in the Department of Missouri, Kansas, and Arkansas. Also includes a catalog of books and papers belonging to Clowry's military files, compiled in 1878.

179

Coe, William P.   Capt., 176th New York Volunteers
    Correspondence, 1862–65. 22 items.
    Transcripts.
    Letters from Coe to his family and friends describe his capture at Bayou Boeuf, La., June 24, 1863, and his life as a prisoner of war at Camp Ford near Tyler, Tex. Letters to Coe from his brother George and from E. F. Coe, John J. Cutter, John Marvin, and Col. Charles C. Nott contain war news and remarks on camp life and desertions.

180

Coffee, Alexander Donelson (b. 1822)   Alabama
    Collection, 1865. 2 items.
    Transcripts.
    Copies of Coffee's pardon, June 16, 1865, and oath of allegiance, June 19, 1865.

181

Coffee, John (1772–1833)
    Family papers, 1816–83. 28 items.
    Includes notebook of Edward A. O'Neal, Jr., volunteer aide to Gen. Robert Rodes, containing remarks on the Chancellorsville and Gettysburg campaigns, and a letter to Gen. Samuel Cooper, Oct. 11, 1864, requesting assignment to the arsenal at Selma, Ala.

182

Coffee, William   Sgt., 3d New York Volunteers
    Letters, 1864. 4 items.
    Letters from Coffee to his brother George (2d California Volunteers), Apr. 16–Nov. 24, 1864, concerning Gen. Thomas Sherman's Port Royal expedition, the capture of Fort Wagner, S.C., and the Siege of Petersburg, Va.

183

Colhoun, Edmund Ross (1821–1897)   Comdr., USN
    Papers, 1839–88. ca. 1,200 items.
    In part, transcripts.
    Official correspondence, orders, circulars, reports, lists of officers, and miscellaneous items relating to Colhoun's command of the U.S.S. *Hunchback*, U.S.S. *Lodona*, U.S.S. *Saugus*, and U.S.S. *Weehawken*, South Atlantic Blockading Squadron. Contains information on the Burnside expedition to North Carolina, vessels captured or destroyed off the coast of South Carolina, attacks on Forts Wagner and Sumter, July–Sept. 1863, prize vessels, discipline, morality, discharges, and promotions. Correspondents include Samuel L. Breese, John A. Dahlgren, Henry K. Davenport, Charles H. Davis, Louis M. Goldsborough, David D. Porter, George W. Rodgers, and Gideon Welles.
    Finding aid available.
    Naval Historical Foundation collection.

184

Collin, William M. (b. 1842)   Cpl., 5th Wisconsin Volunteers
    Papers, 1861–64. 8 items.
    Diary, Jan. 1, 1862–May 9, 1864 (3 v.), concerning troop movements in northern Virginia, the Peninsular Campaign, camp life, and Collin's treatment as a prisoner of war at Libby Prison and Belle Isle in Richmond, Va. Includes a detailed account of the Siege of Yorktown. Also contains Collin's commission as corporal in the 5th Wisconsin, 1861, a statement of health following his release from prison, and his discharge, Feb. 5, 1863.

185

Collis, Charles Henry Tucky (1838–1902)   Capt., USA
    Returns, 1861–62. 1 v.
    "Morning Reports" for Captain Collis' independent company, "Zouaves de Afrique," Aug. 25, 1861–May 21, 1862. Includes information on Gen. Nathaniel P. Banks' Shenandoah Valley Campaign (1862), and camp life, marches, discipline, disease, and deaths.

186
Colvin, Hervey A. (1841–1885)   18th Michigan Volunteers
  Letters, 1862, 1863. 2 items.
  Letters from Colvin to Jacob Baker describing black life and expectations in Kentucky, and a skirmish with forces under Gen. John Pegram (CSA).

187
Comstock, Cyrus Ballou (1831–1910)   Gen., USA
  Papers, 1847–1908. ca. 900 items.
  Official correspondence, reports, orders, and notebooks relating to Comstock's service as assistant and chief engineer in the Army of the Potomac and the Army of the Tennessee, assistant inspector general of the Military Division of the Mississippi, and aide-de-camp to General Grant. Includes engineering reports, a list of the number and type guns at the Siege of Vicksburg, lists of officers, and sketches of various fords, rivers, ferry crossings, and fortifications. Also contains a diary, Oct. 16, 1863–Dec. 9, 1867, containing information on Federal hospitals in Kentucky and Tennessee, tactics in the Chattanooga, Wilderness, Spotsylvania, Petersburg, and Mobile campaigns, Terry's Fort Fisher expedition, the Battle of Cold Harbor (1864), and skirmishes along the North Anna River and Totopotomy Creek, Va.
  Finding aid and microfilm copy (4 reels) available.

188
Conant, Abram F. (d. 1863)   Pvt., 1st Michigan
                                          Engineers and Mechanics
  Family papers, 1845–72. 45 items.
  Contains 15 letters from Conant to his wife written from camps in Kentucky and Tennessee, Oct. 1862–Feb. 1863. Provides information on camp life, marches, morale, diet, skirmishes with Confederate cavalry units, disease, and deaths. Also contains a certificate of Conant's enlistment and death signed by Capt. Marcus Grant.

189
Confederate States of America
  Records, 1858–72. ca. 18,500 items.
  Chiefly official records and correspondence between the Secretary of State (usually Judah P. Benjamin) and Confederate agents in Belgium, France, Great Britain, and Mexico concerning administrative and financial matters, passports, pardons, and domestic matters in the Confederacy. Also, records of the Departments of Justice, Treasury, Navy, War, and Post Office; proclamations, messages, and miscellaneous papers of President Jefferson Davis; acts and resolutions of the Confeder-

ate Congress; and material relating to the Constitution and secession. War Department records comprise the correspondence of the secretary, general orders, returns, muster rolls, payrolls, receipts, quartermaster reports, requisitions, ordnance reports, military passes, and discharge and death certificates. Navy Department records include supply accounts (1863) for the C.S.S. *Sumter*, C.S.S. *Tennessee*, and C.S.S. *Missouri*, ships' logs for vessels in Bermuda and Nassau, 1861–65, pay receipts, reports, and discharge certificates. Correspondents include Bolling Baker, P. G. T. Beauregard, Judah P. Benjamin, John A. Campbell, Clement C. Clay, Lewis Conger, Jefferson Davis, George Dawson, Edwin De Leon, A. J. Guirot, Charles J. Helm, Lewis Heyliger, Henry Hotze, Lucius Q. C. Lamar, Ambrose Dudley Mann, James M. Mason, Christopher G. Memminger, John T. Pickett, John H. Reagan, Raphael Semmes, John Slidell, Alexander H. Stephens, Jacob Thompson, William H. Trescott, Leroy P. Walker, and William L. Yancey.

Finding aid and microfilm copy (70 reels) available.

190
———

Collection, 1862–65. 6 items.

Note concerning an appropriation for the construction of floating defenses on western rivers, Jan. 1862; an order appointing G. W. Newman as medical examiner of conscripts in Louisiana, June 14, 1864; and miscellaneous tax forms filed with the Confederate Government by Dr. Newman, 1864–65.

191
———

Collection, 1861–65. 1 v.

Bonds issued by the C.S. Government, bonds issued by officials in Amherst County, Va., and loan certificates purchased by banks in Lynchburg, Va.

192
———

Collection, undated. 9 items.

Autographs of Confederate officers: Simon B. Buckner (includes a miniature portrait), John B. Gordon, Johnson Hagood, Wade Hampton, John S. Mosby, and Raphael Semmes.

193
Confederate States of America—Army of Northern Virginia
Document, 1865. 1 item.
Photocopy.
Copy of the terms of surrender at Appomattox Courthouse, Apr. 10, 1865, signed by Gens. John Gibbon, Charles Griffin,

and Wesley Merrit for the United States, and Gens. John B. Gordon, James Longstreet, and William N. Pendleton for the Confederate States.

194

Confederate States of America—Army of the Tennessee
    Register, 1861–65. 295 p.
    Microfilm, 1 reel.
    Register of surgeons in the Army of the Tennessee, CSA. Includes hospital assignments and a photograph of Dr. Andrew J. Foard, medical director of the Army of the Tennessee.

195

Congleton, James A. (b. 1844)   Cpl., 105th
                                                  Illinois Volunteers
    Diary, 1862–65. 1 v.
    Entries relate chiefly to the Atlanta, Savannah, and Carolinas campaigns. Includes details on the battles of Resaca, Dallas, Kennesaw Mountain, Chattahoochee River, Peach Tree Creek, and Atlanta during Sherman's march through Georgia, and the battle at Averasboro, N.C., during the Carolinas Campaign. Also contains information on camp life, training, marches in Kentucky and Tennessee in 1863, and the treatment of blacks.

196

Conkling, Roscoe (1829–1888)   U.S. Representative,
                                                    New York
    Papers, 1769–1895. 150 items.
    Includes a military pass and samples of Confederate bonds and currency.
    Microfilm copy (1 reel) available.

197

Conley, Isaiah   Capt., 101st Pennsylvania Infantry
    Papers, undated. 2 items.
    Transcript and photocopy.
    "An Account of Captain Conley's Escape From Prison" (28 p.). Describes Conley's capture near Plymouth, N.C., the movement of prisoners to Andersonville and Camp Oglethorpe military prisons, Conley's escape in South Carolina, aid by Unionists, slaves, and free blacks in South Carolina, North Carolina, and Tennessee, black life, and conscription in the South. Also contains an undated photograph of Conley.

198

Connecticut   12th Connecticut Volunteers
    Document, 1861–65. 1 item.

Roscoe Conkling

Muster roll containing a list of officers and men by company in the 12th Connecticut or "Charter Oaks" Regiment. Includes a record of battles fought and figures on casualties, reenlistments, and desertions.

199

Connecticut Infantry   17th Regiment
     Daybook, 1862–63. 1 v.

Record of rations issued, Sept. 16, 1862–Mar. 10 1863. Also shows the regiment's location during this period.

200

Conrad, Daniel B. (d. 1869)   Surg., CSA and CSN
     Diary, 1853–64. 2 v.

Contains a brief account of Conrad's Civil War experiences, including his arrest in New York as a Confederate sympathizer; his escape and flight to Virginia; service in the 2d Virginia Regiment in Virginia and West Virginia; as chief surgeon, Brock House Hospital, Richmond, Va.; with Comdr. John Taylor Wood in the attack on the U.S.S. *Underwriter*, Feb. 1864; and as fleet surgeon attached to the C.S.S. *Tennessee*, Apr.–Aug. 1864. Provides some information on the capture of Harpers Ferry, W. Va., the Battle of 1st Manassas, and the Battle of Mobile Bay.

     Naval Historical Foundation collection.

201

Cook, George P.   Member of Society of Friends, Maryland
     Letter, 1861. 1 item.

Letter from Cook to Gen. Winfield Scott, May 27, 1861, concerning a Confederate plan to explode a boat in the Potomac River near Washington.

202

Cooke, John Esten (1830–1886)   Writer;
                              Asst. Adj. Gen., CSA
     Papers, 1846–86. 75 items.
     In part, transcripts.

Includes several letters from Cooke to Maria Skelton containing comments on the war in northern Virginia, and a letter to Brig. Gen. Custis Lee concerning Cooke's appointment as Assistant Adjutant General on the staff of Gen. J. E. B. Stuart.

203

Coon, David (1822–1864)   Pvt., 36th Wisconsin Volunteers
     Letters, 1864.
     Microfilm, 1 reel.

Transcripts of letters from Coon to his wife and family,

Feb 28 – Aug. 27, 1864, concerning military bounties, training, hospital care, the Battle of Cold Harbor, and the Siege of Petersburg.

204
Cope, John   Pvt., 98th Ohio Volunteers
    Papers, 1831 – 1919. 190 items.
    Letters from Cope to his family, Jan. 9, 1864 – Apr. 25, 1865, concerning military supplies and skirmishes in the Atlanta Campaign and hospital care at Nashville, Tenn. Also includes a few letters by his brother, Samuel Cope, and his cousin, Clark Bower, concerning military training at Camp Chase, Ohio.

205
Corbin, Henry Clark (1842 – 1909)   Lt. Col.,
                                        14th U.S. Colored Infantry
    Papers, 1864 – 1938. ca. 2,000 items.
    Contains a brief description of Corbin's service in the war and a letter from Corbin to Mrs. Lockman, Nov. 12 [1864], Chattanooga, concerning the death of her husband in a skirmish near Decatur, Ala., Oct. 29, 1864. Also contains a few records of courts-martial and copies of orders issued during the conflict.
    Finding aid available.

206
Cotton, Charles Stanhope (1843 – 1909)   Lt., USN
    Papers, 1860 – 1921. ca. 600 items.
    Includes a letter from Cotton to Comdr. Thomas H. Stevens, Aug. 1, 1864, U.S.S. *Oneida*, Mobile Bay, concerning a reconnaissance expedition ashore and the capture of five members of the 7th Alabama Cavalry, a copy of a letter from Col. Charles D. Anderson (CSA) to Admiral Farragut, Aug. 7, 1864, Fort Gaines [Ala.], proposing the surrender of the fort, orders, newspaper clippings, and a postwar account of the Battle of Mobile Bay.
    Naval Historical Foundation collection.

207
Cotton, Josiah Dexter (b. 1822)   Surg., 92d Ohio Volunteers
    Papers, 1846 – 68. 300 items.
    Letters from Cotton to his wife, May 1863 – Mar. 1865, concerning camp life, casualties, disease, and health care during the Chattanooga, Chickamauga, and Atlanta campaigns. Also includes remarks on devastation in the South and the performance of black soldiers.

208

Covode, John (1808–1871)   U.S. Representative,
                                            Pennsylvania
    Papers, 1854–70. ca. 100 items.
    Includes letters to Covode, 1861–65, concerning military appointments, promotions, casualties and vacancies in the 4th Pennsylvania Cavalry, the capture of his son, Jacob Covode, and the generalship of George G. Meade. Correspondents include William Cochran, A. F. Coon, George H. Covode, Jacob Covode, Riley M. Hoskinson, Lewis McDonald, and C. P. Walker.

209

Cox, Jacob Dolson (1828–1900)   Gen., USA
    Papers, 1868–1940. 15 items.
    Manuscript biography (2 v.) of the "Political Experiences of Major General Jacob Dolson Cox," by William C. Cochran, ca. 1940.

210

Cox, Oliver   Clergyman
    Papers, 1865, 1868. 2 items.
    Military pass issued to Cox to travel from Washington, D.C., to Arlington, Va., Mar. 18, 1865.

211

Craven, John Joseph (1822–1893)   Surg., USA
    Papers, 1849–1939. 75 items.
    Includes a diary kept by Craven's wife Catherine while at Hilton Head, S.C., Mar.–May 1863; a fragment of a diary Craven kept as prison surgeon at Fort Monroe, Va., concerning his care of Jefferson Davis; two letters by Brig. Gen. William S. Walker (CSA), May 20, 1864, concerning his wounds and capture during Gen. B. F. Butler's advance on Petersburg, Va.; and military passes and Confederate currency. A letter from Craven to his wife written from a field hospital near Richmond, Oct. 19, 1864, notes the presence of Clara Barton.

212

Crawford, Samuel Wylie (1829–1892)   Gen., USA
    Papers, 1860–92. ca. 400 items.
    In part, transcripts.
    Includes a diary, Dec. 19, 1860–Apr. 14, 1861, containing a detailed account of the bombardment of Fort Sumter and related correspondence between Gov. Francis W. Pickens, Maj. Robert Anderson, and Gen. P. G. T. Beauregard, and detailed reports and letters on the movements of the Pennsylvania reserves in the Gettysburg Campaign. Also, a letter from Fran-

Samuel Wylie Crawford

cis Pickens to S. Pettigrew, May 18, 1864, describing the career of Pettigrew's brother, Gen. James J. Pettigrew, and miscellaneous letters from Pickens to Jefferson Davis, Maxcy Gregg, Isaac Hayne, Robert E. Lee, Andrew G. Magrath, Christopher G. Memminger, John C. Pemberton, and Roswell S. Ripley.

213

Creamer, David (1812–1887)   Clergyman, Baltimore, Md.
    Diary and notes, 1861–81. 2 items.
    In part, transcripts.
    Diary, June 1861–Dec. 1862, containing Creamer's testimony before a grand jury investigating the Baltimore riot of Apr. 19, 1861, and transcript of the testimony.

214

Cresswell, John Angel James   U.S. Representative,
(1828–1891)   Maryland
    Papers, 1819–85. ca. 6,000 items.
    Includes numerous letters from friends and constituents, 1861–65, concerning Unionist sentiment on Maryland's Eastern Shore, recruitment, military commissions and promotions, discipline, conscription, black volunteers, and emancipation. Also contains a letter from F. A. Macartney to Cresswell, Apr. 14, 1865, describing the situation in Richmond, Va., at the end of the war, particularly the contrasting attitudes of the citizenry toward Jefferson Davis and Robert E. Lee, suffering during the siege, and the restraint exercised by Federal soldiers upon entering the city.
    Finding aid available.

215

Crittenden, John Jordan   U.S. Representative,
(1787–1863)   Kentucky
    Papers, 1782–1888. ca. 2,600 items.
    Includes letters to Crittenden concerning the Crittenden Compromise, enthusiasm for war in the South, recruiting, the conduct of Crittenden's son, Thomas L. Crittenden, in the Battle of Shiloh, a skirmish at West Liberty, Ky., Oct. 23, 1861, Federal policy on the release of prisoners of war, troop dispositions, and the military situation in Virginia during the first year of the war. Correspondents include Don Carlos Buell, Jonathan W. Finnell, John C. Frémont, William Nelson, and P. H. Watson.
    Finding aid and microfilm copy (14 reels) available.

216
Croffut, William Augustus (1835–1915)   Author; Editor; Poet
    Papers, 1774–1933. ca. 7,500 items.
    In part, transcripts.
    Contains copies of the memoir and war correspondence of Gen. Ethan Allen Hitchcock (1798–1870), which Croffut used for his book, *Fifty Years in Camp and Field: Diary of Major-General Ethan Allen Hitchcock, U.S.A.* (1909).
    Finding aid available.

217
Crossly, Sylvanus   USA
    Diary, 1865. 1 item.
    Diary of Crossly's escape from Confederate troops in South Carolina, Feb. 14–20, 1865. Mentions the assistance of blacks living near Columbia, S.C.

218
Cuddy, Thomas C.   Lt., CSN
    Papers, 1858–61. 5 items.
    Includes four letters from Cuddy to his wife and mother, Apr. 5–12, 1861, discussing his appointments as a gunner on a floating battery in Charleston Harbor and as acting lieutenant on the Confederate privateer *Gordon*.

219
Culley, J. A.
    Letter, 1861. 1 item.
    Letter, Apr. 15, 1861, describing the public reaction in Philadelphia to the news of the firing on Fort Sumter, S.C.

220
Curry, Jabez   Lt. Col., 5th Alabama Regiment;
Lamar Monroe (1825–1903)   C.S. Representative, Alabama
    Papers, 1637–1939. ca. 3,900 items.
    In part, transcripts.
    Includes four letters from Augusta Jane Evans to Curry, 1862–64, discussing the quality of Confederate officers, desertions and disaffection in the Confederate Army, and the poor defenses of Mobile, Ala.; a letter from Col. Thomas B. Cooper to Curry, Jan. 20, 1862, concerning Confederate troops wintering at Richmond, Va.; and a letter from Col. John W. Mallet to Curry, Mar. 23, 1862, on the manufacture of saltpeter. Also includes papers concerning Curry's studies on the war and the Confederate Government.
    Finding aid and microfilm copy (4 reels) available.

221

Curtis, Benjamin Robbins   Jurist, Massachusetts
(1809–1874)
    Papers, 1831–79. ca. 450 items.
    In part, transcripts.
    Includes a few copies of letters relating to the arrest and imprisonment of Judge John Archibald Campbell and the investigation of the Lincoln assassination, May–July 1865.

222

Cushing, Caleb (1800–1879)   Statesman, Massachusetts
    Papers, 1785–1906. ca. 120,000 items.
    Contains correspondence, requisitions, bills of lading, invoices, reports, and legal papers relating to Confederate operations in the Trans-Mississippi Department. Also, material concerning prize cases, Mexico's claim for compensation for the seizure of the *Oriente*, and Confederate blockade running, and a series of letters between Christopher Memminger and James Seddon. Cushing's legal papers include statements by Stephen R. Mallory on the purchase and service of the Confederate steamers *Alexandria, Atlanta, Bat, Chickamauga, Owl, Shenandoah, Tallahassee, Texas,* and others.
    Finding aid available.

223

Cushman, Charlotte Saunders (1816–1876)   Actress
    Papers, 1824–1941. ca. 10,000 items.
    Contains a letter (13 p.) from Lt. Samuel Dana Greene (USN) to his parents, Mar. 14, 1862, U.S.S. *Monitor*, describing the voyage of the *Monitor* from New York to Hampton Roads, Va., problems in preparing the vessel for battle, and the engagement with the C.S.S. *Merrimac*.
    Finding aid available.

224

Cushman, William H. (d. 1865)   Engineer, USN
    Papers, 1861–72. 24 items.
    Contains two letters from Cushman to his mother written aboard the U.S.S. *Kearsarge*, June 15 and 19, 1864, before and after the engagement with the C.S.S. *Alabama*. Also, a letter of recommendation for Cushman (1861), pension claim forms, photographs, and papers concerning prize money from the *Alabama*.

John Adolphus Bernard Dahlgren

225

Custer, George Armstrong (1839–1876)   Gen., USA
    Papers, 1865, 1874. 2 items.
    In part, photocopies.
    Includes a printed congratulatory order from General Cus-
ter to the men of the 3d Cavalry Division, Apr. 9, 1865.

226

Cutter, Calvin (1807–1872)   Surg., 21st
                                     Massachusetts Volunteers
    Manuscript, undated. 1 item.
    Transcript.
    Account of Cutter's abolitionist activities in prewar Kansas,
his intimate friendship with John Brown, and his service with
the 21st Massachusetts in North Carolina, Kentucky, and
Virginia.

227

Cutter, Carrie Eliza (1842–1862)   Nurse, USA
    Manuscript, undated. 1 item.
    Transcript.
    Account of Cutter's service as a nurse at the military hospi-
tal in Annapolis, Md., and with the 21st Massachusetts Volunteers during the Burnside expedition to North Carolina.

228

Cutts Family
    Papers, 1755–1905. ca. 100 items.
    Contains five letters by J. Madison Cutts (d. 1863), Comp-
troller's Office, U.S. Treasury Department, concerning military pay.

229

Dahlgren, John Adolphus Bernard (1809–1870)   Adm., USN
    Papers, 1824–89. ca. 10,000 items.
    Contains correspondence, reports, and memoranda relat-
ing to naval ordnance, 1861–62; reports on raids ordered by
Dahlgren against guerrillas operating in Virginia along the
Potomac River and Chesapeake Bay; and letterbooks, logs, and
miscellaneous items maintained by Dahlgren as commander of
the South Atlantic Blockading Squadron, 1863–65—chiefly
official correspondence, orders, reports, lists and records of ships
in the squadron, records of prize vessels, special reports on
ironclad ships, and consular dispatches. Also contains correspondence between Dahlgren and his son, Col. Ulric Dahlgren
(1842–1864) concerning the Shenandoah Valley Campaign of
1862 and the Fredericksburg and Gettysburg campaigns.
    Finding aid available.

Jefferson Davis

Papers, 1843−70. 75 items.

Letter from Dahlgren to "Dear Patty," Sept. 13, 1864, U.S.S. *Philadelphia*. Contains a brief note on expected reinforcements for an attack on Charleston, S.C.

Naval Historical Foundation collection.

231

Dana, Charles Anderson (1819−1897)   Asst. Secretary of War
  Papers, 1859−82. ca. 300 items.
  In part, transcripts.

Chiefly dispatches sent by Dana from the War Office during the Vicksburg, Wilderness, Spotsylvania, Petersburg, and Appomattox campaigns, and during campaigns in Kentucky and Tennessee.

232

Daniels, Josephus (1862−1948)
  Papers, 1806−1948. ca. 331,000 items.

Includes a copy of Stephen R. Mallory's *Report of the Secretary of the Navy* (1864); a photograph from the christening of the U.S.S. *Chattanooga*, Oct. 1864; a postwar sketch of the U.S.S. *Bainbridge* by George H. Rogers (USN); military passes; a medical certificate concerning the health of John Barkley (CSA); and miscellaneous letters by Comdr. Benjamin M. Dove (USN), Col. T. H. Rosser (CSA), and Gideon Welles.

  Finding aid available.

233

Davis, Benjamin
  Military pass, 1861. 1 item.

Pass issued to Davis, Oct. 30, 1861, to travel from St. Louis, Mo., to Baltimore, Md. Signed by Col. John McNeil.

234

Davis, Jefferson (1808−1889)   President, C. S. A.
  Collection, 1835−1913. ca. 500 items.
  In part, transcripts and photocopies of transcripts.

Includes a letter to Gov. Joseph E. Brown of Georgia, Jan. 27, 1863, concerning provisions for the army; a letter from Alexander Walker to Davis, Sept. 13, 1862, accusing Gen. B. F. Butler of numerous atrocities as military governor of New Orleans and describing the plight of various citizens confined at Ship Island, Miss., Fort St. Philip, La., and Fort Pickens, Fla.; and several postwar letters from Davis to C. J. Wright refuting reports that captured Union officers who had commanded black troops had been mistreated, that there had been a Confederate plot to assassinate President Lincoln, and that Davis had been disguised as a woman at the time he was captured.

Microfilm copy (2 reels) available.

235
Davis, John Chandler Bancroft (1822–1907)   U.S. Diplomat
    Papers, 1851–1902. ca. 13,000 items.
    Includes letterbooks and records on the *Alabama* claims.

236
Davis, John E.   5th Pennsylvania Volunteers
    Letter, 1863. 1 item.
    Letter from Davis to his mother, Aug. 24, 1863, concerning the Battle of Gettysburg.

237
Dawes, Henry Laurens (1816–1903)   U.S. Representative,
                                            Massachusetts
    Papers, 1833–1933. ca. 22,000 items.
    Includes a letter from Pvt. Clifton L. Roth, 10th Massachusetts Volunteers, to Dawes, Sept. 18, 1861, concerning Roth's enlistment bounty; a letter from Lt. Col. George Wells to Dawes, July 12, 1862, about a leave of absence from the Army of the Potomac; a letter from Col. J. H. Belknap to Dawes, Dec. 17, 1862, Alexandria, Va., concerning three soldiers being held at a convalescent camp in Virginia; and a letter from Lt. Col. A. W. Dwight to Dawes, Dec. 22, 1862, Falmouth, Va., relating to the resignations of several officers of the 10th Massachusetts Volunteers over the appointment of Maj. Dexter Parker.
    Finding aid available.

238
Dawson, Henry Barton (1821–1889)   Editor; Historian
    Letter, 1872. 1 item.
    Letter from Dawson to Gen. P. G. T. Beauregard, July 11 [1872], Morrisania, N.Y., concerning Maj. Robert Anderson and the surrender of Fort Sumter.

239
Deaderick, David Anderson (1797–1873)   Tennessee
    Collection, 1824–1940. 3 items.
    Transcript and photocopies.
    Chiefly a register of events in the Deaderick family (59 p.). Includes genealogical notes and copies of letters to Deaderick from his sons, Inslee and Robert (East Tennessee Cavalry, CSA), 1861–65, concerning skirmishes in Kentucky and Tennessee,

the battles of Fishing Creek and Murfreesboro, the Siege of Knoxville, the treatment of civilians, depredations, and prison life at Camp Chase, Ohio, Camp Morton, Ind., and Fort Delaware. Also includes photocopies of a sketch and photograph of Deaderick.

240
Deane, Charles H.   Capt., USA
    Order, 1865. 1 item.
    Order relieving Deane from duty as post quartermaster at Chattanooga, Tenn., June 23, 1865.

241
De Leon, Edwin (d. 1891)   C.S. Diplomat
    Papers, 1864–85. 19 items.
    Letters received while serving as Confederate agent in Europe.

242
Denison, George Stanton (1833–1866)   Customs Collector,
                                      New Orleans, La.
    Papers, 1851–84. ca. 300 items.
    Letters from Denison to his family, 1862–65, concerning a trip from New Orleans to Richmond, Va., and his escape north through Tennessee and Kentucky. Provides information on the martial spirit sweeping the South, conscription, the composition of the Confederate Army, the type and availability of weapons, and the military situation in Richmond. Letters written from New Orleans during the Federal occupation relate to the military governorships of Gen. Benjamin F. Butler and Gen. Nathaniel P. Banks. Also contains a few letters between Denison and Salmon P. Chase.
    Indexed.

243
Dennett, Tyler (1883–1949)   Author
    Papers, 1861–1933. ca. 200 items.
    In part, galley proofs.
    Primarily research notes compiled for Dennett's 1933 biography of John Hay and his 3-volume edition of the *Letters of John Hay* (1908).
    Finding aid available.

244
Dewey, George (1837–1917)   1st Lt., USN
    Papers, 1820–1919. ca. 25,000 items.
    Contains an account of Adm. David G. Farragut's attempt to pass Confederate batteries at Port Hudson, La., and the

destruction of the U.S.S. *Mississippi*, Mar. 14, 1863. Written in 1902 by Henry C. Hoskins, CSA.

Finding aid available.

245
Dick, Franklin A.   Provost Marshal Gen., USA
    Document, 1865. 2 items.
"Memorandum of Matters in Missouri in 1861," with a cover letter to Benson J. Lossing, July 6, 1865. Describes the political and military situation in Missouri in 1861, particularly efforts to support the Union and to prevent the St. Louis Arsenal from falling into Confederate hands.

246
Dickinson, Anna Elizabeth   Abolitionist; Actress
(1842–1932)
    Papers, 1860–1932. ca. 8,500 items.
Contains a letter from Samuel Clark Pomeroy to Miss Dickinson, July 2, 1863, concerning Gen. Joseph Hooker's desire to attack Confederate forces under Robert E. Lee before Lee crossed the Potomac River in the Gettysburg Campaign; a letter from Martin Reem to Miss Dickinson, Mar. 31, 1878, recalling an incident in the war in Apr. 1864, between Federal forces in Arkansas and the army of Gen. Kirby-Smith that illustrates the bravery of black troops; and miscellaneous letters to Miss Dickinson, 1861–65, from the U.S. Sanitary Commission, various antislavery societies, and politicians.

Finding aid and microfilm copy (25 reels) available.

247
Dix, John Adams (1798–1879)   Gen., USA
    Papers, 1863, 1873. 2 items.
Includes a letter from Dix to Archibald Dixon, Jan. 19, 1863, Fort Monroe, Va., on winning the war.

248
Dock, Mira Lloyd (1853–1945)
    Papers, 1814–1947. ca. 2,500 items.
Includes a letter from Dr. George Dock to William D. Reinhardt, Oct. 18, 1861, Harrisburg [Pa.], concerning his brief service as a surgeon in the U.S. Army, enthusiasm for war in the North, and the office and location of several mutual friends.

Finding aid available.

249
Dodge, Theodore Ayrault (1842–1909)   Maj., USA
    Diary, 1862–63. 2 v.
    Microfilm, 1 reel.

John Adams Dix

Detailed account of Dodge's service as a lieutenant and adjutant in the 101st and 119th New York Volunteers during the Peninsular, 2d Manassas, Fredericksburg, Chancellorsville, and Gettysburg campaigns. Provides information on camp life, marches, troop movements, foraging expeditions, discipline, disease, casualties, and the use of blacks. Includes sketches of the Chancellorsville and Gettysburg battlefields.

250
Donelson, Andrew Jackson   Lawyer, Memphis, Tenn.
(1799–1871)
    Papers, 1779–1943. ca. 3,200 items.
    Contains several letters written during the war, 1862–64, concerning conditions in Memphis, Tenn., and in northern Mississippi, the death of C. S. Representative John Alexander Wilcox, the death of Capt. John Samuel Donelson of the Hickory Rifles, the murder of Daniel Donelson (CSA), depredations by Union and Confederate troops, the effect of the Federal blockade, and the location of various members of the Donelson family.
    Finding aid and partial index available.

251
Doolittle, James Rood
(1815–1897)   U.S. Senator, Wisconsin
    Papers, 1858–1929. 136 items.
    Letter from Adm. Samuel P. Lee to Doolittle, Feb. 20, 1865, U.S.S. *Black Hawk*, Cairo, Ill., describing his entire war service (North Atlantic Blockading Squadron, Mississippi Squadron, etc.), his stormy relationship with Gustavus V. Fox, his opinion of Adm. David D. Porter, competition between naval officers for commands affording greater opportunity for prize money, interaction between political and military leaders, and efforts of southern politicians to disperse naval vessels around the world during the secession crisis. Also, a letter from Admiral Lee to Doolittle, Mar. 22, 1863, concerning reconnaissance expeditions in the James River and favoritism in promotions; three letters from W. C. Wooling to Doolittle, Feb. 4 and 7, 1864, and undated written from Beaufort and Port Royal, S.C.; and a letter from Edgar T. Welles to an unnamed recipient, July 3, 1864, concerning a visit to Fort Monroe, Va.
    Finding aid and microfilm copy (1 reel) available.

252
Dorman, Orloff M.   Jacksonville, Fla.
    Diary, 1864–86. 7 v.
    "Memoranda of Events that transpired at Jacksonville, Florida, & in its vicinity; with some remarks & comments

thereon: &c." Provides information on skirmishes, depredations, and troop movements in the area.

253

Dornblaser, Benjamin (1828–1905)   Col., USA
    Collection, 1864. 8 items.
    Letter with supporting documents, from Dornblaser to R. A. Kent, Nov. 4, 1864, concerning irregularities in the Commissary Department.

254

Dorsett, Edward Lee (b. 1883)   Collector
    Collection, 1814–1926. 150 items.
    Includes a letter from Capt. Thomas T. Craven to Gideon Welles, Sept. 2, 1861, U.S.S. *Yankee*, concerning the prize sloop *T. J. Evans*, and a letter from Acting Master Henry S. Wetmore to Charles Kendall, Feb. 23, 1864, Cincinnati, Ohio, requesting alterations on the U.S.S. *Fairy*.
    Finding aid available.
    Naval Historical Foundation collection.

255

Doubleday & Company   Publishers, New York
    Collection, 1955–65. ca. 24,000 items.
    Research notes and bibliography compiled by Everett B. Long for Bruce Catton's *Centennial History of the Civil War* (1961–65).
    Finding aid available.

256

Douglas, John Hancock   Associate Secretary, U.S.
(1824–1892)   Sanitary Commission
    Papers, 1861–85. 250 items.
    Includes letters from Douglas to his brother, July 25, 1861–June 7, 1864, concerning his work with the Sanitary Commission, i.e., the acquisition and distribution of medical supplies and the inspection of military hospitals in Pennsylvania, Maryland, Virginia, and Tennessee.

257

Douglass, Frederick (1817?–1895)   Author;
Abolitionist; Orator
    Papers, 1854–1964. ca. 7,300 items.
    Includes a letter from Charles Douglass to his father, Frederick Douglass, July 6, 1863, Camp Meigs; a letter from George Evans to Douglass, June 6, 1863, concerning his service with the 1st Massachusetts Light Artillery; and several letters from the War Department concerning Douglass' work

with the Recruiting Service for U.S. Colored Volunteers.

Finding aid, index, and microfilm copy (34 reels) available.

258
Dow, M. A.
    Collection, 1864. 3 items.
    Military passes issued to Miss Dow for travel from New Berne, N.C., to Norfolk, Va., and New York City, and an all hours pass to and from Morehead City, N.C.

259
Downey, George Darius
(1832–1925)   Official, U.S. Christian Commission
    Diary, 1862–65. 1 v.
    Describes Downey's visits to military camps and field hospitals and his conversations with sick and wounded Federal soldiers and Confederate prisoners of war.

260
Downing, Samuel   Col., CSA
    Papers, 1840–85. 40 items.
    Contains several military passes issued to Richard P. Kenner, a farmer near Camp Hamilton, Va., Kenner's certificate of loyalty, and orders for the protection of his property.

261
Drake, James H.   Col., CSA
    Papers, 1859–63. 7 items.
    Includes a return of Drake's company in the 1st Virginia Cavalry, orders, a military pass, and a letter to Drake concerning horses stolen by Virginia cavalrymen.

262
Draper, John William (1811–1882)   Author; Scientist
    Family papers, 1777–1951. ca. 16,100 items.
    Contains a 235-page postwar account of naval operations along the coast of South Carolina, 1863–64, by Adm. John A. Dahlgren, and letters to Draper from several leading military officers concerning his 3-volume *History of the American Civil War* (1867–70). Correspondents include John A. Dahlgren, David G. Farragut, Quincy A. Gillmore, Ulysses S. Grant, William T. Sherman, Edwin M. Stanton, and Gideon Welles.
    Finding aid available.

263
Draper, William B.
    Papers, 1864. 2 items.
    Letter from Draper to his brother, Oct. 22, 1864, New

Orleans, La., concerning the opening of trade with the Confederacy and the opposition of Gen. Edward Canby, and an article "Our Suffering Trade," [New Orleans] *Daily True Delta*, Oct. 2 [1864].

264
Draper, William Franklin   Lt. Col., 36th Massachusetts
(1842–1910)   Volunteers
    Papers, 1861–1910. 120 items.
    Letters from Draper to his family, 1861–63, concerning military training, General Burnside's expedition to North Carolina, and the Fredericksburg, Vicksburg, and Knoxville campaigns. Includes detailed accounts of the Battle of Roanoke Island, N.C., and engagements at Blue Springs, Campbell's Station, and Fort Sanders, Tenn. Also contains information on camp life, morale, recruiting, army organization, promotions, rank disputes, leadership, and black servants and volunteers.

265
Drayton, A. L.   CSN
    Diary, 1863. 1 v.
    Describes the escape of the C.S.S. *Florida* from Mobile Bay, the capture of the brig *Clarence*, and the cruise of the C.S.S. *Clarence* against Union commerce. Contains a list of prizes captured by the *Clarence* and the *Archer*, along with the name, class, weight, port of origin, cargo, and estimated value of each prize. Also contains verses of the Confederate songs, "Red, White, and Blue" and "Hood's Texas Brigade," and a copy of a letter from Gen. Robert E. Lee to Gen. Louis T. Wigfall, Sept. 21, 1862.

266
Drennan, Daniel O. (ca. 1840–ca. 1905)   Clerk, USA
    Papers 1861–1904. ca. 4,750 items.
    In part, facsimiles and transcripts.
    Correspondence, clippings, reports, proclamations, speeches, memorabilia, and printed matter collected by Drennan as military secretary to Gen. Philip H. Sheridan, 1865–88. Includes clippings on battles, military and political leaders (Abraham Lincoln, Jefferson Davis, Ulysses S. Grant, Robert E. Lee, Philip H. Sheridan, William T. Sherman, and others), prisons, the surrender of Gen. Joseph E. Johnston in Apr. 1865, and the surrender of Gen. Edmund Kirby-Smith at Galveston, Tex., in June 1865. Also includes facsimiles of letters from President Lincoln to Sheridan, copies of Sheridan's correspondence and reports, 1864–67, a muster roll of Capt. John H. Merrill's company of New York Volunteers, Apr. 26, 1861, and a tracing of a map of parts of Alabama and Mississippi used by

Lt. Colonel Prince, 3d Michigan Cavalry.
    Finding aid available.

267
Dungan, William W. (1836–1904)   Engineer, USN
    Collection, 1862–97. 11 items.
    Contains two orders to duty, 1862 and 1864.
    Naval Historical Foundation collection.

268
Dunlop, James (1795–1856)
    Family papers, 1750–1930. ca. 5,000 items.
    Letter from James Buchanan to Judge James Dunlop of
Georgetown, D.C., July 24, 1861, on the legality of the war and
the blockade of southern ports.
    Finding aid available.

269
Dwyer, Ransom O.   2d New York Veteran Cavalry
    Document, 1864. 1 item.
    Commission as chaplain, Jan. 6, 1864.

270
Dyer, Alexander Brydie (1852–1920)
    Papers, 1828–1942. ca. 250 items.
    Chiefly records of the 4th U.S. Artillery Regiment from
the Mexican War and the Civil War. Includes lists of officers
and men in batteries A and M, 1861–65, comments on the
service of batteries A and C in the Civil War, casualty lists, a
manuscript map showing the various stations of battery C,
1861–62, and a manuscript history of the regiment.

271
Eads, James Buchanan   Shipbuilder,
(1820–1887)   St. Louis, Mo.
    Document, 1861. 1 item.
    Agreement between Eads and Gen. Montgomery C. Meigs
for the construction of seven gunboats, Aug. 1861.

272
Early, Jubal Anderson (1816–1894)   Gen., CSA
    Papers, 1829–1930. ca. 5,000 items.
    Includes official correspondence, general and special orders,
reports, returns, and telegrams concerning the battles of 1st
Manassas and Williamsburg, the Gettysburg Campaign, and
the Shenandoah Valley Campaign of 1864. Also, a report on
the performance of Gen. Isaac R. Trimble's brigade in the Battle of 2d Manassas, reports by Gen. Harry T. Hays and Gen.

Clement A. Evans on skirmishes in the Mine Run Campaign, a list of units in Gen. P. G. T. Beauregard's I Corps, Army of Northern Virginia (1862), and a return of troops commanded by Gen. Joseph E. Johnston in the spring of 1862. Principal correspondents include Generals Beauregard, Raleigh E. Colston, Joseph E. Johnston, and Earl Van Dorn.

Finding aid available.

273
Easby—Smith Families
    Papers, 1837–71. ca. 100 items.
    Chiefly correspondence between Lt. Col. William Russell Smith (1815–1896), C.S. Representative from Alabama, and his wife concerning secession and various matters before the Confederate Congress.

274
Eells, Samuel Henry (b. 1836)   Asst. Surg., 12th
                                                 Michigan Volunteers
    Papers, 1862–63. 50 items.
    Chiefly letters from Eells to his family concerning the Battle of Shiloh, the Corinth and Vicksburg campaigns, and a skirmish with troops under Gen. Earl Van Dorn near Middleburg, Tenn., Jan. 1863. Includes information on camp life, troop movements, foraging expeditions, disease, hospital care, the treatment of blacks, desertion in the Confederate Army, and relations between Union soldiers and noncombatants in the South.

275
Eldredge, Charles Augustus
(1821–1896)   U.S. Representative, Wisconsin
    Letter, 1864. 1 item.
    Letter from Eldredge to John E. Thomas, Feb. 7, 1864, Washington, D.C., opposing U.S. Government policy in Arkansas and Tennessee, and Republican policy in general.

276
Ellis and Allan Company   Merchants
    Records, 1795–1889. ca. 80,000 items.
    Includes a daybook containing scattered accounts with the Confederate States Government for military supplies and equipment, 1861–62.
    Finding aid available.

277
Elseffer, Harry S.
(1857–1886), and Family   Engineer, USN
    Papers, 1865–86. ca. 80 items.
    In part, transcripts.

Includes a 20-page letter from Louis Elseffer to his family, Jan. 18, 1865, Pocotaligo, S.C., describing Sherman's Atlanta Campaign, Pvt. Charles Elseffer's certificate of service in the 46th Iowa Volunteers, and letter of Louis Elseffer, Feb. 1885, recalling the Battle of Shiloh and the war in general.

278
Emerson, Bart   USA
    Document, 1862. 1 item.
    Certificate affirming that Elizabeth Copeland of New Orleans, La., took an oath of loyalty to the United States, Sept. 30, 1862.

279
Enslow, Charles Calvin
(1836–1900)   77th Illinois Volunteers
    Letterbook, 1862–63. 1 item.
    Photocopy of transcript.
    Chiefly letters from Enslow to his wife concerning the Vicksburg Campaign and the Battle of Mobile Bay. Includes comments on the occupation of Forts Morgan, Gaines, and Powell (Alabama), camp life, the treatment of prisoners of war at Ship Island, Miss., and New Orleans, La., problems confronting blacks, relations between Union soldiers and noncombatants in the South, and an explosion aboard the *City of Madison*.

280
Ericsson, John (1803–1889)   Shipbuilder, New York
    Papers, 1821–90. ca. 1,500 items.
    Correspondence between Ericsson, Gideon Welles, and various officers and merchants; notes and drawings; and memoranda relating to the construction of the U.S.S. *Princeton*.
    Finding aid available.

281
Este, David Kirkpatrick
(1785–1875)   Lawyer, Cincinnati, Ohio
    Collection, 1804–64. 23 items.
    Letter from Gen. Lewis Wallace to an unnamed recipient, July 4, 1864, Baltimore, Md., on raising emergency forces.

282
Este, William Miller (d. 1900)   Maj., 26th Ohio Volunteers
    Collection, 1862–64. 25 items.
    Correspondence, orders, reports, and telegrams relating in part to the 8th Army Corps. Includes returns of troops at Camp Distribution, Md., Dec. 19, 1863, and Mar. 12, 1864.

283

Eustis, George (1828–1872)   Confederate Agent
    Papers, 1659–1884. ca. 400 items.
    Orders and dispatches from the C.S. Department of State,
1861–63; lists of vessels entering and clearing Confederate
ports, 1861–62; correspondence and accounts concerning the
Trent affair, including copies of letters by John Slidell and
Judah P. Benjamin; notes on slavery and secession; and Eustis'
oath of allegiance, Dec. 12, 1865.

284

Evans, Thomas (d. 1910)   25th Ohio Volunteers
    Diary and note, 1862–1953. 2 items.
    In part, transcript.
    Copy of Evans' diary, Feb. 16, 1862–May 1863, kept dur-
ing Banks' Shenandoah Valley Campaign and the Chancellorsville Campaign. Describes camp life, foraging expeditions,
hospital care, and his treatment as a prisoner of war at Belle
Isle, Va. Also an introductory foreword note written by Evans'
grandson, Lawrence T. Evans, in 1953.

285

Evarts, William Maxwell   Lawyer; Secretary,
(1818–1901)   Union Defense Committee
    Papers, 1835–1908. ca. 12,000 items.
    Includes a few letters to Edward Bates and William Sew-
ard on the legality of the southern blockade, and material on
Civil War prize cases and the trial of Jefferson Davis.
    Finding aid and partial index available.

286

Everett, Edward (1794–1865)   Orator; Educator
    Collection, 1858–64. ca. 150 items.
    In part, photocopies.
    Contains a copy of Everett's Gettysburg oration with photo-
graphs of Gens. Abner Doubleday, Winfield S. Hancock, Oliver
O. Howard, Erasmus D. Keys, John F. Reynolds, John Sedgwick,
Daniel E. Sickles, Henry W. Slocum, and Samuel K. Zook.

287

Ewell, Richard Stoddert (1817–1872)   Gen., CSA
    Papers, 1838–96. ca. 200 items.
    In part, transcripts and photocopies.
    Personal and official correspondence concerning general-
ship in the Confederate Army, Ewell's desire to return to active
duty following the loss of a leg at the Battle of Groveton, Va.,
the recruitment of blacks, his postwar imprisonment at Fort
Warren, Mass., and accusations that he ordered the burning of

Richmond, Va. Principal correspondents include Jefferson Davis, Jubal A. Early, B. S. Ewell, Leczinska Ewell, Henry J. Hunt, Joseph E. Johnston, Robert E. Lee, Lafayette McLaws, Charles Marshall, Dabney E. Maury, Robert E. Rodes, and William T. Sherman.

288
Ewing, Charles (1835–1883)   Gen., USA
    Family papers, 1769–1950. ca. 9,000 items.
    In part, photocopies.
    Contains official and personal correspondence, commissions, reports, general and special orders, an account of Ewing's war service taken from the records of the Adjutant General's Office, and miscellaneous accounts, telegrams, dispatches, and legal records. Also, a report on the participation of Ewing's brigade in the Siege of Vicksburg, diary entries from the Vicksburg Campaign, and a list of Confederate soldiers captured between Black Bayou and Jackson, Miss. Principal correspondents include Thomas Ewing, Jr., Virginia Larwill (Miller) Ewing, Eleanor Boyle (Ewing) Sherman, William T. Sherman, Clement F. Steele, and Maria Theresa (Ewing) Steele.
    Finding aid available.

289
Ewing, George Washington (1803–1866)   Fort Wayne, Ind.
    Papers, 1838–76. ca. 250 items.
    Includes a few letters between George Ewing, Thomas Ewing, and M. Sweetser, 1861–62, concerning secession, the progress of the war, Indian affairs, troop movements, and fortifications.

290
Ewing, Thomas (1789–1871)   Delegate, 1861
                                                  Peace Convention
    Family papers, 1754–1941. ca. 94,000 items.
    Includes the papers of Gen. Thomas Ewing, Jr. (1829–1896)—chiefly official correspondence, reports, accounts, maps, photographs, and scrapbooks relating to the recruitment of the 11th Kansas Volunteers, the battles of Prairie Grove and Pilot Knob (Fort Davidson, Mo.), and military affairs in the "District of the Border" (Kansas and western Missouri) and the St. Louis District. A diary kept by Sgt. Maj. E. Paul Reichhelm, 3d Missouri Volunteers, contains detailed accounts of General Grant's first move against Vicksburg, the Battle of Chickasaw Bluffs, and the Arkansas Post (Fort Hindman) expedition. Also contains letters from Hugh Boyle Ewing, William S. Rosecrans, William H. Seward, and William T. Sherman.
    Finding aid available.

291
_____

Family papers, 1815–72.
Microfilm, 6 reels.
Includes a letter defending Gens. Ulysses S. Grant, William T. Sherman, and Benjamin M. Prentiss against Secretary Stanton's charges of incompetence and misconduct; a letter to President Lincoln suggesting the use of compressed air to power steamships; and material from the William T. Sherman family papers.
Published guide available.
Originals at Notre Dame University Library.

292
Farragut, David Glasgow (1801–1870)   Adm., USN
Papers, 1810–69. 12 items.
In part, photocopies.
General orders issued from Farragut's flagship, U.S.S. *Hartford*, in the Mississippi River, Apr. 17 and 27, 1862, and before New Orleans, Apr. 26, 1862; copy of a letter from Secretary Welles to Farragut, May 10, 1862, on the capture of New Orleans; general order of June 25, 1862, on the bombardment of Vicksburg; and diagram of Farragut's battle formation in the attack on Mobile Bay.

293
_____

Papers, 1816–69. 20 items.
Letterbook kept aboard the U.S.S. *Brooklyn*, 1858–61, containing correspondence concerning the cruising ground of the Confederate privateer *Sumter* and orders from Secretary Welles. Also includes a letter from Farragut to Comdr. Melancthon B. Woolsey, May 13, 1864, placing Woolsey in command of Federal vessels along the Texas coast.
Finding aid available.
Naval Historical Foundation collection.

294
Fay, John   CSA
Manuscript narrative, 1905. 1 item.
Narrative of Lt. Jesse McNeill's capture of Gens. George Crook and Benjamin F. Kelley near Cumberland, Md., Feb. 21, 1865. Based on an account of the event written in the immediate postwar period.

295
Fay, Logan (b. 1830)   Sgt., 7th New York National Guard
Papers, 1861–62. 4 items.

David Glasgow Farragut

Three letters from Fay to his mother, Apr. 26 and 30, and
May 21, 1861, Washington, D.C.; Fay's discharge, Sept. 5, 1862.

296
Feamster Family
    Papers, 1794–1967. ca. 3,000 items.
    Diary of Thomas L. Feamster (1829–1906), 14th Virginia
Cavalry, Jan. 1, 1864–Mar. 21, 1865, kept during campaigns
in Virginia and West Virginia. Also, orderly book containing
muster rolls, returns, and accounts for the 14th Virginia
Cavalry.
    Finding aid available.

297
Fell, Jesse W. (1808–1887)   Maj., USA
    Papers, 1806–1957. ca. 2,100 items.
    In part, photocopies.
    Contains five letters from Fell to his wife, Oct. 1862–Aug.
1863, relating to his service as paymaster of Ohio volunteers;
letter from J. Bailey to Clara Fell, Dec. 24, 1862, concerning
camp life, diet, disease, and deaths among Ohio soldiers stationed near Nashville, Tenn.
    Finding aid available.

298
Fell, Joseph Gove (d. 1863)   Sgt. Maj., 141st
                                              Pennsylvania Volunteers
    Collection, 1863, 1866. 2 items.
    Letter from Adrial Lee to Fell's family, July 17, 1863,
concerning Fell's death in a military hospital near Gettysburg,
Pa.

299
Fenton, Lewis R. (d. 1895)   2d Michigan Cavalry
    Diary and notes, 1863–1960. 2 items.
    Diary, June 23, 1863–Dec. 31, 1864, describing camp life,
discipline, scouting and foraging expeditions, disease, and hospital care during campaigns in Tennessee and northern
Alabama. Also, supplementary information on Fenton and the
war written by Jessie P. Williams, Marquette County, Mich.,
June 1960.

300
Ferguson, John Newton (1838–1919)   2d Iowa Volunteers
    Diary, 1861–66. 4 v.
    Diary, Dec. 11, 1861–Feb. 14, 1866, kept by Ferguson
during the Fort Donelson, Shiloh, Corinth, Atlanta, Savannah,
and Carolinas campaigns. Describes his enlistment and train-

ing in the 2d Iowa, the arrest and detainment of Confederate soldiers and sympathizers in Missouri, marches, foraging expeditions, depredations, the attitude of noncombatants in the South, guerrilla warfare, black life, discipline, and morale. Also includes information on the burning of Columbia, S.C., the occupation of Raleigh and Goldsboro, N.C., skirmishes in northern Mississippi and northern Alabama, and the battles of Resaca, Dallas, and Kennesaw Mountain in the Atlanta Campaign.

301
Ferree, Newton and Joel   36th Ohio National Guard
    Papers, 1812–79. 13 items.
    Diary of Newton Ferree, Jan. 28–Nov. 1, 1864, kept while serving as a temporary clerk in the Paymaster General's Department. Contains remarks on military organization and training and a voyage to Port Royal, S.C., for an exchange of prisoners.

302
Fessenden, William Pitt
(1806–1869)   U.S. Secretary of the Treasury
    Papers, 1832–78. ca. 1,000 items.
    Correspondence relating to abolition, war finance, and the operations of the Treasury Department, 1864–65.
    Finding aid, partial index, and microfilm copy (5 reels) available.

303
Field, S.   Lynchburg, Va.
    Letter, 1864. 1 item.
    Letter from Field to Virginia senator A. T. Caperton, Feb. 7, 1864, protesting a bill passed by the Confederate House of Representatives exempting from military service farmers who provide substitutes.

304
Fillebrown, Thomas Scott (1834–1884)   1st Lt., USN
    Letter, 1861. 1 item.
    Letter from Fillebrown to Gen. Samuel P. Heintzelman, Nov. 26, 1861, U.S.S. *Roanoke*, Old Point [Comfort, Va.], concerning work on the C.S.S. *Merrimac* and the Federal plan of attack when the vessel appears. Includes details on the construction, measurements, and ordnance of the *Merrimac*. Also contains remarks on troops and vessels assembled under Gen. Benjamin F. Butler for operations in Louisiana.
    Naval Historical Foundation collection.

305

Firum, William, et al.   West Virginia
    Testimonial, 1862. 1 item.
    Signed testimonial, Jan. 17, 1862, naming ten dangerous
secessionists: A. G. Davis, D. M. Dent, D. W. Dent, Felix Dent,
George Dent, James Dent, Samuel Dorsenberry, John Jamison,
Milton Stuart, and E. Taylor.

306

Fish, Hamilton (1808–1893)   Chairman, Union
                                            League Defense Committee
    Papers, 1732–1914. ca. 61,000 items.
    Includes seven letters to Fish from Wickham Hoffman
(Assistant Adjutant General to Gen. Thomas W. Sherman),
1862–64, concerning conditions in New Orleans, La., under
military rule, expeditions and skirmishes along the Mississippi River, the Red River Campaign of 1863, the training
and performance of black soldiers, and the generalship of
Nathaniel P. Banks, Benjamin F. Butler, and Thomas W. Sherman. Also, four letters from Capt. Thomas Turner to Fish written
from the U.S.S. *New Ironsides*, 1863–65, concerning the blockade of Charleston Harbor, the bombardment of Fort Sumter,
the construction and performance of Federal monitors, and the
administrative talents of Gustavus V. Fox; two letters from
William Aiken to Fish, Apr.–May 1865, Charleston, S.C., on
the occupation of Charleston; a letter from James P. Holcombe
to Judah P. Benjamin, Nov. 16, 1864, Richmond, Va., on the
Niagara Falls "peace conference"; and a letter from Jacob
Thompson to Judah P. Benjamin, Dec. 3, 1864, Toronto, Canada,
on Confederate activities in Canada and plans by the Knights
of the Golden Circle to seize the steamer *Michigan* in Lake
Erie and free Confederate prisoners of war on Johnson's Island.
    Finding aid available.

307

Fisher, George Purnell   Judge; Public Official,
(1817–1899)   Washington, D.C.
    Papers, 1772–1905. ca. 200 items.
    In part, transcripts.
    Includes a 17-page account of the trial of John H. Surratt
for the assassination of President Lincoln written "by the Judge
who presided at the Trial," and the "Confession of Atzerodt
relative to the Assassination of President Lincoln," by Samuel
B. Arnold.
    Finding aid available.

308

Fisk, Clinton Bowen (1828–1890)   Gen., USA
    Letters, 1862. 2 items.

Letters from Fisk to his mother, Dec. 25, 1862, and 186[2], concerning the defense of Columbus, Ky., and Gens. John Frémont and Henry Halleck.

309
Fisk, Wilbur   2d Vermont Volunteers
    Papers, 1862–65. ca. 100 items.
    Transcripts.
    Diary, 1863–64, and letters to the editor of the Montpelier, Vt., *Green Mountain Freeman*, 1862–65, describing Fisk's service in the 6th Corps, Army of the Potomac, during the Fredericksburg, Wilderness, Spotsylvania, Cold Harbor, and Petersburg campaigns, and Sheridan's Shenandoah Valley Campaign. Includes comments on camp life, morale, military organization, hospital care, foraging expeditions, entertainment, the U.S. Sanitary Commission, furloughs, the performance of black soldiers, and the attitude toward and treatment of non-combatants in the South.

310
Flagler, Daniel Webster (1835–1899)   Capt., USA
    Collection, 1861–91. 14 items.
    Includes three commissions for positions in the Ordnance Department, 1861–63.

311
Fleetwood, Christian Abraham   Sgt. Maj., 4th
(1840–1914)   U.S. Colored Infantry
    Papers, 1797–1945. ca. 400 items.
    Diary, 1862–64 (3 v.), concerning campaigns in Virginia and North Carolina, Aug. 1863–Dec. 1864. Provides information on skirmishes on Virginia's lower peninsula, the Siege of Petersburg, Gen. Benjamin F. Butler's Fort Fisher expedition, camp life, disease, and President Lincoln's visit to the front lines in June 1864. Also includes orders, awards, passes, Fleetwood's discharge, Apr. 27, 1866, a list of officers in the 4th, 5th, 6th, 36th, 38th, and 39th Colored Regiments and the 54th Massachusetts Infantry, the names and service records of 15 black officers, and photographs of black recipients of the Congressional Medal of Honor.
    Finding aid and microfilm copy (1 reel) available.

312
Floyd—McAdoo Families
    Papers, 1806–93.
    Microfilm, 6 reels.
    Includes the diary of William Gibbs McAdoo, Sr. (1820–1894), lawyer and editor of Knoxville, Tenn., and Milledge-

ville and Marietta, Ga. Entries from the war (reels 3–4) describe troop movements, depredations by both Federal and Confederate soldiers, and the social and economic effects of the war in Georgia.

313
Foote, Andrew Hull (1806–1863)   Adm., USN
    Papers, 1838–63. ca. 800 items.
    Correspondence, orders, and reports concerning the gunboat attack on Confederate batteries at Belmont, Mo., the Fort Donelson Campaign, and the capture of the C.S. gunboat *Jeff Davis*. Also contains general orders and ordnance reports. Correspondents include Andrew A. Harwood, Roger N. Stembel, and Gideon Welles.

314
Foote, Lemuel Thomas
(1832–1908)   Chaplain, 151st New York Volunteers
    Papers, 1856–1937. ca. 110 items.
    Contains about 30 letters from Foote to his wife written from camps in Virginia, Aug.–Dec. 1863, chiefly concerning personal affairs, but including remarks on camp life, morale, disease, diet, desertions, depredations, foraging expeditions, religion, inflation, Confederate spies, and the disposition of troops. Also includes an account of the skirmish at Locust Grove, Va., a description of the death of Capt. Sylvanus S. Wilcox, a report on Federal casualties in the Battle of Winchester (Sept. 1864), and miscellaneous passes, orders, and commissions.

315
Forbes, Archibald (1838–1900)   Journalist
    Papers, 1889–98. 19 items.
    Manuscript article with related correspondence on the Grant–Warren–Sheridan controversy over the Battle of Five Forks. Correspondents include John Hay, Wesley Merritt, and James H. Wilson.

316
Forbes Family   Massachusetts
    Papers, 1768–1931.
    Microfilm, 52 reels.
    Contains the correspondence of Robert Bennet Forbes (1804–1889), Massachusetts shipowner and shipbuilder, relating to the construction of gunboats. Correspondents include John A. Dahlgren, Gustavus V. Fox, Louis M. Goldsborough, Francis H. Gregory, Samuel P. Lee, Stephen B. Luce, and Gideon Welles.
    Finding aid available.
    Originals in the Massachusetts Historical Society.

317
Force, Manning Ferguson (1824—1899)   Gen., USV
    Papers, 1835—85.
    Microfilm, 5 reels.
    Diaries, 1861—66, official and personal correspondence, reports, orders, telegrams, and miscellaneous items relating to the Battle of Shiloh and the Vicksburg and Atlanta campaigns. Provides information on camp life, training, diet, discipline, prisoners of war, casualties, generalship, inflation, devastation, and the attitude of noncombatants in the South. Also contains material on the Fitz-John Porter trial.
    Finding aid available.
    Originals in the University of Washington Library.

318
Force, Peter (1790—1868)   Archivist;
          Publisher; Historian
    Papers, 1170—1944. ca. 50,000 items.
    Includes 16 letters to Force from his son, Gen. Manning F. Force, 1862—64, concerning the Fort Donelson Campaign, the Battle of Shiloh, and camp life and marches in southwestern Tennessee. Also contains clippings and printed material on the Battle of Shiloh, and copies of general orders issued at New Orleans, La., Dec. 1863—Feb. 1864.
    Finding aid available.

319
Forney, John Wien (1817—1881)   Journalist; Politician
    Papers, 1841—76. ca. 150 items.
    Contains a few miscellaneous notes and letters relating generally to the war. Correspondents include Montgomery Blair, Simon Cameron, John A. Dahlgren, Thomas L. Kane, Edwin M. Stanton, and Thurlow Weed.

320
Forrest, French (1796—1866)   Flag Officer, CSN
    Letter, 1862. 1 item.
    Letter from Forrest to "My Dear Victor," May 27, 1862, Navy Department, criticizing the Confederate Congress for the passage of a bill creating four new admirals.

321
Forscky, J.
    Letter, 1861. 1 item.
    Letter from Forscky to S. P. Brooks, June 14, 1861, Richmond, Va., praising southerners for their enthusiastic support of the war.

322

Fort Delaware Prison Times
    Collection, 1865. 2 items.
    Photocopies.
    Copy of a prison newsletter, Apr. 1865, showing the name,
rank, and unit of about 30 Confederate prisoners of war.

323

Foulke, William Dudley (1848–1935)   Lawyer; Reformer
    Papers, 1470–1952. ca. 2,500 items.
    Includes letters of R. Moore and D. P. Moore written from
camps near Falmouth, Va., Jan.–Feb. 1863, concerning the
Fredericksburg Campaign, and several letters from Mark E.
Reeves to his family, 1861–63, describing recruitment and
popular support for the war effort in Cincinnati, Ohio.

324

Fowler, Joseph Smith   Educator–Lawyer, Tennessee
(1820–1902)
    Papers, 1865–1903. ca. 300 items.
    Contains a postwar biographical sketch of Gen. Marcus
Joseph Wright and a copy of a photograph of President Lincoln.

325

Frank, Jacob J.   41st New York Volunteers
    Diary, 1862. 1 v.
    Contains comments on camp life, troop movements, skir-
mishes, and entertainment during the Shenandoah Valley
Campaign of 1862 and the 2d Manassas Campaign.

326

Franklin, William Buel (1823–1903)   Gen., USA
    Papers 1861–65. 100 items.
    Chiefly official correspondence, orders, reports, and tele-
grams to Franklin during McClellan's Peninsular Campaign
and the Red River Campaign of 1864. Miscellaneous items
include a medical certificate concerning the wound Franklin
received at Sabine Cross Roads, La., a personal letter from
Gen. Thomas Ransom, May 31, 1864, concerning generalship
and behind-the-lines maneuvering among officers for field
commands, and a complaint by the men of the 1st New York
Cavalry against Col. A. T. McReynolds, Mar. 2, 1862. Principal
correspondents are Ambrose E. Burnside, Albion P. Howe,
Henry J. Hunt, John R. Kenly, George B. McClellan, R. B.
Marcy, John G. Parke, Thomas E. G. Ransom, John F. Reynolds,
Franz Sigel, Henry W. Slocum, William F. Smith, Edwin M.
Stanton, and Orlando B. Willcox.

William Buel Franklin

327

Fraser, P.   Historian
     Manuscript. 1,070 p.
     Unpublished "History of the Great Rebellion and Civil War in the United States, in One Volume."

328

Freeman, Douglas Southall
(1886–1953)   Educator; Author; Lecturer
     Papers, 1900–54. ca. 70,000 items.
     Source material gathered in preparation for Freeman's *R. E. Lee* (1934–35), 4 v.; *The South to Posterity* (1939); and *Lee's Lieutenants* (1942–44), 3 v.; and manuscripts and galley proofs of each work.
     Finding aid available.

329

Frémont, John Charles (1813–1890)   Gen., USA
     Letters, 1862–64. 3 items.
     Letter from Frémont to Maj. Simon Stevens, Apr. 21, 1862, Mountain Department, Wheeling, W. Va., advising Stevens on how to obtain an appointment on his staff.

330

French, Benjamin Brown   Commissioner of Public
(1800–1870)   Buildings, Washington, D.C.
     Papers, 1802–1924. ca. 4,000 items.
     Correspondence, diary, and newspaper clippings describing, in part, life in the Federal Capital during the war. Includes a few details on the Battle of 1st Manassas, observations on soldiers returning to Washington after the battle, public reaction to the Baltimore riots, Lincoln's inauguration and assassination, and Gen. Jubal Early's Washington raid, and a description of Richmond, Va., immediately after the war.
     Finding aid and partial microfilm copy (3 reels) available.

331

Fritsch, Friedrich Otto,
Baron Von (b. 1834)   Capt., 68th New York Volunteers
     Memoir, 1856–1900. 1 v.
     Transcript.
     Unpublished manuscript, "A Modern Soldier of Fortune," edited by Jessie Kaufman. Provides information on camp life, marches, generalship, rank disputes, supply, skirmishes, and the Chancellorsville and Gettysburg campaigns. Includes remarks on interviews with President Lincoln and Edwin M. Stanton on the problems of blacks.

332
Frost, Edward (1801–1868)   Agriculturist–Politician,
                                           South Carolina
      Papers, 1802–66. ca. 1,500 items.
      Contains several letters to Frost from family and friends,
1861–64, concerning the 1st South Carolina Volunteers, coastal
defense, the suffering of the civilian population, Confederate
finance, the relief of families of soldiers, problems with blacks,
and disease and deaths. Correspondents include Edwin P. Frost,
F. H. Frost, Thomas Frost, Simon Lucas, William Miller, and
James D. Tradewell.

333
Fuller, Joseph Pryor   20th Georgia Volunteers
      Papers, 1862–67. 50 items.
      Transcripts.
      Diary, 1864, and letters, 1862–67, concerning prison life
at Rock Island, Ill., and Point Lookout, Md.

334
Furman, Greene Chandler
      Collection, 1862–1954. 3 items.
      Photocopies.
      Letter from Col. Henry Marshall, a member of the Confed-
erate Congress from Louisiana, to his son-in-law, Lt. S. C.
Furman, Mar. 13, 1863, Richmond [Va.], concerning dissatisfaction in Tennessee with Gen. Albert Sidney Johnston and a
petition to President Davis for Johnston's removal. Also a letter from D. E. C. Kemper to Col. Henry Marshall, Dec. 9, 1863,
James Island, S.C., concerning the second disaster aboard the
submarine *H. L. Hunley* and the court-martial of Kemper's
brother, Tip Kemper.
      Naval Historical Foundation collection.

335
Galwey, Thomas Francis
(1846–1913)   Lt., 8th Ohio Volunteers
      Diaries, 1861–1908. 6 v.
      Diary, Jan. 1, 1863–July 6, 1864 (2 v.) and memoir, Apr.
13, 1861–May 27, 1864, concerning skirmishes in West Virginia in 1861, the Shenandoah Valley Campaign of 1862, and
the 2d Manassas, Antietam, Fredericksburg, Gettysburg,
Wilderness, and Spotsylvania campaigns; operations along the
Rapidan and Rappahannock Rivers in late 1863; and the Siege
of Petersburg. Also includes comments on military organization,
camp life, entertainment, a visit to the front lines by President
Lincoln, and various marches and foraging expeditions, as well
as numerous sketches of encampments and battles. Member of
the "Circle of the Irish Brigade."

336
Gardner, Francis R. and George   USMC
    Collection, 1855–1902. 8 items.
    In part, transcripts.
    Includes a postwar account of the reenforcement of Fort
Pickens, Fla., by Union forces, Apr. 12, 1861. Also, transcripts
of official naval correspondence and clippings of Gideon Welles'
version of the event.

337
Garesche, Julius P.   Maj.; Asst. Adj. Gen., USA
    Register, 1861. 1 v.
    Official Army Register, for 1861 (1861). Includes notations
by Garesche to show changes made during the year.

338
Garfield, James Abram (1831–1881), Pres., U.S.
    Papers, 1831–81. 80,350 items.
    Contains official correspondence, reports, general and spe-
cial orders, maps, and miscellaneous items relating to the Sandy
Valley and Shiloh campaigns, and Garfield's command of the
42d Ohio Volunteers and the 18th and 20th brigades, Army of
the Ohio.
    Published index and microfilm copy (177 reels) available.

339
Garfield, Lucretia Rudolph (1832–1918)
    Papers, 1844–1918. ca. 55,000 items.
    Contains four letters from Joe Rudolph to his sister Lucre-
tia (Mrs. James A. Garfield), 1861–65, written from camps in
Ohio, Arkansas, and Louisiana. Provides a detailed account of
the Arkansas Post expedition, particularly the capture of Fort
Hindman.
    Finding aid available.

340
Garrett, Robert (1783–1857),
and Family   Railroad Official; Financier
    Papers, 1820–80. ca. 29,000 items.
    Correspondence and financial papers relating to the opera-
tion of the Baltimore and Ohio Railroad. Includes information
on the movement of troops and supplies, civilian arrests, and
the release of Jefferson Davis from Fort Monroe after the war.
Also, miscellaneous letters between President Lincoln and members of his Cabinet, and letters from various military officers
and political officials.
    Finding aid available.

James Abram Garfield

341

George, Harold C.   Collector
    Collection, 1862–1910. ca. 50 items.
    Contains notes from manuscript and printed sources on
the participation of the VI Corps, Army of the Potomac (particularly the 139th Pennsylvania Volunteers) in the Wilderness
and Spotsylvania campaigns. Also includes details on the action
at " Bloody Angle" in the Spotsylvania Campaign, accounts of
the deaths of Gens. John Sedgwick and Alexander Hays, information on the attitude of soldiers in the Army of the Potomac
toward Gen. Ulysses S. Grant, and miscellaneous poems and
diary extracts.

342

Ghent, William James (1866–1942)   Author; Journalist
    Papers, 1876–1942. ca. 15,000 items.
    Includes a few postwar newspaper clippings and articles
concerning emancipation, President Lincoln, generalship in the
war, various battles and skirmishes, and prisoners of war.
    Finding aid available.

343

Gherardi, Bancroft (1832–1903)   Lt. Comdr., USN
    Letters, 1864. 2 items.
    Letters by Gherardi, U.S.S. *Port Royal*, Mobile Bay, Sept.
17, 1864, concerning the distribution of prize money for cotton
seized when he commanded the U.S.S. *Chocura.*

344

Gibbes, Lewis Reeves (1810–1894)   Educator; Scientist
    Papers, 1793–1894. ca. 5,700 items.
    Contains a few letters from former students at Charleston
College, S.C., concerning recommendations for military commissions or promotions, and letters from friends and acquaintances describing their personal losses and the burning of
Columbia, S.C.
    Finding aid available.

345

Gibson, S. J.   Cpl., 103d Pennsylvania Volunteers
    Papers, 1864. 2 items.
    Diary, Jan. 1–Dec. 24, 1864, concerning the capture of the
Federal garrison at Plymouth, N.C., Apr. 17–20, 1864, and life
as a prisoner of war both on the march and at Andersonville,
Ga., and Florence, S.C. Also a letter from Gibson to his wife
written from Andersonville Prison, June 12, 1864.

346
Gibson—Getty—McClure Families
Papers, 1777–1926. ca. 2,500 items.
Contains the papers of Gen. George W. Getty (1819–1901), Inspector General, Army of the Potomac—official correspondence from the War Department concerning commissions, orders, and other routine affairs; a report on the capture of the Confederate battery at Hill's Point, Va., Apr. 20, 1863; information on Gen. B. F. Butler's Fort Fisher expedition; postwar correspondence on the reinvestigation of the Fitz-John Porter case; and an extract from the diary of Hazard Stevens, Apr. 2, 1865, concerning the Appomattox Campaign. Correspondents include Adelbert Ames, Ambrose E. Burnside, and John G. Foster. Also includes the papers of Col. Charles McClure (1838–1902), USV.
Finding aid available.

347
Giddings, George H. (b. 1823)   Col., CSA
Papers, 1846–1955. 2 items.
Memoir, 1846–1902, published serially by Charles M. Barnes in the San Antonio *Express*, May–June 1902, concerning Giddings' service as a Confederate agent in Mexico, skirmishes with Federal troops near Brownsville, Tex., and his claim to membership in Lincoln's Cabinet. Also, a memorandum by B. F. Dixon, Sept. 1, 1955.

348
Giddings, Joshua Reed (1795–1864)
Papers, 1839–99. ca. 900 items.
Two letters from Gen. John C. Frémont to U.S. Representative George W. Julian, Wheeling, W. Va., Apr. 2 and 21, 1862, concerning Union sentiment in West Virginia, Frémont's desire for reinforcements, and an appointment in the Medical Department; letter from Capt. Benjamin Price (Excelsior Brigade) to Julian, Falmouth, Va., Mar. 29, 1863, criticizing Union officers, advocating complete subjugation of the Confederacy, and outlining Price's own military career; and a military pass.

349
Gilbert, Cass (1859–1934)
Papers, 1841–1961. ca. 9,000 items.
Includes a letter by C. C. Gilbert, in camp near Springfield, Mo., July 15, 1861, concerning the consolidation and disposition of the frontier garrisons, the organization of troops in Missouri under Gen. Nathaniel Lyon, and the generalship of George

McClellan and Irvin McDowell, and various Confederate military leaders.

Finding aid available.

350

Gillett, Simon Palmer (d. 1910)   Lt., USN
    Papers, 1858−76. 12 items.

Contains two letters from Gillett to his wife, Jan. 10 and May 20, 1865, concerning living conditions aboard ironclads and the imprisonment of Confederate leaders; letter to Gillett from his brother Philip, Feb. 7, 1861, on Abraham Lincoln's trip to Washington for the inauguration, assassination attempts, and secession; letter from John Crittenden Watson to Gillett, May 13, 1865, concerning a military pass for his uncle, Col. George B. Crittenden (CSA); two photographs of unidentified Union officers; and a "Schedule of Pay of the Navy."

Naval Historical Foundation collection.

351

Gillette, James Jenkins (d. 1881)   Maj., USA
    Papers, 1857−84. ca. 2,000 items.

Letters and drafts of letters from Gillette to his family and friends in New York concerning his service as an engineer with the 71st New York Militia Regiment, camp life and training, the Battle of 1st Manassas, and life as a prisoner of war at Richmond, Va., July−Dec. 1861; official correspondence concerning military supplies in the Shenandoah Valley Campaign of 1862, and the 2d Manassas, Antietam, Chancellorsville, Gettysburg, and Atlanta campaigns. Includes remarks on troop movements, camp life, generalship, morale, discipline, foraging expeditions, disease, corruption in the Army, hospital care, and devastation in the South. Also contains invoices, vouchers, receipts, accounts, and returns of commissary supplies, a few sketches of battles, a photograph of Gillette taken in 1863, and a report on Gillette's abandonment of commissary supplies at Bolivar Heights, Md., Dec. 10, 1862.

352

Gilpin, E. N.   Clerk, 3d Iowa Cavalry
    Papers, 1861−1911. 76 items.

Diary, Mar. 6−July 5, 1865, and reprint of the published version, "The Last Campaign—A Cavalryman's Journal," *Journal of the U.S. Cavalry Association* (n.d.), describing Gen. James H. Wilson's raid to Selma, Ala., and the capture of Montgomery, Ala., and Columbus and Macon, Ga. Includes remarks on the capture of President Davis. Also contains the diary of Samuel J. B. V. Gilpin, Aug. 1861−Oct. 1864 (5 v.), 3d Indiana Cavalry, kept during the Antietam, Fredericksburg,

Chancellorsville, Gettysburg, Wilderness, Spotsylvania, and Cold Harbor campaigns and the Siege of Petersburg, and operations along the Rappahannock and Rapidan Rivers in the fall of 1863. Provides information on camp life, marches, troop movements, generalship, and the attitude of noncombatants in Maryland and Virginia.

353
Gist Family
　　Collection, 1776–1865. 75 items.
　　In part, photocopies.
　　Letters of Richard J. Gist (d. 1864) and Branford P. Gist, 1862–65, relate to their service in the 6th Maryland Volunteers during the Antietam Campaign, skirmishes along the Rapidan and Rappahannock Rivers in the fall of 1863, the Wilderness Campaign, and the Battle of Cold Harbor. Letters of Col. George W. Gist, 17th Kentucky Volunteers, 1863–65, concern campaigns in east Tennessee and Sherman's Atlanta Campaign. Includes comments on camp life, marches, troop movements, disease, and hospital care.

354
Goldsborough, Louis Malesherbes　　　　　　　Adm., USN
(1805–1877)
　　Papers, 1817–74. ca. 8,000 items.
　　Letters from Goldsborough to his wife and daughter, Sept. 1861–Sept. 1862, concern the blockade of Charleston Harbor, S.C., General Burnside's Roanoke Island expedition, and operations on the James River. Includes information on the scuttling of the *Merrimac* and visits to the front lines by President Lincoln and members of his Cabinet. Also contains miscellaneous orders and newspaper clippings. Principal correspondents are Samuel F. Du Pont and Gustavus V. Fox.

355
Goodnow, James Harrison
(1826–1908)　　　　　　　Lt. Col., 12th Indiana Volunteers
　　Papers, 1847–97. 108 items.
　　Chiefly letters from Goodnow to his wife and family, 1862–64, concerning the Vicksburg and Atlanta campaigns, and campaigns in Kentucky, Tennessee, and Alabama. Provides information on camp life, marches, morale, depredations, foraging expeditions, discipline, disease, new recruits, military bounties, the selection of officers, blacks, and the attitude of noncombatants in the South. Also contains muster rolls, clippings, commissions, and Goodnow's discharge, Sept. 15, 1864.

356
Gorgas, William Crawford (1854–1920)
    Papers, 1857–1919. ca. 12,000 items.
    In part, transcripts.
    Includes a copy of the diary of Gen. Josiah Gorgas (1818–1883), which chronicles the war from the perspective of an officer on the headquarters staff at Richmond, Va., where Gorgas served as chief of ordnance. Contains remarks on generalship, events in Richmond, the flight of Confederate military and political leaders during the Appomattox Campaign, and the problems facing both blacks and whites in the postwar South.
    Finding aid available.

357
Gould, William J.   Sgt., 2d Connecticut Light Artillery
    Papers, 1864–65. 13 items.
    Includes a diary, Mar. 1–July 13, 1865, kept during the Mobile Campaign. Contains comments on camp life, marches, skirmishes, foraging expeditions, the performance of black troops, the effectiveness of Confederate torpedoes, and the attitude of Confederate prisoners of war.

358
Gourdin, Henry   Merchant, Charleston, S.C.
    Papers, 1860–67. 38 items.
    Contains several letters concerning secession, military organization, enlistments, troop movements, the demand for cotton, and the seizure of vessels belonging to Gourdin & Shackleford, particularly the *General Parkhill*.

359
Gove Family
    Papers, 1848–1911. 7 items.
    Includes the diary of Col. Jesse Augustus Gove (1824–1862), 22d Massachusetts Volunteers, Nov. 1, 1861–June 26, 1862. Describes camp life, marches, training, entertainment, morale, discipline, disease, hospital care, reconnaissance balloons and expeditions, generalship in the Army of the Potomac, and the Siege of Yorktown. Also contains a photograph of Gove, a printed memorial entitled "Colonel Jesse A. Gove, U.S.A." (28 p.), and newspaper clippings on Gove's military service.
    Naval Historical Foundation collection.

360
Graham, Henry   177th New York Volunteers
    Memoir, 1862–63. 1 v.
    "A Journal of My Life and Experience as a Soldier," Oct.

27, 1862–Sept. 1, 1863. Describes Graham's military training in New York, a voyage to New Orleans, La., camp life, marches, the conscription and performance of blacks, foraging expeditions, disease, hospital care, operations along the Amite and "Blind" Rivers, the Siege of Port Hudson, and deaths in the 177th New York Volunteers. Also includes a list of officers in the 177th, a list of privates in Graham's company (A), and copies of poems and letters by Graham.

361
Graham, R. H.   Maj., CSA
    Document, 1865. 1 item.
    Parole for Pvt. David Buchanan, 111th Pennsylvania Volunteers, Feb. 2[2?], 1865, signed by Graham.

362
Grand Army of the Republic
    Records, 1883–1928. 7 items.
    Records of the Departments of the Potomac, Florida, and Nebraska. Contains the names of members in each department and service records of members in the Department of the Potomac.

363
Grant, James (1829–1905)   Delegate, U.S.
                                              Christian Commission
    Manuscript narrative, 1862–94. 1 item.
    Manuscript entitled "The Flag and the Cross, a History of the United States Christian Commission," 1894. Includes photocopies of two letters, Sept. 18 and 19, 1862, concerning the care of wounded soldiers during the Antietam Campaign, and photographs of Ulysses S. Grant and J. O. Sloan.

364
Grant, Ulysses Simpson (1822–1885), Pres., U.S.
    Papers, 1844–1922. 47,200 items.
    Includes headquarters records from the six commands held by Grant during the Civil War: Military Districts of Southeast Missouri, Cairo, and West Tennessee; Department of the Tennessee; Military Division of the Mississippi; and General in Chief of the Armies of the United States. Comprises official correspondence, general and special orders, reports, registers, returns, dispatches, accounts, telegrams, and miscellaneous items.
    Published index and microfilm copy (33 reels) available.

365
Grattan, John W. (b. 1841)   Pvt., 47th New York National
                                        Guard; Ens., USN
    Papers, 1862–1937. ca. 300 items.

Ulysses Simpson Grant

Contains a diary, Oct. 1863–May 1865, kept by Grattan while serving as a captain's clerk aboard the U.S.S. *Florida*, U.S.S. *Minnesota*, and U.S.S. *Malvern*, and a memoir, "Under the Blue Pennant, or Notes of a Naval Officer," concerning naval operations on the James River, Oct. 1863–July 1864, and the Fort Fisher expeditions, Dec. 1864–Jan. 1865. Includes details on the loss of the Federal gunboat *Smith Briggs*, the torpedo attack on the U.S.S. *Minnesota*, and the capture of Fort Fisher. Also provides information on black soldiers and refugees, guerrilla warfare, blockade running, discipline, hospital care, visits to the front lines by President Lincoln, the fall of Richmond, Va., the torpedo attack on the C.S.S. *Albemarle*, prize vessels, General Butler's advance on Richmond, the C.S.S. *North Carolina*, and General Schofield's advance on Wilmington, N.C. Additional items comprise letters from Grattan to his father concerning the torpedo attack on the *Minnesota* and the Fort Fisher expeditions; captured Confederate letters concerning camp life and the sinking of the *Albemarle*; photographs of Adm. David D. Porter, Lt. M. W. Saunders, Lt. William B. Cushing, Adm. Samuel P. Lee, Ensign Grattan, and Private Grattan; sketches of the U.S.S. *Malvern*, U.S.S. *Minnesota*, City Point and Bermuda Hundred, Va., Fort Fisher and New Inlet, N.C., the Confederate battery at Howlett's Bluff, Va., and the destruction of the U.S.S. *Shawsheen*; and *Report of General Robert E. Lee, of Operations at Rappahannock Bridge; Also, Report of Lieut. Gen. E. K. Smith of Operations in Lower Louisiana, and Report of Major General Jones of Engagement at Rogersville, Tennessee* (1864).

Naval Historical Foundation collection.

366

Gray, Horace (1828–1902)   Lawyer–Jurist, Massachusetts
   Papers, 1845–1902. ca. 400 items.
   Photocopies.
   Includes a few letters to Gray, 1861–65, concerning the secession crisis, the political situation in Washington, D.C., the Presidential election of 1864, the progress of the war, and morale in the Union Army. Correspondents are C. F. Blake, Wilder Dwight, Manning F. Force, H. L. Hill, Stephen Phillips, L. M. Quincy, Charles Sumner, and William Whiting.
   Microfilm copy (1 reel) available.

367

Grebe, Balzar (1834–1866)   2d Lt., 14th Illinois Volunteers
   Collection, 1861–63 and undated. 4 items.
   Original manuscript (in German) and English translation entitled "Autobiography and Civil War Diary," 1861–63. Provides information on the Shiloh, Corinth, and Vicksburg

campaigns, and maneuvers against Gen. Sterling Price in Missouri. Includes comments on discipline, casualties, depredations, prisoners of war, and Confederate morale and deserters. Also includes a photograph of Grebe in uniform.

368
Greble, Edwin (1806–1883)   Philadelphia, Pa.
   Family papers, 1855–86. ca. 80 items.
   Diary, 1855–72, containing an account of Greble's service in the 196th Pennsylvania Volunteers, chiefly as a guard at the military prison at Camp Douglas, Ill., Aug. 10–Oct. 29, 1864.

369
———
   Papers, 1858–70.
   Microfilm, 1 reel.
   Includes letters by Greble containing descriptions of Confederate cemeteries and prisons. Also contains comments on President Lincoln, Jefferson Davis, and Benjamin F. Butler.

370
Greeley, Horace
(1811–1872)   Journalist–Politician, New York
   Papers, 1826–1928. ca. 1,500 items.
   In part, transcripts.
   Contains Greeley's autobiography and articles, correspondence, lectures, notes, and clippings. Includes material on the slavery issue, the New York *Tribune*, liberal Republicanism, the 1864 Canadian Peace Commission, and a postwar bond for Jefferson Davis.
   Finding aid and partial index available.

371
Greely, Adolphus Washington
(1844–1935)   Capt., 81st U.S. Colored Troops
   Papers, 1753–1959. ca. 45,000 items.
   Contains a diary kept by Greely in 1864 while on guard duty at Port Hudson, La.; a letter to Greely from a cousin in the 1st Massachusetts Cavalry, Feb. 26, 1864, concerning the coming campaign in Virginia; and miscellaneous orders, muster rolls, commissions, and passes.
   Finding aid available.

372
Green, Duff (1791–1875)   Politician; Industrialist
   Papers, 1716–1879. 725 items.
   In part, transcripts.

Includes a few miscellaneous notes and letters to Green from J. M. Baughman, W. R. Daugherty, Jefferson Davis, Burton N. Harrison, and James A. Seddon, 1863–64; letters from Confederate officers held in Libby Prison after the fall of Richmond, Va., Apr. 1865; military passes; and notes on States rights and the Constitution.

Finding aid and microfilm copy (3 reels) available.

373
Green, Joseph F. (b. 1811)   Capt., USN
    Papers, 1828–1960. 60 items.
    In part, transcripts.
    Chiefly official correspondence, 1862–64, concerning the blockade of Charleston Harbor, S.C. Includes information on expeditions to Murrell's Inlet, Dec. 29, 1863–Jan. 2, 1864, and Bull's Bay, Mar. 1864, the attack on Fort Sumter of Sept. 9, 1863, the sinking of the U.S.S. *Housatonic*, blockade runners, desertions, and discipline. Also contains the logbook of the U.S.S. *Mary Sanford*, Dec. 29, 1863–Jan. 2 [1864], instructions and signals for the attack on Murrell's Inlet, sketches of Murrell's Inlet, and miscellaneous orders and reports. Correspondents include James C. Chaplin, John J. Cornwell, John A. Dahlgren, John L. Davis, J. D. Dexter, Samuel F. Du Pont, William Gibson, Charles W. Pickering, and William D. Whiting.
    Naval Historical Foundation collection.

374
Greene, Samuel Dana (1839–1884)   Lt., USN
    Letter, 1862. 1 item.
    Transcript.
    Letter from Greene to his family, Mar. 14, 1862, describing the engagement between the *Monitor* and the *Merrimac.*

375
Greenwood Plantation   South Carolina
    Diary, 1858–64. 1 v.
    Diary of the proprietor of Greenwood plantation, Mr. Gregory, Aug. 1858–Oct. 1864. The diary was picked up by a soldier in the naval brigade and sent to Adm. John A. Dahlgren as a reflection of economic conditions in the South. Includes a forwarding letter from Comdr. George Henry Preble to Dahlgren, Dec. 22, 1864.

376
Greer, Henry I. and Robert   25th South
                                                Carolina Volunteers
    Papers, 1863–64. 32 items.
    Chiefly letters from Henry and Robert Greer to their par-

ents from camps in South Carolina, North Carolina, and Virginia. Describes the defense of Fort Sumter in 1863, the Battle of Drewry's Bluff, Va., the Siege of Petersburg, and the defense of Wilmington, N.C.

377
Gregg, David McMurtrie (1833–1916)   Gen., USA
    Papers, 1716–1936. ca. 500 items.
    Official and personal correspondence, orders, reports, maps, and photographs, chiefly relating to Gregg's service with the Cavalry Division, Army of the Potomac, during the Peninsular, Chancellorsville, and Gettysburg campaigns, the Siege of Petersburg, and operations along the Rapidan River in the fall of 1863. Includes reports on Gen. George Stoneman's raids in Virginia during the Chancellorsville Campaign, accounts of skirmishes at Aldie and Upperville, Va., June–Sept. 1863, copies of letters by William T. Sherman and Ulysses S. Grant concerning Sherman's cavalry during the Atlanta Campaign, and a copy of an unpublished narrative, "Brevet Major General David McMurtrie Gregg," written by a descendant in 1934.

378
Gresham, Walter Quintin (1832–1895)   Gen., USA
    Papers, 1857–1930. ca. 12,000 items.
    Contains letters from Gresham to his wife, 1861–65, relating to the Shiloh, Corinth, Vicksburg, and Atlanta campaigns. Includes remarks on generalship, Confederate deserters, disease, hospital care, slavery, and economic conditions in the South. Also includes a detailed report by Lt. Col. Andrew J. Alexander on the operations of Gresham's 4th Division, 17th Army Corps, in the Atlanta Campaign, May 27–July 20, 1864.
    Finding aid and name index available.

379
Griffith, George Washington Ewing
(b. 1833)   Businessman, Kansas
    Article, 1924. 1 item.
    Transcript.
    Copy of an article, "My Experience in the Quantrill Raid," published in the Lawrence, Kans., *Daily Journal-World*, Aug. 21, 1924.

380
Groening, D. Von   Merchant, Richmond, Va.
    Letterbook, 1861–63. 1 v.
    Contains correspondence, May 24, 1861–July 18, 1863, on economic conditions in the South, the Federal blockade, and various commercial transactions.

381
Gurley, John Addison
(1813–1863)   U.S. Representative, Ohio
    Letter, 1862. 1 item.
    Letter from Gurley to David Chambers, Feb. 24, 1862, criticizing Gen. George B. McClellan.

382
Guslin, M.   Ambulance Corps, USA
    Letters, 1863, 1864. 2 items.
    Letters from Guslin to his wife, July 16, 1863, and Dec. 1, 1864, concerning the Siege of Jackson, Miss., and miscellaneous matters at Camp Russell, Va.

383
Habersham Family
    Papers, 1787–1892. 265 items.
    Contains letters of Richard W. Habersham (CSA), July 19, 1861–Nov. 30, 1864, concerning the performance of Wade Hampton's legion in the Battle of 1st Manassas, the Peninsular Campaign, and the Shenandoah Valley Campaign of 1864. Includes information on camp life, troop movements, marches, the selection of officers, disease, hospital care, hunger in the Confederate Army in 1864, and devastation in the Shenandoah Valley. Letters written by Habersham while serving as chief clerk at a hospital in Richmond, Va., describe life in the Confederate capital in 1862 and 1863. Also includes a few letters of A. M. Habersham of Annapolis, Md., concerning his imprisonment at Fort McHenry.

384
Hahn, Michael (1830–1886)   Gov., Louisiana
    Document, 1864. 1 item.
    Printed copy of the constitution of the State of Louisiana adopted in convention in New Orleans, July 23, 1864, with Governor Hahn's certification.

385
Hall, Angelo (b. 1868)
    Manuscript, 1830–96. 1 v.
    Biography of Chloe Angeline Stickney Hall (1830–1892), completed by her son, Angelo Hall, in 1893. Contains a few observations on life in Washington during the war and public reaction to Gen. Jubal Early's Washington raid. Includes copies and extracts of family correspondence, and a preface dated Sept. 8, 1896.

386
Hall, George Washington
(1841–1912)   14th Georgia Volunteers, CSA
    Memoir and diary, 1861–65. 2 v.
    Transcript.
    Covers the Peninsular, Antietam, Fredericksburg, Chancellorsville, Gettysburg, Wilderness, and Spotsylvania campaigns, and operations along the Rappahannock and Rapidan Rivers in the fall of 1863. Includes information on camp life, enlistments, marches, casualties, disease, hospital care, guerrilla warfare, prisoners of war, deserters, military organization, and life as a prisoner of war at Fort Delaware. Also contains numerous prayers and songs and part of the diary of Pvt. Jacob L. Ellsesser (1831–1909), 38th Pennsylvania Infantry, Jan. 1–June 27, 1862.

387
Halleck, Henry Wager (1815–1872)   Gen. in Chief;
                                                  Chief of Staff, USA
    Papers, 1843–63. 232 items.
    Chiefly drafts of telegrams sent by Halleck concerning affairs in the Department of Missouri and the Department of the Mississippi, Jan.–Mar. 1862. Letters to Halleck, Feb. 5, 1862–Feb. 21, 1863, relate to the treatment of surgeons on the field of battle, General Grant's capture of Fort Donelson, conscription, the movement and disposition of troops, and the overall conduct of the war. Correspondents include Don Carlos Buell, George W. Cullum, John A. Dix, President Lincoln, Thomas A. Scott, and Zealous B. Tower.
    Finding aid available.

388
Hallock, Isaac (1839–1916)   Pvt., 13th New York
                                             Volunteers; Ens., USN
    Papers, 1781–1916. ca. 300 items.
    Correspondence, 1862–65, and diary, 1858–68 (2 v.), describing Hallock's service with the 13th New York Volunteers, Apr.–Aug. 1861, and as an ensign and master's mate aboard the U.S.S. *State of Georgia*, U.S.S. *Mercedita*, U.S.S. *Dragon*, U.S.S. *Don Eureka*, and U.S.S. *Wasp*. Contains information on camp life and training with the 13th New York, General Burnside's Roanoke Island expedition, the Siege of Beaufort, N.C., and the capture of numerous blockade runners.

389
Halpine, Charles Graham (1829–1868)   Journalist; Lt. Col.
                                       and Asst. Adj. Gen.,
                                       New York Volunteers

Henry Wager Halleck

Scrapbooks, 1861–67. 4 v.
Contains clippings of articles by "Pvt. Miles O'Reilley," Halpine's pseudonym, on the conduct of the war and various political and military leaders.

390

Hamilton, Charles Smith (1822–1891)   Gen., USV
    Letter, 1863. 1 item.
    Transcript.
    Letter written by Hamilton, Feb. 11, 1863, Headquarters, Memphis [Tenn.], complaining about the loss of his command. Includes comments on the character and generalship of Ulysses S. Grant, Stephen A. Hurlbut, John A. McClernand, and James B. McPherson.

391
Hamilton, William (1824–1896)   Pvt., 2d Pennsylvania
                                         Cavalry Reserves; 191st
                                         Pennsylvania Volunteers
    Papers, 1838–96. ca. 300 items.
    Chiefly letters from Hamilton to his family, 1861–65, concerning the Antietam, Fredericksburg, Gettysburg, and Appomattox campaigns, operations along the Rappahannock and Rapidan Rivers in the fall of 1863, and the Siege of Petersburg. Provides information on camp life, marches, morale, discipline, disease, hospital care, military organization, generalship, supply problems, the U.S. Sanitary Commission, promotions, Confederate deserters, and the performance and use of black troops. Also contains a few letters of Hamilton's brother, Sgt. John Hamilton.
    Indexed.

392
Hammond, James Henry (1807–1864)   Planter–U.S.
                                      Senator, South Carolina
    Papers, 1774–1875. ca. 8,000 items.
    Contains letters to Hammond from his son, Paul F. Hammond, 1862, concerning the Shiloh and Corinth campaigns, General Kirby-Smith's invasion of Kentucky, the Battle of Richmond, Ky., and Confederate casualties and generalship; letters from James Hammond to Jefferson Davis, Christopher Memminger, and James L. Orr concerning political and financial affairs; a letter from Hammond to Col. A. P. Aldrich, July 22, 1863, concerning captured black soldiers; a letter from P. G. T. Beauregard to Hammond, Dec. 9, 1861, on military appointments; and two letters from John F. Hollenbach to Hammond written from camps in Georgia and Tennessee.
    Finding aid, index, and microfilm copy (20 reels) available.

393

Hammond General Hospital   Point Lookout, Md.
    Collection, 1863 and undated. 2 items.
    Photocopies.
    Sketch of the buildings and grounds of Hammond General
Hospital and copy of the Mar. 31, 1863, issue of the *Hammond
Gazette*.

394

Hampton, Sally S.
    Letter, 1861. 1 item.
    Letter from Hampton to Mr. Ruggles, Woodlands, S.C.,
June 5, 1861, concerning secession, the Fort Sumter affair, and
the martial spirit in Charleston.

395

Hancock, Winfield Scott (1824—1886)   Gen., USA
    Collection, 1864—68. 6 items.
    Includes a letter from Hancock to T. Bailey Myers, Aug. 6,
1864, concerning the Siege of Petersburg, and a copy of a photograph of Gen. U. S. Grant.

396

Hand, George O.
(1830—1887)   Sgt., 1st California Volunteers
    Diary, 1861—64. 1 v.
    Photocopy.
    Account of Hand's service with the California column in
New Mexico Territory, Aug. 15, 1861—May 19, 1864. Describes
marches, skirmishes with Apache Indians, camp life, morale,
leadership, courts-martial, Indian behavior, the attitude of
noncombatants, and living conditions in New Mexico Territory.
Also includes muster rolls for Hand's company (G) for Aug.
1861, Feb. 1863, and when the company was mustered out of
service at Fort Gray, N. Mex., in 1864.

397

Hanna—McCormick Families
    Papers, 1792—1951. ca. 44,500 items.
    In part, photocopies.
    Contains seven letters from Mark Hanna (1837—1925) to
Gussie Rhodes written from Washington, D.C., and vicinity,
1864, concerning camp life, disease, the location of mutual
friends, and personal matters, and two letters from Capt. W. H.
Medill to his sister, Aug. 21, 1862, Yorktown, Va., and Mar. 15,
1863, near Stafford Courthouse, Va., concerning the Peninsular Campaign, morale in the Army of the Potomac, and the
generalship of David M. Gregg, Joseph Hooker, and George B.
McClellan.
    Finding aid available.

398

Hanno, C. B.

Letter, 1861. 1 item.

Letter written by Hanno, June 20, 1861, Washington, D.C., discussing military affairs and troop movements on the eve of the Battle of 1st Manassas.

399

Hanson, George A.

Papers, 1860–64. 4 items.

Includes a letter from Gen. Samuel S. Carroll to Gen. Horatio G. Wright, Aug. 2, 1864, Washington [D.C.], criticizing Gen. David Hunter for his treatment of noncombatants.

400

Hanson, Roger Weightman (1827–1863)   Gen., CSA

Papers, 1856–88. ca. 175 items.

Includes letters from Hanson to his wife, 1862, from Fort Warren and Fort Delaware military prisons; letters of condolence received by Mrs. Hanson following her husband's death in the Battle of Murfreesboro, Tenn., Jan. 2, 1863; a letter from Mrs. Virginia Hanson to her mother, Jan. 21, 1862, on military affairs at Bowling Green, Ky.; and a letter by John J. Crittenden, May 30, 1862, concerning General Hanson's exchange.

401

Hard, Hanson (1821–1896)   Surg., USA

Collection, 1864–1928. 3 items.

Includes a diary, Mar. 25–Apr. 24, 1864, describing an attack on Paducah, Ky., by Confederate cavalry led by Gen. Nathan B. Forrest, and Hard's capture and treatment as a prisoner of war. Also, a letter of introduction to Congressman James A. Garfield written by Capt. J. McKenzie, Feb. 16, 1864, and biographical data on Hard compiled by A. D. Hard in 1928.

402

Hardee, William Joseph (1815–1873)   Gen., USA

Papers, 1861–62. 29 items.

Letters from Hardee to Felicia Lee Shover of Memphis, Tenn., July 2, 1861–June 1, 1862, and undated, concerning the disposition and movement of Confederate troops in western Kentucky, Tennessee, and northern Mississippi.

403

Hardie, James Allen (1823–1876)   Gen., USA

Papers, 1844–86. 395 items.

Includes orders relating to Hardie's appointment and duties on the staff of the inspector general; information on ciphers; a letter from Gen. George Wright to Hardie, May 18, 1863, San Francisco, Calif., concerning the Department of the Pacific; letters by Gens. Joseph Hooker, Randolph B. Marcy, and Ambrose E. Burnside expressing confidence in Hardie; letters concerning the assassination of President Lincoln; and an extract from the *New York Tribune*, July 17, 1865, concerning the visit of Father Walter to Mary E. Surratt shortly before her execution.

Finding aid available.

404
Hardie, R. E.   17th Mississippi Regiment
    Letter, 1862. 1 item.
    Letter from Hardie to his sister, Apr. 17, 1862, Yorktown, Va., describing the Siege of Yorktown.

405
Harlan, John Marshall
(1833–1911)   Col., 10th Kentucky Volunteers, USA
    Papers, 1810–1971. ca. 20,000 items.
    Includes accounts, receipts, invoices, and returns of ordnance, provisions, and camp equipment; muster rolls; payrolls; statements and certificates concerning Harlan's war service; Harlan's resignation as colonel of the 10th Kentucky Volunteers, Mar. 3, 1863; and his pension certificate. Also, essays on the war by Harlan: "Civil War of 1861. The Union Cause in Kentucky. Some Incidents That Occurred in That State," "The Union Cause in Kentucky in 1861 and the Raising of a Regiment by Me for the Volunteer Infantry Service. Some Incidents in That Service," "Some Experiences as a Captain of Home Guards—the Crittenden Union Zouaves of Louisville, Kentucky in 1861," "My Pursuit of Gen. John H. Morgan's Troops . . . December 1862, and the Skirmish . . . at Johnson's Ferry," "Raid by Morgan's Men on Frankfort, Kentucky in the Fall of 1864," "Battle of Hartsville," and "March from Mississippi Into Kentucky."
    Finding aid and microfilm copy (34 reels) available.

406
Harralson, Philip Hodnett (1851–1912)
    Reminiscence, undated. 1 item.
    Transcript.
    Copy of Harralson's "Reminiscence of the War Between the States" (3 p.), which contains remarks on the Siege of Petersburg and conditions in the South during the war.

407
Harrington, Purnell Frederick (1844–1937)   Ens., USN
    Papers, 1861–85. ca. 100 items.

Includes personal and academic records of Harrington's performance as a cadet at the U.S. Naval Academy in the early part of the war, and orders and official correspondence relating to his service on the U.S.S. *Monongahela*, West Gulf Blockading Squadron, 1863–65.

Naval Historical Foundation collection.

408

Harris, Charles A. USA
Letter, 1862. 1 item.
Letter from Harris to his parents, Frankfort, Ky., Oct. 21, 1862, concerning an unsuccessful effort to trap Gen. John Hunt Morgan near Lawrenceburg, Ky.

409

Harris, Isham Green (1818–1897) Gov., Tennessee
Papers, 1861–62. 4 items.
Letterbook, 1861–62, containing copies of letters from various Confederate officers and public officials concerning military supplies, recruits, the treatment of Union sympathizers, troop movements, and the conduct of the war; a document containing the names of political prisoners, a list of Tennessee regiments in service in 1861, and a return of Tennessee troops in the Western Department commanded by Gen. Leonidas Polk; letter from Harris to Gen. Gideon Pillow, June 21, 1861, concerning the defense of Tennessee; and letter from Harris to Beriah Magoffin, Aug. 4, 1861, on Kentucky's neutrality and the recruitment and organization of Union soldiers in Kentucky. Correspondents include P.G.T. Beauregard, Judah P. Benjamin, William H. Carroll, Jefferson Davis, Nathan B. Forrest, Josiah Gorgas, Albert Sidney Johnston, Francis W. Pickens, Leonidas Polk, George W. Randolph, and Lloyd Tilghman.

410

Harrison, Benjamin (1833–1901), Pres., U.S.
Papers, 1787–1938. 69,600 items.
In part, transcripts and photocopies.
Material relating to the Civil War, in which Harrison served as a colonel in the 70th Indiana Volunteers, includes letters from Harrison to his wife written from camps in Kentucky, Tennessee, North Carolina, South Carolina, and Georgia concerning camp life, discipline, desertions, marches, disease, hospital care, courts-martial, and conditions in the South. Includes a few details on battles and skirmishes in the Atlanta Campaign. Also contains Harrison's commissions, a muster roll of the 70th Indiana Regiment, and a manuscript map of DeKalb County, Ga., in 1864.
Published index and microfilm copy (151 reels) available.

411
Harrison, Burton Norvell   Lawyer; Private
(1838–1904)   Secretary to President Davis
    Family papers, 1812–1926. ca. 18,600 items.
    Includes the correspondence and papers of Constance Cary
(1843–1920), whom Harrison married in 1867. Contains information on the movement and training of Confederate soldiers
near Manassas Junction in June 1861, the Battle of 1st
Manassas, the progress of the war, and the effect of the war on
noncombatants in the South. Also, letter to Cary from her
brother, Clarence Cary, C.S.S. *Palmetto State*, Feb. 1, 1863,
describing the attack on the U.S.S. *Mercedita* off Charleston
Harbor; letters to Harrison from his sister in Oxford, Miss.,
discussing troop movements and the effect of the war in northern Mississippi; postwar letters from Harrison to Cary concerning his imprisonment at Fort Delaware and his experiences during the war; and postwar correspondence between
Jefferson Davis and Harrison on the location of letters received
by Davis as President of the Confederacy, the official records of
the C.S. Government, and various events during the war. Miscellaneous items in the collection include an account of the
Battle of Drewry's Bluff, copy of a letter from John C. Breckinridge to President Davis [Apr. 6, 1865] concerning the military
situation on the eve of the Appomattox Campaign; copy of Davis'
address to the Confederate Congress, Feb. 3, 1864; letter from
Thomas C. Reynolds to Davis, Marshall, Tex., Dec. 17, 1864,
criticizing Gen. Sterling Price; copy of a letter from Gen. R. E.
Lee to John C. Breckinridge, Mar. 9, 1865, assessing the over-
all military situation; report and correspondence of Alexander
H. Stephens, Robert M. T. Hunter, and John A. Campbell on
the Hampton Roads Peace Conference; copy of an essay by
C. C. Buell entitled "Who Began the War, and What Was the
Cause of It?" (1887); and military passes, photographs, and
telegrams.
    Finding aid available.

412
Harrison, James O. (1804–1888)   Lawyer–Educator,
                    Kentucky and Louisiana
    Papers, 1803–1912. ca. 5,000 items.
    Includes a few letters from Harrison to his wife, Nov.–Dec.
1864, Richmond, Va., concerning the progress of the war and
events in Richmond; a letter from Harrison's sister-in-law, Ellen
Reily Harrison, on the death of her husband, Jilson Harrison,
in a skirmish near Franklin, La., in 1863; letters from Harrison's son, James O. Harrison, Jr. (1839–1867), Apr. 1861–
Feb. 1862, concerning fortifications at Pensacola, Fla., plans to
attack Federal ships off Fort Pickens, Fla., and camp life,

morale, and suffering during the Peninsular Campaign; and letters by Harrison's son, Albert M. (b. 1848), describing his training as a naval cadet aboard the C.S.S. *Patrick Henry*, Jan.–Oct. 1864.

Finding aid available.

413

Hart, Charles C.

　　Autograph collection, 1476–1942. ca. 100 items.
　　Photocopies.
　　Includes a letter from Gen. George A. Custer to General [Sheridan], Mar. 2, 1865, on the defeat of Gen. Jubal Early's command at Waynesboro, Va.; a note from Comdr. John Rodgers to Gustavus V. Fox, Mar. 9, 1865, Fort Monroe, Va., describing the condition of the U.S.S. *Dictator*; an order by Gen. Robert E. Lee, Oct. 11, 1861, concerning sick soldiers in Gen. John B. Floyd's brigade; a photograph and personal letter of John Wilkes Booth, 1864; and miscellaneous notes by George G. Meade, Oliver P. Morton, Winfield Scott, and Charles Sumner.

Finding aid available.

414

Hartz, Edward L. (1832–1868)　　　　Capt., Asst. Q.M., USA
　　Papers, 1847–1910. 315 items.
　　Contains several letters concerning the secession movement in Texas, 1860–61; letter written as chief assistant quartermaster for the Department of Washington concerning troop movements in the lst Manassas Campaign; and a letterbook kept by Hartz at Chattanooga, Tenn., May 31–July 18, 1864, containing official correspondence on the shipment of supplies during the Atlanta Campaign.

415

Harvey, Charles Henry (1830–1896)
　　Papers, 1835–1965. ca. 265 items.
　　Includes an unsigned letter from a Union soldier in Middletown, Va., to his mother, July 21, 1863, describing camp life and marches in the Shenandoah Valley.

Finding aid available.

416

Harwood Family
　　Collection, 1767–1969.
　　Microfilm, 1 reel.
　　Chiefly autograph letters received by various members of the Harwood family and letters collected by Rear Adm. Andrew Allen Harwood. Includes a letter from Lt. George S. Wilson,

17th Indiana Volunteers, to his brother, July 23, 1861, concerning camp life and the progress of the war in Virginia; Wilson's commission and discharge; a letter from Gen. John A. McClernand to Adm. Andrew H. Foote, Feb. 7, 1862, concerning the capture of Fort Henry; a letter from Gen. Nathaniel P. Banks to Secretary Stanton, May 23, 1863, on the capture of William Luce (Mrs. Harwood's brother); and a receipt for money received by Luce for his service as an engineer. Also contains a few notes on military appointments written by President Lincoln, John G. Nicolay, and Edwin M. Stanton.

Finding aid available.

Originals in the Stanford University Library.

417

Hatch, John Porter (1822–1901)   Gen., USA
    Papers, 1843–68. ca. 150 items.

Includes 10 letters from Hatch to his father written from New Mexico Territory, May–Oct. 1861, concerning the efforts of secessionists in the Southwest, the possible loss of the entire Northwest Territory to the Confederacy, and his personal dissatisfaction with both the U.S. Army and government policy in the West. Also contains about 30 letters from Hatch to his father written from Washington, D.C., Maryland, and Virginia, Dec. 1861–Apr. 1862, concerning his efforts to obtain a field command, the Shenandoah Valley Campaign of 1862, and the 2d Manassas Campaign, particularly the Battle of Cedar Mountain, and the character and generalship of Nathaniel P. Banks, Ambrose Burnside, John C. Frémont, and John Pope.

418
———
    Letter, 1866. 1 item.
    Transcript.
    Letter from Hatch to Comdr. George H. Preble (1816–1865), Oct. 4, 1866, San Antonio, Tex., relating to the service of the Naval Brigade in the Civil War.
    Naval Historical Foundation collection.

419

Hatton, John William Ford   1st Maryland Battery, CSA
    Memoir, 1861–65.
    Microfilm, 1 reel.
    Memoir, 1903, based on a diary kept by Hatton during the Civil War. Contains information on secessionist sentiment on Maryland's Eastern Shore, the Shenandoah Valley Campaign of 1862, the Peninsular, Fredericksburg, Chancellorsville, Gettysburg, Wilderness, and Spotsylvania campaigns, the Siege of Petersburg, and operations along the Rappahannock and

Rapidan Rivers in the fall of 1863. Includes detailed accounts of a skirmish at Bunker Hill, W. Va., 1862, and the battles of Bristoe Station, Mine Run, Cold Harbor, and Malvern Hill, and comments on camp life, marches, morale, and the impact of the war in Virginia.

420

Haupt, Lewis Muhlenberg (1844–1937)
    Family papers, 1861–1923. ca. 3,000 items.
    In part, transcripts.
    Contains a letterbook, Nov. 1862–Aug. 1863, and personal correspondence of Haupt's father, Gen. Herman Haupt (1817–1905). Describes General Haupt's work as military director and superintendent of railroads, particularly railroad construction and the transportation of troops and supplies, and the progress of the war in northern Virginia. Also includes General Haupt's observations on the generalship of Ambrose E. Burnside, Joseph Hooker, George B. McClellan, Irwin McDowell, and John Pope.
    Finding aid available.

421

Hawks, Esther Hill   Teacher, National
                                                Freedmen's Relief Association
    Papers, 1856–67. 515 items.
    Chiefly letters to Hawks, 1862–63, from her husband, Dr. J. Milton Hawks, her brothers, Edward (4th New Hampshire Volunteers), Warren, Sylvester, and L. J. Hill (9th New Hampshire Volunteers), and convalescent soldiers in hospitals at Beaufort, S.C. Letters by Doctor Hawks discuss his work with freedmen, black life, and the progress of the war in South Carolina. Letters by the Hill brothers concern the Port Royal expedition, the occupation of Jacksonville, Fernandina, and St. Augustine, Fla., and camp life. Also contains correspondence between Esther Hawks and members of the Freedmen's Relief Association, returns for the 1st and 3d South Carolina Volunteers, school records (names of blacks taught by Mrs. Hawks, etc.), and military passes.

422

Hawley, Joseph Roswell (1826–1905)   Gen., USV
    Papers, 1638–1906. ca. 13,200 items.
    Official and personal correspondence, orders, telegrams, field returns, battle reports, returns of captured property, lists of Union and Confederate deserters and refugees, requisitions, and company rosters. Letters from Hawley to his wife describe the Siege of Fort Pulaski, the battles of Secessionville, Pocotaligo, Fort Wagner, Olustee, and New Market, the Siege of

Petersburg, and the Fort Fisher expedition of 1865. Includes information on camp life, discipline, morale, casualties, prisoners of war, deserters, rank disputes, disease, and hospital care. Letters to General Hawley from his wife, Harriet Foote Hawley, a nurse with the American Missionary Society, discuss hospital care at Hilton Head, S.C. Several letters to Mrs. Hawley from her brother, S. E. Foote, written aboard the U.S.S. *Penguin* in 1863, relate to the Florida expedition. Also includes material on the Fitz-John Porter trial, sketches of Federal batteries at the Siege of Fort Pulaski, a sketch of fortifications near New Market, Va., Jan. 1864, and routine letters from William Faxon and Gideon Welles.

Finding aid and microfilm copy (29 reels) available.

423
Hay, Eugene Gano (1853–1933)
    Papers, 1770–1933. ca. 13,300 items.
    Includes about 30 letters from John F. Farquhar to his wife, 1861–64, concerning the recruiting and disbursing service in Indianapolis, Ind., military appointments, equipment and supplies, morale, training, and the movement and disposition of Indiana regiments.
    Finding aid available.

424
Hay, John (1838–1905)   Private Secretary
                                           to President Lincoln
    Papers, 1785–1914. ca. 11,290 items.
    In part, transcripts.
    Contains miscellaneous letters, petitions, and newspaper clippings relating to the treatment and exchange of prisoners of war, the Fredericksburg Campaign, finance, and events in Washington, D.C. Also an essay by Charles P. Daly, "Are Southern Privateersmen Pirates?" 1861.
    Finding aid, partial index, and partial microfilm copy (23 reels) available.

425
Hayden, Levi (b. 1813)   Shipwright
    Diary, 1838–77. 2 v.
    Describes Hayden's work under Gen. Ambrose Burnside in clearing obstructions from channels and harbors along the coast of North Carolina, and his service under Adms. John A. Dahlgren and Samuel Phillips Lee in 1863 and 1864. Includes observations on the capture of Forts Clark and Hatteras, the Battle of Roanoke Island, the capture of New Bern, and naval affairs in Virginia and South Carolina. Also contains Hayden's suggestions on the construction of mines and torpedoes, and the improvement of ironclad vessels.

426

Hayden, Nathaniel

Family papers, 1836–80. ca. 500 items.

Contains about 25 letters from members of the Hayden family serving in campaigns in Maryland, Virginia, South Carolina, and Louisiana. Provides some information on camp life, morale, discipline, marches, troop locations, black life, the attitude of noncombatants, enlistments, disease, hospital care, and depredations. Includes a detailed description of New Orleans and vicinity during the war.

427

Heath, Charles Wesley

(1836–1881)   6th Indiana Volunteers

Collection, 1861–1946. 5 items.

Diary, May 1861–Sept. 1864, published in the *Vevay Reveille Enterprise,* Mar. 7–28, 1946. Describes camp life, troop movements, and disease during campaigns in Kentucky, Tennessee, and Georgia.

428

Heintzelman, Samuel Peter (1805–1880)   Gen., USA

Papers, 1822–1904. ca. 1,500 items.

General and official correspondence, diary, telegrams, circulars, returns, commissions, casualty reports, reports on battles and skirmishes, maps, newspaper clippings, and printed material. Relates to the occupation of Arlington Heights and Alexandria, the 1st and 2d Manassas campaigns, the Peninsular Campaign, and the defense of Washington, D.C. Includes details on the battles of Williamsburg, Fair Oaks, Seven Pines, White Oak Swamp, and Malvern Hill, and maneuvers against Big Bethel in Mar. 1862. Correspondents include Henry W. Halleck, Joseph Hooker, Philip Kearny, George B. McClellan, Edwin M. Stanton, and Lorenzo Thomas.

Finding aid and microfilm copy (13 reels) available.

429

Heisler, Henry C. (b. 1845)   Cpl., 48th
                                                     Pennsylvania Volunteers

Papers, 1861–65. 45 items.

Chiefly letters from Heisler to his sister concerning General Burnside's expedition to North Carolina, the 2d Manassas, Fredericksburg, Wilderness, Spotsylvania, and Petersburg campaigns, and campaigns in Kentucky and Tennessee against Gen. John Hunt Morgan. Provides a detailed account of the Siege of Petersburg, and information on camp life, entertainment, marches, desertions, disease, casualties, and the attitude of noncombatants in Virginia and Kentucky. Also includes a "Muster-Out Roll" for Heisler's company (F), July 1865.

430

Herndon, William Henry (1818–1891)   Author, Illinois
    Papers, 1824–1933. ca. 4,600 items.
    In part, transcripts and photocopies.
    Includes a petition by the officers of the 69th New York
State Militia for the exchange of Col. Michael Corcoran; clippings and extracts on prisoner exchange; letters between President Lincoln, Salmon P. Chase, and Gen. Henry Halleck; and a
published letter from Judge Charles P. Daly to Senator Ira
Harris, Dec. 21, 1861, entitled "Are Southern Privateersmen
Pirates?"
    Finding aid and microfilm copy (15 reels) available.

431

Hertz, Emanuel (1870–1940)   Jurist, Illinois
    Collection, 1826–1936. 80 items.
    Chiefly galley proofs of Hertz' *Abraham Lincoln: A New
Portrait* (1931), and speeches and articles about Lincoln.

432

Hewitt, Edward L.   USN
    Notebook, 1864. 1 item.
    Contains drawings and technical notes on steam naviga-
tion prepared by Hewitt aboard the U.S.S. *Mahaska* while on
patrol duty in the St. Johns River, Fla., May 1864.

433

Hickey Family
    Collection, 1803–1900. 41 items.
    Letter from H. H. Pope to Lt. Myron Hickey, July 30, 1863,
La Grange, Tenn., concerning reconnaissance duty in Tennes-
see and deaths in Hickey's former regiment, the 5th Michigan
Cavalry; letter from Lt. Myron Hickey to his family, May 8,
1863, Fairfax Courthouse, Va.; and two letters from Sgt. Andrew
Hickey to his brother Frederick, July 1862 and Feb. 1863, con-
cerning campaigns in Mississippi and Tennessee. Also includes
Andrew Hickey's commission as sergeant in the 3d Michigan
Cavalry, Sept. 1862.

434

Hill, Sara Jane Full (1839?–1914)   Missouri
    Papers, 1861–1952. 2 items.
    Transcripts.
    "Reminiscences of the Civil War," 1861–65. Describes the
secession crisis in Missouri, civil disorder in St. Louis, the contributions of women to the war effort, Union sentiment and
recruitment in St. Louis, and the treatment of runaway slaves.
Also provides information on camp life, morale, entertainment,

disease, hospital care, the capture of New Madrid and Island No. 10, guerrilla warfare, depredations, the Shiloh and Vicksburg campaigns, the treatment of prisoners of war, and inflation.

435
Hills, A. C.   Capt., California Volunteers
    Letter, 1862. 1 item.
    Letter from Hills to Doctor Stedman, July 21, 1862, camp on James River, Va., concerning the Peninsular Campaign, morale, the hardships of war, and the loss of confidence in Gen. George B. McClellan.

436
Hills, William G.   9th New York Cavalry
    Diary, 1864. 1 v.
    Detailed account of campaigns in Virginia, Jan. 1–Nov. 23, 1864. Provides information on the Kilpatrick–Dahlgren raid to Richmond, the Wilderness, Spotsylvania, and Cold Harbor campaigns, the Trevilian raid, the Siege of Petersburg, and the Shenandoah Valley Campaign of 1864—particularly the Battle of Cedar Creek. Also contains comments on camp life, supplies, training, discipline, reconnaissance expeditions, marches, casualties, depredations, guerrilla warfare, black soldiers under General Butler, prisoners of war, Gen. U. S. Grant's assumption of the command of the Army of the Potomac, and reaction to the deaths of Gen. John Buford, Col. Ulric Dahlgren, and Gen. J. E. B. Stuart.

437
Hine, Orrin E. (b. 1836)   Capt., 50th New York
                                              Volunteers; Engineer Brigade
    Papers, 1862–63. 52 items.
    Special orders, telegrams, and communications to Hine, 1862–63, concerning the procurement of supplies, chiefly horses and pontoons, during the Fredericksburg and Gettysburg campaigns. Correspondents include Henry W. Benham, Ambrose E. Burnside, Edward J. Strang, and Daniel P. Woodbury.

438
Hitchcock, Ethan Allen (1798–1870)   Gen., USV
    Papers, 1810–73. ca. 3,000 items.
    Correspondence, orders, returns, telegrams, battle reports, and miscellaneous items concerning appointments, supplies, the treatment and exchange of prisoners of war, and military organization and strategy. Includes official correspondence between General McClellan, President Lincoln, and Secretary Stanton concerning the Peninsular Campaign and the Shenandoah Valley Campaign of 1862; official correspondence between

Ethan Allen Hitchcock

Gen. E. A. Hitchcock and the Navy Department concerning retaliation for the hanging of Spencer Kellogg, son of John Brown of Harpers Ferry fame; and correspondence between Confederate agents Robert Ould and Sidney S. Baxter and Federal agent William P. Wood on the treatment and exchange of prisoners of war. Also includes returns of prisoners of war; extracts of letters by captured soldiers; correspondence relating to the Department of Missouri; and Hitchcock's "Notes Upon the Report of Major General George B. McClellan Upon the Organization of the Army of the Potomac and Its Campaigns in Virginia and Maryland from 26th July, 1861, to November 7, 1862." Miscellaneous items include a report by Col. John A. McDowell on the Battle of Shiloh; a captured letter written by a Confederate sailor aboard the C.S.S. *Bienville*, April 4, 1862, Lake Pontchartrain, describing a naval action at the Rigolets along with a sketch of the defenses of New Orleans; and a letter from Thomas W. Fell to the War Office, Apr. 29, 1862, concerning Federal strategy in Virginia.

Finding aid available.

439

Hitchcock, Henry (1829–1902)   Maj.; Asst. Adj. Gen., USA
    Papers, 1864–65. 40 items.

Letters from Hitchcock to his wife, Oct. 21, 1864–May 26, 1865, and a diary (3 v.), Nov. 11, 1864–Feb. 11, 1865, concerning the Atlanta, Savannah, and Carolinas campaigns. Describes camp life, marches, entertainment, morale, foraging expeditions, the condition and attitudes of whites and blacks in the South, Confederate morale, conditions in the Confederate Army, battles and skirmishes, and the devastation of war. Also contains a few details on the burning of Atlanta and the capture of Savannah, and a letter from Gen. Ethan A. Hitchcock to Hitchcock, May 16, 1864.

440

Hitt, Robert Roberts (1834–1906)   Reporter, Illinois
    Papers, 1830–1905. ca. 2,200 items.

Contains a few shorthand notes on the trials of Col. James Belger, Gen. William A. Hammond, Col. Frederick G. d'Utassy, and others.

Finding aid available.

441

Hodges, James (b. 1843)   Sgt., 9th and 17th New York
                                                        Volunteers
    Papers, 1863–65.
    Microfilm, 1 reel.

Contains three letters from Hodges to Edwin Codet, Mar.

10–Dec. 16, 1864, concerning the Meridian, Atlanta, and Savannah campaigns. Includes remarks on the destruction of public and private property and on conversations with Confederate prisoners. Also contains Hodges' discharge from the 9th New York Volunteers, 1863, and a copy of his service record.

442

Holford, Lyman C.   6th Wisconsin Volunteers
    Papers, 1861–92. 4 v.
    Diary (3 v.), May 18, 1861–Dec. 31, 1864, concerning the 2d Manassas, Antietam, Fredericksburg, Chancellorsville, and Gettysburg campaigns, and service in the Invalid Corps at prisons and hospitals in and around Washington, D.C., in 1864. Provides information on camp life, training, marches, troop movements, discipline, morale, entertainment, supplies, disease, casualties, hospital care, depredations by Confederate soldiers, and battles and skirmishes. Also contains a few poems and miscellaneous notes and accounts.

443

Holmes, George Frederick (1820–1897)   Historian, Virginia
    Papers, 1785–1893. ca. 100 items.
    In part, transcripts.
    Correspondence relating to an unpublished history of the war. Includes a letter from Judah P. Benjamin to Holmes, May 6, 1863, concerning the appointment of Professor Schele, one of Holmes' associates, as special emissary to Germany, and Holmes' response of May 9, 1863; a copy of a letter from Gen. T. J. Jackson to Gen. R. E. Lee, May 2, 1863, on the Chancellorsville Campaign; and postwar letters from Gens. Jubal A. Early, John B. Gordon, and Joseph E. Johnston, and Lt. Col. Charles S. Newable advising Holmes on troop strength and casualties in various campaigns.

444

Holmes, Oliver Wendell
(1809–1894)   Author; Physician; Educator
    Papers, 1846–94.
    Microfilm, 3 reels.
    Letter from John L. Motley to Holmes, Mar. 23, 1862, Vienna, Austria, concerning British attitudes on the American Civil War.
    Originals at the University of Virginia.

445

Holmes, Oliver Wendell
(1841–1935)   Capt., 20th Massachusetts Volunteers
    Papers, 1862–1932. ca. 200 items.

Includes a letter from Charles W. Whittier to an unidentified recipient, Dec. 29, 1862, Falmouth, Va., concerning the Battle of Fredericksburg.

446
Holt, Joseph (1807–1894)   Judge Adv. Gen., USA
        Papers, 1817–95. ca. 20,000 items.
        Official and personal correspondence, diary, notebooks, legal and financial papers, and miscellaneous items concerning the War Department, military justice, the Lincoln assassination, and the trial of the assassination conspirators.
        Finding aid available.

447
Holt, Samuel E. (b. 1838)   Washington Artillery, CSA
        Papers, 1862–65. 8 items.
        Orders, military passes, and discharge certificates.

448
Homsher, Charles Wesley   Pvt., 5th Indiana Cavalry
        Diary, 1864–65. 5 p.
        Photocopy of transcript.
        Describes the treatment of Union soldiers at Andersonville Prison. Includes remarks on diet, deaths, burials, trade with Confederate guards, attempts by Confederate officers to recruit Union prisoners for service in the Confederate Army, and the exchange of prisoners at the end of the war.

449
Hood, Charles Crook
(1841–1927)   Capt., 31st Ohio Volunteers
        Collection, 1862–1913. 10 items.
        In part, transcripts.
        Includes a diary kept by Hood during campaigns in Tennessee, Nov. 5, 1862–Oct. 1863. Describes the Stones River Campaign and skirmishes with Gen. John Hunt Morgan's cavalry. Also contains remarks on camp life, training, discipline, marches, casualties, and the devastation of war. Miscellaneous items include an outline of Hood's military service and an extract of a letter, Dec. 12, 1913, reminiscing about the Battle of Chickamauga.

450
Hooker, Joseph (1814–1879)   Gen., USA
        Papers, 1861–77. 11 items.
        Letter from Hooker to an unidentified recipient, Aug. 15, 1861, concerning the organization and staffing of Hooker's brigade, and orders and official communications from Hooker

Joseph Hooker

to Gen. Joseph Reynolds written during the battles of Lookout Mountain and Missionary Ridge.

451
Horner, Gustavus Richard Brown
(1806–1892)   Surg., USN
    Papers, 1826–1911. ca. 4,900 items.
    Letterbooks (7 v.) maintained by Horner as fleet surgeon, Gulf Blockading Squadron and East Gulf Blockading Squadron, 1861–63, and while assigned to the Brooklyn and Philadelphia Navy Yards, 1863–65. Includes information on medical procedures and supplies, disease, deaths, and routine naval affairs. Also includes a daybook containing records of patients treated by Horner aboard the U.S.S. *Colorado*, June 1861–Feb. 1862; a list of patients aboard the U.S.S. *Niagara*, Mar. 1862; notes on patients treated at the U.S. Marine Hospital in Key West, Fla., Aug.–Sept. 1861; names of candidates examined for entrance to the U.S. Naval Academy, July 1864; names of candidates examined for appointments as engineers and warrant officers, July–Dec. 1863; and miscellaneous medical accounts and invoices. Printed pamphlets and articles concern military hygiene, the diagnosis and treatment of various diseases and injuries, and the management of medical stores.
    Finding aid available.
    Naval Historical Foundation collection.

452
Hotchkiss, Jedediah (1828–1899)   Cartographer; Maj., CSA
    Papers, 1838–1908. ca. 20,000 items.
    In part, transcripts.
    General and family correspondence, diary and diary extracts, orders, battle reports, quartermaster reports, invoices and returns for engineering equipment, and miscellaneous notes relating to the Shenandoah Valley Campaign of 1862, the 2d Manassas, Peninsular, Antietam, Fredericksburg, Chancellorsville, Gettysburg, and Wilderness campaigns, the Battle of Cold Harbor, and operations in the Shenandoah Valley in the summer and fall of 1864. Includes information on strategy, camp life, morale, marches, the disposition of troops, depredations, the selection of officers, the draft, desertions, casualties, prisoners of war, equipment and supplies, battles and skirmishes, and the condition and attitude of noncombatants in Virginia. Also includes an account of the death of Gen. Thomas J. Jackson, remarks concerning Jackson's headquarters staff, a digest of Jackson's letters and orders, and postwar correspondence, newspaper clippings, and articles on the war.
    Finding aid and microfilm copy (61 reels) available.

453

Hotchkiss, Jedediah—McCullough, Samuel   CSA
      Collection, 1846–1912.
      Microfilm, 6 reels.
      Contains four letters from Maj. Jedediah Hotchkiss
(1828–1899) to his daughter, Dec. 1862–Oct. 1863; a note by
Gen. Thomas J. Jackson; an account of "The Seven Days Fighting About Richmond," by Hunter McGuire, medical director of
General Jackson's command; and several postwar maps of battlefields in Virginia. Also contains the diary of Hotchkiss'
son-in-law, Lt. Samuel Thomas McCullough, Aug. 11,
1862–June 22, 1865, kept during the Gettysburg, Spotsylvania,
Cold Harbor, and Petersburg campaigns and while a prisoner
of war at Old Capital Prison and Johnson's Island, and the
diary of Alfred Welton, 9th Indiana Volunteers, Aug. 14,
1861–Oct. 17, 1862. McCullough's diary contains remarks on
camp life, discipline, morale, hospital care, desertions, battles
and skirmishes, and the suffering of noncombatants in Virginia.
      Originals at the University of Virginia.

454

Hotze, Henry (1834–1887)   Diplomat; Journalist; Author
      Papers, 1861–65. 187 items.
      Letterbook, 1862–64, containing correspondence relating
to the *Index*, a Confederate newspaper published in London,
England, and to the London-based Confederate States of Amer-
ica Commercial Agency. Also contains accounts of the C.S.
State Department secret service fund. Principal recipients are
Robert M. T. Hunter and Judah P. Benjamin. Also letterbook,
May 28, 1864–June 16, 1865, containing chiefly personal
correspondence. Includes a few remarks on efforts to recruit
British soldiers whose terms of service were about to expire for
the Confederate Army. Additional items include letters to Hotze,
1863–65, from James D. Bulloch, Edwin De Leon, George
Eustis, George McHenry, Colin John McRae, Ambrose Dud-
ley Mann, Matthew Fontaine Maury, William Preston, and
John Slidell; a letter from Judah P. Benjamin to Edwin De
Leon, Dec. 9, 1864; and three letters from Thomas H. Dudley to
Gideon Welles, July–Oct. 1863.
      Partially indexed.

455

Howe, Hiram P.   10th Missouri Volunteers
      Papers, 1861–64. 76 items.
      Letters from Howe to his family and friends, 1861–64,
concerning camp life and training in Missouri, General
Halleck's advance on Corinth, Miss., the Battle of Iuka, General Grant's first advance on Vicksburg, and the Vicksburg

Campaign. Also includes a diary kept on the Yazoo Pass expedition. Letters written by Howe in late 1863 and 1864 describe his service and experiences as a convalescent in military hospitals in Mississippi and Missouri.

Microfilm copy (1 reel) available.

456
Howe, Letitia T.
     Autograph collection, 1833–71. 78 items.
     Contains a few letters written by President Lincoln relating generally to the war.

457
Howe, Mark Anthony De Wolfe
(1864–1960)   Editor; Author
     Papers, 1929–60. 7 items.
     Letters and clippings relating to Howe's *Marching With Sherman: Passages From the Letters and Campaign Diaries of Henry Hitchcock, Major and Assistant Adjutant General of Volunteers, November 1864–May 1865* (1927).

458
Howe, Samuel Gridley (1801–1876)   Reformer
     Collection, 1862 and undated. 2 items.
     Letter from Howe to Mr. Bird, Mar. 5, 1862, U.S. Sanitary Commission, Washington, D.C., concerning President Lincoln's disillusionment with Gen. George B. McClellan and Lincoln's views on slavery.

459
Howry, Charles Bowen (1844–1928)   Mississippi
     Family papers, 1863–98. 10 items.
     Includes a letter from Jefferson Davis to J. M. Howry of Oxford, Miss., Aug. 27, 1863, expressing surprise at Gen. U. S. Grant's success in Mississippi, faith in the ultimate victory of the Confederacy, and sympathy for the people of Mississippi. Also contains two postwar letters from Davis to J. M. Howry.

460
Hoxie, Vinnie Ream (1847–1914)
     Family papers, 1853–1937. ca. 2,500 items.
     Contains a few letters to Vinnie Ream from wounded Union soldiers and Confederate prisoners of war, including Gen. M. Jeff Thompson; two letters from J. E. Powell, Aug. 26 and 30, 1861, concerning Miss Ream's brother Robert and military activities near St. Louis, Mo.; and two letters from Richard L. Hoxie to his family, July 16, 1862, and Dec. 27, 1863, on the pursuit of Quantrill, military discipline, rank disputes, Hoxie's

appointment to the headquarters staff of the 1st Iowa Cavalry, and the attitude of the civilian population of Little Rock, Ark. Also contains a sketch of Union and Confederate positions before Chattanooga and a field map of northern Alabama and Georgia.

Finding aid available.

461
Hubbard Family
    Papers, 1639–1925. ca. 7,500 items.
    Contains the correspondence and papers of Robert Henry McCurdy (1800–1880). Includes material relating to the activities of the Union Defense Committee in New York, the Southern Relief Committee, the New England Soldiers Relief Association, and various other patriotic and benevolent organizations. Also contains a few letters and documents found by McCurdy in the Senate chambers of the defunct C.S. Government on Apr. 20, 1865, a "Map of a part of the City of Richmond showing the burnt Districts," McCurdy's account of a meeting with President Lincoln, July 11, 1862, a memorandum outlining the composition and strength of Gen. Franz Sigel's XI Corps, Army of the Potomac, on Oct. 10, 1862, and miscellaneous items concerning naval affairs, Gen. Louis Blenker, and the organization, supply, condition, and disposition of New York troops.
    Finding aid available.

462
Hudson, George A.   100th Illinois Volunteers
    Collection, 1863–65. 20 items.
    Letters from Hudson to his family written during campaigns in Tennessee, Alabama, and Georgia, Apr. 1863–Apr. 1865. Contains remarks on camp life, training, discipline, foraging expeditions, marches, desertions, casualties, morale, devastation in the South, the Presidential election of 1864, the attitude of Union soldiers toward blacks, the suffering of noncombatants, and reaction in the South to Lincoln's assassination.

463
Hudson, William Leverreth (1794–1862)   USN
    Papers, 1821–74. ca. 350 items.
    Includes correspondence and notes concerning the sale, purchase, and repair of vessels for the U.S. Navy, drawing of the U.S.S. *Water Witch*, plans for the construction and improvement of gunboats, and miscellaneous items.

464
Hughes, John   Sgt., 28th Iowa Volunteers
    Diary, 1863. 1 item.
    Photocopy.
    Diary, July 1–6, 1863, describing the fall of Vicksburg,
Miss., the suffering of the Confederate garrison, and the num-
ber and type of cannons captured.

465
Hume, Fannie Page (1838–1865)   Orange, Va.
    Diary, 1862. 1 item.
    Transcript.
    Diary kept at Selma plantation, the home of Dr. Peyton
Grymes. Describes the movement of Confederate and Union
troops through Orange, Va., during the 2d Manassas Campaign,
depredations, the suffering of both soldiers and civilians,
skirmishes in the area, and deaths of acquaintances in the
Confederate Army. Also contains war news and the names of
several refugees from Fairfax and Fauquier Counties. Copied
in 1946.
    Indexed.

466
Hunt, Henry Jackson (1819–1889)   Gen., USA
    Papers, 1841–1910. ca. 4,500 items.
    General and official correspondence, orders, reports, tele-
grams, returns, invoices, requisitions, and memoranda relating to Hunt's service in the Reserve Artillery and as chief of
artillery in the Army of the Potomac during the Peninsular,
Antietam, Fredericksburg, Chancellorsville, Gettysburg, and
Wilderness campaigns, and the Siege of Petersburg. Also
includes a letterbook of official correspondence, Sept. 8, 1862–
Sept. 5, 1863; a diary kept at the Siege of Petersburg, May 2,
1864–Mar. 23, 1865, containing sketches of artillery positions,
notes on the progress of the siege, lists of batteries, and copies
of letters and orders; a notebook, May–[July?] 1862; memoranda on the reorganization of artillery; a "List of Disaffected
Non-commissioned Officers and Privates belonging to the 9th
Regiment of New York Cavalry," May 1862, with a petition for
their discharge; a list of officers recommended for brevets for
gallant conduct; and postwar letters from Hunt to Thomas T.
Gantt reminiscing on the war. Correspondents include William F. Barry, Ambrose E. Burnside, Winfield S. Hancock,
George B. McClellan, George G. Meade, John J. Peck, Fitz-
John Porter, Robert O. Tyler, and Seth Williams.
    Finding aid available.

467
Hurja, Emil
Collection, 1841–93. 59 items.
Chiefly official and personal correspondence, orders, vouchers, sketches, and printed matter relating to the Civil War. Includes letters concerning military affairs at Gauley and Cheat Mountain, W. Va., Aug. 1861, Confederate troop strength and troop locations near New Bern, N.C., Mar. 1862, and the Siege of Atlanta; published statements on the Fitz-John Porter trial; and sketches of northwestern Virginia and western Maryland. Correspondents include P. G. T. Beauregard, George Cadwalader, Henry W. Halleck, Schuyler Hamilton, Winfield S. Hancock, Oliver O. Howard, Thomas Jordan, Edmund Kirby-Smith, Samuel P. Lee, James A. Martin, Edward E. Potter, William S. Rosecrans, Lovell H. Rousseau, William T. Sherman, Alexander H. Stephens, George H. Thomas, and John E. Wool.

468
Imboden, John Daniel (1823–1895)   Gen., CSA
Collection, 1861–94. 3 items.
Includes a letter from Imboden to the town council of Winchester, Va., Nov. 27, 1863, concerning atrocities against noncombatants and the need for self-defense.

469
Ingersoll, Robert Green
(1833–1899)   Col., 11th Illinois Cavalry
Papers, 1860–1941. ca. 16,000 items.
In part, transcripts and photocopies.
Contains a letter from Ingersoll to O. H. Wright, Oct. 8, 1861, Peoria, Ill., concerning aid to families of volunteers; a letter from Ingersoll to his brother, Apr. 19, 1862, on sickness in the Army; an order appointing Ingersoll chief of cavalry in Gen. Jeremiah C. Sullivan's division, 13th Corp, Army of the Tennessee; and Ingersoll's resignation from the Army submitted at La Grange, Ga., June 18, 1863.
Finding aid available.

470
Inglis, John Auchinloss
(1813–1878)   Jurist, South Carolina
Collection, 1859–66. 14 items.
Contains two letters from Inglis to Susan H. Muir, 1861–62, concerning the death of his son William, a captain in the 8th South Carolina Volunteers, and the health of his son Charles, also in the 8th South Carolina, and a letter from Inglis

to his daughter Carrie on Confederate prisoners of war and plans in South Carolina to employ blacks as soldiers.

471

Irwin, Bernard John Dowling (1830–1917)   Surg., USA
     Papers, 1850–70. 225 items.
     Chiefly personal and official correspondence, orders, and circulars, 1863–65, relating to Irwin's duties as superintendent of military hospitals in Memphis, Tenn. Also contains a few letters by Irwin's brother Albert, 1861–63, concerning his capture in northern Virginia, his experiences as a prisoner of war, and his exchange, along with a "Precis of the Military History of B. J. D. Irwin." Additional correspondents are James G. Blunt, Joseph B. Brown, Charles H. Crane, Stephen A. Hurlbut, Joseph R. Smith, and Robert C. Wood.

472

Ives, Joseph Christmas (1828–1868)   Col., CSA
     Collection, 1862. 14 items.
     Four letters from Leonard Ives to his brother Joseph, aide to President Davis, Sept.–Oct. 1862, concerning camp life, provisions, training, and troop movements during the Antietam Campaign; three letters from Joseph Ives to his mother, Mrs. L. J. Woods of Dorchester, Mass., Sept.–Oct. 1862, concerning communications with relatives in the North, conditions in Richmond, Va., and the health of Jefferson Davis; letter from Joseph Ives' wife Cora to her mother, Sept. 11, 1862, on the rank, unit, and location of various family members serving in the Confederate Army; letter from Gen. John A. Dix to Richard H. Dana, Oct. 1862, on contraband mail; and two letters from Richard H. Clark to Ned Ives, Oct. 11 and 29, 1862, Washington, D.C., concerning plans for Mrs. Woods to visit her family in Richmond, Va., and the shipment of personal property across enemy lines.

473

Jackman, John S.   9th Kentucky Volunteers, CSA
     Journal, 1861–1908. 1 v.
     Memoir of the period Sept. 1861–May 1865, written from notes taken during the Shiloh, Corinth, Vicksburg, Chickamauga, Chattanooga, and Atlanta campaigns, and Gen. Braxton Bragg's invasion of Kentucky. Describes camp life, marches, morale, troop movements, discipline, entertainment, casualties, disease, hospital care, refugees, the attitude of noncombatants in the South, and the impressment of blacks. Includes sketches of the battles of Rocky Face Ridge, Rasaca, Dallas, and Kenesaw Mountain in the Atlanta Campaign, and details on Admiral Farragut's bombardment of Vicksburg and Gen. Joseph E.

Johnston's attempts to break the Federal siege at Vicksburg and Jackson, Miss. Also includes a description of Jefferson Davis as he appeared shortly after his capture.

Microfilm copy (1 reel) available.

474
Jackson, Theodore (b. 1840)   Pvt., 32d Colored
                                               Regiment, USA
Document, 1863. 1 item.

Jackson's petition for a military discharge, Aug. 22, 1863, Hilton Head, S.C.

475
Jackson, Thomas Jonathan (1824–1863)   Gen., CSA
Papers, 1845–1941. ca. 120 items.

In part, transcripts and photocopies.

Contains letters from Jackson to Gen. Joseph E. Johnston, Feb. 12, 1862, and Alexander R. Boteler, Mar. 5, 1862, concerning the Shenandoah Valley Campaign of 1862; a letter from Jackson to Col. C. J. Faulkner, Nov. 14, 1862, offering Faulkner a position on his headquarters staff; and a letter from Jackson to Gen. Robert E. Lee, May 2, 1863, notifying Lee of his intentions to attack Federal positions near Chancellorsville, Va. Also includes a letter from E. M. Douglas to the Librarian of Congress, May 20, 1941, relating a story on the death of Jackson as told by T. S. F. Saul, a Confederate officer.

476
Jameson, Robert Edwin
(1838–1905)   Surg., 29th Massachusetts Volunteers
Papers, 1857–65. 27 items.

Contains a diary, June 14–Aug. 13 [1863], and 20 letters from Jameson to family and friends, July 1861–May 1865, describing his service as a hospital steward and surgeon at hospitals in and around Washington, D.C., and at field hospitals in the Vicksburg, Knoxville, and Petersburg campaigns. Includes a few details on the Siege of Jackson, Miss., camp life, marches, guerrilla warfare, devastation in the South, and the work of the U.S. Sanitary Commission.

477
Jenckes, Thomas Allen
(1818–1875)   U.S. Representative, Rhode Island
Papers, 1836–78. ca. 42,000 items.

Contains a few letters to Jenckes from soldiers and civilians in the war zone.

Finding aid available.

478

Jewett, George O.   Sgt., 17th Massachusetts Volunteers
    Collection, 1855−65. 57 items.

Contains 17 letters from Jewett to his brother Dexter, 1862−65, concerning the Federal occupation of New Bern, N.C., and marches and skirmishes in the area. Includes remarks on camp life, training, discipline, entertainment, the attitude of noncombatants in New Bern, black life, disease, and hospital care. Also includes letters by John D. Berry (5th Massachusetts Battery), S. H. Brown (32d Massachusetts Volunteers), Edwin B. Daniels (1st Massachusetts Cavalry), Eugene Hadley and Herman C. Stickney (39th Massachusetts Volunteers), John Stafforce (47th Massachusetts Volunteers), Jonathan Blyth, John Harrington, Lebin Stetson, W. D. Tripp, and Charles Weeks.

479

Johnson, Andrew (1808−1875), Pres., U.S.
    Papers, 1814−1900. ca. 40,000 items.

Includes a few letters, reports, and dispatches relating to the war in Tennessee during the period when Johnson served as military governor of Tennessee and as Vice President of the United States.

Printed index and microfilm copy (55 reels) available.

480

Johnson, E. E.   18th Indiana Volunteers
    Diary, 1862. 1 item.
    Transcript.

Describes the campaign against Confederate forces commanded by Gens. Sterling Price and Ben McCulloch in southwest Missouri, Jan. 24−Apr. 21, 1862. Includes details on the Battle of Pea Ridge, and remarks on military organization, morale, discipline, depredations, foraging expeditions, casualties, supplies, and inflation.

481

Johnson, John Augustine
(1847−1918)   Pvt., 13th Massachusetts Battery
    Diary, 1865. 1 v.

Covers the period Mar. 8−July 17, 1865. Describes Johnson's enlistment, a voyage to the Gulf of Mexico, fortifications at Mobile, Ala., and camp life near New Orleans, La.

482

Johnson, Reverdy (1796−1876)   U.S. Senator, Maryland
    Papers, 1830−76. 185 items.

Includes a letter from Gen. George B. McClellan to Johnson,

Mar. 9, 1864, concerning the Battle of Malvern Hill, and several documents from the congressional investigation into the financial affairs of Gens. Benjamin F. Butler and George F. Shepley, i.e., affidavits on the disposition of Confederate deposits in the Bank of Louisiana and authorizations for the shipment of cotton from New Orleans signed by General Shepley and George S. Denison.

483
Johnson, W. C.   89th Ohio Volunteers
    Diary, 1865. 1 item.
    Transcript.
    Diary, "Through the Carolinas to Goldsboro, N.C.," Jan. 20–Mar. 23, 1865. Describes camp life, marches, foraging expeditions, the devastation of war, skirmishes, the Battle of Bentonville, N.C., and the junction of the armies of Gens. John M. Schofield, William T. Sherman, and Alfred H. Terry.

484
Johnson, Waldo Porter (1817–1885)   U.S. Senator, Missouri
    Letter, 1865. 1 item.
    Letter from Johnson to Gov. Thomas C. Reynolds, Jan. 26, 1865, Richmond, Va., concerning political affairs and public morale in Richmond.

485
Johnston, Albert Sidney (1803–1862)   Gen., CSA
    Papers, 1792–1896. 60 items.
    Includes Johnston's commission, Aug. 31, 1861, his letter of acceptance, Sept. 11, 1861, his oath of allegiance to the Confederacy, and the military commissions of his son, Col. William Preston Johnston.

486
Johnston, Georgianna
    Document, 1864. 1 item.
    Military pass issued to Johnston, June 14, 1864, Baltimore, Md.

487
Johnston, Joseph Eggleston (1807–1891)   Gen., CSA
    Papers, 1861–88. 5 items.
    Includes letter from Johnston to Gen. Robert E. Lee, Harpers Ferry, May 28, 1861, suggesting that R. W. Latham, a Washington banker touring the Confederacy, was a Union spy.

488
Johnston, Mercer Green (1868–1954)
    Papers, 1860–1954. ca. 40,000 items.
    Includes 20 letters from Johnston's father, James Steptoe
Johnston, to Mary Green of Sunnyside, Miss., May 7, 1861–Feb.
11, 1863, concerning his service in the 11th Mississippi Volunteers during the Peninsular, 2d Manassas, and Antietam
campaigns, and as drillmaster in Gen. Beverly H. Robertson's
cavalry during operations in North Carolina and Tennessee.
Provides details on the battles of Seven Pines, Malvern Hill,
and Sharpsburg, devastation in the Shenandoah Valley, camp
life, marches, and Unionist sentiment in Maryland. Also contains a few remarks on the conduct of Gen. Roger A. Pryor at
the Battle of Sharpsburg.
    Finding aid available.

489
Johnston, William Preston (1831–1899)   Col., CSA
    Papers, 1852–63. 15 items.
    Letters by Johnston, Dr. Alexander Garnett, and Jasper S.
Whiting, Feb. 1862, concerning Johnston's health and a leave
of absence; official letter notifying Johnston of his appointment
as colonel and aide-de-camp to President Davis, Apr. 19, 1862;
and commissions for the offices of major, 2d Kentucky Volunteers, and lt. colonel, 1st Kentucky Volunteers.

490
Jones, Charles DeHaven
    Papers, 1837–1903. 45 items.
    Contains a "Map of the Southern States, including Rail
Roads, County Towns, State Capitals, County Roads, the Southern Coast from Delaware to Texas, showing the harbors, inlets,
forts and position of blockading ships," Jan. 1862, with inset
portraits of President Lincoln, George B. McClellan, Winfield
Scott, and William H. Seward, and an inset map of Washington,
D.C., and vicinity. Also contains a postwar speech concerning
campaigns in Kentucky and Tennessee.

491
Jones, John Griffith
(1843–1864)   Cpl., 23d Wisconsin Volunteers
    Correspondence, 1862–65. 85 items.
    Transcripts.
    Chiefly letters from Jones to his family written during
campaigns in Kentucky, Tennessee, Mississippi, Louisiana, and
Arkansas. Contains details on the Vicksburg Campaign, particularly the Yazoo Pass expedition and the battles of Champion's Hill and Port Gibson, and the Arkansas Post (Fort

Hindman) expedition. Letters written during marches in southwest Louisiana describe skirmishes at Carrion Crow Bayou and New Iberia, Nov. 1863, and include remarks on camp life, marches, morale, casualties, foraging expeditions, Confederate desertions, Welshmen in the 23d Wisconsin, the performance of black soldiers, and the generalship of Stephen G. Burbridge. Also includes two letters written by Thomas E. Hughes, 23d Wisconsin.

492
Jones, Roger (1625?–1701)
  Family papers, 1649–1896. ca. 7,000 items.
  Includes two letters from Stephen R. Mallory to Lt. Catesby ap R. Jones, Mar. 13, 1862, and Sept. 16, 1864, commending Jones for his work on ordnance for the Confederate Navy.
  Finding aid and microfilm copy (15 reels) available.

493
Jones, Samuel
  Manuscript, undated. 457 p.
  Unpublished narrative of military operations along the coasts of South Carolina, Georgia, and Florida. Contains details on the Port Royal expedition; the capture of Forts Walker, Beauregard, and Pulaski; operations on Morris Island, S.C., particularly the attacks on Fort Wagner (Battery Wagner); the bombardment of Forts Moultrie and Sumter; and the St. Johns River expedition. Incomplete. Supplied title: "The Seige [sic] of Charleston."

494
Jones, Thomas Goode (1844–1914)   Maj., CSA
  Letter, 1864. 1 item.
  Transcript.
  Letter from Jones to his father, Oct. 21, 1864, describing the Battle of Cedar Creek, Va.

495
Kautz, August Valentine (1828–1895)   Gen., USA
  Papers, 1846–99. ca. 500 items.
  Includes general and special orders, a diary, and a memoir—"Reminiscences of the Civil War," 1861–65. Contains information on the battles of Mechanicsville, Hanover Courthouse, and Malvern Hill during the Peninsular Campaign, skirmishes in Kentucky and Tennessee in 1863, the Knoxville Campaign, the pursuit and capture of Gen. John Hunt Morgan in Ohio, the Petersburg Campaign, the fall of Richmond, Va., and the trial of the Lincoln conspirators. Also includes comments on military organization and administration,

August Valentine Kautz

the Cavalry Bureau, camp life, morale, black troops, rank disputes, refugees, Confederate deserters, and the generalship of Ambrose E. Burnside, Benjamin F. Butler, William H. Emory, Quincy A. Gillmore, George L. Hartsuff, William P. Sanders, and William F. Smith.

Finding aid available.

496
Kearny, Philip (1815–1862)   Gen., USA
    Papers, 1861–62. 75 items.
    Chiefly letters from Kearny to his wife, Mar.–Aug. 1862, and to John C. Parker, July 1861–Aug. 1862, concerning skirmishes and marches in northern Virginia, the Siege of Yorktown, and the battles of Seven Pines and Fair Oaks in the Peninsular Campaign. Also contains comments on the administration of the Army of the Potomac, military strategy, casualties, dissension among senior officers, the use of black troops, and the generalship of Nathaniel P. Banks, William B. Franklin, Samuel P. Heintzelman, August V. Kautz, George B. McClellan, Irvin McDowell, William R. Montgomery, Winfield Scott, William F. Smith, Charles P. Stone, and others.

497
Keatinge, Harriette C.
    Collection, 1903–9. 3 items.
    Account of the burning of Columbia, S.C., and Mrs. Keatinge's journey with the army of Gen. William T. Sherman from Columbia to Fayetteville, N.C.; transcript of Col. James G. Gibbs, "The Burning of Columbia," published in *The State*, Feb. 23, 1908; and notes on the burning of Columbia taken from *The Autobiography of Joseph Le Conte* (1903).

498
Keeney, Mrs. George
    Civil War miscellany collection, 1861–89. 14 items.
    Order by Gen. Theophilus H. Holmes, Nov. 28, 1862, concerning the appointment of recruiting officers and the establishment of training camps at various locations in the Trans-Mississippi Department; order by Gen. Joseph E. Johnston, Jan. 23, 1864, concerning rations issued to the Army of the Tennessee; invoice of cargo shipped aboard the *Economist*; and military passes.

499
Keidel Family
    Papers, 1834–1937. ca. 3,000 items.
    Includes about 80 letters from Adj. Herman F. Keidel (b. 1832) to his family in Maryland written from Hammond Gen-

eral Hospital, Fort McHenry, Point Lookout, and Fort Delaware, 1863–65, concerning his service in the 12th Virginia Cavalry and life as a prisoner of war. Also includes secondary accounts of Keidel's war service.

500
Keifer, Joseph Warren (1836–1932) Gen., USV
    Papers, 1861–65. ca. 1,100 items.
    Includes about 385 letters from Keifer to his wife written during campaigns in Virginia, Kentucky, Tennessee, Alabama, and Georgia, concerning camp life, training, morale, discipline, military organization, generalship, troop movements, marches, guerrilla warfare, courts-martial, desertions, casualties, executions, disease, hospital care, depredations, foraging expeditions, black life, prisoners of war, furloughs, visits to the battle zone by officers' wives, reconnaissance expeditions, the treatment and attitude of noncombatants in the South, changes in the attitude of Federal soldiers toward Confederates, recruiting practices, the New York draft riots, reaction in the Army to Lincoln's assassination, and numerous battles and skirmishes. Also includes official correspondence; the headquarters letterbook of the 3d Brigade, 3d and 6th Army Corps, June 16, 1863– June 20, 1865; ordnance and paymaster records; a list of casualties in the 110th Ohio during the Battle of Winchester (1863) and the Mine Run Campaign; reports on the 110th and 122d Ohio in the Battle of Winchester and the pursuit of General Lee after Gettysburg; and reports on operations along the Rapidan and Rappahannock Rivers in late 1863, the Wilderness, Spotsylvania, Cold Harbor, Winchester, Petersburg, and Appomattox campaigns, and the Shenandoah Valley Campaign of 1864. Includes details on the battles of Fisher's Hill, Winchester (1864), Cedar Creek, and Sayler's Creek. Also contains maps of the Petersburg area, "Lloyd's New Military Map of the Border & Southern States" (1863), and miscellaneous printed items relating to the operations of the 3d and 110th Ohio Volunteers.
    Finding aid available.

501
Keim Family
    Papers, 1861–1910. ca. 75 items.
    Contains a photograph of Gen. William H. Keim, a letterbook, June 4–Aug. 14, 1861, kept at the headquarters of General Keim, and clippings of dispatches of D. Randolph Keim published in the *New York Herald, New York Times*, and *Philadelphia Inquirer*.

502
Kelaher, James   9th New York Volunteers
    Letter, 1863. 1 item.
    Letter written by Kelaher during the Fredericksburg Campaign, Jan. 21, 1863. Includes information on battles in which Kelaher's regiment (Hawkins' Zouaves) participated.

503
Kellenberger, Peter B.   10th Indiana Volunteers
    Letters, 1863–65. 5 items.
    Four letters from Kellenberger to A. A. Pollard, Dec. 19, 1863–Aug. 29, 1864, discuss the Chattanooga and Atlanta campaigns, particularly the battles of Lookout Mountain and Missionary Ridge, and Confederate fortifications between Dalton and Marietta, Ga. Includes a sketch of the Battle of Missionary Ridge.

504
Keller, Louis   Pvt., 30th New Jersey Volunteers
    Document, 1892. 1 item.
    Certificate of service.

505
Kellogg, Edward Nealy (1841–1874) and
Edward Stanley (1870–1948)   USN
    Papers, 1859–1937. ca. 500 items.
    Official correspondence and papers of Lt. Edward N. Kellogg, 1861–65. Includes orders, commissions, newspaper clippings, wartime photographs of the U.S. Naval Academy at Annapolis, Md., a chart of the entrance to New York harbor (1862), and a manuscript booklet: "Boat Signals. U.S. Sloop-of-War Marion. Gulf Blockading Squadron." Also, a letter from Kellogg to his father, Aug. 7, 1864, U.S.S. *Oneida*, describing the Battle of Mobile Bay, particularly the capture of the C.S.S. *Tennessee*.
    Finding aid available.
    Naval Historical Foundation collection.

506
Kenner, Duncan Farrar (1813–1887)   C.S. Diplomat
    Collection, 1882–99. 3 items.
    In part, transcripts.
    Two versions (as told by Kenner to different people after the war) of his mission to England and France in 1864–65 to secure diplomatic recognition for the Confederacy. Includes details on his travel in the Northern States with the assistance

of Confederate sympathizers and his meeting with John Slidell and James Mason.

Microfilm copy (1 reel) available.

507

King, Horatio (1811–1897)   U.S. Postmaster General
    Papers, 1832–1906. ca. 3,000 items.
    Letter from J. W. Merriam to King, Apr. 21, 1861, Memphis, Tenn., concerning the rush to arms in the South, plans for the defense of Memphis and the forwarding of weapons from the arsenal at Baton Rouge, La.; letter from William Frazier to King, May 20, 1861, Rockbridge, Va., discussing public sentiment in Virginia after Lincoln's call for troops; military pass issued to King, July 14, 1861; certificate for King's having provided a substitute (Charles Taylor of Alexandria, Va.); and political correspondence with James Buchanan.
    Finding aid available.

508

Kinsley, Edward W.   Capt., 54th Massachusetts Volunteers
    Collection, 1863–65. 12 items.
    Photocopies.
    Correspondence between Captain Kinsley and Gen. Alfred S. Hartwell, Gen. Edward A. Wild, George P. Denny, and G. W. Denhurst, 1863–65, concerning campaigns in North Carolina and South Carolina. Includes comments on the generalship of George B. McClellan, pay for black troops, and morale and casualties in the 54th and 55th Massachusetts.

509

Kintigh, John E.   Cpl., 38th Ohio Infantry
    Document, 1864. 1 item.
    Discharge certificate, Feb. 25, 1864.

510

Kirby-Smith, Edmund (1824–1893)   Gen., CSA
    Letter, 1861. 1 item.
    Letter from Kirby-Smith to Captain Tupper, Sept. 4, 1861, Lynchburg, Va., concerning his recovery from a wound received at the Battle of 1st Manassas and his plans to return to the field.

511

Kirk, John W. (b. ca. 1819)   Ohio
    Papers, 1862–67. 5 items.
    General order, May 25, 1864, concerning the defenses of Covington and Newport, Ky., and an order detailing Kirk to the office of the provost marshal at Cincinnati, Ohio, Sept. 4, 1862.

512

Kirkley, Joseph William

(1841–1912)   Sgt., 1st Maryland Volunteers
    Papers, 1864–1911. 7 items.
    Unpublished history of the 7th Maryland Volunteers, 1861–64; list of commissioned officers in the 7th Maryland; record of Kirkley's war service; and Kirkley's discharge from the 1st Maryland Volunteers, May 23, 1864.

513

Kloeppel, H. Henry   USN
    Diary, 1863. 1 v.
    Diary, Jan.–Dec. 1863, kept aboard the U.S.S. *Patapsco*, South Atlantic Blockading Squadron, concerning a voyage from Philadelphia to South Carolina, activities of Federal ships along the coast of Georgia and South Carolina, attacks on Confederate batteries along the shore, and the bombardment of Forts Moultrie, Sumter, Wagner, and Gregg. Includes the names of some of Kloeppel's shipmates.

514

Knox, Dudley Wright (1877–1960)
    Papers, 1865–1950. ca. 6,500 items.
    In part, photocopies.
    Contains an eyewitness account of the sinking of the C.S.S. *Albemarle*, by Francis H. Swan, paymaster, USN.
    Finding aid available.
    Naval Historical Foundation collection.

515

Knox, James Suydam
    Letter, 1865. 1 item.
    Letter from Knox to his father, Apr. 10, 1865, Washington, D.C., describing the celebration in Washington over the fall of Richmond, Va.

516

Knox, Rose Bell
    Collection, 1861–64 and undated. 20 items.
    In part, transcripts.
    Includes samples of Confederate States currency, 1861–64, and North Carolina currency, 1861.

517

Kock, Charles   Consul for Hamburg,
                                          Germany, at New Orleans, La.
    Letter, 1863. 1 item.
    Letter from Kock to Gen. Cuvier Grover, July 20, 1863,

"Belle Alliance" plantation, complaining of depredations by Federal soldiers.

518
Lair, John A.   Surg., USA
   Collection, 1864–65. 3 items.
   Photocopies.
   Letters from Lair to his family, 1864–65, concerning the Atlanta and Savannah campaigns. Contains information on Federal strategy in the battles of Dalton, Resaca, Dallas, Kennesaw Mountain, Chattahoochee River, and Atlanta, and the Siege of Savannah.

519
Laird, George F.   Lt., 4th Ohio Volunteers
   Diary, 1861. 1 v.
   Covers the period Apr.–Dec. 1861. Describes Laird's enlistment and training in Ohio, marches and skirmishes in West Virginia, and casualties, desertions, and discharges in the 4th Ohio. Also includes a list of officers and enlisted men in the 4th Ohio or Canton Zouaves.

520
Lally, Michael
   Document, 1863. 1 item.
   Petition presented to Judge Roland Jones, July 22, 1863, Caddo Parish, La., for the release of Lally as an illegal conscript.

521
Lander, Frederick West (1821–1862)   Gen., USV
   Papers, 1836–94. ca. 1,250 items.
   Official correspondence, dispatches, telegrams, orders, and miscellaneous items relating to military operations along the upper Potomac River. Also includes numerous newspaper clippings on the military career and death of General Lander. Correspondents include Gens. George B. McClellan, Winfield Scott, and Charles P. Stone.
   Finding aid available.

522
Landis, Allen   116th Pennsylvania Volunteers
   Family papers, 1862–64. 21 items.
   Chiefly letters from Landis to his family concerning the Fredericksburg, Gettysburg, and Spotsylvania campaigns, the Siege of Petersburg, and skirmishes in northern Virginia and West Virginia. Includes comments on camp life, morale, entertainment, marches, the draft, and military diet and pay. Also contains a letter from Aaron Landis to his parents, Sept. 13,

1862, concerning camp life during the Antietam Campaign, and a memorial to Capt. John Teed, 116th Pennsylvania Volunteers, on his exchange as a prisoner of war, Mar. 1864.

523
Larned, Daniel Read (b. 1830)   Capt.; Secretary
                                          to General Burnside, USA
    Papers, 1861–65. ca. 1,100 items.
    In part, transcripts.
    Chiefly letters from Larned to his sisters and brother-in-law concerning General Burnside's expedition to North Carolina. Describes the battles of Roanoke Island, New Bern, Beaufort, and Fort Macon. Also contains information on the Antietam, Fredericksburg, Knoxville, Wilderness, Spotsylvania, Cold Harbor, and Petersburg campaigns; the pursuit of Gen. John Hunt Morgan in Ohio; General Burnside's relationship with Gens. Henry Halleck, George B. McClellan, and William S. Rosecrans; and military organization, rank disputes, discipline, morale, marches, depredations, black life, black troops, entertainment, prisoners of war, foraging expeditions, disease, inflation, furloughs, military appointments, and the effect of the war on noncombatants in the South.

524
Lathers, Richard (1820–1903)   Businessman, New York
    Papers, 1826–1901. ca. 210 items.
    In part, transcripts.
    Contains a few letters to Lathers concerning aid for Confederate prisoners of war held at Fort Delaware, the New York draft riots, the state of the war in July 1863, and the location and condition of Lt. Thomas Ford, 21st South Carolina Volunteers. Seven letters from Gen. John A. Dix to Gens. George B. McClellan, Joseph Mansfield, and Egbert Viele, Secretaries Edwin Stanton and Simon Cameron, and Col. R. Biddle Roberts, 1861–62, concern the release of political prisoners in southeast Virginia and the resumption of commerce at Norfolk. Miscellaneous items include a letter from Thomas Sampson to Col. C. S. Olcott, Feb. 9, 1863, New Providence, Bahama Islands, concerning Confederate shipping in the Bahamas, and a pamphlet: *A Statement of the Facts Concerning the Imprisonment and Treatment of Jefferson Davis While a Military Prisoner at Fort Monroe, Va., in 1865 and 1866* (1902).

525
Latrobe, Osmun
    Papers, 1793–1932. ca. 300 items.
    Includes three letters from R. S. Steuart, Company C, 1st Missouri Cavalry, to his family from various camps in Virginia,

July 1864–Jan. 1865, concerning casualties, morale, uniforms, and the health and location of Latrobe. Also, two military passes to members of the Latrobe family, 1862–63, to visit Latrobe while a prisoner of war at Fort McHenry, Md.

526
Latta, James William (b. 1839)   Capt., 119th
                                              Pennsylvania Volunteers
    Papers, 1854–99. ca. 200 items.
    Includes a diary, Aug. 1862–Apr. 1865 (4 v.), kept by Latta during the Antietam, Fredericksburg, Chancellorsville, Gettysburg, Mine Run, Wilderness, Spotsylvania, and Petersburg campaigns, the Shenandoah Valley Campaign of 1864, the battles of North Anna River, Totopotomoy Creek, and Cold Harbor, Gen. Jubal Early's Washington raid, and Gen. James Wilson's raid to Selma, Ala. (Upton's division). Provides details on camp life, training, discipline, entertainment, disease, desertions, marches, casualties, troop movements, furloughs, courts-martial, depredations, black life, and civilian life in the South during the war. Also contains clippings of an article by Latta on "The Campaign of Wilson's Cavalry Corps Through Alabama and Georgia in the Spring of 1865."

527
Lawton, Henry Ware   Col., 30th
(1843–1899)   Indiana Volunteers
    Papers, 1849–1930. ca. 2,300 items.
    Discharges from the 9th and 30th Indiana Volunteers, commissions for the ranks of 1st lieutenant through colonel in the 30th Indiana, and copies of postwar letters containing remarks on Lawton's service in the war. Also contains a copy of the service record of Lt. A. E. Wood.
    Finding aid available.

528
Leale, Charles Augustus (1842–1932)   Surg., USA
    Report, 1867. 1 item.
    Photocopy.
    Report of Leale (the first physician to reach President Lincoln after he was shot) to the Congressional Assassination Investigation Committee (14 p.).

529
Leavitt, Joshua (1794–1873)   New York
    Papers, 1812–71. ca. 100 items.
    Includes two letters from Leavitt to a brother and sister, Jan. 3 and Dec. 6, 1862, concerning morale, camp conditions,

and the health of New York troops (particularly the Lincoln Cavalry) during encampments near Washington, D.C.

530
Lee, H. I.   Virginia
    Letter, 1864. 1 item.
    Photocopy of a transcript.
    Letter from Mrs. Edmund Jennings Lee to Gen. David Hunter, July 20, 1864, Shepherdstown, W. Va., asking General Hunter to explain his order to burn her home.

531
Lee, Mary Lorrain Greenhow
(b. ca. 1823)   Winchester, Va.
    Diary, 1837–65. 1 item.
    Photocopy.
    Diary kept mainly at Winchester, Va., Mar. 11–Sept. 3, 1862, and Mar. 9, 1863–Nov. 16, 1865. Describes troop movements, depredations, the attitude and suffering of noncombatants, and social life in and around Winchester during the war. Also includes the names of numerous Confederate soldiers.
    Microfilm copy (1 reel) available.

532
Lee, Robert Edward (1807–1870)   Gen., CSA
    Papers, 1830–1913. 166 items.
    In part, transcripts and photocopies.
    Includes Lee's letter of resignation from the U.S. Army, Apr. 20, 1861; a letter from Lee to his cousin, Lt. Roger Jones, Apr. 20, 1861, explaining the reasons for his resignation; a letter from Lee to C. C. Cocke, June 10, 1861, offering Cocke the position of lt. colonel in the 8th Virginia Regiment; a letter from Lee to Capt. M. Dulany Ball, June 29, 1861, concerning Ball's exchange as a prisoner of war; letters from Lee to Gen. Richard S. Ewell, Apr. 27, 1862, on military strategy in northern Virginia and the defense of Fredericksburg, and May 5, 1862, on the arrival and disposition of Gen. Lawrence O. Branch's North Carolina brigade; a letter to Samuel S. Wilson, May 11, 1862, concerning military supplies; a letter to Louis T. Wigfall, Sept. 21, 1862, requesting information on the additional Texas regiments promised by Wigfall; a letter to Mrs. Sarah A. Lawton extending his sympathy on the death of her brother-in-law; a letter from Lee to Gen. William E. Jones, Feb. 13, 1863, concerning operations against Gen. Robert Milroy in the Shenandoah Valley; a letter from Lee to Maj. A. S. Rives, Mar. 26, 1863, on the death of Major Meade; letters from Lee to Gen. John C. Breckinridge, May 16, 1864, ordering Breck-

inridge to follow up on his victory over General Sigel, and Jan. 10, 1865, instructing Breckinridge to destroy bands of deserters and banditti operating in his department; a letter from Lee to Gen. Alexander R. Lawton, Mar. 7, 1865, concerning strategy against an enemy force moving down the Rivanna River; a letter from Lee to Col. A. J. Rives, Mar. 23, 1865, on military appointments; General Grant's letter to Lee, Apr. 9, 1865, stating the terms of surrender at Appomattox; Lee's General Order No. 9, Apr. 10, 1865; and a letter written by Gen. Winfield S. Hancock, Apr. 10, 1865, announcing Lee's surrender.

Finding aid available.

533
___

Collection, 1834–86.
Microfilm, 1 reel.
Chiefly memorabilia. Includes a few rough sketches of military camps, roads, and fortifications along the Potomac River, near Richmond, Va., and at Pensacola, Fla., and portraits of Gens. P. G. T. Beauregard, Joseph E. Johnston, Wade Hampton, Thomas J. Jackson, and R. E. Lee.

534
Lee, Robert W.   Lt. Col., 20th Ohio Volunteers
    Papers, 1862–64. 9 items.
Contains two letters from Lt. Col. Manning F. Force to Lee, Apr. 22 and May 19, 1862, Pittsburg Landing, concerning the Battle of Shiloh, and camp life, disease, and deaths in the aftermath of the battle, and five letters between Lee and Lt. Col. James H. Simpson, May–Nov. 1864, concerning fortifications at Covington and Newport, Ky.

535
Lee, Samuel Phillips (1812–1897)   Adm., USN
    Papers, 1860–69. ca. 19,000 items.
    In part, transcripts.
Official, confidential, and squadron letterbooks, 1862–65; diary of signal officer Lt. M. Miller, May 5–June 14, 1864, concerning activities along the James River; letters of Gen. John Gray Foster, 1863, on coastal defenses and problems with smuggling and discipline in North Carolina and Virginia; letters (to Adm. D. D. Porter) of special agent J. B. Devoe, Feb. 1864–June 1865, on Confederate spies in St. Louis and Chicago, espionage by southern women, Confederate methods of communication with guerrillas, smuggling, and corruption among Federal officials at New Orleans, La.; logbook of the U.S.S. *Mississippi*, 1861–62; logbooks and log extracts of vessels in the North Atlantic Blockading Squadron, 1862–64; sketches

of roads and fortifications near Wilmington, Williamstown, and Roanoke Island, N.C.; lists of persons captured on prize vessels; and printed matter: *Register of the Commissioned and Warrant Officers of the Navy of the Confederate States to January 1, 1864* (1864), and Judah P. Benjamin's *Instructions Upon Neutral and Belligerent Rights* (1864).

Finding aid available.

Naval Historical Foundation collection.

536
_____

Order, 1862. 1 item.

Order from Lee (U.S.S. *Oneida*) to Capt. Edward Donaldson (U.S.S. *Sciota*), May 20, 1862, to prevent the construction of Confederate batteries near Warrenton, Miss.

537
Lee Family

DeButts—Ely Collection, 1749—1916. ca. 900 items.

Photocopies.

Contains the family correspondence of Gen. Robert E. Lee during the war and Mrs. Mary Custis Lee's "My Reminiscences of the War." Describes popular sentiment in Virginia at the outset of the war, personal losses and suffering of the Lee family, and the progress of the war in Virginia.

Microfilm copy (3 reels) available.

538
Leggett, Mortimer Dormer (1821—1896)   Gen., USV

Letter, 1863. 1 item.

Letter from Leggett to Col. David Chambers, Aug. 9, 1863, Vicksburg, Miss., explaining his decision to join the Army.

539
Lester, Joseph   Artisan, Wisconsin Volunteers

Collection, 1860—64. 10 items.

Letters from Lester to his family in England concerning camp life, marches, morale, generalship, disease, prisoners of war, foraging expeditions, depredations, black life, and the attitude of noncombatants in the South. Provides some information on the Battle of Corinth, the Yazoo Pass expedition, the Siege of Vicksburg, and the Chattanooga and Atlanta campaigns. Also contains a diary fragment, Nov. 18—Dec. 17, 1862.

540
Letcher, John (1813—1884)   Gov., Virginia

Papers, 1853—66. 7 items.

In part, transcripts.

Includes three letters from President Davis to Letcher,

Sept.–Dec. 1861, concerning the recruitment and organization of soldiers, and a letter from Gen. Thomas J. Jackson to Letcher, Apr. 20, 1863, asking for a military escort for Mrs. Jackson from Richmond, Va., to his camp near Fredericksburg.

541
Levy, Diana Franklin (b. 1858)
    Collection, 19th century. 1 v.
    Autograph book containing signed photographs of Nathaniel P. Banks, Salmon P. Chase, Schuyler Colfax, Solomon Foote, Ulysses S. Grant, William B. Hazen, Andrew Johnson, Carl Schurz, William H. Seward, Edwin M. Stanton, Thaddeus Stevens, Charles Sumner, Lyman Trumbull, and others.

542
Lewis, Lothrop Lincoln   Pvt., 1st Maine Volunteers
    Collection, 1864–65. 2 items.
    Diary, Aug. 29, 1864–June 26 [1865], kept during the Shenandoah Valley Campaign of 1864, the Siege of Petersburg, and the Appomattox Campaign. Describes camp life, marches, disease, foraging expeditions, discipline, depredations, and Confederate deserters. Includes a few details on the Battle of Cedar Creek and the capture of Petersburg, Va. Also contains a photograph of Lewis taken in Mar. 1865.

543
Lewis, William Delaware   Col., 110th
(d. 1872)   Pennsylvania Volunteers
    Document, 1862. 1 item.
    Proclamation issued by Lewis to the inhabitants of Winchester, Va., Apr. 17, 1862, warning that he would not permit "lying reports and insulting remarks."

544
Libby, Frederick Joseph (1874–1970)
    Papers, 1862–1970. ca. 2,470 items.
    Includes the diary of Dr. Abial Libby, Mar. 8–July 23, 1862, a surgeon with the Army of the Potomac, which contains a list of the questions he asked during the examination of new recruits, and comments on camp life, disease, casualties, medical care, entertainment, morality, depredations, and foraging expeditions during the Peninsular Campaign. Provides names or figures on casualties in the 3d Maine, 38th New York, and 40th New York regiments.

545
Limongi, Felix
    Collection, 1832–80. ca. 240 items.

Letters, briefs, affidavits, petitions, telegrams, notes, judicial decisions, and memoranda from the files of the New Orleans law firm of Durant & Hornor. Includes material relating to the Planter's Life Guard, 1861–62, a list of the officers and crew of the U.S.S. *Chocura*, information on prizes taken by the *Chocura*, material on civilian arrests, and miscellaneous items relating to the administrations of Gens. Nathaniel P. Banks, Benjamin F. Butler, Stephen A. Hurlbut, and George F. Shepley.

546

Lincoln, Abraham (1809–1865), Pres., U.S.
    Papers, 1833–1916. ca. 42,100 items.
    Military and political correspondence, orders, plans, reports, telegrams, circulars, maps, muster rolls and returns, proclamations, petitions, affidavits, speeches, pamphlets, and miscellaneous items. Correspondents include Nathaniel P. Banks, Edward Bates, Montgomery Blair, Benjamin Brewster, Salmon P. Chase, Schuyler Colfax, Ulysses S. Grant, John Hay, Andrew Johnson, Reverdy Johnson, George B. McClellan, George G. Meade, Edwin D. Morgan, John G. Nicolay, William Rosecrans, William H. Seward, Horatio Seymour, Caleb B. Smith, James Speed, Edwin M. Stanton, Charles Sumner, Lyman Trumbull, Lew Wallace, Elihu B. Washburne, and Gideon Welles.
    Published index and microfilm copy (97 reels) available.

547

    Appointment book, 1861.
    Microfilm, 1 reel.
    Covers the period Mar. 5–27, 1861. Includes miscellaneous related documents.

548

    Lincolniana collection, 1849–1954. 29 items.
    Includes a copy of the last photograph of President Lincoln, Apr. 9, 1865.

549

Livingston, Robert R. (1746–1813)
    Papers, 1658–1888.
    Microfilm, 14 reels.
    Includes four letters from Pvt. Eugene Livingston to his father, E. A. Livingston, Apr. 1862, concerning his service in the 95th New York Volunteers, and Eugene Livingston's discharge certificate, Apr. 26, 1862.
    Originals at the New-York Historical Society.

Abraham Lincoln

550
Lockwood, Abram L.   Lt. Col., USA
    Collection, 1865. 2 items.
    Draft of a report by Lockwood on the participation of the
120th New York Volunteers in the Battle of Hatcher's Run,
Feb. 5−7, 1865, and photograph of Gen. John Sedgwick.

551
Lockwood, Jeremiah T.
(1844−1925)   Pvt., 4th New York Heavy Artillery
    Papers, 1829−1922. 12 items.
    Includes a diary, Jan. 1−Nov. 3, 1865, kept during Lock-
wood's convalescence at a military hospital outside Washington,
D.C. Describes hospital care and daily routine, morale, entertainment, deaths, and reaction among convalescents to General Lee's surrender at Appomattox and the assassination of
President Lincoln. Also contains newspaper clippings, photographs, and a map of the operations of the Army of the Potomac and the Army of the James in Virginia and Maryland.

552
Logan, John Alexander (1826−1886)   Gen., USV
    Family papers, 1847−1923. ca. 46,000 items.
    General and official correspondence, headquarters letter-
books, order books, battle reports, returns, telegrams,
dispatches, and circulars relating chiefly to the Vicksburg,
Atlanta, Savannah, and Carolinas campaigns. Provides information on reconnaissance expeditions, troop positions, enlistments and resignations, morale, promotions, disputes between
officers, supplies, ordnance, depredations, courts-martial, prisoners of war, and the defense and operation of military railroads.
Also describes the turmoil in Washington at the beginning of
the war, skirmishes in northern Virginia in 1861, the Battle of
1st Manassas, the Fort Donelson Campaign, casualties in the
Battle of Shiloh, Halleck's advance on Corinth, Miss., and military organization. Includes about 30 sketches and map trac-
ings of parts of Alabama, Georgia, North Carolina, Tennessee,
and Virginia, and sketches of troop positions in the Battle of
Atlanta.
    Finding aid available.

553
Logue, Lloyd Garrison   Sgt. Maj., 7th Ohio Volunteers
    Letter, 1917. 1 item.
    Photocopy.
    Letter from Logue to his daughter, Apr. 17, 1917, recalling
his enlistment and training in the 7th Ohio, his capture at
Cross Lanes, W. Va., and his experiences as a prisoner of war.

554
Long, Breckinridge (1881–1958)
    Papers, 1740–1948. ca. 77,000 items.
    Includes about 30 letters written during the war by Frank
Preston Blair, Jr. (1821–1875), concerning military appointments and organization, generalship, depredations in Maryland,
the Corinth Campaign, and the Arkansas Post (Fort Hindman)
expedition. Also contains postwar reminiscences of William S.
Long concerning his service in the 44th North Carolina Volunteers, 1861–65, and as a clerk on detached duty at Libby Prison
in Richmond, Va. Includes information on the battles of Bristoe
Station and Cold Harbor, the Kilpatrick–Dahlgren raid on
Richmond, prison escapes, the condition of exchanged Union
and Confederate prisoners of war, and camp life, morale, and
marches in the Army of Northern Virginia.
    Finding aid available.

555
Lord, W. W.   Vicksburg, Miss.
    Diary, 1863. 1 item.
    Transcript.
    Copy of Mrs. Lord's "Diary of a Woman During the Siege of
Vicksburg. May to July, 1863." Describes the suffering of noncombatants in Vicksburg, the morale of the Confederate garrison,
disillusionment with Gen. John Pemberton, the behavior of
Union and Confederate soldiers after the capitulation, an interview with General Grant, and devastation in the area.

556
Love, John James Hervey
(1833–1897)   Surg., 13th New Jersey Infantry
    Papers, 1863–94. 50 items.
    In part, transcripts.
    Correspondence, short draft histories of regiments and bat-
teries in the 12th Corps, Army of the Potomac, a general history of the 12th Corps, accounts of the battles of Cedar Mountain, Chancellorsville, and Gettysburg, and printed matter.

557
Lovell, Mansfield (1822–1884)   Gen., CSA
    Letters, 1860–80. 9 items.
    In part, photocopies.
    Includes two letters from Gen. P. G. T. Beauregard to
Lovell, July 28, 1862, and Jan. 21, 1863, the former declining
Lovell's request that he preside over a court of inquiry on the
fall of New Orleans, La., and the latter concerning a command
for Lovell; a letter from Gov. Henry W. Allen to Lovell, Mar.
15, 1864, asking for the return of funds belonging to the city of

New Orleans; a letter from Gen. Joseph E. Johnston to Lovell, Oct. 30, 1864, concerning General Sherman's strategy in the Atlanta Campaign; and a copy of a note from Judah P. Benjamin to Lovell, Oct. 27, 1861.

558
Low–Mills Families
Papers, 1795–1959. ca. 4,000 items.
Includes 36 letters from Capt. George H. Putnam (1844–1930), quartermaster and adjutant, 176th New York Volunteers, to Mary Hillard Loines, Jan. 24, 1863–June 13, 1865, concerning campaigns in southern Louisiana, the Red River Campaign of 1864, the Shenandoah Valley Campaign of 1864 (particularly the Battle of Cedar Creek), and the Carolinas Campaign. Provides information on camp life, marches, foraging expeditions, morale, disease, hospital care, deaths, conscripts, prisoners of war, guerrilla warfare, attacks on transports and supply ships on the Mississippi River, black life, attitudes toward black soldiers, and the effect of the war on noncombatants in Louisiana. Also, wartime entries in the diary of Ellen Low Mills include remarks on the U.S.S. *Monitor*, the Gettysburg Campaign, and the capture of vessels owned by the Low family.
Finding aid available.

559
Lowe, John (1838–1930)   2d Asst. Engineer, USN
Papers, 1860–1945. ca. 600 items.
Includes information on Lowe's service as a private in the 2d Ohio Volunteers, and as assistant engineer on the U.S.S. *Huron*, 1861–64, and the U.S.S. *Shawmut,* 1864–66. Also contains Lowe's discharge from the 2d Ohio, July 31, 1861, and official correspondence and orders.
Finding aid available.
Naval Historical Foundation collection.

560
Lowndes, William (1782–1822)
Papers, 1754–1941.
Microfilm, 2 reels.
Includes a biographical sketch of Lt. J. E. McPherson Washington (CSA); a copy of a letter by Capt. L. M. Shumaker concerning Washington's death on a reconnaissance expedition at Cheat Mountain, W. Va., Aug. 25, 1861; and reminiscences of Thomas Pinckney Lowndes on fortifications and military affairs at Charleston, S.C., and vicinity.
Originals at the University of North Carolina.

561
Luce, Stephen Bleecker
(1827–1917)   Comdr., USN
       Papers, 1799–1938. ca. 8,000 items.
       Includes a diary and letterbooks kept by Luce as 3d
lieutenant, U.S.S. *Wabash*, May–Nov. 1861, and lt. commander,
U.S. Practice Ship *Macedonian*, June–Sept. 1863, U.S.S.
Nantucket, Oct. 1863–July 1864, and U.S.S. *Pontiac*, Sept.
1864–June 1865. Contains lists of officers, names of prize
vessels, information on ship arrivals and departures in the
South Atlantic Blockading Squadron, accounts of the capture
of Forts Hatteras and Clark, N.C., and the Port Royal expedition—particularly the action at Hilton Head, S.C., and
the capture of Forts Beauregard and Walker. Also includes a
detailed report on the participation of the *Nantucket* in operations against Fort Sumter, May 14 and 18, 1864, and remarks
on discipline, courts-martial, naval intelligence, Confederate
deserters, and blacks.
       Finding aid available.
       Naval Historical Foundation collection.

562
Ludwig, Edwin F. (1839–1884)   Telegraph Operator,
                                                         South Carolina
       Diary, 1861. 1 v.
       Covers the period Jan. 1–June 7, 1861. Contains remarks
on the secession crisis, the seizure of Federal forts and arsenals
in the South, Confederate military appointments, and the bombardment and capture of Fort Sumter.

563
Lurton, Horace Harmon
(1844–1914)   Lt., 3d Kentucky Cavalry, CSA
       Papers, 1860–1914. ca. 250 items.
       Contains a note from Lurton to his mother, Feb. 17, 1862,
informing her of his capture at Fort Donelson; a letter from
Gen. Simon B. Buckner to Gen. George W. Cullum, Feb. 19,
1862, requesting Lurton's release as a noncombatant; and
Lurton's certificate of discharge from the 5th Tennessee Regiment, Feb. 4, 1862. Also includes 10 letters from Lurton to A.
B. W. Allen, Mar. 7, 1862–Nov. 14, 1864, concerning prison
life at Camp Chase and Johnson's Island, his personal health,
and the mental and physical suffering of Confederate prisoners
of war; a letter from Lt. John Adams to Lurton, Feb. 17, 1865,
approving the circumstances of Lurton's release from prison;
and a statement of approbation on the means of Lurton's release
signed by 46 Confederate prisoners from Kentucky and
Tennessee. A letter from Lurton to A. B. W. Allen, May 4,

1865, attests to his continued hopes for a Confederate victory and the loyalty of southern women.

Finding aid available.

564

Lyons, Richard Bickerton Pemell,
1st Earl (1817–1887)   British Ambassador
    Letter, 1861. 1 item.
    Letter from Lyons to J. Mandeville Carlisle, July 10, 1861,Washington, D.C., inquiring about legal aspects of the Federal blockade.

565

Lyons, Thomas   Captain's Clerk, USN
    Diary, 1863. 1 v.
    Account of Lyons' service aboard the U.S.S. *Carondelet*, Jan. 8–19, 1863, and the U.S.S. *Lafayette*, Jan. 20–June 25, 1863. Contains details on the Arkansas Post (Fort Hindman) and Yazoo River expeditions, the Battle of Grand Gulf, and the Red River Campaign of 1863. Includes comments on the conduct of Capt. Henry Walke, the outfitting of the *Lafayette*, loyalist refugees, aid to runaway slaves, discipline, disease, casualties, foraging expeditions, illicit trade with Confederates, the sinking of the U.S.S. *Lancaster*, the burning of the U.S.S. *Glide*, and visits aboard the *Lafayette* by Adm. David D. Porter and Gens. Ulysses S. Grant and William T. Sherman.

566

McAdoo, William Gibbs (1863–1941)
    Papers, 1786–1941. ca. 250,000 items.
    Correspondence of the Floyd, McAdoo, and Gibbs families. Letters of William G. McAdoo, Sr. (1820–1894) describe troop movements in the Atlanta Campaign and depredations and plundering by Confederate and Union soldiers, the impact of the war in Georgia, Gen. Ambrose Burnside's advance on Knoxville, Tenn., the sabotage of Confederate railroads by Union sympathizers, and the displacement of Unionists in east Tennessee. Letters of John D. McAdoo discuss the Federal blockade, the defense of Galveston, Tex., recruitment and popular support for the war in Texas, and the impact of the war on the State of Texas. Letters by Lt. Richard S. Floyd concern his enlistment in the C.S. Navy, the blockade of Mobile Bay, and his service on the C.S.S. *Florida*. Letters of Charles R. Floyd (CSN) relate to the activities of the Confederate Navy along the coast of Georgia. Also contains miscellaneous letters concerning the occupation of New Orleans, La., conditions in

Richmond, Va., in Oct. 1864, coastal defenses, black life, and depredations by Federal soldiers.

Finding aid available.

567

McCabe, Flora Morgan   Virginia
    Collection, 1855–78. 69 items.
    Photocopies.
    Includes about 30 letters and documents, 1861–65, concerning camp life, morale, diet, reconnaissance expeditions, supplies, troop positions, disease, and casualties in the 1st Manassas Campaign; popular support for the war in Virginia; and the role of women in the war. Also contains the discharge and exemption certificate (medical) of Sgt. Edward J. Garrett. Correspondents are William H. Carter, Edward J. Garrett, Flora Garrett, John H. Morgan (24th Virginia Volunteers), Margaret A. Morgan, Pvt. William C. Morgan (24th Virginia), and Sgt. Edward T. Walker.

568

McCalla, Helen Varnum Hill
    Diary excerpts, 1863, 1865. 2 items.
    Photocopies.
    Entries describe the draft riots in New York City, July 17–19, 1863, and events in Washington, D.C., from the Lincoln assassination through the trial of the Lincoln conspirators, Apr. 14–May 25, 1865.

569

McCarter, (?)   South Carolina
    Collection, 1860–1946. 3 items.
    Manuscript history, 1860–66, of the secession controversy, the Civil War, and the political, social, and economic effects of the war, particularly in South Carolina; and two brief notes, 1946 and undated, on the author's identity.

570

McCleery, Robert W. (d. 1863)   Engineer, USN
    Papers, 1859–63. 3 items.
    Letter from Peter B. Robinson, assistant engineer, to McCleery, May 25, 1863, U.S.S. *Stettin*, concerning Robinson's promotion, and letter from George D. Emmons to McCleery, June 2, 1863, U.S.S. *Catskill*, concerning repairs to the *Catskill*.
    Naval Historical Foundation collection.

571

McClellan, George Brinton (1826–1885)   Gen., USA
    Papers, 1823–98. ca. 33,000 items.

Chiefly official correspondence, orders, reports, returns, commissions, diaries, receipts, inventories, accounts, telegrams, letterbooks, and memoranda, 1861–62, used by McClellan in his *Report on the Organization and Campaigns of the Army of the Potomac* (1864) and *McClellan's Own Story: The War for the Union* (1887). Relates largely to the Peninsular and Antietam campaigns. Also includes correspondence concerning McClellan's Presidential aspirations and his interest in national political affairs, 1864–65. Correspondents include John Jacob Astor, Jr., Nathaniel P. Banks, John G. Barnard, Don Carlos Buell, Ambrose E. Burnside, Simon Cameron, Leslie Combs, John A. Dix, Millard Fillmore, Henry W. Halleck, Samuel P. Heintzelman, Hiram Ketchum, Abraham Lincoln, Irwin McDowell, Randolph B. Marcy, George G. Meade, Joel Parker, Edwin M. Stanton, Edwin Vose Sumner, Charles M. Swann, Clement L. Vallandigham, Stewart Van Vliet, Daniel W. Voorhees, George W. Weeks, James C. Welling, Henry B. Whipple, John E. Wool, and others.

Finding aid available.

572

McClellan, George Brinton (1865–1940)
    Papers, 1838–1922. ca. 1,200 items.

Includes a letter from an unidentified soldier in the 66th New York Volunteers, Nov. 12, 1862, concerning the pursuit of Confederate troops from Harpers Ferry to Warrenton, Va., and three sketches showing topography and troop positions during the Peninsular Campaign.

Finding aid available.

573

McClintock, James M.   Capt., Signal Corps, USA
    Papers, 1862–64. 84 items.

Messages between Adm. David D. Porter, Gen. William T. Sherman, and Gen. Ulysses S. Grant sent by McClintock during the Vicksburg Campaign, and 23 intercepted Confederate messages sent chiefly from Kennesaw Mountain, Ga., June 15–27, 1864.

574

McConihe, John (d. 1864)   Lt. Col.,
169th New York Volunteers
    Letter, 1863. 1 item.

Letter from McConihe to Martin I. Townsend, May 9, 1863, Suffolk, Va., describing the Siege of Suffolk, devastation in the area, and the service of the 169th New York.

George Brinton McClellan and
Mrs. Nellie Marcy McClellan

575
McCook Family
     Papers, 1827–1963. 3,000 items.
     In part, transcripts and photocopies.
     Correspondence and papers of the "Fighting McCooks," of Ohio. Includes letters and papers of Daniel McCook (1798–1863) concerning the Battle of 1st Manassas and the death of his son, Pvt. Charles M. McCook (1843–1861); Gen. Alexander McDowell McCook (1831–1903) on campaigns in Tennessee and Kentucky, 1861–63; Col. Edwin Stanton McCook (1837–1873) on the Fort Donelson and Corinth campaigns; Col. Anson George McCook (1835–1917) concerning the death of Gen. Robert Latimer McCook (1827–1862) and the Battle of Chickamauga; and Lt. Roderick Sheldon McCook (1839–1886) concerning the battles of Roanoke Island and New Bern, N.C., the Fort Fisher expeditions, and the bombardment and capture of Charleston, S.C. Includes comments on the burning of Charleston and the attitude of noncombatants in the city. Miscellaneous items in the collection relate to the participation of the 126th Ohio Volunteers in the Gettysburg Campaign, the resignation of Gen. Don Carlos Buell, and field and staff officers in the 2d Ohio Volunteers.
     Finding aid available.

576
McCoy, Frank Ross (1874–1954)
     Papers, 1847–1954. ca. 36,750 items.
     Includes a letter from J. C. Smith to his parents, June 13, 1864, concerning the Atlanta Campaign; two letters by Col. Thomas Franklin McCoy, 107th Pennsylvania Volunteers, written during campaigns in Virginia, May 7, 1864, and Jan. 24, 1865; and a postwar essay (39 p.) discussing the Petersburg and Appomattox campaigns.
     Finding aid available.

577
McCullough, James T.
     Collection, 1862–65. 1 v.
     Chiefly printed circulars and decisions on U.S. Treasury Department regulations received by McCullough as collector of Internal Revenue at Elkton, Md.

578
McDonald, William Ogden
(1836–1918)   Lt. Col., Surg., USV
     Papers, 1795–1893. 182 items.
     Chiefly correspondence, general and special orders, passes, requisitions, invoices, receipts, commissions, muster rolls,

affidavits, and miscellaneous items relating to McDonald's service with the 65th New York Volunteers and the 2d Kentucky Cavalry. Includes three postwar narratives concerning the organization and work of the Medical Department, conflicts between the Medical Department and the Christian Sanitary Commission, the development of field hospitals, services performed by chaplains, disease, hospital care, confusion and mismanagement in the Medical Department, and camp life, training, marches, and weapons. Provides numerous details on the Siege of Yorktown, and the battles of Malvern Hill, Sharpsburg, Fredericksburg, Chancellorsville, Chickamauga, Lookout Mountain, Missionary Ridge, and Resaca.

579

McEwen, John   Pvt., 1st Minnesota Volunteers
    Papers, 1861–69. 8 items.
    Contains two letters from McEwen to his family and friends, Oct. 18, 1861, and Jan. 23, 1862, Camp Stone, Md., concerning the Battle of 1st Manassas, the treatment of Federal prisoners of war in Richmond, Va., lack of confidence in Gen. Charles P. Stone, and McEwen's application for a lieutenancy in the 3d Minnesota Volunteers. Also contains an unsigned letter in a different hand portraying the excitement of new recruits at Camp Utley, Wis., in May or June 1861.

580

McGarrah, Gates W. (1863–1940)   Collector
    Presidential letters, 1786–1899. 70 items.
    Photocopies.
    Includes a letter from President Lincoln to Edwin M. Stanton, Jan. 31, 1862; a letter from Gen. Ulysses S. Grant to Gov. David Tod of Ohio, June 7, 1862; and two letters by Chester A. Arthur as Quartermaster General of New York, Aug. 8 and Aug. 18, 1862.
    Finding aid available.

581

McHenry, James (1753–1816)
    Papers, 1775–1862. ca. 3,600 items.
    In part, photocopies.
    Includes three letters from Christopher P. Wolcott to J. Howard McHenry, 1862, concerning visits to prisoners of war at Fort Warren, Mass., and a letter from Frank K. Howard to J. Howard McHenry, Nov. 4, 1862, written from Fort Warren.
    Finding aid available.

582

MacKaye, James Morrison

(1805–1888)   Abolitionist, New York

Papers, 1824–1953. ca. 75 items.

Includes 44 letters to members of the American Freedmen's Inquiry Commission (Dr. Samuel Gridley Howe, Robert Dale Owen, and James M. MacKaye), 1862–63, concerning the condition and treatment of black refugees at Fort Monroe, Va., and various other collection points, the assignment of officers to black regiments, and employment as a residential superintendent of black refugees. Also includes a list of maps and charts furnished to the commission. Correspondents include Francis C. Barlow, LeBaron Russell, Edwin M. Stanton, Charles Sumner, John C. Tucker, and Peter H. Watson.

583

McKean, Thomas Jefferson (ca. 1810–1879)   Gen., USV

Letter, 1864. 1 item.

Letter from McKean to Francisco Moreno, Spanish vice consul at Pensacola, Fla., Dec. 31, 1864, apologizing for Moreno's treatment by Federal soldiers and explaining his government's policy toward noncombatants.

584

McKee, Mary T.   New York

Papers, 1863–64. 5 items.

Account of the imprisonment of John McKee (father of Mary McKee) at Fort Lafayette, N.Y., as a Confederate sympathizer (65 p.); letter from George M. Stoll (CSA) of South Carolina to Mrs. H. A. Barling, Fort Lafayette, May 9, 1864, expressing appreciation for Mrs. Barling's assistance to Confederate prisoners of war; letter, Feb. 2, 1864, concerning military passes to Fort Lafayette; and a sketched emblem of the Knights of the Crimson Cross presented to Mrs. Barling with the signatures of Gens. Franklin Gardner and William Henry Fitzhugh Lee, and others.

585

McKinley, William (1843–1901), Pres., U.S.

Papers, 1847–1902. ca. 131,000 items.

Includes McKinley's discharge as a captain in the 23d Ohio Volunteers, July 26, 1865, a sketch of his military service, and muster-out rolls.

Published index and microfilm copy (98 reels) available.

586

McKinley, William C.   Pvt., 24th Maryland Volunteers

Collection, 1861–62. 13 items.

Letters from McKinley to his wife, Dec. 17, 1861–May 5,

1862, concerning Gen. Ambrose Burnside's expedition to North Carolina. Describes preparations at Annapolis, Md., the landing of troops on Cape Hatteras, N.C., the Battle of Roanoke Island, and the occupation of New Bern. Includes remarks on camp life, disease, casualties, prisoners of war, the attitude of noncombatants in the area, and illiteracy among captured Confederate soldiers.

587
McLennan, Roderick   Engineer, Canada
    Collection, 1864–87. 5 items.
    Photocopies.
    Contains McLennan's parole, Jan. 6, 1864; two passes for travel from Key West, Fla., to New York on the U.S.S. *Continental*; a letter from McLennan to his brother, Dr. Donald McLennan, written from Fort Jefferson, Fla., Nov. 27, 1864; and a postwar letter from McLennan to Donald MacMaster, Dec. 15, 1887, Toronto, Canada, concerning his claims against the United States stemming from his confinement at Fort Jefferson during the Civil War.

588
McManaway, Charles Harvey
(1827–1896)   Sgt., 58th Virginia Regiment
    Account and memo book, 1877–93. 1 v.
    Contains genealogical information on the McManaway family and a description of McManaway's service in the Civil War, particularly during the Shenandoah Valley Campaign of 1862.

589
McMichael, J. C.   5th Regiment,
                                        Pennsylvania Reserve Corps
    Letter, 1862. 1 item.
    Letter from McMichael to his aunt, July 5, 1862, City Point, Va., describing his participation in the battles of Mechanicsville, Gaines Mill, and White Oak Swamp. Includes information on company and regimental casualties and the capture of Gen. George A. McCall.

590
McPherson, Edward
(1830–1895)   U.S. Representative, Pennsylvania
    Papers, 1738–1936. ca. 18,000 items.
    Includes four letters from McPherson to relatives in Pennsylvania, July–Aug. 1861, concerning his service as a volunteer aide to Gen. George A. McCall and as a captain of volunteers assigned to guard railroads in Maryland; and six letters from William Nellis to his family in Pennsylvania written from

Beaufort, S.C., and Jones Landing, Va., Feb.–Nov. 1864, concerning his enlistment in the 29th Connecticut Volunteers, the death of his brother Joseph at Olustee, Fla., the Siege of Beaufort, the Siege of Charleston, S.C., hospital care, and personal needs. Also contains enlistment certificates for Sgt. Randolph Johnston, 27th Regiment, U.S. Colored Troops, and eight volunteers in the 8lst Pennsylvania Volunteers from Cumberland Township, Adams County, Pa.; bounty subscriptions, discharges, and commissions; a list of officers in the 7th Pennsylvania Volunteers; receipts issued to volunteers from Cumberland Township by the Relief Assurance Committee; and postwar clippings, maps, and pamphlets relating to the Battle of Gettysburg.

Finding aid available.

591
McPherson, James Birdseye (1828–1864)   Gen., USV
    Papers, 1848–68. 364 items.

Chiefly personal and official correspondence, telegrams, orders, receipts, quartermaster reports, and ordnance reports. Includes two letters from Lt. James H. Wilson to McPherson, Feb. 20 and Apr. 30, 1862, Port Royal and Hilton Head, S.C., concerning the Siege of Fort Pulaski, military organization, and the generalship of Henry W. Benham, Quincy A. Gillmore, David Hunter, and Thomas W. Sherman; letters from special agents in Louisiana concerning the location, confiscation, and sale of cotton; a report on destitute families in Warren County, Miss., and a summary of rations sold to the citizens of Warren County; a list of quartermaster depots in Mississippi, Nov. 1863; and the signatures of officers in the 7th New Jersey Volunteers and the 30th Illinois Volunteers.

Finding aid available.

592
McPherson, Theodore H. N.   Lt., 107th
                                      Pennsylvania Volunteers
    Collection, 1860–65. 28 items.

Chiefly letters between McPherson and his brothers, George E. (USN) and B. R. McPherson (USN), 1862–63, written from camps in Virginia and aboard the U.S.S. *Norwich*, St. Johns River, Fla. Describes camp life and fortifications along the Potomac River, marches in Virginia, new recruits, morale, and routine duties on the *Norwich*. Also includes a recruiting poster, a duty roster for guards at Camp Curtin, Pa., and McPherson's diary, Oct. 5, 1861–May 19, 1862.

593
Magoffin, Beriah (1815−1885)   Gov., Kentucky
   Letters, 1861. 2 items.
   Letter from Magoffin to Dr. John M. Johnson, May 24,
1861, asking Johnson to present a proclamation of neutrality
at a meeting in Mayfield, Ky., and letter from Magoffin to Gov.
Isham G. Harris of Tennessee, Aug. 12, 1861, assuring Harris
that Union men camped in southern Kentucky would not invade
his State.

594
Magrath, Andrew Gordon
(1813−1893)   Gov., South Carolina
   Collection, 1861−65. 4 items.
   Letters from Magrath to Govs. Joseph E. Brown and
Zebulon B. Vance and Judge Edward Frost concerning mili-
tary organization and supplies, the disposition of troops, and
coastal defenses in South Carolina.

595
Mahan, Alfred Thayer (1840−1914)   Lt., USN
   Papers, 1861−1913. 5 items.
   Letter from Mahan to C. S. Newcome, Oct. 10, 1861, U.S.S.
Pocahontas, on the arrest and imprisonment of secessionist
classmates, the continued presence of southern officers in the
U.S. Navy, attitudes of secessionist women in Maryland, and
the duty stations of mutual friends.
   Naval Historical Foundation collection.

596
Mallory, Stephen Russell
(ca. 1813−1875)   C.S. Secretary of the Navy
   Diary, 1861−66. 2 v.
   Transcript.
   Describes political and social affairs in Richmond, Va., the
progress of the war, the seeming indifference of most Virgin-
ians to the threat of invasion, cabinet meetings, reaction in
Richmond to the policies of Gens. Benjamin F. Butler, David
Hunter, and John W. Phelps, and the deteriorating relation-
ship between President Davis and Gen. Joseph E. Johnston.
Also contains comments on the character of Mrs. Jefferson
Davis, the generalship of P. G. T. Beauregard, the role of Gen.
Leroy Pope Walker as head of the War Department, and naval
affairs.
   Original at the University of North Carolina.

597

Malvern (U.S.S.)
    Notebook, ca. 1863. 1 v.
    Contains regulations for the crew of the U.S.S. *Malvern.*
    Naval Historical Foundation collection.

598

Mangum, Willie Person
(1792–1861)   Jurist, North Carolina
    Papers, 1771–1906. ca. 5,000 items.
    Contains about 200 letters written during the war concerning campaigns in Arkansas and Missouri in 1861, enlistments and training in North Carolina, troop movements, the Battle of 1st Manassas, the death of Mangum's son, William Preston Mangum, camp life, morale, disease, hospital care, prisoners of war, generalship, depredations along the Atlantic coast, fortifications at Memphis, Tenn., and vicinity, the Siege of Petersburg, and the use and abuse of blacks by Confederates. Correspondents include Mangum's brother-in-law James Cain, Col. Wharton Green, Lt. John P. Lockhart, William D. Lunsford, Academus Mangum, Chaplain Addeson M. Mangum, Learned H. Mangum, William Preston Mangum, Josiah Turner, and Maj. Robert F. Webb. Also includes a sketch of the Manassas battlefield.

599

Manigault, Louis (b. ca. 1829)   Medical Assistant, CSA
    Family papers, 1752–1865.
    Microfilm, 1 reel.
    Contains letters of Manigault written partly during his service as secretary to Dr. Joseph Jones concerning conditions at Andersonville Prison, the blockade and bombardment of Charleston, S.C., the death of his brother Alfred (4th South Carolina Cavalry), fortifications in Georgia and South Carolina, and the economic effects of the war; letters of Gabriel E. Manigault (4th South Carolina Cavalry) concerning the engagement at Trevilian Station, prison life at Fort Delaware, and his exchange; and a letter by Alfred Manigault, Oct. 23, 1862, on an engagement at Pocotaligo, S.C. Also includes letters of Dr. Joseph Jones and Dr. Samuel P. Moore (CSA) concerning the administration of the Medical Department and the problem of gangrene among Confederate soldiers and prisoners of war, and letters by Charles Manigault (father of Louis, Gabriel, and Alfred Manigault) describing depredations in Charleston, S.C., and vicinity, the occupation of Charleston, attitudes of noncombatants, and the response of blacks to the war. Miscellaneous items include the diary of Louis Manigault, Nov. 28–Dec. 7, 1863, newspaper clippings, Confederate currency, sketches of Confederate flags, a map of the Savannah River, military

passes, vouchers, certificates, and paroles, letters by Federal soldiers at Andersonville Prison, a pamphlet entitled "Inquiries Upon Hospital Gangrene," by Dr. Joseph Jones, and photographs of Jefferson Davis, Joseph Jones, Alfred and Louis Manigault, and Gens. P G. T. Beauregard, Wade Hampton, Thomas J. Jackson, Joseph E. Johnston, Robert E. Lee, and William T. Sherman.

600
Mann, Mary Tyler Peabody
(1806–1887)   Educator, Massachusetts
     Papers, 1863–76. 75 items.
     Ten letters by Maria R. Mann, Feb. 10–Aug. 14, 1863, describe her work as an agent of the U.S. Sanitary Commission at a freedmen's camp in Helena, Ark. Includes comments on disease and deaths among freedmen, their abuse by soldiers and merchants, black life, efforts to organize black regiments, and the acquisition and distribution of supplies.

601
Mansfield, Joseph King Fenno (1803–1862)   Gen., USA
     Collection, 1853–62. 17 items.
     In part, photocopies.
     Chiefly letters from Mansfield to his wife, Sept. 13, 1861–July 2, 1862, concerning the defense of Washington, D.C., the generalship of George B. McClellan, Mansfield's desire for a field command, the duel between the U.S.S. *Monitor* and C.S.S. *Merrimac* and Mansfield's disagreement with Gen. John Wool over a report on the battle, the attitude of noncombatants in southeast Virginia, the occupation of Norfolk, Va., and routine military affairs at Cape Hatteras, N.C. Also contains a photograph of Mansfield and a telegram from Maj. George D. Ramsay to Mansfield, Aug. 21, 1861, concerning the arrival of arms at the Washington arsenal.

602
Marble, Manton Malone
(1834–1917)   Journalist–Editor, New York
     Papers, 1852–1916. ca. 14,000 items.
     Includes a few letters by soldiers or correspondents in the field concerning the Peninsular and Petersburg campaigns, and miscellaneous letters and documents relating to the U.S. Sanitary Commission.
     Finding aid available.

603
Markland, Absalom H.   Special Agent, U.S. Post Office;
(d. 1888)   Col., USA
    Papers, 1861–1908. ca. 170 items.
    Chiefly letters to Markland from assistant postmasters
John A. Kasson and George W. McLellan concerning the establishment and operation of post offices in federally occupied
territory (Fort Henry, Memphis, and Nashville, Tenn., and New
Orleans, La.), postmaster appointments, mail schedules, traf-
ficking and other irregularities by postal agents, captured Confederate mail, postal receipts, and the delivery of mail to Gen.
William T. Sherman's army during the Atlanta Campaign.
Several letters from Robert C. Gist concern the operation of the
post office at Memphis, Tenn. Also contains an organizational
chart for the Army of the Ohio and miscellaneous telegrams,
receipts, orders, and passes.

604
Marshall, Daniel W. (b. ca. 1830)   Pvt., 1st Rhode
                                            Island Light Artillery
    Papers, 1861–63. 4 items.
    Diary, Jan. 1, 1862–Mar. 8, 1863, kept by Marshall during
the Peninsular and Fredericksburg campaigns; a summary of
Marshall's activities, Aug. 16, 1862–Mar. 8, 1863; furlough
certificate; and military pass, Mar. 7, 1863.

605
Marshall, John Wesley
(1834–1922)   Lt., 97th Ohio Volunteers
    Diary, 1862–65. 1 v.
    Transcript.
    Diary, Sept. 7, 1862–June 10, 1865, kept by Marshall dur-
ing the Stones River Campaign, the Tullahoma, Chickamauga,
Chattanooga, and Atlanta campaigns, and the relief of Knoxville. Includes details on Gen. Braxton Bragg's invasion of
Kentucky, and the Battles of Perryville and Murfreesboro. Also
contains comments on camp life, marches, morale, casualties,
disease, foraging expeditions, supplies, funerals, reenlistments,
Confederate deserters, fortifications around Nashville, Tenn.,
and black camp followers.

606
Marston, John (1796–1885)   Capt., USN
    Papers, 1850–62. ca. 250 items.
    In part, transcripts.
    Chiefly official correspondence, orders, reports, and circu-
lars received by Marston in 1862 as senior officer at Hampton

Roads, Va., and commander of the U.S.S. *Roanoke*. Concerns the Federal blockade, prize vessels *Thomas Watson* and *York*, training, discipline, discharges, desertions, deaths, prisoner exchange, the health of sailors, ship repairs, supplies, the Roanoke Island expedition, and the sinking of the U.S.S. *Cumberland*. Correspondents include James F. Armstrong, John S. Chauncey, Louis M. Goldsborough, Charles Green, Samuel P. Lee, John W. Livingston, Garrett J. Pendergast, William H. Seward, Gideon Welles, and John E. Wool.

Naval Historical Foundation collection.

607

Mart, Charles   Capt., USA
    Certificate, 1863. 1 item.
    Ration certificate for Katharina Keorper, wife of Pvt. Jacob Keorper, 1st Louisiana Volunteers, issued after her husband was wounded at Port Hudson, La.

608

Mason, James Murray (1798–1871)   C.S. Diplomat
    Papers, 1838–70. ca. 3,600 items.
    In part, transcripts and photocopies.
    Contains instructions to Mason from Confederate secretaries Robert M. Hunter and Judah P. Benjamin and assistant secretary William M. Browne; letters and extracts of letters to Mason from the British Foreign Office; dispatches to Mason concerning Confederate victories, the conduct of the war, policy toward Great Britain, and the Federal blockade; correspondence on the *Trent* affair; the log of H.M.S. *Rinaldo*, Jan. 1–14, 1862; letters and documents concerning British merchant vessels; reports on British ships captured or destroyed by the U.S. Blockading Squadron; a report on the attack of the C.S.S. *Merrimac* on Federal ships in Hampton Roads, Mar. 8, 1862; letters to Mason from officers commanding Confederate ships in European waters concerning fuel; and a letterbook, Feb. 2, 1862–May 1, 1865. Correspondents include Judah P. Benjamin, William M. Browne, James D. Bulloch, Robert M. Hunter, W. S. Lindsay, Ambrose Dudley Mann, P. C. Martin, Christopher G. Memminger, Lord John Russell, John Slidell, and James Spence.

609

Massachusetts
    Civil War records, 1861–64. 10 items.
    Contains a list of volunteers from North Reading in the 32d, 33d, and 35th Massachusetts Volunteers, July 10, 1862; a list of volunteers from North Reading in Company D, 50th Massachusetts, Sept. 19, 1862; a partial list of volunteers in

Company E, 39th Massachusetts, Sept. 5, 1862; muster rolls for Companies A and G, 59th Massachusetts, 1864; and pay records for Company F, 13th Massachusetts, 1862–64. Also, a volume begun as a "Complete Record of the Names of all the Soldiers and Officers in the Military Service and of all the Seamen and Officers in the Naval Service of the United States, during the Rebellion begun in 1861," but containing the names and abbreviated service records of only 113 men.

610
Massey, R. H.   Capt., Chaplain, 40th Illinois Volunteers
    Collection, 1863–64. 15 items.
    Consists of a report by Massey on the condition and service of the 40th Illinois during the Atlanta Campaign; a list of the soldiers in the 40th Illinois killed or wounded in the Battle of Resaca; an inventory of the effects of Lt. Col. R. L. Barnhill, who was killed at Kennesaw Mountain; a copy of a war correspondent's report on the Battle of Kennesaw Mountain; an inventory of equipment in Massey's charge; orders concerning reenlistments and the property and treatment of noncombatants; and a letter from Massey to President Lincoln, May 28, 1863, La Grange, Tenn., requesting permission to organize and command a black regiment.

611
Matthewson, Arthur (1837–1920)   Surg., USN
    Papers, 1861–65. 9 items.
    Official correspondence concerning duty assignments, commissions, and examinations for promotion. Correspondents include Thornton A. Jenkins, Gideon Welles, and William Whelan.
    Naval Historical Foundation collection.

612
Maury, Betty Herndon (1835–1903)   Fredericksburg, Va.
    Diary, 1861–63. 1 v.
    Provides comments on Maury's move from Washington, D.C., to Fredericksburg in 1861, preparations for war in Virginia, jealousy between regular and volunteer forces, contributions of Confederate women to the war effort, disagreement between Matthew F. Maury and President Davis, efforts by M. F. Maury to torpedo Federal vessels on the Potomac and James Rivers, popular support for the war, inflation, troop movements, raids and skirmishes in the area around Fredericksburg, the occupation of Falmouth and Fredericksburg, the suffering of noncombatants, black life, and the response of blacks to the war.
    Microfilm copy (1 reel) available.

613

Maury, Dabney Herndon (1822–1900)   CSA
    Collection, 1862. 2 items.

    Letter from Maury to Gen. Earl Van Dorn, June 25, 1862, concerning the disposition of Union troops in northern Mississippi and Alabama, Confederate supplies, and rumors of the removal or resignation of Gen. P. G. T. Beauregard; letter from Maury to Van Dorn, July 8, 1862, on the strength of Gen. Sterling Price's division, reinforcements, and generalship in the Confederate Army.

614

Maury, Matthew Fontaine   Comdr., CSN; Special Agent
(1806–1873)   to Great Britain
    Papers, 1825–1927. ca. 14,500 items.

    Includes correspondence of Maury concerning the secession crisis, an invitation to make his home in Russia, the manufacture of torpedoes, plans for the construction of gunboats and shore batteries in Virginia, the acquisition of ships for the Confederate Navy, the security of his family, and affairs in Richmond, Va.; letters of William A. Maury concerning the situation in Richmond and his appointment to a military court; letters of Gen. Dabney H. Maury and other members of the Maury family concerning the location or possible death of Lt. John H. Maury; miscellaneous letters concerning the suffering of noncombatants in Virginia, plundering by Federal soldiers, the capture and burning of Richmond, and the attitude of the South in defeat. Also contains about 30 letters of Maj. Richard L. Maury (24th Virginia Regiment) written chiefly to his mother describing camp life, training, discipline, enlistments, military organization, entertainment, the economic effects of the war, skirmishes in northern Virginia, the Siege of Richmond, and the character and behavior of Confederate soldiers. Additional items comprise letters received by M. F. Maury as special Confederate agent in London and as an immigration official for southern expatriates in Mexico.

    Finding aid available.

615

May, John Frederick (1812–1891)   Physician
    Essay, 1887. 1 item.

    Manuscript essay, "The Mark of the Scalpel," recounting May's identification of the body of John Wilkes Booth, a former patient, and arguing that Booth was insane when he shot President Lincoln.

616
Mayo, Joseph (1795–1872)   Mayor, Richmond, Va.
    Letter, 1865. 1 item.
    Transcript.
    Letter from Mayo to Gen. Godfrey Weitzel, Apr. 3, 1865, surrendering the city of Richmond to Union forces.

617
Mazzini, Giuseppe
(1805–1872)   Revolutionist–Journalist, Italy
    Collection, undated. 4 items.
    Autograph literary manuscript, "La Concordia," in Italian, bound, donated by Mazzini during the Civil War to be sold for the benefit of wounded soldiers. Includes an English translation and two engravings and one photograph of Mazzini.

618
Mead, Rufus (1836–1922)   Sgt., 5th
                                  Connecticut Volunteers
    Papers, 1861–1943. 233 items.
    Chiefly letters from Mead to his brother David and various members of the Mead family, May 25, 1861–May 9, 1865, concerning the Commissary Department, sutlers, casualties, morale, marches, plundering by Federal soldiers, enlistments, training, camp life, diet, disease, prisoners of war, generalship in the Union Army, the attitude of noncombatants in the South, and the changing attitude of Federal soldiers toward southerners. Also describes the Battle of Chancellorsville, the Atlanta Campaign, the Savannah Campaign, and the Shenandoah Valley Campaign of 1862, particularly the Battle of Winchester, and the activities of Unionists in Atlanta. A diary (5 v.), Aug. 28, 1861–May 29, 1865, contains remarks on the arrest of two female soldiers, Unionists in Virginia, the arrest of Confederate spies, reconnaissance balloons, Union morale after the 2d Manassas Campaign, foraging expeditions, depredations by Federal soldiers, the Antietam, Gettysburg, and Carolinas campaigns, and operations along the Rapidan and Rappahannock Rivers in late 1863. Also includes a biographical sketch of Mead written in 1943 by Mrs. Jennie C. Mead.

619
Meade, William (1789–1862)   Episcopal Bishop, Virginia
    Papers, 1822–62. 50 items.
    Contains 11 letters from Meade to John Stewart of Richmond, Va., written from Millwood, Meade's home in Clark County, Va., July 1861–Jan. 1862, concerning Federal and Confederate strategy in the Battle of 1st Manassas, troop movements and skirmishes in the Shenandoah Valley, the activities of J. E. B. Stuart, generalship and morale in the Confederate

Army, depredations, casualties among volunteers from Clark County, and the care of sick and wounded soldiers.

620

Meagher, Thomas Francis (1823–1867)   Gen., USV
    Collection, 1859–65. 3 items.
    Letter from Meagher to John F. Coyle, New York, Sept. 27, 1861, concerning the appointment of sutlers for the 4th and 5th New York Volunteers and Meagher's reasons for entering the Army. Also includes a pass issued to Meagher, Apr. 23, 1865, to serve as an honor guard for the body of President Lincoln.

621

Mearns, Edgar Alexander (1856–1916)
    Papers, 1864–1918. ca. 5,850 items.
    Includes a letter by Gen. John A. Dix, Oct. 20, 1864.
    Finding aid available.

622

Meigs, Montgomery Cunningham
(1816–1892)   Q.M. Gen., USA
    Papers, 1849–1968. ca. 4,000 items.
    In part, transcripts.
    Includes two letterbooks, Apr. 1, 1861–Feb. 26, 1862, and Apr. 2–29, 1864, containing copies of incoming and outgoing correspondence; newspaper clippings relating to the war; a pamphlet: *Instructions for Officers on Outpost and Patrol Duty*; sketches of portable barracks and war scenes; notes on equipment and supplies; miscellaneous accounts; a report on the death of Meigs' son, Lt. John Rodgers Meigs; remarks on the economic effects of the war and the changing attitudes of Federal soldiers toward the South; and a diary, 1861–64, containing brief references to Cabinet meetings, conferences with Gens. Ambrose E. Burnside, Henry W. Halleck, George B. McClellan, William S. Rosecrans, William T. Sherman, and others, trips to the front lines, inspection tours, and problems with Secretary Stanton over fraud in the Quartermaster Department.
    Finding aid available.

623

Meigs, Return Jonathan (1740–1823)   Tennessee
    Family papers, 1772–1862. 72 items.
    Includes a letter by Return J. Meigs (1801–1891), Feb. 10, 1861, Nashville, concerning Unionist sentiment in Tennessee and public rejoicing in Nashville over the apparent Union victory in the election of delegates to the State convention.
    Microfilm copy (1 reel) available.

Montgomery Cunningham Meigs

624

Méjan, Eugene   French Consul, New Orleans, La.
    Papers, 1862. 85 items.
    Chiefly correspondence and reports of Méjan, Gov. Thomas
O. Moore, Mayor John J. Monroe, and various officers of the
French brigade, Feb.–May 1862, concerning the service of foreign volunteer organizations in New Orleans before and during the Federal occupation, efforts to maintain French neutrality,
and the departure of the steamer *Milan.* Also includes Adm.
David G. Farragut's assurance not to interfere with the foreign
police guard in New Orleans. Largely in French.

625

Meredith, William D. (b. 1844)   Pvt.,
                                        134th Indiana Volunteers
    Documents, 1864. 2 items.
    Discharge, Sept. 2, 1864, and certificate of honorable
service, Dec. 15, 1864.

626

Merwin, James Burtis (1829–1917)   Chaplain, USA
    Collection, 1861–1910. 6 items.
    Transcripts and facsimiles.
    Diary, May 10–Sept. 5, 1864, describing Merwin's service
aboard the hospital ship *Thomas P. Way,* the arrival and care
of wounded soldiers at the "Transit Hospital" at Willets Point,
N.Y., the dispersal of convalescents to hospitals from Maine to
New Jersey, efforts to locate missing and wounded soldiers,
and efforts to notify the families of deceased soldiers. Also contains a copy of a letter by Merwin, July 5, 1910, concerning a
discussion he witnessed between President Lincoln and Gen.
Benjamin F. Butler on what to do with 180,000 black soldiers
after the war; facsimiles of orders issued by Gen. Winfield
Scott and President Lincoln granting Merwin free access to
military camps; copy of an order by Charles McDougall, May
19, 1863; and a published postwar photograph of Mervin.

627

Miers, Earl Schenck (1910–1972)   Editor; Author
    Papers, 1951–60. 3 items.
    Manuscripts of *The General Who Marched to Hell; William
Tecumseh Sherman and His March to Fame and Infamy* (1951),
The Web of Victory; Grant at Vicksburg (1955); and Miers and
Paul M. Angle, *The Tragic Years, 1860–1865; a Documentary
History of the American Civil War* (1960).

628

Miles, William Porcher (1822–1899)   C.S. Representative, South Carolina

   Collection, 1861. 1 item.
   Transcript.
   Letter from Miles to Gov. Francis W. Pickens, Feb. 9, 1861, Montgomery, Ala., announcing the selection of Jefferson Davis as President of the new Confederate States of America and Alexander Stephens as Vice President, and urging delay in the planned attack on Fort Sumter.

629

Miles—Cameron Families

   Correspondence, 1860–1945. ca. 1,000 items.
   Includes a few letters to Gen. Nelson A. Miles (1839–1925), 1863–65. Correspondents include Thomas C. Cox and Gens. John C. Caldwell and Winfield Scott Hancock.
   Finding aid available.

630

Miller, Allen Woods
(ca. 1834–1864)   Capt., 36th Iowa Volunteers

   Diary, 1863–1940. 1 v.
   Transcript.
   Covers the period Jan. 1, 1863–Aug. 18, 1864. Describes troop movements along the Mississippi River between Memphis, Tenn., and Helena, Ark., the Yazoo Pass expedition, the Battle of Fort Pemberton, Miller's capture at Moro Creek, Ark., Apr. 25, 1864, his suffering as a prisoner of war near Starrville, Tex., and his escape and flight north through Arkansas. Includes an introductory biographical statement prepared by Miller's grandnephew, L. S. Shockley, Dec. 26, 1940.

631

Miller, Marshall Mortimer
(b. 1827)   1st Lt., 1st Michigan Light Artillery

   Collection, 1862–1903. ca. 50 items.
   Transcripts and photocopies.
   Chiefly letters from Miller to his wife and family, Mar. 26, 1862–June 24, 1865, concerning the role of the 1st Michigan Light Artillery in Kirby-Smith's invasion of Kentucky, the Siege of Knoxville, and the Atlanta, Franklin and Nashville, and Carolinas campaigns. Provides details on the Battle of Richmond, Ky., in which Miller was wounded and captured, skirmishes and battles in the Atlanta Campaign, discipline, morale, training, diet, entertainment, foraging expeditions, depredations, guerrilla warfare, Confederate deserters, casualties, disease, generalship, and the treatment of noncombatants. Also

contains a wartime photograph of Miller and photocopies of his commission, parole, and service record.

632
Milton, George Fort (1894–1955)   Journalist; Author
        Papers, 1828–1963. ca. 30,000 items.
        Includes source material and notes for *The Eve of Conflict* (1934), and *Abraham Lincoln and the Fifth Column* (1942).
        Finding aid available.

633
Minor, Mary and Marietta
        Pass, 1863. 1 item.
        Military pass issued to Mary and Marietta Minor to travel from Washington, D.C., to Virginia and return, Nov. 23, 1863.

634
Minor, Smith
        Pass, 1865. 1 item.
        Military pass issued to Smith Minor to travel from Washington, D.C., to Virginia and return, May 5, 1865.

635
Mitchell, Benjamin   Comdr., USN
        Papers, 1861–1926. ca. 200 items.
        Chiefly orders, circulars, court records, reports, correspondence, and miscellaneous items relating to Mitchell's service as acting ensign on the U.S.S. *Ottawa* and commander of the U.S.S. *Clover*, South Atlantic Blockading Squadron. Contains information on the disposition of various ships in the squadron, skirmishes with shore batteries, the loss of the U.S.S. *Water Witch*, training, discipline, and sanitation aboard naval vessels, prisoners of war, promotions, discharges, ship repairs, and deaths.

636
Mitchell, Charles D.   Lt., USA
        Memoir, 1865. 1 item.
        Transcript.
        "Extract From Field Notes of the Civil War: The Selma Campaign," Mar. 15–May 14 [1865]. Describes Mitchell's service on the headquarters staff of Gen. Andrew J. Alexander, preparations for the Selma Campaign, skirmishes at Montevallo and Selma, Ala., and Columbus, Ga., the occupation of Montgomery, Ala., and Macon, Ga., depredations, foraging expeditions, the attitude and suffering of noncombatants, Confederate deserters, black life, the recruitment and organization of

black troops, and relations between returning Confederate soldiers and Union troops immediately following the cessation of hostilities.

637
Mitchell, James B.   1st Lt., 34th Alabama Volunteers
    Papers, 1859–1913. 65 items.
    Chiefly letters from Mitchell to his parents written during campaigns in Tennessee and Mississippi, 1862–63, and as a prisoner of war at Johnson's Island, Ohio, 1864–65. Includes a detailed account of the participation of the 34th Alabama in the Battle of Stones River (Murfreesboro), and comments on military leadership, training, camp life, morale, supplies, casualties, entertainment, disease, and prison life.

638
Mitchell, James S.   1st Lt., 84th Pennsylvania Volunteers
    Papers, 1864. 6 items.
    Invoices and returns of ordnance and ordnance stores received by Mitchell during the Siege of Petersburg, Va., Dec. 1864, and a military pass, July 8, 1864.

639
Mitchell, Marcellus   11th Illinois Cavalry
    Letters, 1864, 1865. 2 items.
    Letters from Mitchell to "Rebecca," Sept. 18, 1864, Vicksburg, Miss., and Sept. 11, 1865, La Grange, Tenn.

640
Montgomery, James H. (b. 1833)   Capt., 33d Ohio Volunteers
    Diary, 1862–64. 3 v.
    Describes operations in Kentucky and Tennessee in 1862, the Stones River Campaign, the occupation of Huntsville, Ala., and the Atlanta Campaign. Includes details on the Battle of Murfreesboro; comments on camp life, marches, training, discipline, entertainment, casualties, disease, hospital care, prisoners of war, furloughs, and the death of Gen. William Nelson; and miscellaneous accounts and notes.

641
Montgomery Family
    Papers, 1771–1974. ca. 12,000 items.
    Includes about 40 letters from Lt. Col. Frank Henry Peck, 12th Connecticut Volunteers, to his parents and relatives, 1862–64, and 135 letters from Col. Newton W. Perkins, 13th Connecticut Volunteers, to his mother, 1862–65, written chiefly during campaigns in southern Louisiana and the Shenandoah Valley Campaign of 1864. Provides details on the capture of

Forts Jackson and St. Philip, the occupation of New Orleans, reconnaissance expeditions and skirmishes west of New Orleans, the Port Hudson Campaign, and the Red River campaigns of 1863 and 1864. Also describes camp life, training, marches, discipline, military supply, entertainment, guerrilla warfare, foraging expeditions, depredations, the attitude and treatment of noncombatants, resistance to conscription in the North, disease, hospital care, black life, the recruitment and performance of black soldiers, Confederate deserters, prisoners of war, and the generalship of Nathaniel P. Banks, Benjamin F. Butler, Edward R. S. Canby, Philip H. Sheridan, and Godfrey Weitzel.

Finding aid available.

642

Moran, Benjamin (1820–1886)   U.S. Diplomat, London
Diary, 1851–75. 44 v.

Describes conversations or chance meetings with American secessionists in England, instructions from the U.S. Government, the arrival of Confederate warships and privateers (some with prizes), British reaction to the war and to Confederate privateering in European waters, the activities of Confederate emissaries, problems over the Federal blockade, and numerous related matters.

643

——

Letter, 1864. 1 item.

Letter from Moran to Comdr. George H. Preble, Jan. 4, 1864, concerning the possible closure of British ports to both Union and Confederate vessels, the changing attitude of "John Bull" toward the U.S. Government, and the presence of the C.S.S. *Florida*, C.S.S. *Rappahannock*, and C.S.S. *Georgia* (ex-*Japan*) in France.

644

Moran, Frank E. (d. 1892)
Collection, undated. 1 item.

Account of the role of Col. Ulric Dahlgren in the abortive Kilpatrick–Dahlgren raid on Richmond, Va., Feb. 28–Mar. 4, 1864. Taken in part from the statement of Lt. [Reuben?] Bartly, Colonel Dahlgren's signal officer, and in part from the memoir of Adm. John A. Dahlgren.

645

Mordecai, Alfred (1804–1887)   Maj., USA
Papers, 1790–1948. ca. 3,700 items.

Contains several letters from Mordecai to his family and

friends, May 1861, concerning his decision to resign from the U.S. Army; letters to Mordecai from various officers expressing their dilemma over the war and their reasons either for resigning their commissions or remaining in service; letters to Mordecai from his sister Ellen in Richmond, Va., concerning friends and relatives in the Confederate Army, public morale, and efforts by women in Richmond to manufacture tents and uniforms; and two letters to Mordecai from his son, Lt. Alfred Mordecai II, Apr. 16, 1864, Hilton Head, S.C., and July 31, 1864, Bermuda Hundred, Va., on camp life and the Siege of Petersburg.

646
More, E. J.   Pennsylvania Militia
    Collection, 1836–77. 20 items.
    Photocopies.
    Includes four letters from More to his wife, June 16–21, 1863, Harrisburg, Pa., on camp life, fortifications, Confederate prisoners of war, and a black company from Philadelphia during the early stages of the Gettysburg Campaign, and seven letters written from Harrisburg, Allentown, and Norristown, Pa., and Washington, D.C., Feb. 22–June 7, 1864, on the overall military situation and political affairs in Washington. Also contains a letter by Emanuel Lookingbeal, 4th Maryland Volunteers, Mar. 1, 1865.

647
Moreno, Francisco   Spanish Vice Consul, Pensacola, Fla.
    Collection, 1864. 1 item.
    Transcript.
    Letter from Moreno to Gen. Thomas J. McKean, Dec. 28, 1864, Pensacola, Fla., protesting his treatment at the hands of black soldiers.

648
Morgan, George Washington (1820–1893)   Gen., USA
    Collection, 1849 and undated. 2 items.
    Includes a photocopy of a biographical sketch of General Morgan (23 p.), with remarks on the capture of Cumberland Gap, the Battle of Chickasaw Bluffs, the Arkansas Post (Fort Hindman) expedition, and the use of black troops.

649
Morgan, James Morris (1845–1928)   Midshipman, CSN
    Manuscript, undated. 8 p.
    Transcript.
    Concerns Clarence Cary's tours of duty on the C.S.S. *Nashville,* C.S.S. *Mississippi*, C.S.S. *Chickamauga*, and C.S.S.

Teaser, and at Fort Jackson, La., and Fort Fisher, N.C. Constitutes p. 17–24 of an unidentified larger work.
    Naval Historical Foundation collection.

650

Morley, Edward Williams   Scientist; Official,
(1838–1923)   U.S. Sanitary Commission
    Papers, 1833–1923. ca. 1,200 items.
    Contains about 50 letters from Morley to his family written from Fort Monroe, Va., and vicinity, Oct. 11, 1864–June 13, 1865, concerning the work of the Sanitary Commission, relations between commission officials and hospital surgeons, hospital management, the care of sick and wounded soldiers, camp life, medical supplies, the attitude of noncombatants in southeast Virginia, the treatment of Jefferson Davis during his confinement at Fort Monroe, Confederate prisoners of war, problems with black soldiers, the arrest of several members of the "Knights of the Golden Circle," reaction among soldiers and civilians to the Lincoln assassination, and the arrest of Samuel Arnold, an accomplice of John Wilkes Booth. Also contains a few letters by Pvt. Myron A. Munson (USA) on camp life and training in Indiana and Maryland.
    Finding aid available.

651

Morrell, Charles W.   USA
    Letters, 1864–65. 3 items.
    Transcripts.
    Letters from Morrell to his brother, Aug. 23, 1864–Apr. 17, 1865, describing the Siege of Petersburg, the capture of Richmond, Va., and the reaction in Richmond to the assassination of President Lincoln.

652

Morrill, Justin Smith
(1810–1898)   U.S. Representative, Vermont
    Papers, 1825–1923. ca. 10,600 items.
    Includes a letter from Lt. Col. Oscar A. Hale, 6th Vermont Volunteers, to Morrill, May 21, 1864, concerning the death of Col. Elisha L. Barney, casualties and reenforcements in the 6th Vermont, and his desire for promotion. Also contains several letters from Vermont soldiers seeking commissions or reporting the results of the 1864 Presidential election among the Vermont troops.
    Finding aid and microfilm copy (52 reels) available.

653

Morris, Martha Elizabeth Wright (d. 1919)
    Papers, 1911–30. 3 items.
    Draft of an address given by Martha Morris in 1916, with additions to 1919, describing various war-related experiences, i.e., her acquaintance with the Confederate spy, Rose O'Neal Greenhow, casual meetings with President Lincoln, life in New Orleans, La., under the military governorship of Gen. Nathaniel P. Banks, and her work with the U.S. Sanitary Commission. Also contains a clipping with a picture of Mrs. Greenhow and her daughter.

654

Morris—Popham Families
    Papers, 1667–1892. ca. 770 items.
    Contains three letters from Charles Fleming to his parents, May–July 1861, concerning camp life and training at the Washington Navy Yard; and a letter by Charles R. Carmer(?), 71st New York State Militia, Aug. 5, 1862.
    Finding aid available.

655

Morse, Samuel Finley Breese
(1791–1872)   Artist; Inventor
    Papers, 1793–1944. ca. 10,000 items.
    Includes a few letters to Morse concerning the effect of the war on his business interests in the South, chiefly the confiscation of telegraph equipment by Confederate authorities.
    Finding aid and microfilm copy (35 reels) available.

656

Morse Family
    Papers, 1806–65. ca. 75 items.
    Contains the commission of Charles N. Morse as 1st lieutenant in the 1st Louisiana Artillery Regiment, Apr. 17, 1862; miscellaneous orders; an ordnance invoice; and printed rules and regulations concerning ordnance.

657

Mosby, John Singleton (1833–1916)   Partisan Ranger;
                                         Col., Virginia Cavalry
    Papers, 1861–86. 70 items.
    Photocopies.
    Correspondence, orders, commissions, reports, and circulars concerning the organization and activities of Mosby's Rangers. Contains remarks on public enthusiasm for the war in 1861, the treatment of prisoners of war, casualties, the death of Maj. John Pelham, the capture of Gen. Edwin H. Stoughton,

and raids and skirmishes in northern Virginia. Correspondents include Gens. J. E. B. Stuart and Robert E. Lee, and Henry E. Peyton.

658
Moss, Helen Palmer Hess (1840–1931)   Washington, D.C.
    Descriptive account, undated. 1 item.
    Transcript.
    Describes chance meetings with President Lincoln and John Wilkes Booth on Apr. 14, 1865, and reaction in Washington to Lincoln's assassination.

659
Myer, Albert James
(1829–1880)   Col.; Chief Signal Officer, USA
    Papers, 1851–1933. ca. 300 items.
    Contains 20 letters from Myer to his wife, 1862–65, concerning the organization and performance of the Signal Corps, particularly in the coordination of land and sea forces during the Peninsular Campaign and the Red River Campaign of 1864, camp life, morale, the Seven Days' Battles, competition from the "Telegraph and Railroad Combination," and the generalship of Edward Canby. Also includes photographs of Myer and his staff and of a reconnaissance balloon taken during the Peninsular Campaign; the *Annual Report of the Signal Officer of the Army to the Secretary of War* (1863); and an article on "The Army Signal Corps," published in the *Philadelphia Press* [1862].
    Finding aid and microfilm copy (1 reel) available.

660
———
    Papers, 1816–80.
    Microfilm, 4 reels.
    Official and personal correspondence, general and special orders, photographs, printed matter, and miscellaneous items. Includes a plan for increasing the Regular Army, May 1861; remarks on the resignations of southern officers from the U.S. Army at the outset of the war; instructions in the use of signals; photographs of the Signal Corps headquarters staff; and a pamphlet, *The Spirit of Washington: or McClellan's Vision. A Wonderful Revelation of the Present Rebellion* (1862). Correspondents include Samuel Cushing, J. L. Donaldson, James A. Hardie, Andrew Harwood, Leonard F. Hephorn, and Gideon Welles.
    Finding aid available.
    Originals at the U.S. Army Signal Corps Museum, Fort Monmouth, N.J.

661

Neely, McGinley M.   Capt., 16th Kansas Cavalry
    Papers, 1863–65. 16 items.
    Miscellaneous commissions and orders, official abbrevia-
tions and orders concerning the "Signal Detachment," accounts
for the Department of Kansas, "Rules and Explanations for the
Use of Cipher Discs," and photographs of Neely and Capt. John
R. Wright, 2d Colorado Cavalry.

662

Nelson, Thomas Henry
(1823–1896)   Lawyer; U.S. Minister to Chile
    Papers, 1861–66. ca. 1,000 items.
    Transcripts.
    Chiefly correspondence, instructions, and dispatches with
enclosures between Secretary of State William H. Seward and
Nelson concerning U.S.–Chilean relations, the outfitting of
privateers in Chile for use by the Confederacy, the offer of a
loan to the Confederacy by a private firm, and the defense of
American institutions.
    Microfilm copy (1 reel) available.

663

New Jersey Infantry—7th Regiment   USA
    Records, 1862–64. 9 items.
    Muster rolls for Company K, 7th New Jersey Regiment,
Oct. 1862–Feb. 1864.

664

New York—5th Cavalry   USA
    Orderly book, 1861–62. 1 v.
    Contains general, special, and regimental orders; proceed-
ings for military courts; lists of signals; and guard rosters,
Aug. 16, 1861–May 19, 1862.

665

New York City—Draft Board
    Records, 1861–63. 83 items.
    Applications, affidavits, and miscellaneous items relating
to exemption from military service due to physical disability.

666

New York State Volunteers—16th Regiment
    Diary, 1861–62. 1 v.
    Probably the diary of the regiment quartermaster, A. P.
Smith, Sept. 1861–Nov. 1862. Describes the enlistment and
organization of the 16th New York, camp life, marches, discipline, disease, diet, training, morale, the reaction of soldiers to

orders for the return of runaway slaves, the attitude of noncombatants in Virginia, reconnaissance expeditions, and black life.

667
Newburger, Alexander (b. 1842?)   Lt., 4th
                                              New York Cavalry
    Diary, 1864. 1 v.
    Diary, Apr.–July 1864, kept by Newburger during the Wilderness, Spotsylvania, and Cold Harbor campaigns. Contains comments on camp life, marches, skirmishes, casualties, prisoners of war, entertainment (gambling, drinking, and horse racing), guerrilla warfare, hospital care, the acquisition and distribution of supplies, and the use of blacks in the Army of the Potomac.
    Microfilm copy (1 reel) available.

668
Newcomb, Simon (1835–1909)   Scientist
    Papers, 1854–1936. ca. 46,000 items.
    Diaries kept by Newcomb during the war contain some information on the progress of the war and political and military affairs in Washington, D.C.
    Finding aid available.

669
Newlin, William Henry   1st Lt., 73d Illinois Volunteers
    Manuscript, 1907. 1 item.
    Manuscript, "The North Western Confederacy," concerning the hope of Confederate officers for an alliance with people living in the region drained by the Mississippi and Ohio Rivers. Ascribes the frustration of this alliance to the action of Gen. Emerson Opdycke's brigade at the Battle of Franklin, Tenn., Nov. 30, 1864. Also contains remarks by Lt. William R. Lawrence, 73d Illinois, on life as a prisoner of war at Atlanta, Ga., in 1863.

670
Newman, G. W.   Physician, Louisiana
    Papers, 1863–65. 5 items.
    Includes three orders concerning Newman's service in the examination of conscripts.

671
Nichols, Charles Henry   Supt., St. Elizabeths Hospital,
(1820–1889)   Washington, D.C.
    Papers, 1857–83. 82 items.
    Contains about 40 letters to Nichols concerning the Battle of 1st Manassas, generalship in the Union Army, the promo-

tion and assignment of officers, insane soldiers sent to St. Elizabeths, black troops at Fort St. Johns, La., the performance of the 16th Maine Volunteers in the Battle of Fredericksburg and in campaigns in Louisiana and Mississippi, problems with sutlers, and military pay. Correspondents include Daniel Butterfield, William Dwight, Joseph Hooker, John H. Varney, and Robert C. Wood.

672

Nicholson, Robert Livingston (b. 1883)   Writer; Collector
      Collection, 1940–45. 32 items.
      Transcripts.
      Includes sketches of Gens. P. G. T. Beauregard, Albert Sidney Johnston, Joseph E. Johnston, and Robert E. Lee; notes on Gen. Philip Sheridan's horse Rienzi; notes on the number of soldiers in the Union Army between 10 and 21 years of age; and part of the memoir of Mrs. Louise Babcock Clack (1830–1901) concerning her escape from New Orleans during the Federal occupation, her flight from Columbia, S.C., before Sherman's army, and her sojourn at Warm Springs, Ga., with numerous other refugees. Also describes the smuggling of contraband in Louisiana, Confederate morale, women's life during the war, depredations, inflation, and transportation.

673

Nicholson, Sommerville (1822–1905)   Lt., USN
      Papers, 1839–81. 70 items.
      Contains about 30 items relating to the war, chiefly official correspondence, orders, reports, and memoranda concerning Nicholson's command of the U.S.S. *Marblehead* and U.S.S. *Galatea,* 1861–65. Correspondents include Samuel F. Du Pont, Louis M. Goldsborough, John S. Missroon, Joseph P. Sanford, Cornelius K. Stribling, and Gideon Welles.
      Naval Historical Foundation collection.

674

Nicolay, John George   Private Secretary to President
(1832–1901)   Lincoln; Historian
      Papers, 1811–1943. ca. 5,500 items.
      Includes correspondence, notebooks, scrapbooks, and miscellaneous material relating to Nicolay's tenure as secretary to President Lincoln and research notes for his works on Lincoln.
      Finding aid available.

675

Niles, Peter H.   Signal Corps,
                                    23d Massachusetts Volunteers
    Diary, 1862. 1 v.
    Chiefly describes General Burnside's expedition to North
Carolina. Includes a few details on the Battle of New Bern and
the Siege of Beaufort, N.C.

676

Noble, John Willock (1831–1912)
    Certificate, 1891. 1 item.
    Pension certificate for Pvt. George W. Gray, 125th and 82d
Pennsylvania Volunteers, signed by Secretary of Interior Noble
on Dec. 16, 1891.

677

North Carolina Infantry—11th Regiment   CSA
    Records, 1863–64. 3 items.
    Clothing receipts for Companies B and K, Feb.–Mar. 1864,
and muster roll and payroll for Company A, Oct. 1863. Identifies a few sick, wounded, and captured soldiers.

678

Noyes, Isaac R.   New Jersey
    Collection, 1864. 1 item.
    Letter from Noyes to Rev. George Allen of Worcester, Mass.,
May 3, 1864, expressing sympathy over the death of Allen's
son, George Allen, Jr., in the war.

679

Nye, James Warren (1814–1876)   Maj., Washington
                                              Clay Guards
    Letter, 1861. 1 item.
    Photocopy of a transcript.
    Letter from Nye to Simon Cameron, Apr. 27, 1861, Wash-
ington, D.C., asking that the Washington Clay Guards be
allowed to return to their homes.

680

Ogden, Robert Curtis
(1836–1913)   Businessman; Philanthropist
    Papers, 1843–1913. ca. 10,000 items.
    In part, transcripts.
    Includes three letters from Adrian R. Root (lt. colonel,
21st New York Volunteers, and colonel, 94th New York Volunteers) to Ogden, 1861–63, written from various camps in
Virginia; three letters from Charles E. Benson (7th Michigan
Volunteers) to Ogden, 1862–64, concerning camp life and

morale among Union soliders in Virginia; a letter from James M. Green (48th New York Volunteers) to Ogden, Feb. 22, 1862, Daufuskie Island, S.C., on the Port Royal expedition, fortifications, the Siege of Fort Pulaski, and black life; and a letter from John B. Lord to Ogden, Jan. 28, 1862, Paducah [Ky.], describing camp life, morale, marches, and entertainment.

Finding aid available.

681
Old, William W.   Capt., CSA
     Diary, 1864. 9 p.
     Describes maneuvers and skirmishes in Maryland and Virginia, June–Aug. 1864, including Gen. Jubal A. Early's Washington raid and the Shenandoah Valley Campaign of 1864. Also contains a few comments on the movements of Gens. John C. Breckinridge, John B. Gordon, John D. Imboden, Stephen D. Ramseur, and Robert E. Rodes.

682
Oliphant, Benjamin F. and Catherine (d. 1916)
     Papers, 1861–1916. 22 items.
     Contains Benjamin Oliphant's commission as 1st sergeant in the 3d Maryland Volunteers, July 2, 1864; discharges of both Oliphant and his wife Catherine, a laundress and nurse with the 3d Maryland during the Red River Campaign; a military pass; signed statements attesting to the service and character of both Benjamin and Catherine Oliphant; and postwar correspondence concerning a military pension for Catherine Oliphant.

683
Oliver, John F.   Capt., USA
     Papers, 1863. 17 items.
     Dispatches received by Oliver as provost marshal, 4th District of Ohio, concerning Gen. John Hunt Morgan's Ohio raid, July 1863.

684
Oliver Family
     Papers, 1419–1946.
     Microfilm, 28 reels.
     Includes two letters by Arthur Lawrence written from Chattanooga and Knoxville, Tenn., Sept.–Oct. 1864, relating generally to the war.
     Originals at the Massachusetts Historical Society.

685

Olmsted, Frederick Law   General Secretary,
(1822–1903)   U.S. Sanitary Commission
    Papers, 1777–1952. ca. 27,000 items.
    Includes personal and official correspondence concerning
the organization and operation of the U.S. Sanitary Commission,
particularly the acquisition and distribution of medical supplies,
the establishment of military hospitals, hospital ships, and the
care and transport of sick and wounded soldiers. Letters written in the field contain Olmsted's observations on morale and
leadership in the Union Army, President Lincoln and his
Cabinet, the care of blacks, camp life, troop movements, and
the defense of Washington, D.C. Several letters written from
Louisiana by Sgt. Alfred H. Olmsted, 25th Connecticut Volunteers, 1862–63, discuss camp life, disease, diet, foraging
expeditions, marches, training, the organization and use of black
troops, hospital care, and the burning of the State House at
Baton Rouge, La. A few letters from Maj. George S. Waring,
Jr., to Olmsted discuss the situation in southeast Missouri
under Gens. John C. Frémont and John W. Davidson, and
letters from A. J. Dallas to Olmsted, May–June 1861, describe
war sentiment in Washington, D.C., military appointments,
and troop movements.
    Finding aid and microfilm copy (60 reels) available.

686

O'Neil, Charles (1842–1927)   Master's Mate;
                                                    Acting Master, USN
    Papers, 1833–1927. ca. 4,500 items.
    Contains O'Neil's manuscript autobiography and memo-
randa and notes relating to the war. Provides information on
the destruction of the Norfolk Navy Yard before the city was
abandoned to the Confederates, the C.S.S. *Merrimac,* the capture of Forts Hatteras and Clark, blockade duty along the Florida coast and the Bahama Islands, Gen. Ambrose E. Burnside's
expedition to North Carolina, the Peninsular Campaign, and
the Fort Fisher expeditions of 1864 and 1865. Also contains the
diary of Lt. Anthony Francis O'Neil (1840–1872) kept during
his service with the Gulf Coast Blockading Squadron and Mississippi Squadron, 1861–63. Describes fortifications at Key
West, Fla., and Ship Island, Miss., the capture of Forts Jackson
and St. Philip, Admiral Farragut's bombardment of Vicksburg,
operations on the Mississippi River, engagements with the
C.S.S. *Arkansas,* black life, smuggling, prize vessels, diet, the
occupation of New Orleans, naval leadership, depredations,

guerrilla warfare, the exchange of prisoners, and the attitude of noncombatants along the Mississippi River.

Finding aid available.

Naval Historical Foundation collection.

687

Osborn, Joseph Bloomfield   Cpl., 26th New Jersey
(1842–1876)   Volunteers; USN

Family papers, 1857–65. 295 items.

Diary, Aug. 31, 1862–July 1, 1863, and correspondence, 1861–65, concerning enlistments, camp life, training, marches in Maryland and Virginia, foraging expeditions, diet, morale, depredations, discipline, the conduct of field officers, the attitude and condition of Confederate prisoners of war, Confederate generalship, weapons, casualties in the 26th New Jersey, disease, hospital care, and the effect of the Emancipation Proclamation on Federal troops. Includes details on the Peninsular, Fredericksburg, and Chancellorsville campaigns; Osborn's service aboard the U.S.S. *Vanderbilt* in the North Atlantic and the South Atlantic Blockading Squadrons; and the Fort Fisher expedition of Jan. 1865.

688

Otis, Elwell Stephen (1838–1909)   Gen., USA

Letter, 1888. 1 item.

Letter from Otis to Maj. Fowler Prentice, Dec. 26, 1888, containing recollections of the Wilderness Campaign, particularly the events of May 5, 1864.

689

Ott, Mary E.

Pass, 1863. 1 item.

Military pass issued to Mary Ott, Harpers Ferry, W. Va., Sept. 5, 1863.

690

Ott, Thomas

Pass, 1864. 1 item.

Military pass issued to Thomas Ott, Harpers Ferry, W. Va., May 23, 1864.

691

Owen, Robert Dale (1801–1877)   Reformer

Letter, 1862. 1 item.

Letter from Owen to Edwin M. Stanton, July 23, 1862, discussing the purpose and nature of the war and advocating emancipation with remuneration to slave owners as the only effective way to terminate the conflict between North and South.

692
Owen, William Miller
(1832–1893)   Washington Artillery, CSA
     Quotations, undated. 4 p.
     Extracts from William M. Owen's *In Camp and Battle With the Washington Artillery of New Orleans* (1885).

693
Owner, William   Washington, D.C.
     Diary, 1860–67. 9 v.
     Pro-South commentary on military, political, and diplomatic events in the war as reported in newspapers and magazines. Includes newspaper clippings and a few maps.

694
Palmer—Loper Families   Merchants–Shipbuilders,
                                               Connecticut
     Papers, 1767–1900. ca. 4,000 items.
     Includes correspondence and documents relating to the sale and lease of ships to the U.S. Government; a partial list of vessels used in the Peninsular Campaign and Gen. Ambrose E. Burnside's expedition to North Carolina; letters written by W. S. Palmer concerning his efforts to claim vessels stranded in New Orleans, La., at the outbreak of the war, negotiations with Gen. Benjamin F. Butler, and the attitude of noncombatants in Louisiana; material on R. F. Loper's defense against charges of profiteering on ship leases; a biographical sketch of R. F. Loper; and a certificate of enlistment for Edward Sheridan, 48th New York Volunteers, Jan. 17, 1862.
     Finding aid and partial microfilm copy (1 reel) available.

695
Park, Maud Wood (1871–1955)
     Papers, 1864–1978. ca. 3,500 items.
     Includes the Civil War memoir and notes of James Rodney Wood, Sr. Describes Wood's enlistment and service in the 1st Massachusetts Regiment, interviews with President Lincoln and Secretary Stanton, his transfer to the 6th U.S. Cavalry, and the participation of the 6th Cavalry in the Peninsular and Wilderness campaigns, Stoneman's raid (Chancellorsville Campaign), and the Kilpatrick–Dahlgren raid on Richmond. Provides a detailed account of Wood's treatment as a prisoner of war, his escape, and the service and death of Col. Ulric Dahlgren.
     Finding aid available.

696
Parmenter, Abram Verrick (b. 1830)   Cpl., 7th Veteran
                                            Reserve Corps, USA
    Collection, 1865. 3 items.
    Includes a diary, Mar. 20–Dec. 31, 1865, concerning activities at Camp Blair, Mich., in the final weeks of the war, the execution of Henry Wirz, and the reinterment of Col. Ulric Dahlgren.

697
Parsons, Byron   Maj., 94th New York Volunteers
    Collection, 1864–65. 3 items.
    Includes a diary, Jan. 1, 1864–Oct. 14, 1865 (2 v.), concerning the movement of troops from New York to Virginia, the Siege of Petersburg, life as a prisoner of war at Libby Prison in Richmond, Va., and at Salisbury, N.C., and Danville, Va., and the exchange of prisoners. Also includes a list of Federal soldiers captured at Reams' Station, Va., a partial list of officers confined at Libby Prison in 1864, and a list of noncommissioned officers and privates in the 94th New York.

698
Parsons, Henry Chester
(1840–1894)   Capt., 1st Vermont Cavalry
    Manuscript, undated. 1 item.
    Draft of Parsons' "Farnsworth's Charge and Death," *Battles and Leaders of the Civil War* (1888), v. 3.

699
Patrick, Marsena Rudolph (1811–1888)   Gen., USA
    Diary, 1862–65. 3 v.
    Diary kept by Patrick as inspector general of New York Volunteers and provost marshal general, Army of the Potomac, Jan. 1, 1862–June 16, 1865. Contains remarks on the 2d Manassas, Antietam, Fredericksburg, Chancellorsville, Gettysburg, Mine Run, Wilderness, Spotsylvania, Cold Harbor, and Petersburg campaigns, Gen. George Stoneman's raids during the Chancellorsville Campaign, the Kilpatrick–Dahlgren raid on Richmond, and the occupation of Fredericksburg. Provides details on military politics, discipline, generalship, corruption among officers, entertainment, morale, disease, depredations, female soldiers, the attitude of southern women, prisoners of war, reconnaissance expeditions, and refugees. Edited and pub-

lished by David S. Sparks, *Inside Lincoln's Army: The Diary of Marsena Rudolph Patrick, Provost Marshal General, Army of the Potomac* (1964).

700
Patterson, George Washington
(1799–1879)   Farmer, New York
    Papers, 1864. 3 items.
    Includes a letter from Col. J. C. Drake to Patterson, Apr. 24, 1864, Gloucester Point, Va., concerning the 112th New York Volunteers and Drake's disappointment over being replaced as senior colonel in his brigade; and a letter from Chaplain William L. Hyde to Patterson, White House Landing, Va., concerning Drake's death and arrangements for the return of his body to New York.

701
Patterson, Theodore Cuyler   Financier, Pennsylvania
    Collection, 1861–1927. 3 items.
    In part, photocopies.
    Includes an account of the events in which Patterson's father, Joseph Patterson (1808–1887), influenced the banking establishment of Philadelphia to loan the U.S. Government $50 million to finance the war; and a facsimile of the original agreement sent to Secretary Salmon P. Chase, July 22, 1861.

702
Patterson, William Franklin (1826–1886)   Capt., USA
    Papers, 1812–1937. ca. 230 items.
    Contains about 50 letters from Patterson to his wife, 1862–64, written during his service with an independent company in the occupation of Cumberland Gap, and as a military engineer in campaigns in Kentucky, Tennessee, Mississippi, Arkansas, and Texas. Provides information on the Vicksburg Campaign, military organization, generalship, camp life, diet, guerrilla warfare, disease, medical care, desertions, problems with prostitution and drinking in New Orleans, La., and military supplies. Also contains miscellaneous orders and notes and Patterson's discharge certificate, Jan. 22, 1865.
    Finding aid and microfilm copy (1 reel) available.

703
Patton, John   98th Ohio Volunteers
    Memoir, 1862–64. 27 v.
    Describes Patton's enlistment and early training in Ohio, Federal reaction to Gen. Edmund Kirby-Smith's invasion of Kentucky and Gen. John Hunt Morgan's raid on Columbia, Ky.; the fortification of Louisville, Ky.; the aftermath of the Battle of Perryville and the pursuit of Gen. Braxton Bragg in

Kentucky; the Battle of Chickamauga, and the Chattanooga and Atlanta campaigns. Includes details on the battles of Lookout Mountain and Missionary Ridge, camp life, discipline, morale, marches, foraging expeditions, disease, casualties, hospital care, guerrilla warfare in Kentucky, prison life, slavery, and the attitude of rank and file Confederate soldiers toward the war.

704
Paxton, James Dunlop (1860–ca. 1947)
Reminiscence, undated. 1 item.
An account of how Paxton's father, a Presbyterian minister in Pittsburgh, Pa., successfully intervened to stop the execution of a parishioner's son for desertion from the Army of the Potomac through a direct appeal to President Lincoln and Secretary Stanton.

705
Pease, David   111th New York Volunteers
Collection, 1863. 2 items.
Letter from David and Solomon Pease to their father, Mar. 1, 1863, and letter from David Pease to his brother Solomon, Apr. 10, 1863, written from Camp Jim Walker near Centreville, Va. Describes a skirmish near Centreville, camp life, morale, inflation, and the suffering of the civilian population.

706
Peckham, Rufus Wheeler (1809–1873)   Lawyer, Minnesota
Family papers, 1838–94. ca. 800 items.
Includes three letters from Capt. M. T. Dana to Peckham, Oct. 27–Nov. 23, 1861, written from camp along the Potomac River near Edwards Ferry, and a letter by Gen. Willis A. Gorman, Dec. 21, 1861, on the appointment of an Assistant Adjutant General for Gorman's brigade.

707
Pelham, William   Landsman, USN
General order, 1864. 1 item.
Order issued Dec. 31, 1864, awarding the Medal of Honor to servicemen who performed distinguished service in the Battle of Mobile Bay.
Naval Historical Foundation collection.

708
Pemberton, John Clifford (1814–1881)   Gen., CSA
Papers, 1862–1937. 5 items.
Transcripts and photocopies.
Unfinished postwar letter from Pemberton to Major Walt-

hall refuting charges of misconduct in the defense of Vicksburg; copy of a letter by T. J. Wharton published in the *New York Herald*, Aug. 17, 1881, concerning an interview with President Davis after the fall of Vicksburg and Davis' reasons for the appointment of Pemberton as commander of the Department of Mississippi, Tennessee, and East Louisiana; and copies of letters by Pemberton, Dec. 31, 1862–Dec. 4, 1866.

709
Pendleton, Edward   Pvt., 27th Massachusetts Volunteers
    Reminiscences, 1862–65. 1 item.
    Describes Pendleton's enlistment and early training in Massachusetts, the Federal occupation of New Bern, N.C., the Siege of Petersburg, and service under Gen. John Schofield in the Carolinas Campaign. Includes remarks on camp life, marches, casualties, hospital care, and his treatment as a prisoner of war in North Carolina.

710
Perham, Aurestus S.   Writer; Lecturer
    Papers, 1882–1923. ca. 2,100 items.
    Documents assembled to vindicate the military record of Gen. Gouverneur K. Warren, who was relieved of his command by Gen. Philip H. Sheridan at the Battle of Five Forks, Va. Includes correspondence, notes, maps, photographs, and printed material.

711
Perkins, Edward Thomas
(1826–1872)   Surg., 71st New York Volunteers
    Family papers, 1822–1901. ca. 100 items.
    Includes a letter to Perkins from the surgeon of the 73d New York (Excelsior brigade), Dec. 4, 1863, Brandy Station, Va., concerning marches and skirmishes along the Rapidan River, medical care, and the suffering of convalescents; a recommendation for Perkins by Col. William R. Brewster, July 4, 1864; miscellaneous orders and returns; and photographs of Perkins and Col. William O. Stevens.

712
Perkins, George Hamilton (1835–1899)   Lt. Comdr., USN
    Isabel Perkins Anderson collection of the papers of George Hamilton Perkins, 1857–1936. 500 items.
    Includes notes and published accounts of Perkins' service in the war, a photograph of Perkins as a midshipman, and a list of documents, photographs, clippings, and souvenirs collected by Isabel Perkins.
    Naval Historical Foundation collection.

713
Perkins, Henry Welles (d. 1890)
Letters, 1865. 1 item.
Letter from Perkins to Captain Lacy, Apr. 13, 1865, Raleigh, N.C., concerning the movement of quartermaster supplies.

714
Petigru, James Louis (1789–1863)   Lawyer–State Official,
                                                   South Carolina
Papers, 1812–68. ca. 400 items.
In part, transcripts.
Correspondence and papers of a Unionist family in South Carolina during the war. Includes about 50 letters from Petigru to his daughters, Sue Petigru King and Caroline Petigru Carson, concerning politics in the South, public unity over the secession crisis, the progress of the war, devastation along the coast of South Carolina, acquaintances and friends in the Confederate Army, and the attitude and suffering of noncombatants. Also contains a letter from Gen. William T. Sherman to Mrs. Carson, Jan. 20, 1865, Savannah, Ga., on the protection of the Petigru family and property in South Carolina; a letter from Gen. Winfield Scott to Secretary Stanton, May 27, 1863, soliciting Stanton's assistance for Mrs. Carson to visit her family in South Carolina; and a letter from Millard Fillmore to J. Chamberlin(?), Apr. 4, 1863, Buffalo [N.Y.], on Petigru's political appointment during his administration.

715
Phelps, Winthrop Henry   Chaplain, 2d Connecticut
(1818–1865)   Heavy Artillery
Diary, 1864–1945. 1 v.
Transcript.
"A Chaplain's Life in the Civil War: The Diary of Winthrop Henry Phelps," edited by Ethel L. Phelps, 1945. Covers the period May 15, 1864–Dec. 31, 1865, with a "Résumé of Regiment Activities During 1863." Describes the participation of the regiment in the Spotsylvania, Cold Harbor, and Appomattox campaigns, the Siege of Petersburg, and Sheridan's Shenandoah Valley Campaign. Includes details on the battles of Winchester (1864), Fisher's Hill, and Cedar Creek, and remarks on military organization, discipline, marches, desertions, disease, casualties, medical care, foraging expeditions, religion, and the suffering of noncombatants. Also contains photographs of Phelps, the officers of the 19th Connecticut Infantry, Col. Elisha S. Kellogg, Lt. Bradley D. Lee, the Fairfax Theological Seminary (used as a military hospital), maps of

Washington and vicinity, and a genealogical and statistical table on the men of the 2d Connecticut Heavy Artillery published in Apr. 1864.

716
Phillips, Philip (1807–1884)   Washington, D.C.,
                                                         and New Orleans, La.
    Family papers, 1826–1914. ca. 7,000 items.
    In part, transcripts.
    Includes the diary of Phillip's wife, Eugenia Yates Levy Phillips (1820–1902), a southern sympathizer and suspected spy, describing her arrest and imprisonment in Washington, her parole and return to the South, conflict with Federal authorities in New Orleans, La., life as a prisoner on Ship Island, Miss., and her work with sick and wounded Confederate soldiers at La Grange, Ga.; and the autobiography of Philip Phillips concerning the secession movement, the arrest and imprisonment of his wife, and life in New Orleans and La Grange during the war. Also contains two letters from Phebe Levy to Eugenia Phillips written from a military hospital near Richmond, Va., June 25 and Sept. 13, 1863, concerning the progress of the war, troop movements, inflation, and the attitude of women in the South; four letters from Eugenia's brother, S. Yates Levy, to his father, July 28, 1864–May 16, 1865, Johnsons Island, Ohio, concerning prison life and family matters; and a letter from C. C. Clay, Jr., to Gen. James H. Wilson, May 10, 1865, La Grange, Ga., written in response to an order for his arrest as a possible conspirator in the Lincoln assassination.
    Finding aid available.

717
Pickard, Alonzo C.
(1938–1910)   112th New York Volunteers
    Papers, 1856–87. ca. 150 items.
    Chiefly letters from Pickard to his fiance written during campaigns in Virginia, 1861–65. Contains information on fortifications near Suffolk, camp life, morale, marches, discipline, supplies, prisoners of war, religion, conscription, reconnaissance expeditions, disease, deaths, hospital care, and generalship. Also includes letters relating to the war by E. P. Putnam, R. Tyler, and F. A. Pickard, and a detailed account of the engagement at Dranesville, Va., Dec. 20, 1862, written by an unidentified participant.

718
Pickens—Bonham   Govs., South Carolina
    Papers, 1837–1920. ca. 400 items.
    In part, photocopies.
    Chiefly official correspondence, telegrams, proclamations, petitions, reports, extracts from the journals of the executive council, and newspaper clippings from the administrations of Govs. Francis W. Pickens (1805–1869) and Milledge L. Bonham (1813–1890). Provides information on military organization, the acquisition of arms and ammunition, coastal fortifications, Fort Sumter, authority over South Carolina, runaway slaves, and the use of blacks in the construction of military works and in the militia. Correspondents include P. G. T. Beauregard, Judah P. Benjamin, Martin J. Crawford, Jefferson Davis, James A. Seddon, H. P. Walker, Leroy P. Walker, and James H. Witherspoon.
    Microfilm copy (2 reels) available.

719
Pickett, John Thomas (1822–1884)   Col, CSA; Diplomat
    Papers, 1849–84. ca. 4,000 items.
    Correspondence and letterbooks relating primarily to Pickett's service as Confederate agent to Mexico. Includes comments on the progress of the war, economic conditions in the South, and Confederate morale and finance. Also includes two letters from General Beauregard to Judah P. Benjamin, Oct. 5 and 8, 1861, suggesting areas along the southern coast vulnerable to attack; a letter from General Beauregard to Gen. Mansfield Lovell, Oct. 9, 1861, Fairfax Courthouse, Va., outlining the best ways to defend New Orleans, La., and recommending people that might prove helpful to Mansfield; and a letter from R. R. Barrow to Col. D. F. Kenner, Sept. 11, 1862, concerning military activities near Bayou Des Almonds, La., and a plan for infecting Federal troops in New Orleans with yellow fever.

720
Pierce, Franklin (1804–1869), Pres., U.S.
    Papers, 1820–69. ca. 2,300 items.
    In part, photocopies.
    Material for the Civil War period includes a few letters requesting Pierce's support in obtaining military or political office, and suggestions for peace negotiations.
    Index and microfilm copy (7 reels) available.

721
Pierpont, Francis Harrison
(1814–1899)   Gov., Virginia and West Virginia
    Letter, 1862. 1 item.
    Letter from Pierpont to Maj. Francis Darr, Feb. 5, 1862,

Wheeling [W. Va.], concerning the arrest of Confederate volunteers upon their return home.

722
Pike, James Shepherd (1811–1882)   U.S. Minister to
                                                    the Netherlands
        Collection, 1849–69. 56 items.
        Includes 16 letters from Pike to William P. Fessenden written chiefly from The Hague, June 1861–Feb. 1865, concerning the effects of the war on the European economy and public sentiment in Europe.

723
Pillow, Gideon Johnson (1806–1878)   Gen., CSA
        Letters, 1847–61. 3 items.
        Letter from Pillow to Gov. Beriah Magoffin, May 13, 1861, Memphis, Tenn., on the defense of Kentucky; and letter from Pillow to Gov. Isham Harris, July 3, 1861, concerning fortifications on the Mississippi River and subsistence for Pillow's troops.

724
Pinkerton's National Detective Agency
        Papers, 1861–83. ca. 2,000 items.
        Includes letterbooks, Aug. 21–Nov. 26, 1861 (2 v.), of E. J. Allen, alias Allan Pinkerton (1819–1884), as head of the secret service for the Army of the Potomac. Contains summaries of field investigations by Pinkerton agents, reports and recommendations on soldiers and civilians accused of various crimes, estimates of Confederate troop strength in Virginia, and detailed reports from agents inside Confederate lines on the strength, disposition, and movement of troops, travel conditions, public support for the war, and inflation.
        Finding aid and microfilm copy (3 reels) available.

725
Pinkney, Ninian (1811–1877)   Surg., USN
        Papers, 1830–78. ca. 900 items.
        Includes personal and official correspondence of Pinkney as fleet surgeon and medical adviser, Mississippi Squadron, 1863–64, concerning the outfitting of hospital ships, the Vicksburg Campaign, including the Yazoo Pass and Port Hudson expeditions, black life, the establishment and management of military hospitals at Memphis, Tenn., the use and performance of black troops, abolition, the generalship of Ulysses S. Grant, Samuel P. Lee, George B. McClellan, John A. McClernand, and William T. Sherman, and routine affairs in the Medical Department. Also contains letters from Pinkney to his wife writ-

ten from Frederick, Md., Sept. 23, 1862, and Washington, D.C., Nov. 11, 1862, describing the Antietam battlefield, the care and suffering of wounded soldiers, and his indignation over the dismissal of General McClellan. Miscellaneous items comprise photographs of the staff of a hospital ship, the U.S.S. *Red Rover*, the Federal camp at White River Station, Ark., the State House at Baton Rouge, La., the commandant's house at Mound City, Ill., the U.S.S. *Louisville*, U.S.S. *Lexington*, U.S.S. *Black Hawk*, U.S.S. *Ozark*, U.S.S. *Essex*, and U.S.S. *Indianola*, and a print of the bombardment of Island No. 10.

Finding aid available.

Naval Historical Foundation collection.

726

Pleasants, Archibald (1839–1862)   Lt., CSA
   Inscription, 1862. 1 item.
   Copy of the inscription on Pleasants' tomb, Richmond, Va.

727

Pleasonton, Alfred (1824–1897)   Gen., USA
   Collection, 1862–92. 9 items.

Includes seven letters from Pleasonton to Gen. John F. Farnsworth, Oct. 1862–July 1863, chiefly concerning the performance of his former command, the 8th Illinois Cavalry, in the Fredericksburg, Chancellorsville, and Gettysburg campaigns, the organization of the U.S. cavalry, the generalship of Julius Stahel, and the death of Gen. Elon J. Farnsworth. Also includes a letter from General Farnsworth to Gen. [Joseph Hooker], June 23, 1863, complaining of a lack of support for Pleasonton during the Gettysburg Campaign and criticizing the performance of Stahel.

728

Plumb, Edward Lee   President,
(1827–1912)   Mexican Pacific Company
   Papers, 1826–90. ca. 3,600 items.

Chiefly business correspondence and papers of the Mexican Pacific Coal and Iron Mining and Land Company. Includes observations on Confederate–Mexican relations and French activity in Mexico.

729

Poe, Orlando (1832–1895)   Gen., USA
   Papers, 1852–1900. ca. 8,400 items.

Contains about 500 items relating to the war, chiefly official and personal correspondence, letterbooks, reports, orders, and diaries. Includes about 300 letters from Poe to his wife, 1861–65, written during his service as chief topographical engineer on the staff of Gen. George B. McClellan during the West Virginia Campaign and the defense of Washington, D.C., as colonel of the 2d Michigan Volunteers during the Peninsular, 2d Manassas, and Fredericksburg campaigns, as assistant engineer in the Military Division of the Mississippi, Dec. 1863–Apr. 1864, and as chief engineer under Gen. William T. Sherman during the Atlanta and Carolinas campaigns. Also includes memorabilia on Poe's military service collected by his wife. Provides information on the organization and training of troops in Ohio early in the war, enthusiasm for the war in the North, the organization and performance of McClellan's Army of the Potomac, rank disputes, Confederate morale, depredations and plundering by General Sherman's army in Georgia and South Carolina, casualties, the surrender of Gen. Joseph E. Johnston, the suffering of Unionists in the South, the psychological effects of battle, conscription in the South, and the attitude and behavior of southern women.

730
Polk, Leonidas (1806–1864)   Episcopal Bishop; Gen., CSA
    Papers, 1856–68. 40 items.
    Chiefly correspondence, orders, and miscellaneous items relating to military affairs in Kentucky, Tennessee, Missouri, and Mississippi. Includes a report on the skirmish near Belmont, Mo. Correspondents include Braxton Bragg, Jefferson Davis, Nathan B. Forrest, Joseph E. Johnston, Sterling Price, and Louis T. Wigfall.
    Microfilm copy (1 reel) available.

731
Polsley, John J. (1831–1866)   Lt. Col.,
                                        7th West Virginia Cavalry, USA
    Collection, 1862–73. 4 items.
    Includes a letter from Polsley to his wife, June 10, 1862, concerning the Battle of Port Republic, Va., and a letter from Polsley to Maj. Hedgeman Slack, Jan. 21, 1864, Libby Prison, expressing concern for his regiment and his hope for an early exchange.

732
Poole, Edmund Leicester (b. 1845)   USA
    Letter, 1865. 1 item.
    Photocopy.
    Letter from Poole to his parents, Apr. 5, 1865, describing the celebration in Washington, D.C., over the fall of Richmond, Va.

David Dixon Porter

733
Porter, Albert Quincy (1825–1904)   Musician, 33d
                                                 Mississippi Volunteers
 Collection, 1864–1944. 3 items.
 Transcripts.
 Diary, Jan. 20–July 7, 1864, and Feb. 2–May 30, 1865,
kept by Porter during operations against Gen. William T. Sherman in the Meridian, Atlanta, and Carolinas campaigns. Contains comments on casualties, disease, hospital care, inflation,
discipline, desertions, depredations by both Union and Confederate soldiers, stealing from Confederate supply depots, the
contribution of southern women to the war effort, and the displacement of blacks. Also includes a few biographical notes on
Porter.

734
Porter, David Dixon (1813–1891)   Adm., USN
 Papers, 1790–1899. ca. 7,000 items.
 Official and family correspondence, orders, reports, newspaper clippings, memoirs, printed matter, and miscellaneous
items concerning the capture of New Orleans, La., the Vicksburg Campaign, operations on the Mississippi and Red Rivers,
the Fort Fisher expeditions of 1864 and 1865, and the evacuation and occupation of Richmond, Va. Also includes the report
of Lt. Col. Edward Higgins (CSA) on the mutiny of the garrisons at Forts Jackson and St. Philip; a list of Confederate
steamers, gunboats, and rams on the Yazoo, Ouachita, Big
Black, and Red Rivers; a list of 41 men from Pine Bluff, Ark.,
who passed Confederate lines to serve the Union; and a detailed
report on Confederate fortifications at New Orleans with related
correspondence.
 Finding aid available.

735
Porter, Fitz-John (1822–1901)   Gen., USA
 Papers, 1830–1949. ca. 13,100 items.
 In part, transcripts.
 Chiefly correspondence, orders, telegrams, reconnaissance
and battle reports, maps, photographs, financial and legal
papers, and printed material relating to Porter's commands in
the Peninsular, 2d Manassas, and Antietam campaigns, and to
his subsequent court-martial. Also contains information on the
situation in Texas in Apr. 1861, resignations by officers in the
Regular Army at the beginning of the war, efforts to protect
northern railroads, Gen. Robert Patterson's failure to prevent
reinforcements from reaching General Beauregard at the Battle of 1st Manassas, and extracts from the diaries of Washing-

Fitz-John Porter

ton A. Roebling, Aug. 21–30, 1862, and Gouverneur K. Warren, Aug. 14–Nov. 11, 1862.
Finding aid available.

736
Porter, Horace (1837–1921)   Lt. Col., USA
Papers, 1854–1921. ca. 1,500 items.
Chiefly correspondence relating to the Port Royal expedition (including the capture of Hilton Head and Forts Walker and Beauregard), the siege and capture of Fort Pulaski, the occupation of Beaufort, S.C., the Battle of Secessionville, the Tullahoma and Chickamauga campaigns, and the Siege of Petersburg. Contains comments on camp life, casualties, ordnance, disease, Union sentiment in the South, black life, the organization and service of black troops, morale in the Confederate Army, the attitude of noncombatants in the South, depredations, foraging expeditions, and the generalship of Henry W. Benham, Quincy A. Gillmore, and Thomas W. Sherman.

737
Porter Family
Papers, 1811–81. ca. 600 items.
Includes a letter from Gideon Welles to David Dixon Porter, Aug. 11, 1861, informing Porter of his appointment to the rank of commander in the U.S. Navy; a letter from D. D. Porter to Secretary William H. Seward, U.S.S. *Powhatan*, Apr. 21, 1861, explaining his failure to enter Pensacola Bay; and a letter from Porter to his wife, New Orleans, La., June 6, 1862, concerning the attitude of noncombatants, the generalship of Benjamin F. Butler, and the failure of the Navy Department to encourage Union sentiment in the area.
Finding aid available.
Naval Historical Foundation collection.

738
Potter, William F.   Pvt., 3d Louisiana Volunteers
Records, 1865. 2 items.
Material from Potter's trial on the charge of desertion from the Confederate Army, Feb.–Mar. 1865.

739
Powel, Mary Edith (1846–1931)   Collector
Collection, 1747–1922. ca. 32,000 items.
Contains photographs or engravings of Col. Ulric Dahlgren, Adm. David D. Porter, and Gen. Gouverneur K. Warren; articles and clippings on the duel between the U.S.S. *Monitor* and C.S.S. *Merrimac*, ordnance, and various officers and inventors:

John Ericsson, David G. Farragut, Andrew H. Foote, David D. Porter, George H. Preble, and Cornelius K. Stringham; and miscellaneous letters by Henry H. Bell, S. Livingston Breese, Gustavus V. Fox, Francis H. Gregory, Samuel P. Lee, and William H. Seward.

Finding aid available.

Naval Historical Foundation collection.

740
Powell, John F.   Physician, Baltimore, Md.
    Collection, 1862–63. 2 items.
    Photocopies.
    Medical accounts with the U.S. Government for the treatment of political prisoners in the Baltimore City jail, Oct. 1862–May 1863.

741
Pratt, Richard Henry
(1840–1924)   Capt., 11th Indiana Cavalry
    Papers, 1862–1924. 3 items.
    In part, transcripts.
    Chiefly Pratt's manuscript autobiography. Includes a copy of Pratt's diary, Mar. 1862–Feb. 1863, kept during the Shiloh Campaign, the Battle of Munfordville, Ky., and skirmishes with Gen. John Hunt Morgan in Tennessee. Includes comments on camp life, training, marches, entertainment, foraging expeditions, depredations, Confederate and Union morale, casualties, disease, hospital care, and Union sentiment in Tennessee.

742
Pratt, William Veazie (1869–1957)
    Papers, 1862–1963. ca. 200 items.
    Includes a few orders and routine letters to Pratt's father, Nicholas Pratt (USN).
    Naval Historical Foundation collection.

743
Preston, John Thomas Lewis
(1811–1890)   Lt. Col., 9th Virginia Volunteers
    Diary, 1861. 1 v.
    Covers the period July 21–Sept. 22, 1861. Describes garrison duty on Crany Island, Va., discipline and morale in the 9th Virginia, the use of blacks to build fortifications, ordnance, disease, the attitude of noncombatants in southeast Virginia, and visits from women living in the North whose husbands served the Confederacy.

744
Preston Family of Virginia
    Papers, 1727–1896.
    Microfilm, 14 reels.
    Includes a letter from Maj. William Preston Johnston to his wife, Oct. 3, 1861, in camp near Fairfax Courthouse, describing an expedition to Mason's Hill, discipline among Mississippi regiments, depredations, and the attitude of noncombatants in Fairfax County.

745
Procter, A. C.   Kentucky
    Letter, 1865. 1 item.
    Letter from Mrs. Procter to her brother, Nov. 26, 1865, Perryville, Ky., concerning her personal losses from the war, the attitude and behavior of Federal officers, and the murder of numerous Confederate soldiers returning to Kentucky.

746
Proctor, Wilbur Huntington   Musician, 10th
                                                   New York Volunteers
    Diary, 1864–74.
    Microfilm, 1 reel.
    Contains comments on Proctor's enlistments in the 20th Massachusetts Volunteers and the 10th New York Volunteers, military bounties, profiteering by civilian recruiters or "bounty brokers," camp life, entertainment, marches, diet, discipline, foraging expeditions, and battles and skirmishes in the Wilderness, Spotsylvania, and Petersburg campaigns.

747
Public Archives of Canada
    Papers, 1791–1885. 47 v.
    Photocopies.
    Material for the Civil War period includes correspondence of British Ministers at Philadelphia and Washington, D.C., concerning such matters as the recruitment of British subjects for the U.S. Army, the southern blockade, the purchase of privateers and blockade runners, passports, commerce, alleged Confederate forces in Canada, and the treatment of Englishmen living or trading in the war zone.

748
Quincy—Wendell—Upham—Holmes Families
    Papers, 1866–1910.
    Microfilm, 67 reels.
    Includes about 100 letters from Samuel Miller Quincy to his family, 1861–65, written during campaigns in Maryland,

Virginia, and Louisiana. Contains details on the occupation of Harpers Ferry and Charles Town, W. Va., the engagement at Dranesville, Va., Dec. 6, 1861, the Shenandoah Valley Campaign of 1862, the Battle of Chancellorsville, and the Port Hudson Campaign. Also provides information on camp life, training, morale, marches, reconnaissance and foraging expeditions, depredations, discipline, entertainment, casualties, hospital care, guerrilla warfare, generalship, the treatment and exchange of prisoners of war, the attitude of noncombatants, slavery, black life, and the training and employment of black troops during Quincy's service as colonel of the 73d U.S. Colored Infantry.

Published guide available.

Originals in the Massachusetts Historical Society.

749

R. Hoe & Company   Printers—Manufacturers, New York
   Records, 1830–1935. ca. 5,100 items.
   In part, transcripts.
   Includes a few family letters relating generally to the war, and material concerning the manufacture of rifling machines.
   Finding aid and microfilm copy (17 reels) available.

750

Radford, William (1809–1890)   Comdr., USN
   Papers, 1847–90. 53 items.
   Contains 23 items relating to the war, chiefly official correspondence and orders concerning Radford's command of the U.S.S. *Cumberland* and U.S.S. *New Ironsides*, 1862–65. Includes Radford's report of Mar. 10, 1862, on the loss of the *Cumberland* at Hampton Roads; a letter from Col. John Harris to Radford, Dec. 7, 1863, concerning an effort in Congress to transfer the Marine Corps to the Army as an additional regiment; a letter from Adm. David D. Porter to Radford, Jan. 17, 1865, commending Radford on the performance of the *New Ironsides* in the Fort Fisher expedition; and a letter from Gustavus V. Fox to Radford, Feb. 10, 1865, on the utility of monitors.
   Naval Historical Foundation collection.

751

Ramsey, Margaret Lawrence (1840?–1922)
   Collection, 1864–1977. 7 items.
   In part, transcripts.
   Contains the diary of Margaret L. Lindsley, Oct. 29, 1864–May 28, 1865, concerning the Siege of Nashville, Dec. 1864, and life in Washington, D.C., in the final weeks of the war. Includes comments on the behavior of Union troops in Nashville, the attitude of noncombatants, and generalship. Also

contains copies of letters to Margaret (Maggie) Lindsley; the published version of the diary; miscellaneous orders; a map of "Part of Cobb County, Georgia" (1864); and recommendations for promotion of numerous officers who served under Gen. George H. Thomas, Feb. 18, 1866, with details on the wartime service of each officer named.

752
Randall, James Garfield (1881–1953) and Ruth P.
    Papers, 1850–1952. ca. 13,400 items.
    In part, photocopies.
    Correspondence, notes, drafts, outlines, memoranda, and printed matter relating to J. G. Randall's studies of Lincoln and the Civil War.
    Finding aid available.

753
Randolph, George Wythe
(1818–1867)   C.S. Secretary of War
    Letter, 1862. 1 item.
    Transcript.
    Letter to the editors of the *Richmond Whig*, July 17, 1862, Richmond, appealing for assistance in apprehending deserters and absentees from the Confederate Army.

754
Randolph, William B. (b. 1793)   Agriculturist
    Papers, 1696–1884. ca. 7,500 items.
    Includes three letters from N. Harrison to Randolph, June 1–Oct. 21, 1862, concerning the military situation in Monroe County, W. Va., and the generalship of Henry Heth and John B. Floyd; and a letter from Randolph to an unidentified recipient, Nov. 6, 1864, commenting on military affairs in Virginia and the health of Gen. George E. Pickett and his headquarters staff.
    Finding aid available.

755
Ransom, Robert (1828–1892)   Gen., CSA
    Letter, 1863. 1 item.
    Letter from Ransom to Gov. Zebulon Vance, Apr. 13, 1863, Winston, N.C., concerning conscription in North Carolina and the excessive number of militia officers in the State.

756
Read, John Meredith
(1837–1896)   Adj. Gen., New York
    Family papers, 1706–1906. ca. 1,000 items.

Includes a few routine letters from Simon Cameron to Read, May 14–20, 1861, on the mustering of volunteers, and drafts of legislation on enlistments, conscription, and military regulations.

757
Read, Thomas Buchanan
(1822–1872)   Artist–Poet, Ohio
    Collection, 1864. 3 items.
    Includes a poem on the war entitled "The Oath."

758
Reed, Charles Wellington   Pvt., 9th Massachusetts
(1841–1926)   Light Artillery; Topographic
                              Engineer, Army of the Potomac
    Papers, 1849–1920. ca. 1,200 items.
    Chiefly correspondence, drawings, maps, photographs, a diary, and printed matter relating to the war. Includes about 700 sketches of battles and skirmishes, military camps and camp scenes, black refugees, Confederate prisoners of war, fords, settlements and points of interest (Bealeton Station, Gainesville, Bethesda Church, Laurel Hill, Burke's Station, Nottoway Station, Belle Isle, and the Petersburg mine explosion), ordnance, and various military and political leaders: Gens. Henry Baxter, Ambrose E. Burnside, Ulysses S. Grant, and Paul J. Semmes (CSA), and President Lincoln. Also includes about 200 letters (many with sketches on the letterhead) from Reed to his family and friends in Massachusetts, 1862–65, describing camp life, training, discipline, diet, military organization, marches, entertainment, ordnance, ethics, furloughs, disease, casualties, competition between regiments, and the attitude of recruits toward officers. Provides information on the Gettysburg, Mine Run, Wilderness, Spotsylvania, Cold Harbor, Petersburg, and Appomattox campaigns. Miscellaneous items include manuscript essays on the role of the 8th Vermont Volunteers in the Battle of Cedar Creek, and the role of the 9th Massachusetts Light Artillery at Gettysburg. Diary entries cover the period Jan. 1–Oct. 25, 1864.
    Finding aid available.

759
Reed Family of Indiana and Kentucky
    Papers, 1795–1891.
    Microfilm, 1 reel.
    Contains about 65 letters from Chaplain George J. Reed to his wife, 1861–62, concerning his ministry to soldiers in the 1st (renamed the 2d) Kentucky Cavalry, camp life, morale, marches, depredations by Confederate soldiers, discipline, the

disposition of Federal troops in Kentucky, the attitude of noncombatants, guerrilla warfare, disease and deaths in the regiment, hospital care, the treatment of runaway slaves, generalship, Gen. Don Carlos Buell's forced march to Pittsburg Landing, and casualties from the Battle of Shiloh.

760
Reichhelm, Edward Paul   Sgt. Maj., 3d
                                                  Missouri Volunteers
    Collection, 1862–63. 2 items.
    In part, transcripts.
    Diary, Dec. 1862–Jan. 1863, kept during the Vicksburg Campaign. Describes Gen. William T. Sherman's move down the Mississippi River from Helena, Ark., to Millikens Bend, including guerrilla attacks on Federal transports and retaliatory raids on towns and plantations along the river; the Yazoo Pass expedition; and the Battle of Chickasaw Bluffs. Includes comments on camp life, marches, morale, depredations, casualties, and the generalship of Charles E. Hovey and John A. McClernand. Also describes the Arkansas Post (Fort Hindman) expedition.

761
Reid, Samuel Chester (1783–1861)
    Family papers, 1807–1963. ca. 2,450 items.
    Includes the diary of Samuel Chester Reid, Jr. (1818–1897), Feb. 5, 1862–Apr. 9, 1865, kept during travels in the South as a war correspondent. Contains some information on travel conditions, troop movements, generalship, personal difficulties with Gen. Braxton Bragg, and the Atlanta Campaign. Also contains a few military passes, and the following essays: "An Appeal to the Democracy of the South," "The Cause and Origin of the War Between the North and the South," "An Ex-Confederate on the Late Rebellion," and "A Forthcoming Secret History of the Confederacy."
    Finding aid available.

762
Reid Family
    Papers, 1795–1973. ca. 60,050 items.
    Includes the papers of Whitelaw Reid (1837–1912), war correspondent for the *Cincinnati Gazette*. Material relating to the war consists chiefly of newspaper clippings of Reid's dispatches written in Washington, D.C., and in the field, and popularly known as the "Agate" letters.
    Finding aid and microfilm copy (237 reels) available.

763

Remey, George Collier (1841–1928)   Lt., USN
     Papers, 1902–35. 1 item.
     Reminiscences of Remey's experiences in the war, 1863–64.
Describes the capture of Confederate blockade runners *Cherokee*
and *Secesh*, operations against Fort Sumter and Fort Wagner,
S.C., life as a prisoner of war at Charleston and Columbia,
S.C., and the execution of a Union spy. Includes a sketch of the
Columbia jail and the names of several other prisoners.
     Naval Historical Foundation collection.

764

Remey Family
     Papers, 1855–1932. 1,225 items.
     In part, transcripts.
     Includes official and personal correspondence, orders, and
reminiscences of Lt. George Collier Remey (1841–1928).
Describes Lieutenant Remey's service on the U.S.S. *Marblehead*
in the Peninsular Campaign and with the South Atlantic Blockading Squadron, as executive officer on the U.S.S. *Canandaigua*,
South Atlantic Blockading Squadron, and operations against
Fort Wagner and Fort Sumter, S.C. Also describes Remey's
experiences as a prisoner of war at Charleston and Columbia,
S.C., and Richmond, Va., the suffering of Federal prisoners at
Savannah, Ga., and Florence, S.C., and Union sentiment
among the middle and lower classes in the interior parts of
South Carolina. Miscellaneous items include a printed list of
officers and men of the U.S. Navy exchanged at Cox's Landing,
Va., Oct. 16, 1864. Correspondents include John A. Dahlgren,
Samuel F. Du Pont, Quincy A. Gillmore, William Reynolds,
and Gideon Welles.
     Finding aid available.

765

Remsen, Tredwell W.   48th New York Volunteers
     Collection, 1861–64. 5 items.
     Three letters from Remsen to his sister, 1861–64, written
from Washington, D.C., and South Carolina, concern Army life
and morale, the Siege of Fort Pulaski, and events in Washington; an undated letter from Remsen to his grandfather discusses troop strength at Annapolis, Md.

766

Revere Family
     Papers, 1746–1964.
     Microfilm, 15 reels.
     Includes the correspondence and papers of Lt. Col. Paul
Joseph Revere and Dr. Edward Hutchinson Robbins Revere,

both of the 20th Massachusetts Volunteers, 1861–63. About 75 letters from Lt. Colonel Revere to his wife and family discuss his capture at the Battle of Balls Bluff, prison life, his exchange, and the participation of the 20th Massachusetts in the Peninsular, Antietam, and Gettysburg campaigns. Includes remarks on camp life, morale, marches, discipline, supplies, casualties, promotions, disease, slavery, and black life. Also contains letters to Revere from various officers in the regiment during his convalescence from a wound received at the Battle of Sharpsburg.

Originals at the Massachusetts Historical Society.

767
Reynolds, Alexander Welch (1817–1876)   Gen., CSA
   Poem, 1864. 1 item.
   Signed poem from Reynolds to Mrs. Hardee, written near Dalton, Ga., Mar. 21, 1864.

768
Reynolds, Charles   Capt., 12th Wisconsin Volunteers
   Order book, 1864–65. 1 v.
   Covers the period Jan. 14, 1864–July 16, 1865. Contains circulars and special orders from the War Department, military codes, orders from the headquarters of Gens. William T. Sherman and James B. McPherson during the Atlanta and Savannah campaigns, figures on votes cast by soldiers in the Presidential election of 1864, copies of congratulatory letters from Gen. U. S. Grant and President Lincoln to General Sherman on his successful campaigns in the South, and orders on enlistments, discharges, foraging expeditions, plundering, special details, and the arrest of stragglers.

769
Reynolds, Thomas Caute (1821–1887)   Gov., Missouri
   Papers, 1856–66. ca. 1,100 items.
   Official and private letterbooks of Reynolds, Dec. 27, 1862–Apr. 15, 1865, and Apr. 13, 1863–Aug. 6, 1864. Contains letters to various officers and statesmen concerning military organization, the appointment of officers, recruitment, supplies, guerrilla warfare, the disposition of troops, and numerous related problems. Letters written from Marshall, Tex., Shreveport, La., Little Rock, Ark., and Richmond, Va., concern chiefly the situation in the southern Trans-Mississippi area.

Microfilm copy (1 reel) available.

770
Reynolds, William (1815–1879)   Adm., USN
   Collection, 1877–1880. 2 items.

Reprint of J. G. Rosengarten's *William Reynolds, Rear-Admiral U.S.N., John Fulton Reynolds, Major-General U.S.V., Colonel Fifth U.S. Infantry. A Memoir* (1880).
Naval Historical Foundation collection.

771
Rhodes, James Ford (1848–1927)   Historian
    Manuscripts, 1912. 3 items.
    Drafts of three lectures on the Civil War.

772
Rice, David A. (d. 1863)   Pvt., 108th
                                    New York Volunteers
    Collection, 1862–65. 6 items.
    Diary, Aug. 19, 1862–Apr. 18, 1863, kept by Rice both as a foot soldier and a wagoner in the Antietam and Fredericksburg campaigns. Describes the capture of over 300 Confederate soldiers who became ill after partaking of the Maryland harvest during the Antietam Campaign, camp life, diet, disease, and hospital care. Also includes three letters from Rice to his family and relatives in New York, 1862–63.

773
Richardson, Charles H.   2d Vermont Volunteers
    Diary, 1862–68. 3 v.
    Contains two volumes relating to the war: Mar. 12–Oct. 22, 1863, and Feb. 10, 1864–Apr. 21, 1867. Describes morale, entertainment, discipline, and hospital care at the Patterson Park Hospital near Baltimore, Md.; preparations against the Confederate invasion of 1863 (Gettysburg Campaign); and the impressment and treatment of blacks as laborers. Also describes acute drunkenness in the Army of the Potomac, the Wilderness Campaign, guerrilla attacks on wounded Federal soldiers, and casualties in the 2d Vermont. Includes a record of Richardson's correspondence.

774
Richmond, Lewis (d. 1894)   Capt., USA
    Document, 1862. 1 item.
    Military pass for the transportation of eight telegraph operators aboard the *Alice Price*, Sept. 1, 1862.

775
Riggs Family
    Papers, 1763–1945. ca. 100,000 items.
    Includes official correspondence and papers of George W. Riggs, Jr., agent for paying U.S. military pensions, 1856–62.
    Finding aid available.

776

Ripley, Josiah W.   Pvt., 18th Massachusetts Volunteers
    Papers, 1862, 1931. 2 items.
    Diary, May 16–Aug. 21, 1862, kept by Ripley during the
Peninsular Campaign. Contains remarks on camp life, training,
marches, and routine affairs. Includes a few details on the
evacuation of the peninsula. Also contains a record of Ripley's
service in the war obtained from the Massachusetts attorney
general's office in 1931.

777

Rittenhouse, Benjamin F.   Maj., USA
    Article, undated. 1 item.
    Transcript.
    "The Battle of Gettysburg as Seen From Little Round Top."
Includes a note in the margin indicating that this account var-
ies from the published version.

778

Rives, William Cabell
(1793–1868)   Member, C.S. Congress
    Papers, 1674–1939. ca. 50,400 items.
    In part, transcripts and photocopies.
    Official and family correspondence concerning Confeder-
ate politics, finance, and trade, public support for the war,
military and political leadership, military appointments and
promotions, the attitude of the southern clergy, life in Richmond during the war, the general progress of the war, and
enlistments and casualties in the Confederate Army. Also contains requests for aid from numerous Confederate prisoners of
war, biographical and autobiographical material on Rives, miscellaneous photographs, and letters from Alfred S. Rives (CSA)
to his wife and parents concerning the defenses of Richmond,
casualties, and the Chancellorsville, Petersburg, and Appomattox campaigns. Correspondents include Robert E. Lee, Christopher G. Memminger, Prince Camille Armand Jules Marie de
Polignac, and James A. Seddon.
    Finding aid and microfilm copy (7 reels) available.

779

Robert, Henry Martyn (1837–1923)   Engineer; Capt., USA
    Papers, 1853–1927. ca. 5,000 items.
    Includes a few miscellaneous letters and orders, 1861–64,
pertaining to the construction of fortifications and Robert's ill
health. Correspondents are Gen. Richard Delafield and Gen.
Joseph G. Totten.
    Finding aid available.

780
Robert J. Lowry and Company
    Records, 1862–63. 10 items.
    Letters concerning, in part, the purchase and distribution of military supplies and problems with Union raiding parties.

781
Roberts Family
    Papers, 1734–1944. 433 items.
    Includes eight letters from Pvt. Junius B. Roberts (28th U.S. Colored Infantry) to his family, 1864–65, concerning his service as an orderly in a military hospital in Alexandria, Va. Provides some information on deaths, disease, and hospital care. Miscellaneous items comprise "Perrine's New Military Map Illustrating the Seat of War," by C. O. Perrine (1862); a manual of arms; and a "Prison Song. Lines written by Dr. Sutherland, . . . 92d N.Y. Regiment, who was captured . . . during the battle of 'fair Oaks,' . . . being a correct history of his capture, and their confinement, treatment and suffering, while prisoners; also, a hint at the habits and customs of the Southern Confederacy" (n.d.).

782
Rockwell, Almon Ferdinand (b. 1835)   Maj., USA
    Papers, 1852–1900. ca. 2,000 items.
    In part, transcripts.
    Includes a diary kept by Rockwell, Oct. 1861–Sept. 1862, during Gen. Don Carlos Buell's occupation of Nashville, the Shiloh Campaign, the Corinth Campaign, marches and skirmishes in northern Alabama, and the pursuit of Gen. Braxton Bragg in Kentucky. Contains remarks on camp life, training, morale, marches, discipline, entertainment, disease, medical care, Confederate deserters, casualties, southern Unionists, prisoners of war, the death of Gen. William Nelson, generalship, and the removal and reinstatement of General Buell. Also contains an autobiographical sketch (10 p.) of Rockwell; a letter from T. J. Bush to Rockwell, Nov. 14 [1862], Indianapolis [Ind.], on General Buell's spirits while awaiting a court of inquiry on his conduct in the Battle of Perryville; and a letter from Buell to [Rockwell], July 10, 1864, concerning his resignation from the Army.

783
Rodgers Family
    Papers, 1740–1957. ca. 11,150 items.
    Material relating to the war consists chiefly of letters from Col. John N. Macomb to his wife, 1861–62, concerning his service as chief of the army topographical engineers, his associ-

ation with Gens. Irvin McDowell and John Pope, the occupation of Fredericksburg, Va., and the 2d Manassas Campaign. Miscellaneous items include a few letters by Gen. Montgomery C. Meigs, a letter by Comdr. John Rodgers describing his engagement on the U.S.S. *Galena* with Confederate batteries near City Point, Va., a letter by Ann Minerva Macomb, Apr. 17, 1865, concerning the excitement in Washington following the assassination of President Lincoln, and the war record of Capt. R. H. Montgomery.

Finding aid available.

784
—————

Papers, 1788–1944. ca. 15,500 items.

Includes official, general, and family correspondence of Capt. John Rodgers (1812–1882), U.S. Navy, along with orders, returns, telegrams, receipts, inventories, accounts, intelligence and battle reports, and miscellaneous items. Relates to the construction and staffing of gunboats for duty on the Ohio and Mississippi Rivers (U.S.S. *Tyler*, U.S.S. *Conestoga*, and U.S.S. *Galena*), reconnaissance expeditions along the Mississippi River, and Rodgers' command of the U.S.S. *Galena* during the Peninsular Campaign, the U.S.S. *Weehawken* during blockade duty off the coasts of South Carolina and Georgia, and the U.S.S. *Dictator* during its trial voyage. Provides information on the pillage of Beaufort, S.C., black life, the treatment and performance of black soldiers, drug addiction in the Army of the Potomac, prize vessels, the movement and disposition of vessels in the South Atlantic Blockading Squadron, the capture of Forts Walker and Beauregard, attacks on Fort McAllister, weapons, entertainment, discipline, and the Fort Fisher expedition of 1865. Correspondents include Andrew J. Drake, Samuel F. Du Pont, David G. Farragut, Andrew H. Foote, Gustavus V. Fox, George B. McClellan, Matthew Fontaine Maury, Montgomery C. Meigs, John S. Missroon, R. J. Oglesby, Samuel L. Phelps, Roger N. Stembel, and Gideon Welles. Miscellaneous items include captured Confederate letters and documents, a letter from Gen. John C. Frémont to James B. Eads, Oct. 3, 1861, a report on the capture of the C.S.S. *Atlanta*, a comparative evaluation of monitors and ironclads, and sketches of Charleston Harbor, Fort Darling, and Fort Fisher and vicinity.

Finding aid available.

Naval Historical Foundation collection.

785
Roe, Francis Asbury (1823–1901)   Lt. Comdr., USN
Papers, 1842–1901. ca. 500 items.
In part, transcripts.

Includes proof sheets for Roe's *Naval Duties and Discipline With the Policy and Principles of Naval Organization* (1865); and an account of the action between the U.S.S. *Sassacus* and C.S.S. *Albemarle* near the mouth of the Roanoke River, May 5, 1864, written by Roe from his diary and notes in 1899.

Finding aid available.

Naval Historical Foundation collection.

786
Roedel, Josephine Forney (1825–1904)
    Collection, 1863–64. 2 items.
    Diary kept by Roedel during travels in Virginia, Maryland, and Pennsylvania, Oct. 28, 1863–July 13, 1864. Includes comments on depredations and the effects of war in the Shenandoah Valley, inflation, the attitude of noncombatants in Virginia, Pennsylvania, and Maryland, morale among soldiers from Wythe County, Va., the Gettysburg Address, and Gen. Jubal Early's Washington raid. Also includes an offprint of Roedel's diary published in the *Pennsylvania Magazine of History and Biography* (Oct. 1943).

787
Roelofson, William J.   Pvt., 145th Illinois Volunteers
    Document, 1864. 1 item.
    Certificate of service as a 100-day volunteer, Dec. 15, 1864.

788
Rogers, Henry J. (1811–1879)
    Papers, 1844–75.
    Microfilm, 1 reel.
    Includes a letter from Comdr. Homer C. Blake to Commodore Andrew A. Harwood, Dec. 18, 1863, endorsing the use of Rogers' "Semophoric Telegraphic Signals" in the U.S. Navy; a letter from Harwood to Adm. Charles H. Davis, Dec. 30, 1863, on a successful test of the signals at sea; and copies of signals between the U.S.S. *Wachusett* and U.S.S. *Sangamon* in Feb. 1864.

789
Roman, Alfred (b. 1824)   Col., Louisiana Militia
    Papers, 1861–90. 150 items.
    In part, transcripts.
    Includes official correspondence between Gen. P. G. T. Beauregard and various officers and officials, 1861–62, concerning military appointments, the Battle of 1st Manassas, supplies, reinforcements, military organization, Gen. Ambrose E. Burnside's expedition to North Carolina, recruits, strategy, transportation, and the need for more officers. Also contains

military telegrams concerning the Franklin and Nashville Campaign and the defense of Charleston, S.C., in 1865, and Roman's report on Gen. Joseph Wheeler's cavalry corps written as assistant inspector general, Military Division of the West, Dec. 28, 1864. Correspondents include William B. Bate, Judah P. Benjamin, John A. Calhoun, James Chestnut, Samuel Cooper, Jefferson Davis, John B. Hood, Joseph E. Johnston, Thomas Jordan, James L. Kemper, Mrs. Augusta Mason, William P. Miles, Abraham C. Myers, Roger A. Pryor, Richard Taylor, and Jacob Thompson.

790
Roosevelt, Robert Barnwell
(1829–1906)   71st New York Volunteers
    Papers, 1862. 75 items.
    Letters from Roosevelt to his wife, June 4–23, 1862, describe the abuse of the men of the 71st New York by government officials, military officers, and citizens in Washington, D.C., as a result of their refusal to enlist in the Regular Army for three years or for the war—the regiment had been dispatched from New York to Washington in the face of Federal reversals in the Peninsular and Shenandoah Valley campaigns. Also contains a list of officers in the 71st New York, newspaper clippings on the war, and a detailed account of the trip from New York to Washington.

791
Roosevelt, Theodore   Recruitment Commissioner,
(1831–1878)   New York
    Family papers, 1810–1919. ca. 300 items.
    Contains a few letters and documents relating to the appointment of commissioners to issue military certificates in New York, and the recruitment of volunteers.

792
Roosevelt, Theodore (1858–1919), Pres., U.S.
    Papers, 1759–1920. ca. 276,000 items.
    In part, transcripts.
    Includes a copy of an article in the Portland, Maine, *Evening Courier*, Mar. 8, 1862, on "General McClellan's Dream," a facsimile of President Lincoln's letter to Mrs. Lydia Bixby, Nov. 21, 1864, and a copy of the war record of William Allen.
    Published index and microfilm copy (485 reels) available.

793
Rose, Luther A.   Operator, U.S.
                                        Military Telegraph Service
    Diary, 1863–66. 1 v.
    Contains information on the operation of the U.S. Military

Telegraph Service during the Chancellorsville, Gettysburg, Mine Run, Wilderness, Spotsylvania, Cold Harbor, and Petersburg campaigns. Includes comments on the frequent relocation of the telegraph service, the progress of the war, camp life, deserters, devastation in Virginia, casualties, prisoners of war, entertainment, generalship, and various battles and skirmishes.

794

Rose, Solomon D.   Pvt., USA
    Letter, 1865. 1 item.
    Letter from Rose to his mother, Mar. 20, 1865, concerning camp life and patriotism in the Army of the Potomac.

795

Rosecrans, William Starke (1819–1898)   Gen., USA
    Collection, 1862, 1865. 2 items.
    Includes a letter from Rosecrans to Dr. Jacob Boyers, Feb. 5, 1862, Wheeling, [W.] Va., encouraging the arrest and prosecution of Confederate sympathizers in Monogalia County.

796

Rowan, Stephen Clegg (1808–1890)   Comdr., USN
    Papers, 1826–90. 4 items.
    Includes a letterbook, Feb. 22, 1854–Jan. 21, 1880, containing about 250 copies of letters and reports on the war, including attempts by the U.S.S. *Pawnee* to reach Fort Sumter in Apr. 1861, the engagement of the U.S.S. *Pawnee* and U.S.S. *Thomas Freeborn* with Confederate batteries at Aquia Creek, Va., the capture and occupation of Alexandria, Va., the action at Mathias Point, Va., June 27, 1861, Gen. Ambrose E. Burnside's expedition to North Carolina, and the Battle of New Bern, N.C. Also includes miscellaneous reports and comments on the activities of the North Atlantic and South Atlantic Blockading Squadrons, loyalist refugees, blockade runners, prize vessels, the torpedo attack on the U.S.S. *New Ironsides*, the sinking of the U.S.S. *Housatonic*, naval morale, discipline, ship repairs, and the bombardment of Forts Sumter, Wagner, Moultrie, and Gregg. Correspondents include John A. Dahlgren, Gustavus V. Fox, Louis M. Goldsborough, David D. Porter, Cornelius K. Stribling, Silas H. Stringham, Alfred H. Terry, and Gideon Welles.
    Finding aid available.
    Naval Historical Foundation collection.

797

Rowan, W. H.   Capt., Kentucky Battalion, CSA
    Letter, 1861. 1 item.
    Photocopy.

William Starke Rosecrans

Letter from Rowan to his mother, July 22, 1861, concerning casualties and captured stores and equipment from the Battle of 1st Manassas.

798
Ruffin, Edmund (1794–1865)   Agriculturist–Writer, Virginia
      Diary, 1856–65. 14 v.
      Observations on secession, Confederate and Union politics, and battles and skirmishes, including the Fort Sumter affair and the battles of 1st and 2d Manassas. Also includes copies of letters, maps, pamphlets, clippings, and fragmentary essays.
      Microfilm copy (7 reels) available.

799
Rupley, Samuel K. (b. 1844)   Pvt., 150th
                                      New York Volunteers
      Papers, 1863–1908. 78 items.
      Chiefly miscellaneous telegrams and drafts of messages, 1863–65, concerning military appointments, troop positions, supplies, furloughs, passes, and visits of public officials to the war zone. Includes a copy of the official announcement from the War Department of the death of President Lincoln.

800
Russell, John Henry (1827–1897)   Lt. Comdr., USN
      Collection, 1861–75. 18 items.
      Chiefly official correspondence and orders, 1861–64, concerning blockade duty with the Gulf Coast and South Atlantic Blockading Squadrons, and operations on the Mississippi River. Includes a sketch of Admiral Farragut's order of battle for the attack on Forts Jackson and St. Philip, a sketch showing the position of several vessels in Farragut's fleet in the bombardment of Vicksburg, and a letter from Comdr. Henry H. Bell to Russell, Oct. 14, 1862, on the blockade of Mobile Bay. Other correspondents are Adms. John A. Dahlgren and David G. Farragut, and Comdr. Cadwalader Ringgold.
      Naval Historical Foundation collection.

801
Russell, William R.   USA
      Papers, 1858–89. ca. 90 items.
      Includes a letter to Russell from his mother, July 3, 1861, concerning the military presence in Washington, D.C., and President Lincoln; and a letter from a soldier at Norfolk, Va., to his parents, June 10, 1862, describing camp life and morale among the 13th New York State Militia, also known as the 13th New York National Guard.

802

Ryan, George Parker (1842–1877)   1st Lt., USN
    Papers, 1860–1952. 75 items.
    Includes 12 letters from Ryan to his brother, U.S.S. *Sacramento,* European Squadron, July 25, 1864–Mar. 28, 1865, concerning Confederate privateers, the search for the C.S.S. *Alabama,* efforts to capture the C.S.S. *Rappahannock,* and an encounter with the C.S.S. *Stonewall.* Also contains a description of the *Stonewall,* an explanation as to why the *Sacramento* did not attack it, and an undated photograph of the U.S.S. *Monongahela.*
    Naval Historical Foundation collection.

803

Ryan, Patrick   Sgt., 132d New York Volunteers
    Diary, 1863–65. 1 v.
    Covers the period May 30, 1863–June 3, 1865. Describes Ryan's enlistment in New York City, garrison duty in New Berne, N.C., and vicinity, marches and skirmishes in the area, guerrilla warfare (the mining of roads and railroads), Gen. George E. Pickett's attack on New Bern, Feb. 1, 1864, and the Carolinas Campaign. Includes a few details on the Battle of Kinston, N.C., Confederate deserters, camp life, training, prisoners of war, and discipline.

804

St. John, Bela T. (b. 1843)   Pvt., 46th Illinois Volunteers
    Papers, 1861–66. 108 items.
    Chiefly letters from St. John to his family and relatives, 1862–66, and a diary, Nov. 7, 1861–Sept. 16, 1866 (9 v.), relating to the Fort Donelson, Shiloh, Corinth, and Vicksburg campaigns, the Siege of Jackson, Miss., and the Siege of Mobile, Ala. Also describes St. John's enlistment and training in Illinois, camp life, morale, discipline, marches, the selection of officers, military organization, casualties, disease, hospital care, foraging expeditions, guerrilla warfare, Confederate deserters, the use of blacks in the U.S. Army, generalship, the dismissal of incompetent officers, and speculation in cotton by officers. Additional items include remarks on the movement of troops and supplies on the Mississippi River, life in New Orleans, La., during the war, an expedition up the White River (Arkansas) in Sept.–Oct. 1864, the capture of Spanish Fort and Fort Blakely, Ala., and the Battle of Mobile Bay as viewed from shore. Two letters by Sgt. John D. St. John, Mar. 26–27 and Apr. 14, 1862, discuss the Fort Donelson and Shiloh campaigns, black life, and the presence of women in battle.

805

Saint John, Theodore Edgar

(1831–1887)   Pvt., 14th Wisconsin Volunteers
    Papers, 1862–92. ca. 20 items.
    Photocopies.
    Chiefly letters from Saint John to Jane Cecelia Harries, 1862–65, written during operations in northern Mississippi, Oct.–Nov. 1862, and in the Vicksburg, Atlanta, Savannah, and Carolinas campaigns. Includes remarks on camp life, morale, marches, foraging expeditions, deaths, and prisoners of war. Also contains Saint John's discharge, May 27, 1865, miscellaneous orders, a poem on the death of Gen. James B. McPherson by a surgeon on McPherson's staff, pension records, and biographical notes.

806

Sanborn, Fred G.   Capt., 5th Maine Volunteers
    Papers, 1864. 75 items.
    In part, transcripts.
    General and special orders, returns, battle reports, clippings, and miscellaneous items relating to campaigns in Virginia in 1864. Includes some information on the Wilderness, Spotsylvania, and Cold Harbor campaigns.

807

Sanders, George Nicholas

(1812–1873)   Confederate Agent; Revolutionist
    Papers, 1833–79. 27 items.
    Contains a letter from Henry S. Foote to Sanders, Mar. 26, 1861, concerning recognition of the Confederacy and Foote's efforts to carry Tennessee out of the Union; and a letter from Judah P. Benjamin to Mrs. G. N. Sanders, Oct. 6, 1863, on a proposed plan for sending secret dispatches.

808

———

    Papers, 1854–65.
    Microfilm, 2 reels.
    Correspondence, clippings, and pamphlets concerning the secessionist crisis, the organization of the Confederate Government, the progress of the war, the bombardment of Charleston, S.C., inflation, and politics.
    Originals at the National Archives.

809

Sands, Frank T.   Mortician, Washington, D.C.
    Collection, 1862–65. 8 items.
    Includes "Articles of Agreement" between Sands and Capt.

Edward L. Hartz for the burial of deceased soldiers, and photographs of both Sands and Hartz.

810

Sanger, Donald Bridgman (1889–1947)   Author
        Papers, 1932–37. ca. 1,000 items.
        Draft of Sanger's thesis, "General James Longstreet and the Civil War," submitted to the University of Chicago in 1934, and later edited, expanded, and published by Thomas R. Hay. Also includes notes, articles, and lectures on Longstreet.

811

Santee (U.S.S.)
        Logbook, 1861–62. 2 v.
        Chiefly navigational records kept during service in the Gulf Blockading Squadron, June 9, 1861–Aug. 23, 1862. Also contains a list of officers aboard the *Santee,* an inventory of stores and equipment, names of prize vessels, an account of the attack on the *Royal Yacht,* and comments on discipline, desertions, deaths, and prisoners of war.

812

Sargent, John Osborne (1811–1891)   Journalist; Lawyer
        Papers, 1831–1912.
        Microfilm, 4 reels.
        Contains clippings and extracts from various newspapers on the progress of the war, Confederate generals, emancipation, and the trial of Henry Wirz.
        Originals in the Massachusetts Historical Society.

813

Sargent, Winthrop (1753–1820)
        Family papers, 1772–1948.
        Microfilm, 7 reels.
        Contains a copy of the proceedings of the military trial of Pvt. Amsel Harmen, 4th Illinois Cavalry, for the murder of George Washington Sargent at Natchez, Miss., in 1864. Also tried with Harmen were Pvts. Alexander McBride, David Greer, and William Thomas.
        Originals in the Massachusetts Historical Society.

814

Savage, John (1828–1888)   69th New York
                                                Militia Regiment
        Letter, 1861. 1 item.
        Letter from Savage to George P. Morris, July 31, 1861, relating to his service as a three-month volunteer in Washington, D.C., and Virginia.

815
Saxton, Rufus (1824–1908)   Gen., USA
     Collection, 1862–89. 3 items.
     Letter from Saxton to the Board of Home Missions, Oct.
22, 1862, Beaufort, S.C., concerning the transfer of Rev. J.
Kennedy from Beaufort to Fernandina, Fla., where the garrison needed a minister; and a letter from Saxton to the American Medical Association, June 18, 1863, Beaufort, S.C., thanking the association for its interest in his work in behalf of
freedmen in his department.

816
Sayre, Francis Bowes (1885–1972)
     Papers, 1861–1961. ca. 8,100 items.
     Contains about 50 letters from Capt. Wilberforce Nevin,
79th Pennsylvania Volunteers, to his family and relatives, Oct.
14, 1861–Jan. 4, 1864, concerning campaigns in Kentucky,
Tennessee, and Alabama. Includes comments on camp life,
marches, morale, discipline, troop movements, foraging expeditions, the treatment of prisoners of war, guerrilla warfare,
depredations by both Union and Confederate soldiers, the attitude and conduct of noncombatants, black life, the attitude of
blacks toward the war, the use and treatment of blacks by
Union soldiers, southern Unionists, inflation, disease, spies,
military organization, and generalship. Also contains information on the battles of Perryville, Ky., and Murfreesboro, Tenn.,
and a skirmish at Rowlett's Station, Ky., Dec. 17, 1861; and a
short history of the 79th Pennsylvania written by Captain
Nevin in Dec. 1864.
     Finding aid available.

817
Schaumburg Family
     Collection, 1795–1865. 3 items.
     In part, photocopies.
     Military pass issued to Orleana Christy Schaumburg (Mrs.
Charles W. Schaumburg), Jan. 18, 1865, to enter the South,
and signed by President Lincoln. Also a personal letter from
Gen. P. G. T. Beauregard to Mrs. Schaumburg.

818
Scholossen, Peter   Pvt., USA
     Document, 1863. 1 item.
     Discharge certificate, Mar. 2, 1863.

819
Schnell, Joseph (1840–1914)   Pvt., 2d
                                                        Pennsylvania Reserves
      Papers, 1844–1914. ca. 100 items.
      Includes Schnell's enlistment certificate, Apr. 17, 1861; a
letter from Schnell to his sister, Sept. 18, 1861, on his work
with the military telegraph, troop reviews by President Lincoln,
Gen. George B. McClellan, Gov. Andrew Curtin, and Simon
Cameron, and discipline in Gen. George A. McCall's Pennsylvania Reserves Corps; miscellaneous telegrams; and an autograph
book.

820
Schofield, John McAllister (1831–1906)   Gen., USA
      Papers, 1837–1906. ca. 30,000 items.
      Contains orders, dispatches, reports, returns, telegrams,
maps, court-martial records, and official correspondence concerning Schofield's command of the Army of the Frontier and
the Department of the Missouri, and operations in the Atlanta
and Franklin and Nashville campaigns. Cartographic items
comprise maps of the battlefields of Totopotomoy Creek, Beth-
esda Church, North Anna, the Wilderness, and Spotsylvania; a
map of Sparta, Tenn., and vicinity (1863); and a topographical
sketch of Bowling Green, Ky., and environs. Also includes a
postwar account of the Franklin and Nashville Campaign by
Capt. William M. Wherry, aide-de-camp to Schofield; and a
diary, Aug. 26-Oct. 29, 1863, kept by Schofield as commander
of the Department of the Missouri. Diary entries concern the
generalship of Samuel R. Curtis, popular support for Gen.
Thomas Ewing, the political situation in Missouri, radical
opposition to Schofield, military organization, recruitment, and
black recruits. Also includes copies of letters from President
Lincoln to Schofield, Oct. 1, 1863, on Federal policy in Missouri,
and from Charles D. Drake, Oct. 5, 1863, stating the President's
reasons for not removing Schofield from command. Correspondents include Francis P. Blair, Jr., Montgomery Blair, John A.
Campbell, Cyrus B. Comstock, Jacob D. Cox, Ulysses S. Grant,
Henry W. Halleck, John C. Kelton, John Pope, Fitz-John Porter,
William S. Rosecrans, Philip H. Sheridan, William T. Sherman,
Edwin M. Stanton, Alfred H. Terry, George H. Thomas, and
Edward D. Townsend.
      Finding aid available.

821
Schonborn, Harry F.
      Notebook, 1861–63. 1 item.

John McAllister Schofield

Contains drawings of fortifications at Battery Douglass, Fort Totten, Fort Mahan, and Fort Saratoga, and payrolls for labor and supplies used in construction of these works.

822

Schoonmaker, Cornelius Marius
(1839–1889)   1st Lt.; Executive Officer, USN
    Papers, 1833–1931. ca. 1,400 items.
    Official and personal correspondence, orders, reports, and miscellaneous items relating to Schoonmaker's service on the U.S.S. *Minnesota* (1861), U.S.S. *Pawnee* (1861), U.S.S. *Wyandotte* (1861), U.S.S. *Octorara* (1862), U.S.S. *Pinola* (1863), U.S.S. *Manhattan* (1864), U.S.S. *Augusta* (1864), and U.S.S. *Catskill* (1865). Also includes an unpublished biography of Schoonmaker by his father, Marius Schoonmaker, consisting chiefly of his son's personal letters to his family concerning training, discipline, the dilemma confronting southern officers during the secession crisis, war fever in the North, the Federal blockade, torpedo warfare, prize vessels, the treatment of prisoners of war, Gen. Ambrose E. Burnside's expedition to North Carolina, the generalship of Benjamin F. Butler, rank disputes, the Siege of Fort Pulaski, ship construction, the advantages and disadvantages of ironclads, contraband trade with Nassau, the Battle of Mobile Bay, and the attitude of southerners toward U.S. seamen.
    Finding aid available.
    Naval Historical Foundation collection.

823

Schouler, William (1814–1872)   Adj. Gen., Massachusetts
    Collection, 1864. 2 items.
    Photocopies.
    Letter with attached note from Schouler to Gov. John A. Andrew, Sept. 24, 1864, Boston, Mass., concerning the discharge of one of five sons of John Otis Newhall. Includes remarks on Mrs. Lydia Bixby.

824

Schuckers, Jacob William (ca. 1832–1901)   Author
    Papers, 1836–1900. ca. 200 items.
    Includes letters by Dr. S. M. Smith, Gustav C. Weber, and B. P. Baker, Dec. 12, 1862–Jan. 12, 1863, concerning positions in the Medical Department, USA.

825

Schurz, Carl (1829–1906)   Gen., USV
    Papers, 1842–1932. ca. 23,000 items.
    In part, transcripts and photocopies.

Correspondence and papers concerning military appointments, diplomatic affairs, recruits, the organization and disposition of troops, training, morale, discipline, desertions, President Lincoln, generalship, Federal policy toward blacks in the war zone, and the battles of 2d Manassas and Chancellorsville. Also includes clippings, battle reports, returns, a diary, June 2, 1862–Feb. 1, 1863, concerning, in part, the Shenandoah Valley Campaign of 1862, and miscellaneous postwar maps and pamphlets. Correspondents include Ambrose E. Burnside, Simon Cameron, Samuel P. Chase, John C. Frémont, John Hay, David Hunter, Abraham Lincoln, Irvin McDowell, Halbert E. Paine, William H. Seward, Franz Sigel, Julius Stahel, and Charles Sumner.

Finding aid and microfilm copy (120 reels) available.

826
Schuyler, Louisa Lee (1837–1926)   Social Worker
    Collection, 1852–1915. 17 items.
    Includes a pamphlet by Georgina Woolsey, *What We Did at Gettysburg* (1863), on the care of sick and wounded soldiers after the battle.

827
Scott, John White (1837–1917)   21st Virginia Volunteers;
                                                   Clerk, CSA
    Papers, 1861–1917. 250 items.
    Includes a photograph of Scott in Confederate uniform, postwar clippings relating to his service in the 21st Virginia, and notes concerning his arrest and imprisonment as a Confederate spy. Also contains letters from a political prisoner, Representative T. Parker Scott (Maryland) to his wife, Sept. 1861–Nov. 1862, written from Forts Monroe, Warren, and Lafayette, concerning his arrest and imprisonment, prison morale, entertainment, and health. Miscellaneous items include a medical discharge for John W. Scott, Jan. 3, 1862; a letter from Charles H. Blair to Scott, Mar. 25, 1862, on Scott's appointment as a clerk on the C.S.S. *Arkansas*; and a letter from John A. Wilson to Scott, July 24, 1862, on naval activities near Vicksburg, Miss.

828
Seabrook, Edward M.   Lt., CSA
    Papers, 1858–64. 25 items.
    Commission, July 8, 1864, and miscellaneous accounts and receipts.

829
Searcher, Victor   Author
     Article, ca. 1960. 1 item.
     Draft of the unpublished appendix to Searcher's *Lincoln's
Journey to Greatness* (1960).

830
Secession Conventions
     Collection, 1860–61. 4 items.
     Photocopies and facsimiles.
     Ordinances of secession adopted by the States of Virginia,
Louisiana, Florida, and South Carolina.

831
Seeley, Francis Webb   Capt., 4th U.S. Artillery
     Collection, 1871. 2 items.
     Letter from Seeley to Gen. John Watts de Peyster, Sept.
19, 1871, concerning de Peyster's request for information on
the Battle of Fredericksburg, and Seeley's account of the battle
(13 p.).

832
Selfridge, Thomas Oliver (1804–1902)   Comdr., USN
     Papers, 1809–1927. ca. 750 items.
     In part, transcripts.
     Official correspondence, orders, reports, and printed matter.
Includes copies of orders issued by Selfridge as commander of
the U.S.S. *Mississippi*, Mississippi Squadron, 1861; the log of
the *Mississippi*, May 18, 1861–Feb. 16, 1862; orders from William Mervine and William W. McKean to Selfridge, 1861–63,
concerning the Gulf Blockading Squadron; information on ship
sightings and seizures; letters from Thomas Selfridge, Jr., Dec.
16 [1862], describing the sinking of the U.S.S. *Cairo* in the
Yazoo Pass expedition, and Sept. 6 [1864], on the design and
performance of the U.S.S. *Vindicator*; instructions by Adm.
David D. Porter, Dec. 17, 1864, on the plan to explode a vessel
loaded with powder off Fort Fisher, N.C.; proceedings from
Selfridge's trial for supposed negligence of duty on the Gulf
Blockade; and a letterbook, Feb. 3, 1863–Aug. 12, 1864, con-
taining Selfridge's official correspondence as commandant at
Mare Island, Calif. Printed items include the *Defence of Com.
Charles Wilkes, U.S.N., Late Acting Rear Admiral in Com-
mand of the West India Squadron* (1864), and *The Navy in
Congress: Being Speeches of the Hon. Messrs. Grimes, Doolittle,
and Nye; of the Senate. and the Hon. Messrs. Rice, Pike,
Griswold, and Blow; of the House of Representatives* (1865).
     Finding aid available.
     Naval Historical Foundation collection.

833

Selfridge, Thomas Oliver (1836–1924)   Comdr., USN
    Papers, 1852–1927. ca. 1,900 items.
    In part, transcripts.
    Includes a copy of a letter from James M. Mason to Judah
P. Benjamin, July 6, 1864, London, concerning the Great Seal
of the Confederate States of America; and a letter from Jacob
Thompson to Benjamin, Dec. 3, 1864, Toronto [Canada], concerning the organization and activities of the Sons of Liberty in
the northwestern United States, plans for a general uprising in
Illinois, Indiana, and Ohio by Confederate sympathizers, the
loss of arms stored at Indianapolis, plans to take over the
steamer *Michigan* and free Confederate prisoners of war at
Johnson's Island, efforts to disrupt northern finance by buying
and exporting gold, and other subversive activities.
    Finding aid available.
    Naval Historical Foundation collection.

834

Sellers, David Foote (1874–1949)
    Papers, 1830–1949. ca. 6,500 items.
    Includes the scrapbook and diary of Joseph E. Nourse, pro-
fessor of ethics and English studies at the U.S. Naval Academy
at Newport, R.I. Contains a few remarks on sick and wounded
soldiers, deaths of servicemen, and troop departures.
    Finding aid available.
    Naval Historical Foundation collection.

835

Sewall, Joseph (1795–1851)
    Papers, 1832–1907. ca. 3,700 items.
    Includes miscellaneous correspondence and papers of
Sewall's son, Col. Frederick Drummer Sewall, 19th Maine Volunteers and 3d Veteran Reserve Corps. Consists of official correspondence with the provost marshal's office, circulars, telegrams, orders, commissions, receipts, and invoices.
    Finding aid available.

836

Seward, William Henry
(1801–1872)   U.S. Secretary of State
    Collection, 1834–71. 40 items.
    In part, facsimiles.
    Includes Seward's instructions to Charles Francis Adams
as Minister to England, May 21, 1861, with alterations by
President Lincoln.

837

Shackleford, W. C.   Asst. Surg., 2d Virginia Cavalry
    Letter, 1906. 1 item.
    Photocopy.
    Letter from Shackleford to J. P. McCabe, Stony Point, Va.,
Feb. 4, 1906, describing an amputation he performed on McCabe
in 1863 and the death of Doctor Nelson, also an assistant surgeon with the 2d Virginia Cavalry.

838

Shafter, William Rufus
(1835–1906)   Col., 17th U.S. Colored Infantry
    Papers, 1864–1906. 6 items.
    Includes a letter by Shafter's wife, Mrs. Harriet Grimes
Shafter, Dec. 20, 1864, Nashville, Tenn., on the performance of
the 17th Colored Infantry in the Battle of Nashville, and the
death of Capt. J. H. Aldrich; and a letter written by a black
soldier, Samuel Jones, to Colonel Shafter, Dec. 26, 1864, Little
Rock, Ark.

839

———

    Papers, 1862–1938.
    Microfilm, 14 reels.
    Includes a few orders, circulars, and letters relating chiefly
to the participation of the 17th U.S. Colored Infantry in the
Franklin and Nashville Campaign.
    Originals at Stanford University.

840

Shaler, Alexander   Gen., USA
    Collection, 1863–64. 1 v.
    Record of court-martial proceedings in Shaler's brigade,
with miscellaneous clippings.

841

Shaler, William   CSA
    Family papers, 1809–1916. 47 items.
    Letter from Albert S. Berry, commander of the Marine
Guard on the C.S.S. *Charleston*, to his father, Nov. 10, 1863,
and a "Certificate of Non-liability" for military service through
the procurement of a substitute, Aug. 26, 1864.

842

Shankland, William F.   Comdr., USN
    Diary, 1862. 1 v.
    Diary kept by Shankland in the form of a log while com-
manding the U.S.S. *Currituck*, Feb. 27–Dec. 4, 1862. Describes

the voyage of the *Currituck* from New York to Hampton Roads as an escort to the U.S.S. *Monitor*, the destruction of the U.S.S. *Congress* and U.S.S. *Cumberland*, blockade duty in Chesapeake Bay, reconnaissance and patrol duty on the James and York Rivers during the Peninsular Campaign, assistance rendered to runaway slaves and Unionist refugees, the capture of Confederate blockade runners *American Coaster* and *Planter*, and skirmishes with Confederate shore batteries.

843

Shaver, W. T.   Adj., 12th Missouri Cavalry
    Memoir, undated. 8 p.
    Transcript.
    Describes the organization and service of the 12th Missouri Cavalry, Nov. 1863–Apr. 1866. Includes remarks on skirmishes at Holy Springs, Tallahatchie River, and Abbeville, Miss., and the Franklin and Nashville Campaign.

844

Shaw, Lemuel (1781–1861)
    Family papers, 1648–1923.
    Microfilm, 61 reels.
    Includes three letters from Philip Dolan to Mrs. Shaw written from the U.S.S. *Merrimac* and from camps in North Carolina, 1862–63, concerning the voyage of the 43d Massachusetts from Boston to North Carolina, camp life, training, and morale, and sentiment in the Army toward Gens. George B. McClellan, David Hunter, and John G. Foster. Also contains a few military passes issued to Sgt. Herbert B. Cushing in 1861.
    Published guide available.
    Originals in the Massachusetts Historical Society.

845

Shellenberger, John K.   Capt., USA
    Papers, 1862–1913. 20 items.
    Chiefly postwar letters to Shellenberger written in response to his articles on the Battle of Franklin, Tenn. Correspondents, mostly participants, include Capt. A. P. Baldwin, Gen. Mendal Churchill, Col. Joseph Conrad, Maj. Ephraim C. Dawes, Col. John Q. Lane, Lt. Col. William G. Le Duc, Gen. Stephen D. Lee, Gen. David S. Stanley, Henry Stone, Capt. Edward G. Whitesides, and Gen. Thomas J. Wood. Also includes copies of two letters by Gen. John D. Cox concerning a promotion for Col. Emerson Opdycke for his performance in the Battle of Franklin.

846

Sheridan, Philip Henry (1831–1888)   Gen., USA
    Papers, 1853–88. ca. 18,000 items.
    In part, transcripts.
    Contains official correspondence, letterbooks, orders, dispatches, battle and reconnaissance reports, and clippings relating to the Stones River, Tullahoma, Chickamauga, Chattanooga, Shenandoah Valley (1864), and Appomattox campaigns, as well as telegraph books, lists of battles and skirmishes, notes on the Union spy, Rebecca Wright, of Winchester, Va., and a draft of the *Personal Memoirs of P. H. Sheridan* (1888). Correspondents include George A. Forsyth, James W. Forsyth, Ulysses S. Grant, Abraham Lincoln, and William T. Sherman. Also contains miscellaneous letters by William H. Emory, David M. Gregg, Henry W. Halleck, Andrew A. Humphreys, George G. Meade, Wesley Merritt, Edwin M. Stanton, John D. Stevenson, Lorenzo Thomas, Seth Williams, and James H. Wilson, and a captured letter from Braxton Bragg to Jubal Early with an enclosed report on Early's command, Aug. 29, 1864.
    Finding aid available.

847

Sherman, John (1823–1900)   U.S. Senator, Ohio
    Papers, 1836–1900. ca. 130,000 items.
    In part, photocopies.
    Contains political, military, and family correspondence on the war. Includes numerous solicitations for military appointments and promotions, suggestions on military organization and strategy, appeals for exchange from Union and Confederate prisoners of war, reports on the condition, location, and performance of the Sherman brigade (64th and 65th Ohio Regiments), and letters concerning military pay and bounties, sutlers, the return of runaway slaves, the Siege of Fort Pulaski, generalship, guerrilla warfare, the Shiloh and Corinth campaigns, the attitude and treatment of noncombatants in the South, and the Presidential election of 1864. Also includes dispatches and telegrams from soldiers in the field, Sherman's correspondence as chairman of the Senate Finance Committee, correspondence with the Adjutant General and Quartermaster General of Ohio on recruits and supplies, and a copy of the diary of Colonel Worthington (USA), Mar. 26–Apr. 5, 1862, kept during the Battle of Shiloh. Correspondents include Daniel Butterfield, Simon Cameron, Charles A. Dana, Thomas Ewing, Gustavus V. Fox, James A. Garfield, Quincy A. Gillmore, Willis A. Gorman, John H. Hammond, James A. Hardie, William B. Hazen, Oliver O. Howard, John A. Logan, Joseph K. F. Mansfield, Montgomery C. Meigs, James S. Robinson, Robert C. Schenck, Winfield Scott, John W. Sprague, David S. Stanley,

Philip Henry Sheridan

Lorenzo Thomas, Stewart Van Vliet, and Gideon Welles.
Finding aid available.

848
———

Papers, 1848–93.
Microfilm, 2 reels.
Contains a letter from Fitz-John Porter to Sherman, June 28, 1861, concerning Confederate spies in western Maryland, troop positions, and strategy; a letter from Fitz-John Porter to Sherman, July 26, 1861, defending himself against criticism for his failure to prevent Gen. T. J. Jackson from reaching the Manassas battlefield; and miscellaneous letters relating to the war from Samuel F. Du Pont, James A. Garfield, Henry W. Halleck, James A. Hardie, William S. Rosecrans, Gideon Welles, and John Wool.

849
Sherman, Thomas West (1813–1879)   Gen., USA
Collection, 1860–62. 2 items.
Letter from Sherman to his former aide-de-camp, Adam Badeau, Apr. 3, 1862, Port Royal, S.C., thanking Badeau for his services during the Port Royal expedition.

850
Sherman, William Tecumseh (1820–1891)   Gen., USA
Papers, 1810–96. ca. 18,000 items.
In part, transcripts.
Political and military correspondence between General Sherman and Senator John Sherman, letters from Mrs. Ellen Ewing Sherman to Senator Sherman, 1861–62, concerning her husband's health and career, and official correspondence on the situation in Kentucky in 1861, General Sherman's attitude toward newspaper correspondents, the Shiloh, Corinth, and Vicksburg campaigns, the Arkansas Post expedition, military organization, the treatment of blacks, discipline, generalship, conscription, military strategy, rank disputes, appointments and promotions, and the suffering of noncombatants in the South. Also contains information on the relief of General Burnside at Knoxville, Tenn., the Meridian Campaign, the Battle of Missionary Ridge, Sherman's role in the Battle of 1st Manassas, and the Atlanta Campaign. Miscellaneous items comprise military accounts, telegrams, intelligence reports, orders, clippings, maps, drafts of the *Memoirs of General William T. Sherman* (1875), the *Report of Lieutenant General U. S. Grant of the Armies of the United States—1864–65* (1865), "Particulars of the Death of Maj. Gen. James B. McPherson," by William E. Strong, 1876, and certificates commemorating Sherman's role at

the Battle of Shiloh and the capture of Atlanta. Principal correspondents during the war include Robert Anderson, Nathaniel P. Banks, Frank P. Blair, Don Carlos Buell, Ambrose E. Burnside, Eugene A. Carr, Samuel P. Chase, George W. Cullum, Samuel R. Curtis, William Dennison, John A. Dix, Grenville M. Dodge, Thomas Ewing, Ulysses S. Grant, Henry W. Halleck, John H. Hammond, Stephen A. Hurlbut, Richard W. Johnson, Thomas W. Knox, Jacob G. Lauman, Mortimer D. Leggett, Abraham Lincoln, George B. McClellan, Robert H. Milroy, Edward O. C. Ord, David D. Porter, Lovell H. Rousseau, John M. Schofield, Carl Schurz, William Sooy Smith, Frederick Steele, George Stoneman, David Stuart, George H. Thomas, Lorenzo Thomas, David Tod, and Cadwallader C. Washburn.

Finding aid and microfilm copy (51 reels) available.

851
———

Papers, 1808–91.
Microfilm, 15 reels.

Chiefly personal correspondence and papers of the Sherman and Thomas Ewing families. Includes military orders, drafts of Sherman's military reports, letters from Sherman to his wife concerning his role in the war, and miscellaneous related items. Provides some information on the Shiloh, Vicksburg, Chattanooga, Atlanta, Savannah, and Carolinas campaigns, generalship, and the politics of war.

Published guide available.
Originals at the University of Notre Dame.

852
Shields, J. E.   Lt., USA
Letter, 1861. 1 item.

Letter from Shields to Col. J. B. Thurman(?), Oct. 1, 1861, Cape Girardeau, Mo., concerning the rental of the steamboat *Luella*. A note on the verso by Gen. U. S. Grant approves Shields' rejection of the requested rental price and orders the vessel retained in government service if needed.

853
Shiner, Michael   Mechanic, Washington, D.C., Navy Yard
Diary, 1813–69. 1 v.

Contains remarks on the arrival of various regiments in Washington, the organization of workers at the Washington Navy Yard to help oppose Gen. Jubal A. Early in July 1864, the arrival of British and French warships, and visits by President Lincoln to troops along Washington's defensive perimeter.

854
Shippen Family
    Papers, 1671–1936. ca. 6,500 items.
    Includes three letters to Dr. Edward Shippen, surgeon, 1st
Pennsylvania Artillery Reserves, 1862–63, from William
T. W. Ball, Thomas P. Parry, and Robert M. West.
    Finding aid and microfilm copy (15 reels) available.

855
Shortelle, James Edward (d. 1871), and Family
    Collection, 1851–64. 11 items.
    Includes four letters from Robert Shortelle (6th Pennsylva-
nia Reserves) to his family, written from camps in Maryland
and Virginia, 1861–63, and two letters from Parly Colburn
(USA) to his wife, 1863–64, concerning camp life, disease,
discipline, and morale. Also contains a photograph of James
Shortelle in uniform.

856
Shorter, John Gill (1818–1872)   Gov., Alabama
    Collection, 1862. 2 items.
    Letter by Shorter, Apr. 4, 1862, Montgomery, concerning
military organization and recruiting in Alabama, the location
of military camps in the State, public support for the war, and
the defense of Mobile, Ala., and Pensacola, Fla.; letter from
Shorter to Gov. Francis W. Pickens, May 2, 1862, Montgomery,
concerning Shorter's personal commitment to the Confederacy,
conscription, the manufacture of arms and ammunition, and
Confederate finance.

857
Shriver, William H. (b. 1887)   Author
    Collection, 1863 and undated. 5 items.
    Transcripts.
    Letter from Miss S. C. Shriver to her sister, Mrs. Elizabeth
Shriver Myer, June 29, 1863, Union Mills, Md., concerning
troop movements, depredations, casualties, and the attitude of
noncombatants in the area around Gettysburg during the Gettysburg Campaign; an explanation of J. E. B. Stuart's late
arrival at the Battle of Gettysburg; an account of how W. H.
Shriver's father located the exact spot where Stuart dismounted
at Gettysburg; and an essay by Shriver, "My Father Led General J. E. B. Stuart to Gettysburg."

858
Shufeldt, Robert Wilson   Diplomat; Comdr., USN
(1822–1895)
Papers, 1836–1910. ca. 15,000 items.
In part, transcripts.
Letters and copies and extracts of letters to Shufeldt as U.S. consul general at Havana, Cuba, concerning the presence of Confederate blockade runners; a list of vessels in the South Atlantic Blockading Squadron (1862); signals and instructions for blockading ships; copies of official letters and reports concerning the quarantine of vessels bound for New Orleans, La., during the military rule of Gen. Benjamin F. Butler; letters from Adm. David G. Farragut to Shufeldt, Jan.–Feb. 1863, concerning the C.S.S. *Alabama*, C.S.S. *Alice*, C.S.S. *Florida*, and C.S.S. *Harriet Lane*; official correspondence and orders relating to Shufeldt's command of the U.S.S. *Conemaugh* and U.S.S. *Proteus*; a list of Confederate and blockade running vessels at Nassau, Apr. 21, 1864; and miscellaneous diplomatic correspondence.
Finding aid available.
Naval Historical Foundation collection.

859
Shuler, M.   Capt., 33d Virginia Regiment
Collection, 1862. 2 v.
Diary, June 11–Dec. 12, 1862, kept during the Peninsular, 2d Manassas, Antietam, and Fredericksburg campaigns. Provides information on casualties, marches, discipline, supplies, depredations, and morale. Includes a few details on the battles of Malvern Hill, Cedar Mountain, Groveton, and Sharpsburg; the capture of Harpers Ferry; and the burning of public buildings at Martinsburg, W. Va. Also includes a list of men in the 33d Virginia killed or wounded in the Antietam Campaign, and miscellaneous accounts.

860
Sicard, Montgomery (1836–1900)   USN
Papers, 1800–1948. ca. 1,200 items.
Includes a letter from Sicard to his wife, Feb. 23, 1865, U.S.S. *Malvern*; notes and sketches on ordnance and armaments; and postwar sketches of the U.S.S. *Swatara*.
Finding aid available.
Naval Historical Foundation collection.

861

Sickles, Daniel Edgar (1819–1914)   U.S. Representative,
                                          New York; Gen., USA

Papers, 1845–1914. ca. 1,100 items.

In part, transcripts.

Includes 14 letters and documents, 1861–64, concerning military appointments, strategy, reinforcements for the Excelsior brigade, Sickles' mistaken arrest of Federal spies, his temporary removal from command in 1862, and the death of Gen. David B. Birney. Correspondents include Randolph B. Marcy, Gershom Mott, Henry L. Potter, and Lorenzo Thomas.

Microfilm copy (5 reels) available.

862

Sigel, Franz (1824–1902)   Gen., USV

Collection, 1862–70. 2 items.

Letterbook, 1862–65, containing a copy of a personal letter by Sigel, Mar. 27, 1863, on the promotion of Capt. Joseph M. Kennedy, 9th New York Cavalry.

863

Simmons, James Fowler
(1795–1864)   U.S. Senator, Rhode Island

Papers, 1788–1939. ca. 21,000 items.

Includes a letter from S. W. Macy to Simmons, July 12, 1861, describing the Confederate privateer *Echo* and tactics used by privateers, and routine letters from soldiers and civilians seeking commissions or promotions, or promoting new and improved weapons.

Finding aid available.

864

Simpson, Matthew (1811–1884)   Bishop, Methodist
                                        Episcopal Church

Papers, 1829–1929. ca. 5,000 items.

Includes about 40 letters written chiefly to Simpson, 1861–64, concerning the appointment of officers and chaplains, promotions, the Christian Sanitary Commission, discrimination against Methodist soldiers, upper class support for the war in the South, conflicting claims for church property, military use of church buildings, black troops, secessionist sentiment at Murfreesboro, Tenn., and conditions in east Tennessee. Correspondents include Chaplain W. H. Black, Lt. Col. Dexter E. Clapp, N. J. Cramer, Chaplain William Earnshaw, Col. William Gamble, Senator James Harlan, Charles M. Hayes, C. Holman, J. W. Hoover, Chaplain Joseph Jones, Chaplain H. A. Pattison, Thomas Rinson, D. H. Whitney, and Dr. William Wright.

Finding aid available.

Daniel Edgar Sickles

865

Sisson, Lewis E.   Poet
      Collection, 1939. 2 items.
      Poem "Shiloh" commemorating the Battle of Shiloh. Dedicated to the author's grandfather, Capt. Lewis E. Sisson, 77th Ohio Volunteers. Also a printed map of the battlefield.

866

Smith, Charles Ferguson (1807–1862)   Gen., USA
      Papers, 1825–62. 16 items.
      Contains commissions, a chart showing the organization of regular and volunteer troops according to act of Congress, July 29, 1861, and a resolution by city officials in Philadelphia providing for the interment of Smith's body.

867

Smith, Daniel Angell (1839–1901)   Acting Asst.
                                                   Paymaster, USN
      Collection, 1863–1905. 38 items.
      Includes about 20 letters from Smith to his sister, 1863–64, concerning his service on the U.S.S. *Nahant*, South Atlantic Blockading Squadron. Provides information on torpedo attacks on the U.S.S. *New Ironsides* and U.S.S. *Weehawken*; naval attacks on Forts Moultrie, Sumter, Wagner, and Gregg; black troops, and the naval brigade.
      Naval Historical Foundation collection.

868

Smith, George Boyd (1839–1893)   Pvt., CSA
      Diary, 1861–64. 1 v.
      Photocopy.
      Contains a few random entries on the war, notably Smith's enlistment in Tennessee, Sept. 7, 1862, and his service at the Siege of Vicksburg.

869

Smith, Howard Malcolm (1838–1890)   Maj.,
                                              1st New York Dragoons
      Collection, 1862–1914. 3 items.
      In part, transcripts.
      Copy of Smith's diary, Aug. 12, 1862–July 1, 1865 (185 p.), kept chiefly during campaigns in Maryland and Virginia. Includes copies of letters from Smith to his future wife, Mary E. Joslyn. Contains information on the Federal defense of Suffolk, Va., in 1863, the Gettysburg, Wilderness, Spotsylvania, Cold Harbor, Petersburg, and Appomattox campaigns, Gen. Jubal A. Early's Washington raid, the Shenandoah Valley and Loudoun Valley campaigns of 1864, and the Trevilian raid.

Also describes camp life, training, discipline, morale, marches, disease, hospital care, foraging and reconnaissance expeditions, the attitude of noncombatants, the use of blacks, black life, the condition and treatment of Confederate prisoners of war, casualties, guerrilla warfare, Confederate deserters, military organization, and generalship. Additional items include a brief biographical sketch of Smith and a membership badge from the 1914 meeting of the 1st New York Dragoons Association.

870
Smith, James Power (1837–1923)   CSA
    Collection, 1861–64. 20 items.
    In part, transcripts.
    Official correspondence, orders, and reports. Includes a report by Capt. William R. Garrett on the performance of the Williamsburg Light (Lee) Artillery in an attack on Fort Magruder, May 5, 1862; Gen. John Bell Hood's report on the engagement at Eltham's Landing, Va., May 7, 1862; reports on the Battle of Williamsburg by Lt. William I. Clopton, Richmond-Fayette Artillery, Capt. Robert M. Stribling, Fauquier Artillery, Capt. James Dearing, Lynchburg Artillery, Gen. George E. Pickett, Gen. Cadmus M. Wilcox, and Lt. Col. J. Thompson Brown. Also includes a letter from Gen. Braxton Bragg to Joseph E. Johnston, Feb. 25, 1863, Tullahoma, explaining his plan for an attack on Franklin, Tenn.; a letter from Dr. Samuel P. Moore to James A. Seddon, Jan. 5, 1863, Richmond, Va., on pay for soldiers detained in the Medical Department; reports by Gen. Braxton Bragg on the Battle of Chickamauga; and miscellaneous items by Gen. Cadwallader C. Washburn, Gen. George H. Thomas, and Stephen R. Mallory.

871
Smith, John Cotton (1765–1845)
    Papers, 1805–64. 6 items.
    Includes a letter from Julius Nichols, an official with the U.S. Sanitary Commission, to Miss Helen Smith, [Mar. 16, 1864], Washington, D.C., containing remarks on Gens. Ulysses S. Grant and Hugh J. Kilpatrick.

872
Smith, Jonathan Bayard (1742–1812)
    Family papers, 1686–1903. ca. 530 items.
    Includes a personal letter by Gen. George B. McClellan, Nov. 21, 1861; a letter from Gen. Joseph E. Johnston to Capt. John R. Tucker, May 1, 1862, concerning transportation for sick soldiers; a personal letter by John Slidell, Aug. 23, 1862, Paris [France]; a letter by James D. Halyburton(?), Sept. 16, 1863, Richmond [Va.], on hardships endured by soldiers; Col.

John S. Mosby's farewell letter to his Partisan Rangers, Apr. 21, 1865; and miscellaneous letters by Gens. P. G. T. Beauregard, George H. Steuart, and James A. Walker.

873
Smith, Orren Randolph   2d North
(1827–1913)   Carolina Battalion, CSA
    Papers, 1846–1913. ca. 400 items.
    Includes a scrapbook and folder containing postwar notes, clippings, and pamphlets supporting Smith's claim as the designer of the Confederate flag, the Stars and Bars.

874
Smith, Oscar (b. 1843)   Pvt., U.S. Marine Corps
    Diary, 1861–62. 1 v.
    Transcript.
    Covers the period May 19, 1861–Dec. 24, 1862. Describes Smith's training and service on the U.S.S. *Hartford* early in the war, a sea voyage to Louisiana, the capture of Forts Jackson and St. Philip, and the surrender of New Orleans, guerrilla warfare along the Mississippi River, Adm. David G. Farragut's bombardment of Vicksburg, and the burning of Grand Gulf, Miss., and Donaldsonville, La.

875
Smith, Samuel (1752–1839)
    Papers, 1772–1869. ca. 2,700 items.
    Includes a list of Confederate soldiers and sailors from Maryland, along with their rank, county, and service record; clippings and miscellaneous notes and letters on the war; and information on officers and men from the State of Maryland killed or wounded in the war.

876
Smith, Stuart Farrar (1874–1951)
    Papers, 1860–1951. ca. 300 items.
    Contains a few leaves from a notebook containing data on vessels used in the war: measurements, tonnage, builder, designer, ordnance, cost, etc.
    Naval Historical Foundation collection.

877
Smith, William Farrar (1824–1903)   Gen., USA
    Letter, 1863. 1 item.
    Letter from Smith to Prof. Dennis H. Mahan, Dec. 7, 1863, Chattanooga, Tenn., on the state of the war in east Tennessee. Provides details on supply problems and military strategy.

878
Smith, William Wrenshall
    Diary, 1863. 1 v.
    Transcript.
    Observations on the war made by Smith, a cousin of Julia
Dent Grant, during a visit with Gen. Ulysses S. Grant, Nov.
3–Dec. 2, 1863. Describes travels through Kentucky and Tennessee and the effects of the war in those States, the occupation
of Nashville, profiteering by sutlers, the apparent absence of
religion among soldiers, the atmosphere and routine around
General Grant's headquarters, morale, foraging expeditions,
and the generalship or character of John C. Frémont, Ulysses
S. Grant, Clark B. Lagow, John A. Rawlins, William F. Smith,
and James H. Wilson. Includes a few details on the battles of
Chattanooga, Lookout Mountain, and Missionary Ridge.

879
Smith—Carter Families
    Papers, 1669–1880.
    Microfilm, 6 reels.
    Includes five letters from William V. Smith to his parents,
July 1864–May 1865, concerning a skirmish with Confederate
forces along the coast of South Carolina, Gen. William Birney's
expedition to Jacksonville, Fla., and morale and health care at
a military hospital in southeast Virginia.
    Originals in the Massachusetts Historical Society.

880
Smith—Townsend Families
    Papers, 1670–1890.
    Microfilm, 1 reel.
    Includes two letters from Mrs. B. Smith to her daughter
written from Chesapeake Military Hospital near Fort Monroe,
Va., Aug.–Sept. 1864, concerning the welfare of her son, Capt.
William Smith, who was wounded at the Siege of Petersburg.
    Originals at the Massachusetts Historical Society.

881
Snow, Elliot (1866–1939)
    Papers, 1790–1942. ca. 9,450 items.
    In part, transcripts and photocopies.
    Includes copies of documents concerning the futile efforts
of Capt. George H. Preble to prevent the C.S.S. *Florida* (alias
Oreto) from entering Mobile Bay, and miscellaneous letters
and clippings concerning Preble's dismissal and reinstatement.
Also contains the papers of Horatio D. Smith (1845–1918), an
officer in the U.S. Revenue Cutter Service.
    Finding aid available.
    Naval Historical Foundation collection.

882
Society of the Army of the Potomac
    Minutes, 1869–70. 1 v.
    Contains speeches by former officers in the Army of the
Potomac concerning their wartime experiences.

883
South Carolina—Adjutant and
Inspector General's Office
    Document, 1862. 1 item.
    Transcript.
    Extract from a resolution of the Governor and council,
July 21, 1862, concern– ing the punishment of anyone failing
to respond when summoned to serve in the 1st Corps, South
Carolina Reserves. Endorsed by Col. J. H. Witherspoon, 8th
South Carolina Reserve Regiment.

884
Sowers, Isaac M.
(1840–1920)   Lt., 9th Pennsylvania Reserves
    Papers, 1861–1920. 15 items.
    Commissions, enlistment and discharge certificates, mis-
cellaneous accounts and receipts, muster roll for Company A,
and a table showing casualties, desertions, discharges, and new
recruits in Company A, Apr. 20, 1864. Also contains a diary,
May 6, 1861–Dec. 16, 1862, describing the organization of the
Pennsylvania Reserves, the selection of officers in the 9th
Pennsylvania, recruits in Company A, morale, marches in
Maryland and Virginia, foraging expeditions, an engagement
at Dranesville, Va., Dec. 20, 1861, the participation of the 9th
Pennsylvania in the Peninsular and 2d Manassas campaigns,
and Sowers' capture and brief confinement at Libby Prison.

885
Spalding, Mrs., et al.
    Pass, 1862. 1 item.
    Military pass issued to Mrs. Spalding, Mrs. Parker, and
Mr. Davis to travel to Alexandria, Va., and return, Jan. 4, 1861
[1862]. Signed, Capt. M. T. McMahon, Army of the Potomac.

886
Spaulding Family
    Papers, 1838–1928. ca. 320 items.
    Transcripts and photocopies.
    Includes the diary of Col. Oliver Lyman Spaulding (1833–
1922), 23d Michigan Volunteers, Sept. 17, 1862–Nov. 14, 1863,
and Jan. 1–Nov. 14, 1865, concerning camp life, marches,
entertainment, foraging expeditions, Unionists in Kentucky
and east Tennessee, the death of Gen. Jefferson C. Davis, the

Battle of Perryville, black life, the attitude of blacks toward the war, problems with slave owners, Confederate prisoners of war, guerrilla warfare, generalship, and the Knoxville and Carolinas campaigns.

Originals at the University of Michigan.

887
Spears, Stewart (b. 1834)   Pvt., 24th
                                                    New Jersey Volunteers
Documents, 1861–63. 3 items.

Discharge certificates from the 4th New Jersey Militia Regiment, July 31, 1861, the 5th New Jersey Volunteers, Mar. 15, 1862, and the 24th New Jersey Volunteers, June 29, 1863.

888
Spencer Family
Papers, 1856–1914. ca. 1,300 items.

Includes the diary of Lyman Potter Spencer (1840–1915). Entries during the war (3 v.), Sept. 12, 1863–June 14, 1865, describe his service as an assistant quartermaster in the 2d Ohio Heavy Artillery. Provides information on the Battle of Munfordville, Ky., Col. John Thomas Wilder's surrender to Gen. Braxton Bragg, and the Battle of Nashville (1864). Includes remarks on camp life, disease, discipline, entertainment, slavery, black life, religion in the Federal Army, guerrilla warfare, supplies, the displacement of noncombatants, foraging expeditions, the attitude of noncombatants, troop movements in Kentucky and Tennessee, and the persecution of Confederate veterans after the war. Also contains a sketch of fortifications at Varnell's Station, Ga.

889
Sperry, Charles Stillman (1847–1911)   Midshipman, USN
Papers, 1862–1912. ca. 2,300 items.

Includes five letters written by Sperry during his voyage on the training ship U.S.S. *Macedonian*, June–Sept. 1863, and a letter from Sperry to his sister, Nov. 20, 1864, concerning the capture of the Confederate blockade runner *Lucy*.

Finding aid available.

890
Spofford, Ainsworth Rand
(1825–1908)   Librarian of Congress
Papers, 1819–1970. ca. 600 items.

Includes two military passes, July 1861, and a letter from Spofford to his wife, July 23, 1861, describing the panic among Federal troops at the Battle of 1st Manassas.

Finding aid available.

891
Spooner, John Coit
(1843–1919)   Maj., 50th Wisconsin Volunteers
   Papers, 1855–1909. ca. 10,000 items.
   Includes muster rolls for the 50th Wisconsin at Benton
Barracks, Mo., Mar.–Dec. 1865.
   Finding aid available.

892
Sprague, Homer Baxter (1829–1918)   Capt., 13th
                                         Connecticut Volunteers
   Papers, 1862–1919. ca. 2,000 items.
   Diary, Jan. 31, 1862–Mar. 6, 1864 (2 v.), kept during campaigns in Louisiana. Contains information on the Port Hudson
and Red River (1863) campaigns, the Battle of Irish Bend, the
recruitment and performance of black troops, camp life, morale,
discipline, disease, deaths, desertions, black life in Louisiana,
Confederate spies, depredations, and the treatment of noncombatants. Diary entries also include a muster roll of the 13th
Connecticut, miscellaneous accounts, a complete list of the men
who served in the regiment, and details on the origin, health,
physical appearance, and service of each recruit.

893
Squier, Ephraim George
(1821–1888)   Archeologist; Diplomat
   Papers, 1841–88. ca. 2,500 items.
   Includes a letter from Col. Charles K. Graham, 74th New
York Volunteers, to Squier, Jan. 16, 1862, written from camp
near Falmouth [Va.].
   Finding aid available.

894
Squires, Charles W.
(1841–1900)   Capt., Washington Artillery, CSA
   Autobiography, 1894. 1 item.
   Transcript.
   Describes Squires' enlistment in the Washington Artillery,
service under Gen. Jubal A. Early in the Battle of 1st Manassas,
an attack on the barge canal at Great Falls, Md., and the
participation of the Washington Artillery in the Peninsular, 2d
Manassas, Antietam, Fredericksburg, and Gettysburg cam-
paigns, the Red River Campaign of 1864, and campaigns in
Arkansas under Gens. John H. Forney and John B. Magruder.
Includes brief descriptions of Gens. P. G. T. Beauregard, Jubal
A. Early, John H. Forney, Thomas J. Jackson, Joseph E.
Johnston, David R. Jones, Stephen D. Lee, James Longstreet,
and John B. Magruder. Also contains remarks on camp life,

entertainment, marches, desertions, discipline, his capture and exchange in May 1863, and the movement of the Washington Artillery from Petersburg, Va., to Texas in 1864.

895
Stahel, Julius (1825–1912)   Gen., USV
    Papers, 1861–1916.
    In part, transcripts.
    Microfilm, 1 reel.
Chiefly commissions, orders, dispatches, and letters concerning Stahel's military career. Also contains pension records, obituaries, and a biographical essay (24 p.). Correspondents are Gens. Darius N. Couch, Samuel P. Heintzelman, George B. McClellan, Carl Schurz, and Franz Sigel.

896
Stanton, Edwin McMasters
(1814–1869)   U.S. Secretary of War
    Papers, 1831–70. ca. 7,600 items.
Chiefly correspondence relating to Stanton's service as Secretary of War under Presidents Abraham Lincoln and Andrew Johnson, particularly the organization and management of the War Department. Also includes letterbooks, 1863–65, the proceedings of the Board of War, Mar. 1862, a draft of the annual report of the Secretary of War for 1863, maps and charts, reports from various military departments and commands, letters concerning morale and discipline in the U.S. Army, the use of runaway slaves as soldiers, generalship, the Lincoln assassination, ordnance reports, field returns, memoranda from consultations with various generals, letters and reports on the exchange of prisoners of war, plans and suggestions for campaigns, and miscellaneous items. Correspondents include Benjamin F. Butler, Simon Cameron, Charles A. Dana, John A. Dix, Thomas Ewing, William P. Fessenden, Andrew H. Foote, Gustavus V. Fox, John C. Frémont, Reverdy Johnson, Abraham Lincoln, George B. McClellan, Thomas A. Scott, Charles Sumner, and Gideon Welles.
    Finding aid, partial index, and microfilm copy (14 reels) available.

897
Stanton, Elizabeth Cady
(1815–1902)   Reformer; Feminist
    Papers, 1814–1946. ca. 1,000 items.
Several letters from Stanton's husband, Henry B. Stanton, written from Washington, D.C., and New York City in 1861, describe troop arrivals and war fever in Washington, war finance, and his opinion of Gen. George B. McClellan. Also

Edwin McMasters Stanton

includes a letter by Susan B. Anthony, Feb. 14, 1865, Leavenworth, Kans., noting the presence of black refugees.
Finding aid and microfilm copy (5 reels) available.

898
Starr, George H. Capt., 104th
New York Volunteers
Scrapbooks, 1864–1910. 2 v.
Chiefly articles, speeches, and clippings relating to Starr's
experiences in the war. Includes copies of addresses concerning
his capture at the Battle of Gettysburg and his treatment at
Libby Prison in Richmond, Va., and articles and obituaries on
various officers with whom he was associated.

899
Steiner, Walter Ralph (1870–1942)
Autograph collection, 1780–1937. 10 items.
In part, transcripts.
Includes a copy of the diary of Francis A. Boyle, 32d North
Carolina Volunteers, 1864–65. Describes the Wilderness and
Spotsylvania campaigns and prison life at Point Lookout, Md.,
and Fort Delaware. Provides information on the conduct of
black guards at Point Lookout Military Prison, prison morale,
diet, disease, deaths, hospital care, entertainment, escapes, and
dishonesty among prison guards. Also contains the names, units,
and home addresses of 16 Confederate officers, and a published
bibliography of prison narratives.

900
Stephens, Alexander Hamilton
(1812–1883) C.S. Vice President
Papers, 1784–1886. ca. 27,000 items.
Contains correspondence relating to secession, the Confederate provisional government, the C.S. Government, and the
conduct of the war. Also includes a manuscript autobiography
of Stephens.
Finding aid and microfilm copy (57 reels) available.

901
———
Correspondence, 1834–91.
Microfilm, 6 reels.
Chiefly correspondence between Stephens and his brother,
Judge Linton Stephens. Includes about 200 letters and tele-
grams concerning the secession crisis, preparations for war in
the South, Linton Stephens' service as lt. colonel in the 15th
Georgia Regiment, Apr.–Dec. 1861, the 1st Manassas Cam-
paign, camp life, morale, disease, hunger in the Confederate

Army, the generalship of Robert Toombs, the effect of conscription in Georgia, a plot to assassinate President Davis, Confederate politics, the Atlanta Campaign, and the Hampton Roads Peace Conference.

902
Stephenson, Nathaniel Wright
(1867–1935)   Historian; Journalist
    Papers, 1922–30. 28 items.
    Notes on blacks in the Civil War and on Jefferson Davis, scenarios for "Lee and the Confederacy" and "For the Union," photoplays in *The Chronicles of America* series, and scenario notes for "Lincoln."

903
Stevens, Hazard (1842–1918)   Col., 1st Loyal
                                                Eastern Virginians
    Family papers, 1835–97.
    Microfilm, 2 reels.
    Official and personal correspondence, orders, commissions, and reports relating to the service of Stevens and his father, Gen. Isaac Ingalls Stevens. Contains details on the Battle of Secessionville, S.C., the Siege of Suffolk, Va., the Shenandoah Valley Campaign of 1864, the Petersburg Campaign, and the Battle of Sayler's Creek, Va. Also contains letters and documents on the recruitment of the 1st Loyal Eastern Virginia Volunteers, guerrilla warfare in Virginia and North Carolina, reconnaissance and foraging expeditions, prisoners of war, generalship, the death of General Stevens, response to General Early's Washington raid, depredations, camp life, marches, morale, and the effectiveness of Union cavalry and weapons. Miscellaneous items include an incomplete biography, "Life of Gen. I. I. Stevens by his son Hazard Stevens."
    Originals at the University of Washington.

904
Stevens, Thaddeus (1792–1868)   U.S. Representative,
                                                Pennsylvania
    Papers, 1813–69. ca. 4,750 items.
    Contains about 30 letters to Stevens, 1861–64, from relatives serving in the Union Army, soldiers in various Pennsylvania regiments, constituents, military and political prisoners, and office seekers concerning the Battle of Shiloh, marches and skirmishes in Tennessee, the attitude of noncombatants at Nashville, Tenn., the release or exchange of prisoners, military appointments and commissions, generalship, furloughs, and the service of black troops.
    Finding aid available.

905
Stevens Family
    Papers, 1810–1952. 35 items.
    In part, photocopies.
    Includes a letter by Lt. Pendleton G. Watmough, U.S.S. *Potomska*, Jan. 6 [1862]; a letter by Christopher R. Perry Rodgers, U.S.S. *Wabash*, Feb. 8 [1864]; and a copy of the Great Seal of the Confederate States of America.
    Naval Historical Foundation collection.

906
Stewart, D. W.   Surg., 38th Illinois Volunteers
    Papers, 1862. 5 items.
    Miscellaneous receipts, a medical invoice, and a list of soldiers in the 38th Illinois killed and wounded in the Battle of Murfreesboro, Tenn., July 13, 1862.

907
Stickney, Frank L. (1858–1940)
    Papers, 1840–1940. ca. 1,000 items.
    Material relating to Stickney's father, Francis H. Stickney (warrant clerk, USN), includes two letters from Asa C. Winter written aboard the U.S.S. *E. B. Hale*, Nov. 21–23, 1861, on the shipment of supplies and increasing hostilities in Virginia; a letter from an unidentified sailor aboard the U.S.S. *Ossipee*, May 19, 1864, on the blockade of Mobile, Ala.; two letters from Frank S. Hesseltine, Jan. 1862, concerning activities in the 13th Maine Volunteers; a letter by Henry Lewis, 121st Ohio Volunteers, July 2, 1864, on camp life in the Atlanta Campaign; a letter by J. O. Bradford, Dec. 29, 1862, U.S.S. *Colorado*; and official orders of Gideon Welles, 1865.
    Finding aid available.

908
Stimson, William R.   3d Iowa Volunteers
    Collection, 1862–1961. 6 items.
    Includes four letters from Stimson to his wife and family, Mar.–June 1862, concerning the Shiloh and Corinth campaigns. Contains comments on casualties in the 3d Iowa and the desperate plight of the Federal Army on the first day of the Battle of Shiloh.

909
Stone, Jasper Jay (b. 1847)   Pvt., 35th Iowa Volunteers
    Collection, 1862–1908. 1 v.
    Poems and songs, 1862–94, commemorating the war and Stone's experiences as a "high private" in the 35th Iowa.

910

Strait, N. A.   Collector
    Records, 1860–65. ca. 1,800 items.
    Provides information on the service of various Union regu-
lar and volunteer regiments. Pertains chiefly to regiments from
Massachusetts and New York.

911

Strong, Hayward & Company   Boston, Mass.
    Scrapbook, 1857–69. ca. 220 items.
    Contains five letters from Adj. R. M. Bearden (Turner
Ashby's cavalry) while a prisoner of war at Johnson's Island,
Ohio, appealing for aid from his prewar business acquaintance,
Alexander Strong, Aug.–Nov. 1863.

912

Stuart, Alexander Hugh Holmes
(1807–1891)   Statesman, Virginia
    Collection, 1790–1868. 34 items.
    Includes five letters to Stuart, May 7, 1861–Jan. 20, 1865,
concerning the secession crisis, the Peninsular Campaign, the
political situation in Virginia in Dec. 1862, Whig prospects in
Virginia after the war, and the desperate political and economic situation in Virginia in Jan. 1865. Correspondents are
James D. Armstrong, John B. Baldwin, John Letcher, William
Cabell Rives, and Williams C. Wickham.

913

Stuart, George Hay   President,
(1816–1890)   U.S. Christian Commission
    Collection, 1792–1930. ca. 550 items.
    Miscellaneous letters and documents relating to the war.
Includes a letter from Gen. Isaac P. Rodman to his sister, Aug.
15, 1861, on the Battle of 1st Manassas, a letter from Stuart to
President Lincoln, Dec. 11, 1861, on the origins and service of
the Christian Commission, a letter from Gen. D. H. Hill to
General Beauregard, Dec. 16, 1861, calling for the execution of
Federal soldiers and Tories for the pillage and murder of
noncombatants, and a note by Gen. Robert E. Lee, Aug. 1861,
on an exchange of prisoners. Also contains letters concerning
generalship, promotions, reinforcements, conscription, prisoners of war, cavalry tactics, supplies, religion among soldiers,
and the 2d Manassas, Antietam, and Fredericksburg campaigns, and the Shenandoah Valley Campaign of 1862. Miscellaneous items comprise a manuscript map of the battlefield at
Gettysburg, a return of soldiers in the 56th Pennsylvania
Volunteers, July 16, 1863, military passes, orders, receipts,
and requisitions, and a photograph of Gen. Amiel W. Whipple.

Other correspondents include William W. Averell, Francis Barbour, John Buford, Simon Cameron, Silas Casey, John Cochrane, Darius N. Couch, John A. Dix, Samuel F. Du Pont, David G. Farragut, Edward Ferrero, Andrew H. Foote, William B. Franklin, Ulysses S. Grant, William A. Hammond, Joseph Hooker, Oliver O. Howard, Andrew A. Humphreys, Thomas J. Jackson, William E. Jones, Erasmus D. Keyes, Abraham Lincoln, George B. McClellan, Joseph K. F. Mansfield, George G. Meade, Thomas F. Meagher, Montgomery C. Meigs, Christopher Memminger, George W. Morell, Robert Ould, Marsena R. Patrick, Fitz-John Porter, John F. Reynolds, Joseph J. Reynolds, William S. Rosecrans, William Seward, Thomas W. Sherman, William T. Sherman, Daniel E. Sickles, Gustavus W. Smith, William F. Smith, Edwin M. Stanton, George Stoneman, Charles Sumner, Gouverneur K. Warren, Gideon Welles, and Julius White.

914

Stuart, James Ewell Brown (1833–1864)   Gen., CSA
    Letters, 1861–62. 8 items.
    Photocopies.
    Seven letters from Stuart to Laura Ratcliffe written from camps in Virginia, 1861–62, and a letter from Gen. Robert E. Lee to Stuart, Aug. 18, 1862, on cavalry movements.

915

Stull, Lydia J.   Nurse, Special Relief Service,
                                         U.S. Sanitary Commission
    Papers, 1865. 23 items.
    Chiefly letters to Stull from Union soldiers held in military prisons in and around Washington, D.C. (Old Capital Prison, Fort Whipple, Va., etc.) for crimes committed during the war. Provides the names and units of about 20 prisoners.

916

Sturgeon, Robert   Capt., 25th New York Volunteers
    Document, 1861. 1 item.
    Special order accepting Sturgeon's resignation from the Army, Oct. 30, 1861.

917

Sturgis, Samuel Davis (1822–1889)   Gen., USA
    Collection, 1861–81. 6 items.
    In part, transcripts.
    Contains an account of the Battle of Wilson's Creek copied from the *Franklin Repository and Transcript*, Oct. 9, 1861.

918
Sullivan, John T.
    Papers, 1831−67. 12 items.
    Photocopies.
    Letter from J. H. M.(?) to Sullivan, July 18, 1861, Vichy, France, on the response of French bankers to loan requests by the Confederacy.

919
Surratt, Mary Eugenia Jenkins
(1820−1865)   Alleged Conspirator
    Letter, 1865. 1 item.
    Photocopy.
    Letter from Mrs. Surratt to an unnamed recipient, July 9, 1865, Washington, D.C., proclaiming her innocence in the Lincoln assassination.

920
Susquehanna (U.S.S.)
    Collection, 1853−65. 3 items.
    Transcript, photocopy, and photograph.
    Photograph of 17 officers and men on the U. S. S. *Susquehanna* taken shortly after the second Fort Fisher expedition.
    Naval Historical Foundation collection.

921
Suydam, Charles Crooke   Asst. Adj. Gen., 4th Corps,
(1836−1911)   Army of the Potomac
    Papers, 1859−64. ca. 200 items.
    Correspondence, clippings, telegrams, intelligence reports, inventories, orders, dispatches, military passes, and a diary relating chiefly to Suydam's duties as Assistant Adjutant General to Gen. Erasmus D. Keyes, as chief of staff for Gen. Alfred Pleasonton, and as colonel of the 3d New Jersey Cavalry. Includes information on courts-martial, the suffering of noncombatants, marches, training, discipline, casualties, guerrilla warfare, rank disputes, appointments and promotions, drunkenness, and desertions. Miscellaneous items include a report on the organization of General Keyes' command at Yorktown, an outline of Suydam's military career, lists of marches in which Suydam participated, and a diary kept during the Peninsular Campaign, Apr. 4−June 2, 1862, and as colonel of the 3d New Jersey Cavalry during the Shenandoah Valley Campaign of 1864. Principal correspondents include Gens. David Birney, John A. Dix, William B. Franklin, Joseph Hooker, Erasmus D. Keyes, Rufus King, Randolph B. Marcy, John J. Peck, and George Stoneman.

922

Swann, John S.   West Virginia
    Reminiscences, 1876. 1 item.
    Transcript.
    Account of Swann's experiences as a prisoner of war at
Fort Delaware, 1864–65.

923

Swindler, Albert Clayton   12th Virginia Cavalry, CSA
    Records, 1862–63. 1 v.
    Record book captured from the 5th Connecticut Volunteers.
Contains morning reports on the 5th Connecticut for May 5,
1862, and on the 12th Virginia Cavalry for Jan.–Mar. 1863.
Includes comments on troop movements and the condition of
the 12th Virginia Cavalry.

924

Swisher, Carl Brent (1897–1968)   Historian
    Collection, 1836–1962. ca. 12,250 items.
    In part, transcripts and photocopies.
    Research notes, clippings, and copies of letters and docu-
ments. Includes information on slavery, emancipation, and the
war, and military and political leaders such as Salmon P. Chase,
Roger B. Taney, and Gideon Welles.
    Finding aid available.

925

Taft, William Howard (1857–1930), Pres., U.S.
    Papers, 1810–1930. ca. 675,000 items.
    Contains 17 items relating to the war, chiefly official corre-
spondence and orders of Maj. Thomas D. Sedgwick, 2d Kentucky Regiment, 1861–62, concerning campaigns in West Virginia and Tennessee, and miscellaneous letters to Alfonso Taft,
1862–63, on the progress of the war in southeast Virginia,
Confederate recruiting in Campbell County, Ky., the death of
Gen. William Nelson, and the role of Lt. Col. Bassett Langdon
in the Battle of Missionary Ridge.
    Published index and microfilm copy (657 reels) available.

926

Talbot, Theodore (d. 1862)   Capt., USA
    Papers, 1837–67. ca. 200 items.
    Includes 26 letters from Talbot to his mother and sister,
Feb. 26, 1860–Apr. 2, 1861, detailing the situation of the Federal garrison at Forts Moultrie and Sumter, i.e., the attitude of
inhabitants and officials in South Carolina, negotiations for
the surrender of the forts, the move of the garrison from Fort
Moultrie to Fort Sumter, morale, and supplies. Also, a receipt
for supplies delivered to General Sigel's corps, July 25, 1862.

927
Taylor, Henry Clay (1845–1904)   USN
    Papers, 1862–1904. ca. 300 items.
    In part, transcripts.
    Contains two letters from cadet Taylor to his father, Apr. 3 and 5, 1863, U.S. Naval Academy, concerning future service with the South Atlantic Blockading Squadron and the advantages and disadvantages of sailing, steam, and "combination" vessels, and a letter by Comdr. C. R. P. Rodgers, U.S.S. *Wabash*, off St. Augustine, Fla., Mar. 21, 1862.
    Finding aid available.
    Naval Historical Foundation collection.

928
Taylor, Henry S.
(d. 1863)   Capt., 3d Kentucky Volunteers
    Document, 1863. 1 item.
    Affidavit affirming Taylor's death at the Battle of Chickamauga, Sept. 20, 1863. Signed by Col. Henry C. Dunlap, 3d Kentucky Volunteers.

929
Taylor, Thomas W.   Unionist, Kentucky
    Letters, 1862, 1864. 2 items.
    Contains two letters from Taylor to his sisters in Massachusetts, Oct. 25, 1862, and June 6, 1864, concerning Confederate foraging in Kentucky, problems with guerrillas, and his arrest for destroying his own mill.

930
Taylor, Walter Herron   CSA
    Letter, 1864. 1 item.
    Letter from Taylor to Gen. Richard H. Anderson, June 6, 1864, Gaines Mill, Va., on troop positions in the Siege of Petersburg.

931
Taylor, Zachary (1784–1850), Pres., U.S.
    Papers, 1814–1931. 631 items.
    In part, transcripts.
    Includes a letter from Gen. Benjamin F. Butler to Gen. Joseph P. Taylor, July 28, 1862; a copy of a petition from the officers of the 9th Louisiana Regiment to Gen. Richard Taylor, July 30, 1862, asking to remain under Taylor's command despite his recent promotion and reassignment; and a copy of a letter of appreciation from the officers of Maj. Edward Waller's battal-

ion of Texas volunteer cavalry to Gen. Richard Taylor, Dec. 22, 1863.

Published index and microfilm copy (2 reels) available.

932
Ten Broeck, R. C.
Narrative, undated. 1 item.
Transcript.
Describes the efforts of Confederate agents to obtain a loan of $1 million from German merchants and bankers.

933
Thatcher, Henry Knox (1806–1880)   Adm., USN
Document, 1866. 1 item.
Agreement between Thatcher and S. Colburn concerning the salvage of two torpedo boats sunk in Mobile Bay.
Naval Historical Foundation collection.

934
Thomas, Calvin H.
(b. 1834)   1st Lt., 51st Illinois Volunteers
Collection, 1863–66. 35 items.
Miscellaneous commissions, orders, passes, and accounts.

935
Thomas, Joseph Conable (1833–1906)   Clergyman
Papers, 1855–1905. ca. 400 items.
Chiefly correspondence concerning Thomas' work with the U.S. Christian Commission and the Sanitary Commission in establishing libraries at military hospitals for convalescents from the Army of the Cumberland.

936
Thomas, Lorenzo (1804–1875)   Gen., USA
Collection, 1848–64. 3 items.
Letter from Thomas to his cousin, Feb. 28, 1864, Louisville, Ky., on the use and abuse of blacks in the Union Army.

937
Thompson, Ambrose W.   Businessman; Inventor
Papers, 1847–1960. ca. 12,000 items.
Contains seven letters from Lt. Col. Ambrose Thompson (USA) to his father, A. W. Thompson, May 1862–Mar. 1864, concerning the organization, equipment, and work of the Pontoon brigade, Army of the Potomac; personal differences with Gen. James Shields; the Gettysburg Campaign; and his desire for promotion and separate command. Also includes miscella-

neous accounts and receipts, and a "Proposed Plan to secure the Military Service of the Negroes to the United States during the term of the War."

Finding aid available.

938

Thompson, Gilbert

(1839–1909)   Cpl., Topographic Engineers, USA
     Memoir, 1857–1901. 1 v.

Based on a diary kept by Thompson during the war, Nov. 1861–Nov. 1864. Provides information on camp life, diet, training, morale, disease, medical care, entertainment, casualties, foraging expeditions, skirmishes, generalship, and recruits during the Peninsular, 2d Manassas, Antietam, Fredericksburg, Chancellorsville, Gettysburg, Spotsylvania, Wilderness, Cold Harbor, and Petersburg campaigns. Also contains copies of letters; sketches of military camps, soldiers' tents and huts, pontoon and log bridges, equipment, accoutrements, Gen. Philip Kearny, and Gilbert Thompson; and photographs (chiefly clippings from books and magazines) of John G. Barnard, Henry W. Benham, Ambrose E. Burnside, James C. Duane, Joseph Hooker, Andrew A. Humphries, Thomas J. Jackson, George B. McClellan, George G. Meade, Nathaniel Michler, Gilbert Thompson, and Gouverneur K. Warren, various officers in the engineer battalion, corduroy roads and bridges, Federal batteries at the Siege of Yorktown, and the pontoon bridges at the Siege of Fredericksburg.

939

Tidball, John Caldwell (1825–1906)   USV
     Reminiscence, undated. 67 p.

Contains comments on President Lincoln, Gens. Robert E. Lee, Albert S. Johnston, and John B. Magruder, war fever in the Washington area, Confederate sympathizers in the District of Columbia, the progress of the war, and Tidball's service in William F. Barry's Light Artillery.

940

Tidd, Charles Plummer (1832–1862)   Orderly Sgt., 21st
                                                    Massachusetts Volunteers
     Biography, undated. 15 p.

Brief account of Tidd's life. Mentions Tidd's association with Dr. Calvin Cutter and John Brown in prewar Kansas, his involvement in John Brown's raid on Harpers Ferry, and his service and death in Gen. Ambrose Burnside's expedition to North Carolina.

941

Tod, David (1805–1868)   Gov., Ohio
    Letters, 1862. 2 items.

Letters from Tod to Adj. Gen. George B. Wright, July 15 and Sept. 9, 1862, concerning aid to loyalists in Kentucky, the security of Ohio's southern border, and troop positions.

942

Todd, Oliphant Monroe
(1821–1897)   Chaplain, 78th Ohio Volunteers
    Diary, 1862. 1 v.

Contains some information on marches, discipline, depredations, and disease during the Fort Donelson, Shiloh, and Corinth campaigns, and the response of soldiers to Todd's ministry.

943

Tompkins, Aaron B.   1st New Jersey Cavalry
    Letters, 1863–64. 6 items.

Letters from Tompkins to his mother written from camps in Maryland and Virginia. Mentions problems with Mosby's Rangers.

944

Toner, Joseph Meredith
(1825–1896)   Physician; Historian; Collector
    Papers, 1741–1896. ca. 75,000 items.

Includes a medical certificate for Capt. John Hastings, 106th Pennsylvania Volunteers, Sept. 11, 1862, who was wounded at the Battle of 2d Manassas; a letter from Frank Piers to Toner, Oct. 18, 1862, discussing marches of the 91st Pennsylvania Volunteers in the Antietam Campaign; a note from Capt. R. E. Taylor to Toner, June 19, 1861, appealing for help for a Pennsylvania soldier lying ill at Alexandria, Va.; a letter from Chaplain R. C. Christy to Toner, Mar. 1, 1864, concerning his dismissal from the 78th Pennsylvania at Chattanooga, Tenn.; and a letter from H. Riley(?) to Toner, Apr. 9, 1864, Chattanooga, Tenn., on the progress of the war.
    Finding aid available.

945

Toombs, Robert Augustus (1810–1885)   Gen., CSA
    Collection, 1837–62. 12 items.

Includes a letter from Toombs to Mr. Crawford, Feb. 20, 1862, Richmond, Va., critical of the ability of President Davis to deal with the present crisis and voicing his own optimism on the final outcome of the war.

946
Torrey, Charles Oscar
(b. 1836)   Sgt., 27th Iowa Volunteers
    Papers, 1862–1913. 196 items.
    Chiefly letters from Torrey to his wife, 1862–65, written
during campaigns in Tennessee, Arkansas, and Mississippi,
the Red River Campaign of 1864, and the Siege of Mobile.
Includes observations on diet, disease, deaths, medical care,
and morale at military hospitals in Mississippi and Tennessee,
written while Torrey served in the ambulance corps, as well as
remarks on camp life, marches, generalship, guerrilla warfare,
deserters, prisoners of war, loyalist volunteers in Arkansas,
blacks, and the political attitude of soldiers. Also contains
Torrey's diary, Jan. 1, 1863– Dec. 31, 1865 (3 v.), commission,
discharge, and pension papers.

947
Townsend, George Alfred
(1841–1914)   Journalist; Author
    Scrapbook, 1865–99. ca. 20 items.
    Clippings, notes, and sketches compiled by Townsend under
the pseudonym "Gath," concerning, in part, the Lincoln assassination and the escape and death of John Wilkes Booth.

948
Treadway, Allen Towner (1867–1947)
    Collection, 1787–1865. 15 items.
    Contains $20.00 in Confederate money.

949
Treat, Samuel (1815–1902)   Jurist; Educator
    Collection, 1856–63. 9 items.
    Includes a letter from Treat to Mr. Greenough, Mar. 14,
1863, on the organization and disposition of Missouri troops
(USA), generalship, and the loyalty of noncombatants in
Missouri.

950
Tredway, Thomas Thweatt   C.S. Representative, Virginia
    Collection, 1857–65. 3 items.
    Includes a letter from Tredway to his daughter, Feb. 16,
1865, Richmond, Va., concerning the state of the war, possible
service for representatives, and Confederate morale.

951
Trenholm, George Alfred
(1807–1876)   C.S. Secretary of the Treasury
    Papers, 1853–97. ca. 400 items.

Miscellaneous accounts, records of delinquent accounts, lists of officers whose accounts are in arrears or unreported, correspondence concerning Confederate finance, and a copy of an order by Gen. William T. Sherman, Jan. 16, 1865, Savannah, Ga.

952
Trigg, Connally F.   District Judge
      Papers, 1862–66. 4 items.
      Contains a letter from James A. Irvine to Trigg, May 2, [1862], Johnson's Island, Ohio, concerning a petition for the release of James Irvine and William McFall (formerly in the Tennessee Cavalry, CSA); a letter from Samuel L. Foute to Trigg, Apr. 9, 1862, Camp Douglas, Ill., on his exchange or release; and a letter to Trigg from his son, E. C. Trigg, Mar. 26, 1862, concerning a recent skirmish in Kentucky.

953
Trumbull, Lyman (1813–1896)   Jurist;
                                                 U.S. Senator, Illinois
      Papers, 1843–94. ca. 4,520 items.
      Includes numerous letters to Trumbull, 1861–65, from Illinois soldiers concerning the organization, strength, and location of Illinois regiments, equipment and supplies, appointments, promotions, rank disputes, generalship, resignations, prisoners of war, medical care, and conflict between Gens. John A. McClernand and Ulysses S. Grant. Also contains information on the Battle of Pea Ridge, the Peninsular, Corinth, Meridian, Chattanooga, Atlanta, and Petersburg campaigns, and various military affairs in Alabama, Mississippi, Louisiana, and Texas.
      Finding aid, partial index, and microfilm copy (22 reels) available.

954
Tucker, Nathaniel Beverley
(1820–1890)   Confederate Agent
      Collection, 1859–63. 2 items.
      Letter from Tucker to John Coyle, Oct. 20, 1863, Toronto, Canada, revealing Tucker's undercover address—A. Dixon & Son, Hardware Merchants, Toronto, Canada.

955
Turner, Justin G.   Collector
      Autograph collection, 1701–1972. ca. 1,300 items.
      In part, transcripts.
      Contains letters by Maj. Robert Anderson, Lucius Q. C. Lamar, Christopher G. Memminger, William P. Miles, Francis

W. Pickens, Maj. P. F. Stevens, and Leroy P. Walker, Jan.–Apr. 1861, concerning preparations for war in Georgia and South Carolina. Also includes three reports on interviews conducted by Benjamin Lossing with participants in the defense of Fort Sumter.

956
Tyler, John (1790–1862), Pres., U.S.
    Papers, 1691–1918. ca. 1,400 items.
    Includes a few letters touching on the morale and strength of Virginia soldiers, public support for the war in Virginia, and the confidence of the South in victory.
    Published index and microfilm copy (3 reels) available.

957
Underwood, John Curtiss (1809–1873)   Jurist; Lawyer
    Papers, 1856–73. 165 items.
    Includes a scrapbook of clippings relating to Underwood's capture by Confederate guerrillas, his recruitment and organization of a black company, the progress of the war in Virginia, a letter from Gen. Edward Canby to Underwood, Feb. 7, 1864, on the abduction and abuse of blacks, and a letter from Underwood to President Lincoln, Feb. 17, 1862, on the organization and service of loyalists in eastern Virginia.

958
Unidentified Manuscripts Collection
    Letters, 1863–64. 3 items.
    Letter by an unnamed soldier in the 15th Massachusetts Volunteers, Apr. 27, 1864, written from a camp near Brandy Station, Va., and two letters by unnamed soldiers at Fort March, Va., Jan. 23 and 24, 1863, concerning morale, diet, disease, and discipline.

959
U.S. Army—Commissary Department Miscellany
    Records, 1862–63. 1 v.
    Contains requisitions, reports, orders, and correspondence relating to commissary departments at St. Helena and Folly Island, S.C., and Scranton, Pa., May 3–31, 1862, and Mar. 7–Aug. 26, 1863.

960
U.S. Army—Engineers
    Letterbook, 1862–65. 1 v.
    Correspondence of Edward Frost (1801–1868) and A. Grant Childs concerning the defenses of Washington south of the Poto-

mac River, May 9, 1862–June 8, 1865. Includes a few sketches of fortifications, reports on the condition of various works, and comments on available black laborers in Washington, D.C.

961

U.S. Army—Judge Advocate General Miscellany
    Letterbook, 1862–63. 1 v.
    Copies of letters by special commissioners at Camp Chase, Ohio, Sept. 1, 1862–June 10, 1863, investigating the cases of civilian prisoners from Virginia, Kentucky, and Tennessee. Concerns various charges of disloyalty to the Union: refusing to take an oath of allegiance to the Federal Government, aiding or abetting guerrillas, and refusing to join the U.S. Army.

962

U.S. Army—Medical Department
    Letterbook, 1862–65. 1 v.
    Includes the correspondence of Charles Frederick Crehore, surgeon, 37th Massachusetts Volunteers, with Dr. C. N. Chamberlain, Dr. Silas A. Holman, Dr. Charles O'Leary, and others concerning practices detrimental to the health of soldiers, efforts to secure housing for sick and wounded soldiers, medical discharges, the organization and operation of military hospitals, and the symptoms and treatments of various diseases. Also contains orders, circulars, and instructions on medical procedures, lists of sick and wounded soldiers, an invoice of hospital property, and the names of a few hospital nurses, stewards, and cooks.

963

U.S. Army—Quartermaster's Department
    Order book, 1865–66. 1 v.
    Extracts of orders and copies of military passes issued to Cpl. William Farrow and Lt. W. J. Kyle, 25th Ohio Volunteers.

964
———
    Papers, 1865–68. ca. 50 items.
    Correspondence and reports on military cemeteries. Includes infomation on the size and maintenance of cemeteries in Tennessee, plans for national military cemeteries, and records of disinterments.

965

U.S. Christian Commission
    Notebooks, 1865. 2 v.
    Contains the names and requests of wounded and dying soldiers, miscellaneous accounts, lists of goods and supplies

distributed to convalescing soldiers, remarks on blacks, hospital ships, and wounds, and the names of several hospitals in Virginia. Also contains sketches of the Christian Commission offices at Goldsboro, N.C., and a list of commission delegates at New Bern, Goldsboro, Raleigh, Wilmington, and Smithville, N.C.

966
U.S. Finance Miscellany
    Collection, 1761–1897. ca. 2,500 items.
    Reports, accounts, and miscellaneous items. Includes a descriptive list of North Carolina Confederate currency, and a letter from Gen. George B. McClellan to Edwin M. Stanton, May 6, 1862, concerning the Battle of Williamsburg, Va.

967
U.S. Lincoln Sesquicentennial Commission
    Records, 1957–60. ca. 33,000 items.
    In part, transcripts.
    Chiefly drafts and copies of *Lincoln Day-by-Day: A Chronology, 1808–1865*, compiled by Earl Schenck Miers, William E. Baringer, and C. Percy Powell (1960), 3 v. Also includes research notes and an incomplete Lincoln bibliography.
    Finding aid available.

968
U.S. Navy
    Collection, 1899–1933. 6 items.
    In part, transcripts.
    Includes a copy of an unsigned letter by a former Confederate soldier to the U.S. Navy Department, July 23, 1920, concerning the capture and treatment of several Confederate soldiers by a Federal landing party on Edisto Island, S.C., and the capture of the U.S.S. *Isaac Smith* on Jan. 30, 1863.
    Naval Historical Foundation collection.

969
U.S. Sanitary Commission
    Papers, 1863–64. ca. 900 items.
    Miscellaneous material relating to the services provided by the Commission for soldiers in the field and at home: clippings, posters, photographs, and sketches of military hospitals, soldiers' homes, and refreshment saloons; the rules and regulations of the "Union Volunteer Refreshment Saloon"; welcome cards and tickets to the Central Sanitary Fair; clippings on various fairs sponsored by the Commission, and a sketch of the Commission chapel in the field near Petersburg, Va.

970
U.S. Work Projects Administration
  Federal Writers Project.
  Microfilm, 1 reel.
  Narratives of ex-slaves living in Ohio in 1937. Includes recollections of the treatment of noncombatants in the South, the treatment of blacks by Union soldiers, depredations and foraging expeditions, black soldiers, and black life during the war.
  Originals in the Ohio Historical Society.

971
Usher, John Palmer (1816–1889)   U.S.
                                                     Secretary of the Interior
  Letter, 1865. 1 item.
  Transcript.
  Letter from Usher to his wife, Apr. 16, 1865, concerning the death of President Lincoln.

972
Van Cise, Edwin A.   2d Lt.,
(1842–1914)   41st Iowa Volunteers; Lawyer
  Papers, 1857–1904. 26 items.
  Diary entries for the period May 4–Sept. 14, 1864, describe Van Cise's service as a 100-day volunteer in the 41st Iowa. Includes remarks on military organization, training, discipline, morale, marches, entertainment, disease, medical care, deaths, guerrilla warfare, reconnaissance expeditions, and generalship during operations along the Mississippi River between St. Louis, Mo., and New Orleans, La. Also contains information on black life and the behavior of black soldiers.

973
Van Dorn, Earl (1820–1863)   Gen., CSA
  Papers, 1858–63. ca. 80 items.
  Chiefly official correspondence, orders, intelligence reports, and telegrams concerning civilian and military appointments in the Confederacy, military organization, the movement and disposition of troops, the Corinth and Vicksburg campaigns, military supplies, and black unrest on plantations along the Mississippi River. Includes a few details on the defense of Port Hudson, La. Correspondents include P. G. T. Beauregard, Braxton Bragg, John C. Breckinridge, George W. Carter, Jefferson Davis, William W. Loring, Dabney A. Maury, John C. Pemberton, John J. Pettus, Daniel Ruggles, Martin L. Smith, and John B. Villepigue.

974
Van Dyke, Richard Smith (1840–1864)   CSA
    Papers, 1861–1940. 3 items.
    Photograph of Van Dyke with his class at Princeton
University, 1861, and biographical notes on his service and
death in the war.

975
Van Horn, Arthur   78th Ohio Volunteers
    Family papers, 1705–1865. 75 items.
    Contains 24 letters from Van Horn to his wife, 1863–64,
concerning campaigns in Tennessee and Mississippi, particularly the sieges of Vicksburg and Jackson, Miss. Includes
remarks on Confederate deserters, the performance of black
troops, favoritism toward black soldiers, foraging expeditions,
the attitude of noncombatants living near Vicksburg, and camp
life, morale, and disease. Also contains 10 letters from Albert,
David, and Joseph Hall to Arthur and Mary Van Horn, 1861–
64, written during campaigns in West Virginia, Kentucky,
Tennessee, and Alabama. Includes comments on the murder of
Union prisoners in the West Virginia campaign (1861), the
capture of Fort Donelson, camp life, morale, and guerrilla
warfare.

976
Van Norman, C. R.   Pvt., 4th Wisconsin Volunteers
    Collection, 1861. 2 items.
    Letters from Van Norman to his aunt, July 4 and Sept. 19,
1861, concerning camp life and training in Pennsylvania and
Maryland.

977
Vance, Robert B. (1828–1899)   Gen., CSA
    Letter, 1863. 1 item.
    Letter from Vance to his brother, Oct. 9, 1863, Asheville,
N.C., requesting assistance in retaining conscripts in the border counties to maintain order in western North Carolina, and
the impressment of all foreigners.

978
Waddel, John Newton (1812–1895)   Clergyman–Educator,
                                                Tennessee
    Diary, 1862–64. 3 v.
    Covers the period Oct. 20, 1862–May 14, 1864. Contains a
detailed account of the Federal occupation of La Grange, Tenn.
Includes comments on troop movements, foraging expeditions,
depredations, the suffering of noncombatants, inflation, the
confiscation of private homes for officers' quarters and military

hospitals, the treatment of blacks by Union soldiers, black life, and illegal trade in military supplies. Also contains comments on the situation of Waddel's friends and relations in the Confederate Army, and observations on the effects of the war in Mississippi, Alabama, and Georgia.

979
Wade, Benjamin Franklin (1800–1878)   U.S. Senator, Ohio
    Papers, 1832–81. ca. 3,500 items.
    Contains about 100 letters and documents concerning the recruitment, organization, supply, leadership, and service of Ohio troops; military pay, enlistments, discipline, appointments, and promotions; the treatment of noncombatants; the conduct of the war; reinforcements; and slavery and emancipation. Includes a few details on the Battle of Ball's Bluff, the Arkansas Post expedition, the Siege of Petersburg, the capture of Island No. 10, and the service of the 29th Ohio Volunteers in the Shenandoah Valley Campaign of 1862. Also contains miscellaneous returns for the 6th U.S. Colored Cavalry; V. P. Corbett's "Map of the Seat of War showing the battles of July 18th, 21st, and Oct 21st, 1861"; a sketch of the battlefield at Chickamauga; and a quarterly report, Mar. 1, 1864, to the Confederate surgeon general on conditions at the hospital for prisoners of war in Richmond, Va. Correspondents include James S. Brisbin, James A. Garfield, Joseph Hooker, George W. Morgan, Henry Wade, and James F. Wade.
    Finding aid and microfilm copy (11 reels) available.

980
Wadsworth, James (1768–1844)
    Family papers, 1730–1952. ca. 7,000 items.
    Material from the Civil War consists chiefly of letters and documents relating to the service and death of Wadsworth's son, Gen. James Samuel Wadsworth. Includes official orders and commissions; a letter from General Wadsworth to his daughter on the Battle of Chancellorsville; a copy of Wadsworth's report on the Battle of Gettysburg; an account of the Gettysburg campaign, with accompanying sketches of troop positions and maneuvers; a telegram announcing Wadsworth's death in the Battle of the Wilderness; copies of official reports on Wadsworth's death; and letters of condolence to his wife, Mrs. Mary Wharton Wadsworth, from Gens. George G. Meade, Andrew A. Humphreys, and Gouverneur K. Warren, and various public and private citizens. Also includes letters by Robert E. Lee and Wade Hampton on the return of Wadsworth's body and personal effects; memorials and addresses on the life of General Wadsworth; correspondence with the U.S. Treasury Department on the settlement of Wadsworth's accounts; and letters

Benjamin Franklin Wade

from Capt. Craig W. Wadsworth and James W. Wadsworth to their parents, Aug.–Oct. 1863, concerning generalship and discipline in the Union Army, the suffering of noncombatants, and attitudes toward blacks. Miscellaneous items include a letter from President Lincoln to Horace Greeley, July 9, 1864, promising safe conduct to anyone carrying peace proposals from Jefferson Davis; correspondence of the Union Defense Committee of New York; and an album containing about 200 signed photographs of military and political leaders on both sides of the war. Additional correspondents are John Dix, T. E. Ellsworth, James B. Fry, Preston King, Edwin D. Morgan, H. J. Raymond, Edwin M. Stanton, and Benjamin F. Wade.

981
Walker, Andrew J.   55th Illinois Infantry
    Collection, 1856–78. 44 items.
    Contains three letters from Walker to his family and friends, Oct.–Dec. 1861, concerning recruiting and training in Illinois; a letter from Pvt. George Fitch to William Walker, Oct. 1, 1861, relating to the defense of Washington, D.C.; and an unidentified soldier's letter written from Savannah, Tenn., Mar. 22, 1862.

982
Walker, James   Pvt., USA
    Letter, 1862–63. 1 item.
    Transcript.
    Serial letter from Walker to his family in England, Dec. 28, 1862–Jan. 3, 1863, Nashville, Tenn., concerning marches in Mississippi, Alabama, and Tennessee, skirmishes near Nashville, the care of wounded soldiers and prisoners of war from the Stones River Campaign, camp life, discipline, and supplies.

983
Walker, Nicholas   Pvt., 74th Pennsylvania Volunteers
    Document, 1864. 1 item.
    Discharge certificate, Oct. 17, 1864, Grafton, W. Va.

984
Walker, Robert John (1801–1869)   Gov., Kansas Territory
    Papers, 1815–1936. ca. 3,000 items.
    Includes scrapbooks containing clippings on the war.

985
Wallace, Lewis (1827–1905)   Gen., USV
    Collection, 1864–96. 5 items.
    In part, photocopies.
    Letter from Benjamin Lossing to Wallace, Apr. 27, 1864;

Lewis Wallace

letter from Wallace to Col. John P. Nicholson, Apr. 1896, Crawfordsville, Ind., defending his conduct in the Battle of Shiloh. Also includes copies of three printed maps of the battle showing Wallace's line of march.

986
Wallach, Richard (1816–1881)   Washington, D.C.
    Family papers, 1800–68. 40 items.
    In part, photocopies.
    Includes an authorization for a letter of marque to be granted to the *Pembroke*, owned by R. B. Forbes, Oct. 8, 1861.

987
Walton, John T.   Alabama
    Letter, 1865. 1 item.
    Letter from Walton to Dr. J. C. Nott of Mobile, Ala., Mar. 24, 1865, requesting that he treat Walton's son, an 18-month veteran home from campaigns in Virginia.

988
Wanamaker, Winfield S.
(b. 1846)   Pvt., 17th Illinois Cavalry
    Document, 1865. 1 item.
    Discharge certificate, Dec. 18, 1865.

989
Ward, James Thomas
(1820–1897)   Clergyman; Author; Educator
    Papers, 1841–97. ca. 36,000 items.
    Includes a diary which Ward continued throughout the war. Contains information on the Federal occupation of Alexandria, Va., the attitude and morale of noncombatants at Alexandria, Va., and Libertytown, Md., civilian arrests, troop movements, women accompanying their husbands in the field of war, the suppression of Union sentiment in northern Virginia, depredations by soldiers from the Union and Confederate armies, prisoners of war, deaths, generalship, and sundry battles and skirmishes. Also contains clippings on the war. Entries for the period Sept. 20, 1862–Feb. 12, 1864, are missing.

990
Ward, John   12th New York Volunteers
    Collection, 1861–62 and undated. 3 items.
    Letter from Ward to his brother Charles, May 3, 1861, Washington, D.C., concerning the organization and accommodation of the 12th New York, conditions in Washington, public attitudes toward the war, a meeting with President Lincoln, and the conduct of the New York Fire Zouaves; letter from

[John Ward?] to his brother, New York, Nov. 7, 1862, describing his capture at Harpers Ferry, the treatment of prisoners of war, skirmishes at Bolivar Heights and Maryland Heights, and the appearance and habits of Gen. Thomas J. Jackson.

991
Ward Family of Richmond County, Va.
    Papers, 1830−65. ca. 2,600 items.
    Contains family and personal correspondence relating to the war, and letters from Confederate soldiers, 1861−65. Includes remarks on public support for the war in Virginia and South Carolina, the organization and composition of the Wade Hampton Legion, fortifications at Charleston, S.C., and at various locations in Virginia, Confederate casualties and troop locations, depredations and foraging by Federal soldiers, disease and deaths in the Confederate Army, prisoners of war, desertions, problems with slaves abandoning plantations, and the Fort Donelson, Peninsular, 2d Manassas, Antietam, Fredericksburg, Chancellorsville, and Gettysburg campaigns. Also contains five captured letters concerning soldiers in the 18th Maine Volunteers. Correspondents in the Confederate Army include R. L. T. Beall, D. E. Goodwyn, John Hooff, W. Lewis, W. A. Little, George W. Richardson, L. B. Smith, James Pegram Ward, William N. Ward, Jr., William N. Ward, Sr., and James H. Weeks.

992
Washburn, Israel (1813−1883)   U.S. Representative, Maine
    Papers, 1838−1908. ca. 300 items.
    Includes seven letters to Washburn, 1861−64, concerning military appointments, promotions, morale, and generalship, and casualties in the 16th Maine at the Battle of Fredericksburg. Correspondents include Gens. Ambrose E. Burnside and Thomas Meagher. Also contains a letter from Col. Simon Jones to Maj. Christian T. Christensen, Aug. 11, 1864, Berwick Bay, La., discussing a skirmish near Patterson, La., depredations, and the performance and discipline of black troops.

993
Washburne, Elihu Benjamin
(1816−1887)   U.S. Representative, Illinois
    Papers, 1829−82. ca. 37,000 items.
    Contains a few letters to Washburne, 1861−65, concerning military appointments, promotions, supplies, armaments, and the progress of the war.
    Finding aid available.

994
Washington Family
>Collection, 1582–1915. ca. 800 items.
>In part, photocopies.
>Includes a letter from John A. Washington to his son, Lawrence Washington, May 20, 1861, Richmond [Va.], on fortifications and military activities at Norfolk, and three military passes for Capt. George Washington Ball, Mar.–June 1862.
>Finding aid available.

995
Watkins, Louise Ward (1890–   )
>Autograph collection, 1801–99. 45 items.
>Includes a letter from William H. Seward to Gideon Welles, Oct. 15, 1861, Washington, D.C., urging that the C.S.S. *Nashville* carrying John Slidell and James M. Mason be intercepted; a letter from R. A. Ford to R. S. Montague, Jan. 14, 1864, Northumberland County, Va., concerning the transfer of his son, Clement R. Ford, from the 40th Virginia Regiment to the Confederate Navy and the arming of senior citizens to oppose Federal raiding parties in Northcumberland County; and a list of taxable property and tax rates in Mobile County, Ala., 1861.

996
Watson, John Crittenden (1842–1923)   Lt., USN
>Papers, 1845–1960. ca. 1,500 items.
>Includes letters from [John J. Crittenden] to Watson, May 31 and July 7, 1861, Frankfort, Ky., appealing to Watson to remain loyal to the Union; letters from John J. Crittenden to his son, Gen. Thomas L. Crittenden, Oct. 2, 1861, and May 23, 1863, concerning Gen. Felix K. Zollicoffer's threatened attack in southeastern Kentucky and Gen. Ambrose E. Burnside's Knoxville Campaign; letters from Gen. Thomas L. Crittenden to J. J. Crittenden and J. C. Watson, July 10 and Dec. 11, 1863, on the progress of the war, the generalship of Don Carlos Buell, and troop locations; and an official letter from the headquarters of Gen. U. S. Grant approving Gen. T. L. Crittenden's resignation from the Army. Also contains official letters and orders to Watson, 1861–64; a sketch of the U.S.S. *Hartford*; photographs of John C. Watson and Adm. David G. Farragut; and printed matter: *Officers of the Western Gulf Blockading Squadron, Register of the Commissioned and Warrant Officers of the Navy of the Confederate States, to January 1863,* and *Farragut and Mobile Bay—Personal Reminiscences.*
>Finding aid available.
>Naval Historical Foundation collection.

997
Watterson, Henry (1840–1921)   Journalist; Author
    Papers, 1863–1920. ca. 9,000 items.
    Includes six routine letters to Watterson from Gen. William B. Bate, Gen. Joseph E. Johnston, Gen. Leonidas Polk, Alexander Stephens, Andrew Ewing, and George D. Prentice.
    Finding aid available.

998
Waud, Alfred R.   USA
    Papers, 1862–80. 7 items.
    Includes a letter by Waud, July 5, 1862, Camp Lincoln, James River, concerning hardships and disease during the Peninsular Campaign; a letter to Waud, Oct. 3, 1864, apparently written by a brother (Paul Waud?) who was working in the field as an artist or photographer with the Army of the James; and a letter from Gen. G. K. Warren to Waud, Sept. 29, 1863.

999
Wayman, Dorothy Godfrey (1893–1975)   Journalist; Author
    Papers, 1862–1971. ca. 6,000 items.
    Includes a postwar manuscript, "Civil War Frogman," based on the diary of Washington Hobbs Godfrey.
    Finding aid available.

1000
Weaver, Henry Clay (1840–1904)   Capt.,
                                     16th Kentucky Volunteers
    Papers, 1861–1945.
    Microfilm, 1 reel.
    Chiefly letters from Weaver to Cornelia S. Wiley, 1861–65, concerning marches and skirmishes in Kentucky and Tennessee, the Siege of Knoxville, and the Atlanta, Franklin and Nashville, and Carolinas campaigns. Includes remarks on camp life, training, discipline, disease, morale, depredations by Confederate soldiers, the treatment of loyalists by Confederate guerrillas and soldiers, resignations and promotions, and generalship. Also discusses the attitude of noncombatants in Knoxville, Tenn., conflict between veteran soldiers and new recruits in the Carolinas Campaign, the attitude of Federal soldiers toward slavery, and the effect of the assassination of President Lincoln on Gen. William T. Sherman's army.

1001
Weaver, Willis (1846–1929)
    Collection, 1892. 2 items.
    Transcripts.
    Letter from Weaver to the editor of the *National Tribune*

concerning President Buchanan's Cabinet crisis of Dec. 1860; and notes on Gen. Benjamin F. Butler's New Orleans expedition, with emphasis on the role of Secretary Stanton in the origin and implementation of the plan.

1002
Webb, Charles Henry (1834–1905)   Correspondent, *New York Times*

Papers, 1859–1924. ca. 320 items.

Includes a military pass issued to Webb, June 25, 1862, and a letter from Gen. Rufus King to Webb, Oct. 21 [1862], on the character and ability of Gen. James S. Wadsworth.

1003
Webster, Harrie (1843–1921)   3d Asst. Engineer, USN

Papers, 1889–1913. ca. 50 items.

In part, transcripts.

Includes a copy of Webster's autobiography describing his escape from a farm in Falls Church, Va., during the Battle of 1st Manassas, his employment at the U.S. Navy Yard in Washington, D.C., service on various ships of war in the blockade of Wilmington, N.C., the Battle of Port Hudson, the blockade of Mobile Bay, conditions on monitor class vessels, the surrender of Fort Morgan, and two interviews with Adm. David G. Farragut. Also includes a copy of a published article by Webster, "An August Morning With Farragut at Mobile Bay."

Naval Historical Foundation collection.

1004
Weed, Thurlow (1797–1882)   Journalist; Politician

Papers, 1821–94. ca. 125 items.

Contains a few letters concerning military appointments and the effect of the war on the economy.

Finding aid available.

1005
Weeks, Benjamin Franklin   Q.M. Sgt., 28th
(b. 1838)   Massachusetts Volunteers

Papers, 1861–67. ca. 450 items.

Chiefly records from the Commissary Department—invoices, orders, receipts, provision returns, vouchers for supplies issued to various units, and miscellaneous items.

1006
Welles, Gideon (1802–1878)   U.S. Secretary of the Navy

Papers, 1777–1911. ca. 15,000 items.

General correspondence, official letterbooks, Welles' diary, drafts and copies of articles on the war, newspaper clippings, and biographical notes on Welles. Contains information on the location and duty assignment of numerous officers, ship stations, vessels comprising flotillas and squadrons; naval guns and munitions, monitors, prize vessels, naval battles, and the number of officers (by rank) in the U.S. Navy. Articles by Welles discuss the capture of James Mason and John Slidell, the reinforcement of Fort Pickens, the abandonment of the U.S. Navy Yard near Portsmouth, Va., the capture of New Orleans, emancipation, the Lincoln administration, the use of monitors, and Civil War politics. Miscellaneous items include a report by a Confederate deserter on the manufacture and importation of weapons, ship construction, the production of railroad iron (rails), and the armor and firepower of the *Merrimac*.

Finding aid and partial index available.

1007
Wells, David Ames
(1828–1898)   Public Official, New York
    Papers, 1795–1898. ca. 5,000 items.

Contains several proposed designs, with accompanying correspondence, Jan.–Apr. 1862, for the official seal and flag of the Confederacy.

Finding aid and microfilm copy (9 reels) available.

1008
Wells, James Madison (1808–1899)   Gov., Louisiana
    Document, 1865. 1 item.

List of 22 names of office holders appointed by Wells, Mar.–May 1865, with comments on the loyalty or military service of each appointee.

1009
Wentworth, Edwin Oberlin   Pvt., 37th
(1833–1864)   Massachusetts Volunteers
    Papers, 1862–90. ca. 120 items.

Chiefly letters from Wentworth to his wife, July 1862–May 1864, concerning the Fredericksburg, Chancellorsville, Gettysburg, and Wilderness campaigns, and operations along the Rappahannock River in the fall of 1863. Provides information on camp life, training, morale, discipline, enlistments, marches, bounties, desertions, diet, disease, medical care, foraging and reconnaissance expeditions, sutlers, depredations, generalship, the attitude of soldiers toward blacks and emancipation, the treatment of noncombatants, and trading between Union and Confederate pickets. Also includes a list of officers and men in Company I, 37th Massachusetts, details on casualties in the 37th Massachusetts, a photograph of Wentworth, drafts of articles written for *The Reveille*, a camp paper edited by Wentworth during the 1864 winter bivouac near Brandy Station, Va., and miscellaneous poems and pension records.

1010

West, James B.   USA
    Collection, 1864. 4 items.
    Countersigns used by Gen. Rufus Saxton, Jan.–Apr. 1864, Port Royal, S.C.

1011

Westervelt, H. C.   USA
    Collection, 1863. 3 items.
    Letters from Westervelt to his wife, July–Aug. 1863, concerning generalship, Confederate sympathizers in Maryland, and wounded prisoners of war.

1012

Whaley, Daniel (b. 1829)   Pvt., 6th New York Artillery
    Document, 1864. 1 item.
    Military pass, Jan. 15, 1864, Camp Hunt, Va.

1013

Wheeler, Henry (b. 1844)   Pvt.,
                                             5th Connecticut Volunteers
    Document, 1864. 1 item.
    Discharge certificate, July 21, 1864, Hartford, Conn.

1014

Wheeler, John Hill (1806–1882)   Diplomat;
                                          Historian; Public Official
    Papers, 1828–82. ca. 100 items.
    Diary, 1854–82, and scrapbooks of a Confederate sympathizer. Contains information on the service of Wheeler's two sons, Lt. Charles Scully Wheeler (USA) and Capt. Woodbury Wheeler (CSA), military activities in northern Virginia, reaction in Washington to the Battle of 1st Manassas, travel in the Confederacy, meetings with Confederate officers and officials, operations in West Virginia in 1861, public morale in the South, the effect of the war on noncombatants, generalship, Federal prisoners of war, the use of blacks by the Confederacy, camp life, and disease. Also describes Wheeler's voyage to Europe, 1863–64, including the running of the Federal blockade at Wilmington, N.C.
    Finding aid and microfilm copy (5 reels) available.

1015
White, B. F.   Pvt., CSA
    Letter, 1862. 1 item.
    Photocopy.
    Letter from White to his parents, Sept. 24, 1862, Hampstead County, Ark., concerning problems with disease, discipline, and desertion.

1016
White, John Chester
(1841–1921)   1st Lt., 11th U.S. Infantry
    Memoir, 1861–1921. 2 v.
    Transcript.
    Covers chiefly White's service with the 17th, 19th, and 21st Pennsylvania Volunteers, and the 11th U.S. Infantry during the Chancellorsville, Gettysburg, and Wilderness campaigns, and the Siege of Petersburg. Includes details on enlistments, promotions, bounties, the recruitment of criminals, behavior of Indian soldiers, morality, entertainment, discipline, desertions, generalship, problems with drunkenness and gambling, casualties, disease, medical care, depredations, guerrilla warfare, the treatment of prisoners of war, and White's exchange and parole. Also contains a photograph of White, and notes from his obituary published in the Boston *Morning Globe*, Jan. 18, 1921.

1017
Whiting, Jasper S.
    Letter, 1861. 1 item.
    Letter from Whiting to Gen. P. G. T. Beauregard, [Apr. 10, 1861], Morris Island, complaining about the lack of organization among troops deployed against Fort Sumter, S.C.

1018
Whiting, William Henry (1843–1925)   USN
    Family papers, 1731–1952.
    Microfilm, 1 reel.
    Includes a few miscellaneous clippings relating to the war.
    Finding aid available.

1019
Whitman, Walt (1819–1892)   Poet
    Collection, 1850–1912.
    Microfilm, 2 reels.
    Contains a few letters from Whitman to his mother and brother, and letters written to or for wounded Federal soldiers. Includes comments on visits to military hospitals in Washington and observations on President Lincoln. Also contains an

exchange of letters with Capt. William Cook, Feb. 1865, concerning the location of Whitman's brother, Capt. George W. Whitman, a prisoner of war in the Confederacy.

Originals at Yale University.

1020
Whitten, John   Pvt., 5th Iowa Volunteers
    Diary, 1862–65. 1 v.
Contains information on the participation of the 5th Iowa in the Battle of Iuka, Miss., the Siege of Corinth, the Vicksburg Campaign (particularly the battles of Champion's Hill and Jackson), and a detailed account of Whitten's experiences as a prisoner of war at Libby Prison, Belle Isle, and Andersonville. Includes comments on the arrival, transfer, and exchange of prisoners, escape attempts, disease, deaths, and the release of prisoners at Andersonville, Ga., at the end of the war.

1021
Wigfall, Louis Trezevant
(1816–1874)   Gen., CSA; C.S. Senator, Texas
    Family papers, 1858–1909. ca. 550 items.
Contains about 75 letters to Wigfall from his son, Lt. F. Halsey Wigfall, concerning the Peninsular, Antietam, Fredericksburg, Chancellorsville, Atlanta, and Franklin and Nashville campaigns, and operations along the Rapidan and Rappahannock Rivers in the fall of 1863. Includes remarks on camp life and fortifications in northern Virginia during the winter of 1861–62, training, marches, morale, casualties, diet, supplies, entertainment, the organization and strength of various artillery units, disease, medical care, appointments and promotions, generalship, furloughs, the suffering of noncombatants, and reaction in the army to the removal of General Johnston during the Atlanta Camgaign. Also includes a detailed account of the movements of Gen. John Bell Hood after the fall of Atlanta and a copy of Hood's preliminary report on the Franklin and Nashville Campaign. Letters from Gen. Joseph E. Johnston to Wigfall, 1862–65, discuss Johnston's frustrations with officials in Richmond, his personal feud with Jefferson Davis, military organization and strategy, appointments and promotions, troop morale, generalship, reinforcements, and various aspects of the Peninsular, Vicksburg, Chickamauga, Chattanooga, and Atlanta campaigns. Miscellaneous items comprise letters to Wigfall on military affairs from P. G. T. Beauregard, Clement C. Clay, Richard S. Ewell, Wade Hampton, John Bell Hood, Robert M. T. Hunter, Ralph Izard, Robert E. Lee, James Longstreet, Francis Pickens, Leonidas Polk, Robert Barnwell Rhett, and John A. Wharton; copies of letters in the papers of the Confederate War Department, Feb. 18–Mar. 13, 1865, by

John C. Breckinridge, John H. Claiborne, Samuel G. French, Josiah Gorgas, Robert E. Lee, Richard Morton, B. P. Nolan, and Isaac Munroe St. John; and letters from Mrs. Lydia Johnston to Mrs. L. T. Wigfall, 1862–74, relating generally to the war.

1022
Wight, Frederick H.   9th New York Volunteers
    Collection, 1860–62. 11 items.
    Includes nine letters written by Wight from camps in Maryland and Virginia, Aug. 21, 1861–Feb. 12, 1862, concerning camp life, marches, morale, discipline, disease, hospital care, and military organization.

1023
Wilcox, Cadmus Marcellus
(1824–1890)   Gen., CSA
    Papers, 1846–87. ca. 1,200 items.
    In part, transcripts and photocopies.
    Includes copies of official reports on the battles of Williamsburg, Fair Oaks, Gaines Mill, White Oak Swamp, 2d Manassas, Fredericksburg, Salem Church, and Gettysburg, extracts of reports on the Gettysburg, Spotsylvania, and Wilderness campaigns, notes on the Siege of Petersburg, casualty reports, clippings on the war, and an autobiography for the period June 8, 1861–Apr. 1865. Also contains letters from General Wilcox to his brother, John A. Wilcox, 1861–65, concerning Confederate morale, fortifications, casualties, conscription, pillage by Confederate soldiers, depredations by Union soldiers, the suffering of noncombatants, disease, discipline, supply shortages, weapons, and his feelings toward his former friends in the U.S. Army.

1024
Wild, Edward Augustus (1825–1891)   Gen., USV
    Letter, 1863. 1 item.
    Letter from Wild to Rev. William A. Green, Nov. 5, 1863, Norfolk, Va., concerning Green's appointment as chaplain in the 3d Regiment, African brigade.

1025
Wilda, R. W. A.
    Index, undated. 1 v.
    "Index to Volumes, First Series of the Official War Records." Incomplete.

1026

Wilder, William Frank

(1831–1917)   Capt., 46th Illinois Infantry
    Collection, 1903–27. 3 items.
    In part, transcripts.
    "Reminiscences of the Civil War," written in 1903. Includes comments on the Fort Donelson, Corinth, and Vicksburg campaigns, northern optimism at the beginning of the war, the sobering effect of the 1st Manassas Campaign, enlistments, training, camp life, disease, casualties, slavery, black life, the attitude of Union soldiers toward blacks, depredations, discipline, entertainment, and Confederate deserters.

1027

Wiley, Harvey Washington

(1844–1930)   Cpl., 137th Indiana Volunteers
    Papers, 1854–1944. ca. 70,000 items.
    Includes diary kept by Wiley during marches in Kentucky and Tennessee, May 30–Sept. 17, 1864. Contains comments on camp life, diet, morale, discipline, disease, morality, the occupation of Nashville, guerrilla warfare, and the activities of loyalist cavalry units from east Tennessee.
    Finding aid available.

1028

Wilkes, Charles (1798–1877)   Comdr., USN
    Papers, 1607–1959. ca. 6,500 items.
    General, official, and family correspondence, diary, and autobiography concerning the *Trent* affair, and Wilkes' command of the James River and Potomac River flotillas and the West India Squadron. Also contains letterbooks, court-martial records, and miscellaneous maps and photographs.
    Finding aid and microfilm copy (26 reels) available.

1029

Willard Family
    Papers, 1800–1955. ca. 80,000 items.
    In part, transcripts and photocopies.
    Items relating to the war comprise chiefly letters and documents relating to the career of Maj. Joseph C. Willard, aide-de-camp to Gen. Irvin McDowell, and personal and family correspondence of the accused Confederate spy, Antonia Ford, the future Mrs. J. C. Willard. Includes a diary kept by Willard during the 2d Manassas Campaign and containing remarks on camp life, marches, foraging expeditions, depredations, and the activities of General McDowell; letters from Antonia Ford to

Willard and her family concerning the effects of the war on noncombatants, the location and health of her brother and acquaintances in the Confederate Army, and her secret romance with Willard; and miscellaneous telegrams, clippings, orders, receipts, commissions, and military passes.

Finding aid available.

1030
Willey, Henry Stevens (b. 1844)   16th Vermont Regiment
    Collection, 1915. 2 items.
    Transcripts.
    Reminiscences: "The Story of My Experiences During the Civil War, 1862–1863" (25 p.) and "Additional Items From the First Draft of the Story of My Experiences During the Civil War" (7 p.). Describes the attitude of northern "mudsills" and "greasy mechanics" toward the South, the effect of the attack on Fort Sumter in the North, Willey's enlistment in the 16th Vermont, military organization, the selection of line and field officers, camp life, training, diet, equipment and supplies, disease, hospital care, the conduct and treatment of sutlers, the generalship of Edwin Henry Stoughton, the Gettysburg Campaign, and the death of Gen. William Barksdale (CSA).

1031
Williams, John L.   CSA
    Papers, 1846–62. 9 items.
    Letter from Williams to his niece, July 18, 1862, Camp Douglas, Ill., on life as a prisoner of war.

1032
Williams, Margaret D.
    Collection, 1921. 2 items.
    Transcripts.
    Contains "A Brief Reminiscence of the First Inauguration of Abraham Lincoln as President," with comments on the assassination plot (10 p.).

1033
Williams, William W.   Pvt., 27th
                                              Alabama Regiment
    Document, 1865. 1 item.
    Photocopy.
    Military parole issued to Williams at Salisbury, N.C., May 2, 1865.

1034
Willis, Edward   Maj., CSA
    Papers, 1860–65. ca. 4,000 items.

Quartermaster records, official correspondence, clippings, pamphlets, orders, reports, and letterbooks. Provides information on defensive operations along the coasts of South Carolina and Georgia, the Siege of Petersburg, and troop movements in Georgia, Mississippi, and Alabama. Miscellaneous items include photographs of prisoners of war at Fort Warren, Mass., plans for the manufacture of various types of torpedoes, *The Soldier's Pocket Bible*, engraved views of the bombardments of Fort Sumter, Fort Walker, Fort Beauregard, and Port Royal, S.C., poems, the diary of Capt. J. E. Edings, a manuscript history of Gen. Thomas F. Drayton's brigade, engraved portraits of Jefferson Davis, Braxton Bragg, Hannibal Hamlin, James Longstreet, J. E. B. Stuart, Leonidas Polk, and Ben McCulloch, and postwar articles and clippings on Confederate blockade running. Pamphlets include W. A. Harris, *The Record of Fort Sumter, From Its Occupation by Major Anderson, to Its Reduction by South Carolina Troops* (1862)*; Report of the Chief of the Department of the Military of South Carolina* (1862)*; Report of the Adjutant and Inspector General of South Carolina* (1863)*; Operations on Morris Island* (1863)*; Report of the Congressional Committee on the Operations of the Army of the Potomac* (1863)*;* and *General Washington and General Jackson, on Negro Soldiers* (1863).

1035
Wills, David (1831–1894)
    Papers, 1863–1940. 13 items.
    In part, transcripts.
    Includes a letter from Gen. George G. Meade to Wills, Nov. 13, 1863, on the dedication of Gettysburg National Cemetery, and Wills' recollections of the Gettysburg Address.

1036
Wilson, Henry
(1812–1875)   U.S. Senator, Massachusetts
    Papers, 1851–75. ca. 200 items.
    Includes a letter from Gen. Willis A. Gorman to Wilson, Dec. 22, 1861, concerning charges that Gorman flogged and returned fugitive slaves; a letter from Gen. Joseph Hooker to Wilson, Apr. 4, 1862, on rank disputes, depredations, and problems with blacks in the Peninsular Campaign; a letter from Gen. Benjamin F. Butler to Wilson, May 7, 1864, on the progress of his army in the Siege of Petersburg; and a personal letter from Gen. Edward Ferrero to Wilson, Feb. 18, 1865.

1037
Wilson, James Harrison (1837–1925)   Gen., USA
    Papers, 1861–1923. ca. 25,000 items.
    In part, transcripts.
    Includes official correspondence and dispatches, Dec. 1864–June 1865, concerning military equipment and supplies, desertions, reinforcements, and preparations for Wilson's raid to Selma, Ala.; a "Consolidated Report of Cavalry serving in the Military District of the Mississippi," Aug. 1864; and miscellaneous returns. Also includes copies of dispatches from the War Department to Gen. U. S. Grant, July 11–24, 1864, concerning reinforcements and troop movements, and copies of the dispatches of Charles A. Dana to Edwin M. Stanton, 1863–64, reporting on generalship, troop strength and dispositions, casualties, morale, discipline, supplies, desertions, guerrilla warfare, tactics, and the treatment of noncombatants in the Vicksburg, Chickamauga, Chattanooga, Wilderness, Spotsylvania, Cold Harbor, and Petersburg campaigns, and the Siege of Knoxville.
    Finding aid and partial index available.

1038
Wilson, Lawrence (b. 1842)   Sgt., 7th Ohio Volunteers
    Papers, 1861–65. 6 items.
    Diary, June 30, 1862–Dec. 15, 1864 (3 v.), kept during the 2d Manassas, Fredericksburg, Chancellorsville, Gettysburg, Chattanooga, and Atlanta campaigns. Describes camp life, marches, discipline, depredations, casualties, guerrilla warfare, courts-martial, furloughs, reconnaissance expeditions, prisoner exchanges, and problems with drunkenness. Also includes an advertisement for the Soldiers' Home in Cleveland, Ohio, and a roll book containing the names of officers and privates in Company D, 7th Ohio, along with details on casualties, discharges, transfers, and deaths; pay and allowances; equipment and supplies; and a copy of a letter written by a Confederate soldier at the Battle of Resaca.

1039
Wilson, Samuel Lewis
(1844–1879)   Midshipman, USN
    Papers, 1862–1939. 22 items.
    Includes a few letters from Wilson to his family and relations written while a student at the U.S. Naval Academy and aboard the U.S.S. *Macedonian*, 1864.
    Naval Historical Foundation collection.

1040

Wilson, Thomas   Gen., USA
	Collection, 1865. 2 items.
	Letter from Wilson to his wife, Apr. 9, 1865, [Appomattox
Courthouse, Va.] describing the scene in the Army of the Potomac when the surrender of Gen. R. E. Lee's army was an-
nounced; and a photograph of Meade with his staff reviewing
his troops near Appomattox Courthouse.

1041

Winslow, John Ancrum (1811–1873)   Capt., USN
	Collection, 1864–88. 10 items.
	In part, photocopies.
	Account of the battle between the U.S.S. *Kearsarge* and
C.S.S. *Alabama* copied from entries in the log of the *Kearsarge*
for June 14–21, 1864; postwar account of the battle with a steel
engraving of Captain Winslow; pamphlet, *The Cruise of the
Kearsarge* (1888); list of subscribers to an award for Captain
Winslow, Nov. 16, 1864; and photographs of five officers who
served on the *Kearsarge*: William H. Bedlam, chief engineer
Cushman, Hayard Marsh, Frederick L. Miller, and sailing master Stoddard.
	Naval Historical Foundation collection.

1042

Winthrop Family
	Papers, 1537–1904.
	Microfilm, 53 reels.
	Contains notes or memoranda by Robert C. Winthrop writ-
ten during a visit to Washington, D.C., in Oct. 1861. Provides
information on meetings with President Lincoln, William
Seward, Winfield Scott, and Robert Anderson, and observations on public morale, generalship, and the conduct of the
war. Also contains a military pass issued to Winthrop by General Scott, Oct. 21, 1861; an undated letter from Robert Anderson to Winthrop on fortifications and camp scenes near Washington, and problems between Generals Scott and McClellan;
and miscellaneous letters by Nathaniel P. Banks, Edward
Everett, George B. McClellan, William C. Rives, and D. M.
Sargent.
	Published finding aid available.
	Originals in the Massachusetts Historical Society.

1043

Wirz, Henry (d. 1865)   Commandant, Andersonville Prison;
                                                     Maj., CSA
	Collection, 1865. 14 items.
	Material relating to Wirz' trial.

1044
Wise, Henry Alexander
(1806–1876), and Family   Gen., CSA
    Collection, 1836–1928. ca. 350 items.
    Includes a letter from Wise to Gov. Henry T. Clark of
North Carolina, Jan. 18, 1862, assessing the military situation
along the Carolina coast and suggesting a plan of defense.
    Microfilm copy (1 reel) available.

1045
Wise, Henry Augustus (1819–1869)   Comdr., USN
    Papers, 1850–69. 90 items.
    Includes several letters from Wise to Mrs. John L. Worden
and an unnamed recipient, May–Nov. 1861, concerning the
exchange of Mrs. Worden's husband, a prisoner of war at
Montgomery, Ala., and a letter from Harriet M. Kennard to
[Mrs. Worden], Apr. 30, 1861, Montgomery, Ala., assuring Mrs.
Worden that her husband, a prisoner in the city, was well.
    Naval Historical Foundation collection.

1046
Wiser, Angelo   Sgt., 15th
                                      Pennsylvania Cavalry
    Maps, 1865. 1 v.
    "Complete Map of the march of the 1st Brigade 1st Cav-
alry Divn. Dept. of Cumberland on the Stoneman expedition
through Tenn., Va., N.C., S.C., Geo., & Ala. March to June
1865." Consists of a series of sketches showing roads, towns
and villages, bridges, mills, farms and estates, and various
places of interest.

1047
Wittenmyer, Annie   Agent, Iowa
                                   Sanitary Association
    Collection, 1862–66. 5 items.
    In part, photocopies.
    Military passes signed by Edwin Stanton and President
Lincoln, letter of introduction to Gen. William T. Sherman,
June 28, 1863, and instructions from the assistant surgeon
general at Louisville, Ky., to the medical directors under his
command to assist Mrs. Wittenmyer in introducing a diet she
developed for wounded soldiers.

1048
Women's Loyal National League   New York
    Document, 1863. 1 item.
    Circular signed by Susan B. Anthony and S. E. Draper,

June 20, 1863, requesting aid in gathering signatures on petitions.

1049
Wood, Henry Clay (1832–1918)   Col., USA
   Papers, 1838–1907. ca. 300 items.
   In part, photocopies and transcripts.
   Includes some material concerning the Battle of Wilson's Creek; miscellaneous orders, accounts, and receipts; Wood's commission as colonel in William Adams' 1st Missouri Cavalry; official correspondence regarding Wood's service in the 11th U.S. Infantry; and information on recruiting, supplies, and military organization in northeast Missouri in 1861.

1050
Wood Family
   Papers, 1836–1906. 28 items.
   In part, transcripts.
   Contains the papers of William W. Wood (1816–1882) and his son, Thomas Newton Wood (1854–1919). Includes three letters to W. W. Wood, Apr.–Nov. 1864, concerning the construction of naval vessels and torpedoes; a letter from John Lenthall to Adm. Francis H. Gregory, Apr. 29, 1864, on a contract for the construction of launches and torpedo boats; and a naval contract with the Clute brothers of Schenectady, N.Y., for six picket boats designed by Wood.
   Naval Historical Foundation collection.

1051
Woodbury, Levi (1789–1851) and
Charles Levi (1820–1898)
   Papers, 1638–1899. ca. 18,350 items.
   Includes the diary of Virginia Woodbury Fox (wife of Assistant Secretary of the Navy, Gustavus V. Fox), which contains numerous references to Cabinet meetings, troop reviews, war plans, political and military leaders, the arrival and departure of various warships, and troop movements.
   Finding aid available.

1052
Woodford, Stewart Lyndon (1835–1913)   Col., USA
   Collection, 1865–1908. 4 items.
   Includes a petition from J. T. Welsman to Woodford, Apr. 21, 1865, Charleston, S.C., requesting permission to go north on parole on family and business matters, and Woodford's negative response, Apr. 29, 1865, Hilton Head, S.C.

1053

Woodman, Harry   Bucks County, Pennsylvania
    Papers, 1861–65. 9 items.

Letters to Woodman, Nov. 1861–Jan. 1865, concerning camp life, enlistments, the progress of the war, and the return of bodies of deceased soldiers. Correspondents are Henry D. Franklin, Charles L. Smith, Fred L. Smith, and Jeremiah Worthington.

1054

Woodson, Carter Godwin (1875–1950)   Author; Editor
    Collection of Negro papers and related documents, 1796–1936. ca. 5,000 items.

Includes a letter by Jacob C. White, Aug. 19, 1862, Philadelphia, Pa., on the recruitment of black regiments in the North; a letter by Lewis [Douglas?], July 20, 186[3], Morris Island, S.C., on the performance of black troops at Fort Wagner; a letter from Christian A. Fleetwood to his father, June 23, 1863, Baltimore, Md., on the impressment of blacks to work on the city's fortifications; and a letter from Sgt. Maj. Christian A. Fleetwood to Robert Hamilton, June 28, 1864, written at the Siege of Petersburg, concerning the performance of the 4th U.S. Colored Infantry.

Finding aid and microfilm copy (10 reels) available.

1055

Woodwell, Charles H.   Pvt., 5th Massachusetts Volunteers
    Diary, 1862–63. 1 v.
    Transcript.

Discusses the recruitment, organization, and training of the 5th Massachusetts; leadership, discipline, and morale; skirmishes near Kinston, White Hall, and Goldsborough, N.C.; the defense of Fort Washington; and marches through Beaufort and Craven Counties. Also contains remarks on casualties, disease, medical care, sutlers, the effect of the Emancipation Proclamation, and public support for the war in Massachusetts.

1056

Woodworth, Selim Edwin (1815–1871)   USN
    Papers, 1851–65. 4 items.
    Photocopies.

Photograph of Woodworth; list of battles in which Woodworth participated; and postwar letter (unsigned) outlining Woodworth's naval career.

Naval Historical Foundation collection.

1057
Worden, John Lorimer (1818–1897)   Comdr., USN
    Papers, 1861–98. 65 items.
    In part, transcripts.
    Includes a letter from Worden to Gideon Welles, Apr. 15,
1861, Montgomery, Ala., concerning his arrest and imprisonment after delivering dispatches from the War Department to
Fort Pickens; two letters from Welles to Mrs. Olivia Worden,
1861; a letter from Adm. Samuel F. Du Pont to Worden, Apr.
13, 1863, Port Royal, S.C., relieving Worden of his command of
the U.S.S. *Montauk*; and a photograph of Worden with his family taken shortly after he was blinded in the battle between the
U.S.S. *Monitor* and C.S.S. *Merrimac*.
    Naval Historical Foundation collection.

1058
Wragg, Thomas L.   8th Georgia Regiment
    Collection, 1861–63. 11 items.
    Nine letters from Wragg to his father and sister written
from camps in northern Virginia, July 1861–July 1862, concerning the participation of the 8th Georgia in the Battle of 1st
Manassas, casualties in the 8th Georgia, camp life, morale,
disease, supplies, the attitude of Federal prisoners of war, and
the skirmish at Dranesville, Va., Dec. 20, 1861. Also includes a
sketch of the Manassas battlefield, and a letter from Wragg to
his father written from Fort Warren Prison in Boston Harbor,
Nov. 17, 1863.

1059
Wright, Benjamin Hall (1801–1881)   Civil Engineer
    Papers, 1839–80. 63 items.
    Includes a letter from Gen. Henry W. Halleck to Wright,
Apr. 10, 1863, acknowledging Wright's suggestions on the conduct of the war, and a personal letter from Gen. Robert Anderson to Wright, June 4, 1862.

1060
Wright, Nathaniel (1789–1875)   Lawyer, Ohio
    Family papers, 1787–1917. ca. 23,400 items.
    Contains about 30 letters relating to the war. Includes
four letters from Col. Rutherford B. Hayes to R. H. Stephenson,
1861–63, concerning enlistments, morale, casualties, and
health in the 23d Ohio Volunteers during campaigns in western Virginia; eight letters from Edward F. Noyes to Stephenson,
1861–64, describing the pursuit of Confederate forces under
Gen. Martin E. Green in Missouri, guerrilla warfare in Missouri,
the participation of the 39th Ohio Volunteers in the Chattanooga and Atlanta campaigns, and hospital care following the

loss of a foot near Kennesaw Mountain; and five letters from Edward, Nathaniel, and William Wright, 1862–64, written during campaigns in Kentucky, Tennessee, and Georgia. Also contains letters relating to the war by George K. Cox, J.H.H. Daniel, John B. Elliott, Jackson Lane, William Owen, Thomas S. Rope, Willard Storres, and E. H. Tatem.

Finding aid available.

1061
Wright, William W.   Engineer, USA

Papers, 1863–70. 10 items.

Chiefly orders and commissions, 1863–64, concerning Wright's duties as superintendent of military railroads in the Department of the Susquehanna, as chief engineer of construction, Military Division of Mississippi, and as colonel, 42d U.S. Colored Infantry Regiment.

1062
Wyndham, Percy   Col., USA

Note, 1863. 1 item.

Concerns the transmission of a message to Washington, May 14, 1863.

1063
Yoder, Samuel S. (1841–1921)   128th Ohio Volunteers

Family papers, 1841–1907. ca. 500 items.

Includes about 100 letters by Yoder's brothers, Noah W., Moses F., and Jacob Yoder, 1861–64, written during campaigns in Kentucky, Tennessee, and Georgia. Provides information on the occupation of Nashville; the Stones River, Chickamauga, Chattanooga, and Atlanta campaigns; and the deaths of Moses and Jacob Yoder. Also contains comments on the service of the 51st Ohio Volunteers, camp life, morale, generalship, marches, discipline, entertainment, disease, casualties, hospital care, prisoners of war, morality of soldiers, and the attitude of Federal soldiers toward blacks.

1064
Young, John Russell
(1841–1899)   Editor, *Philadelphia Press*

Papers, 1843–98. ca. 11,000 items.

Includes a letter from Simon Cameron to Gen. Irvin McDowell, July 20, 1861, on reinforcements; letters from John W. Forney to Young, 1861–64, on the progress of the war and events in Washington, D.C.; a letter from Col. John H. Taggard to Young, May 22, 1862; a letter from Edward Zane Carroll Judson (alias, Ned Buntline) to John W. Forney, Sept. 20 [1863], and photographs of Edwin and John Wilkes Booth.

Finding aid available.

INDEX

15th, 88; 27th, 1033;
34th, 637
Albemarle(C.S.S.): battle with
U.S.S.
Sassacus, 785; destruction
of, 365, 514, 785
Aldie, Va.: skirmish at, 162,
377
Aldrich, A. P., 392
Aldrich, J. H., 838
Aldrich, Nelson Wilmarth, 8
Alexander, Andrew J., 378,
636
Alexander, Edward Porter, **9**
Alexandria (blockade runner),
222
Alexandria, Va.: capture and
occupation of, 428, 796,
989; attitude and morale
of inhabitants of, 33, 989;
mentioned, 507, 885, 944
Alice (C.S.S.), 858
Alice Price (U.S. transport),
774
Allatoona, Ga.; *see* Franklin
and Nashville Campaign
Allatoona Hills, Ga.; *see*
Atlanta Campaign
Allen, A. B. W., 563
Allen, Charles Julius:
reminiscences and
autobiographical writings
of, 14
Allen, E. J., 33, 724
Allen, George, 678
Allen, George, Jr.: death of,
678
Allen, Henry Watkins, **10**,
557
Allen, Isaac Jackson, **11**
Allen, Samuel E., **12**
Allen, William: war record of,
792
Allen, William A. H., **13**
Allen family, **14**

Allentown, Pa., 646
Alsop's Farm; *see*
Spotsylvania Campaign
Alston, Jacob Motte, 15
Alston family, **15**
Alvord, Augustus V., **16**
Alvord, Jabez, **17**
Ambulance Corps (U.S.
Army), 382, 946
American Coaster (blockade
runner), 842
American Freedmen's Inquiry
Commission, 582
American Institute of
Aeronautics and
Astronautics, 18
American Medical
Association, 815
American Missionary Society,
422
Ames, Adelbert, 346
Amherst County, Va.: bonds
issued in, 191
Amite River, La.: operations
along, 360
Anderson, Charles D., 206
Anderson, Finley, 78
Anderson, Frank Maloy, **19**
Anderson, Isabel Perkins, 712
Anderson, John Emerson, **20**
Anderson, Richard H., 930
Anderson, Robert, **21**;
correspondence of, 212,
238, 850, 955, 1042, 1059;
notes from Cabinet meet-
ings concerning
Anderson, 87; mentioned,
1034
Anderson T. M., 21
Anderson—Moler families, **22**
Anderson County, Kans., 22
Andersonville Prison:
conditions at, 599; letters
of prisoners, 599; list of
U.S. soldiers buried at, 54;

release of prisoners, 1020;
treatment of prisoners at,
345, 448, 1020; mentioned,
197; *see also* Wirz, Henry

Andrew, John Albion, 91, 823

Anglin, John S., 23

Annapolis, Md.: Burnside
expedition prepared at,
586; sick and wounded
soldiers at, 12; mentioned,
765

*Annual Report of the Signal
Officer* (1863), 659; *see
also* Signal
communications

Anonymous, 24

Anthony, Susan B., 897, 1048

Antietam Campaign, 33, 335,
351-53, 363, 386, 391,
442, 452, 466, 472, 488,
522-23, 526, 571-72, 578,
618, 699, 725, 735, 766,
772, 859, 894, 912, 938,
944, 991, 1021; *see also*
Sharpsburg, Battle of

"An Appeal to the Democracy
of the South," 761

Appomattox Campaign, 25,
112, 162, 193, 346, 391,
500, 542, 576, 715, 758,
778, 846, 869; condition of
C.S. Army on eve of, 411;
U.S. dispatches concern-
ing, 231; attitude of C.S.
and U.S. soldiers during,
636

Appomattox Courthouse, Va.:
General Lee's surrender
at, 193, 532; effect of
surrender on Lee's army,
159; mentioned, 1040;
see also McLean House

Aquia Creek, Va.: skirmish at,
796; *see also* Battle of
Aquia Creek, Va.

Archer (C.S.S.): list of vessels
captured by, 265

*Are Southern Privateersmen
Pirates?* (1861), 424, 430

Arkansas (C.S.S.): engagements with enemy vessels,
686; mentioned, 246

Arkansas: campaigns in, 41,
44, 46, 48, 339, 491, 598,
630, 702, 894, 946; *see
also* Fort Hindman expe-
dition; Pea Ridge, Battle
of. Impact of the war on,
156; Indian volunteers
from, 61; Unionist
volunteers from, 946;
opposition to Federal
policy in, 275; skirmish in,
246

Arkansas Post expedition; *see*
Fort Hindman expedition

Arlington Heights, Va.:
occupied by Federal
soldiers, 428

Arms and ammunition, 94,
242, 578, 784, 803, 903,
1006, 1023; imported by
the Confederacy, 1006;
manufacture of, 220, 749,
856, 1006; procurement of,
132, 718; promotion of new
and improved weapons,
863; returns and reports
on, 189, 405, 492, 500,
507, 552, 591, 638, 736,
743, 758; rules and regulations concerning, 656;
seizure of, 105, 507, 562;
see also Arsenals;
Torpedoes

Armstrong, James D., 912

Armstrong, James F., 606

Army; *see* Confederate States
Army; U.S. Army; Black

troops; various State
troops

"The Army Signal Corps," 659;
see also Signal communications

Arnold, John Carvel, **25**

Arnold, Samuel: arrest of, 650

Arnold, Samuel B., 307

Arsenals: seizure of, 105, 507,
562

Arthur, Chester Alan, **26**, 580

Arthur, William, **26**

Artillery: (C.S. Army) 147,
419, 447, 656, 692, 870,
894, 939; organization and
strength of, 1021; (U.S.
Army) 11, 16, 94, 108,
112, 257, 270, 357, 466,
551, 604, 631, 715, 758,
831, 854, 888, 1012;
see also various State
troops and names of indi-
vidual units

Asbill, J. J., **27**

Ashby, Turner, 911

Asheville, N.C., 977

Assassination; *see* Lincoln
assassination; Booth, John
Wilkes; Surratt, Mary

Associated Survivors of the
Sixth U.S. Army Corps, **28**

Association of Acting Assistant
Surgeons, **29**

Aston, Ralph, **30**

Astor, John Jacob, 571

Atlanta (C.S.S.): purchase of,
222; capture of, 84, 784

Atlanta, Battle of, 195, 467;
Federal strategy in, 518;
certificate commemorating
Sherman's role in, 850;
sketch of troop positions
in, 552; burning of, 439;
see also Atlanta
Campaign; Sherman,

William T.

Atlanta, Ga.: Unionist activities in, 618; treatment of
Federal prisoners of war
at, 669

Atlanta Campaign, 20, 80, 94,
103, 116, 133, 148, 174,
195, 204-205, 207, 277,
300, 317, 353, 355, 377-78,
410, 439, 441, 473, 518,
539, 552, 566, 576, 578,
605, 610, 618, 631, 640,
703, 729, 733, 768, 805,
820, 850-51, 901, 907, 953,
1000, 1021, 1038, 1060,
1063; Federal strategy in,
518, 557; Confederate fortifications, 503; Con-
federate reaction to
removal of J. E. Johnston,
1021; Federal cavalry operations in, 146, 377; report
on service of 4th Division,
17th U.S. Army Corps,
378; report on service of
40th Illinois Infantry,
610; death of James B.
McPherson, 64; supplies
in, 351, 414; *see also*
individual battles
and skirmishes of the campaign

Attorney General (U.S.),
58, 87

Atzerodt, George, 307

"An August Morning With
Farragut at Mobile Bay,"
1003

Augusta (U.S.S.), 822

Autobiographies: Allen, Isaac
J., 11; Burt, Elizabeth
J. R., 133; Grebe, Balzar,
367; Greeley, Horace, 370;
Pratt, Richard Henry, 741;
Webster, Harrie, 1003;

Barnwell, Robert Woodward, 47

Barracks: portable, 622

Barritt, Jasper N., 48

Barron, Wesley, 49

Barrow, R. R., 719

Barry, William F., 466, 939

Barstow, Wilson, 50

Bartlett, Ezra, 52

Bartlett, Joseph Jackson, 51

Bartlett family, 52

Bartly, Reuben, 644

Barton, Chauncey E., 53

Barton, Clara Harlowe, 54, 211

Barton, Seth M., 55

Barton–Jenifer families, 55

Bat (blockade runner), 222

Batchelder, John Davis, 56

Bate, William B., 789, 997

Bate, William R., 59

Bateman, Francis Marion, 57

Bates, Edward, 58, 285, 546

Baton Rouge, La.: burning of State House at, 685; photograph of State House, 725; Federal camps at, 123; seizure of Federal arsenal at, 105, 507

Battery Douglass, 821

Battery Wagner; *see* Fort Wagner, S.C.

Battle of Aquia Creek, Va., 59

Battle of Cedar Creek, Va., 60

"The Battle of Gettysburg as Seen from Little Round Top," 777

"Battle of Hartsville," 405

Battle of Thompson's Station, Tenn., 61

Battles, lists of, 846

Battles and Leaders of the Civil War (1888), 698

Baughman, J. M., 372

Baxter, Henry: sketch of, 758

Baxter, Sidney S., 438

Bayard, Thomas Francis, 62

Bayou Boeuf, La.: skirmish along, 179

Bayou Des Allemands, La.: skirmish at, 137; military operations near, 719

Bealeton Station, Va.: sketch of, 758

Beall, R. L. T., 991

Beard, Daniel Carter, 63

Beard, Harry, 63

Beard, Richard, 64

Bearden, R. M., 911

Beardslee, Lester Anthony, 65

Beatty (C.S.S.), 109

Beaufort, N.C.: Siege of, 388; Battle of, 523; letters written from, 1

Beaufort, S.C.: Siege of, 590, 675; occupation and plunder of, 784; mentioned, 815

Beauregard, Pierre Gustave Toutant, 66; correspondence of, 21, 82, 143, 189, 212, 238, 272, 392, 409, 467, 557, 718-19, 817, 872, 913, 973, 1017, 1021; generalship of, 596; plan for defense of New Orleans, 719; resignation and removal rumored, 613; description of, 894; sketch of, 672; photographs of, 533, 599; mentioned, 735

Beck, R. B., 175

Beckwith, W. W., 67

Bedford, Wimer, 68

Bedlam, William H.: photograph of, 1041

Bee, Barnard Elliott: death of, 174

936, 957; treatment of free blacks, 140; sketches of, 758; U.S. Government policy toward, 34, 825; U.S. citizenship for, 81; *see also* Black troops; Freedmen; Slavery

Blaine, James Gillespie, 89, 167

Blair, Charles H., 827

Blair, Francis Preston, 90-91, 554, 820, 850

Blair, Montgomery, 91, 319, 546, 820

Blair family, **91**

Blake, Charles Follen, 92, 366

Blake, Homer C., 788

Bledsoe, Albert, 43

Blenker, Louis, 461

Blind River, La., 360

Bliss, Alexander, 41

Blockade, 45, 70, 132, 354, 358, 566, 606, 608, 822, 842; effects of, 75, 250; legality of, 268, 285, 564; problems with Great Britain over, 608, 642, 747; squadrons, 3, 13, 30, 65, 70, 84, 92, 105, 121, 156, 158, 183, 229, 251, 262, 293, 373, 407, 451, 505, 513, 535, 561, 635, 686-87, 764, 784, 796, 800, 811, 832, 858, 867, 927, 1028; *see also* North Atlantic Blockading Squadron; South Atlantic Blockading Squadron; Gulf Blockading Squadron; East Gulf Blockading Squadron; West Gulf Blockading Squadron; European Squadron

Blockade running, 45, 222, 358, 365, 373, 606, 1014,

1034; vessels, 283, 358, 373, 763, 796, 842, 889; tactics, 157; captured vessels, 388, 763, 842; *see also* Prize vessels

Blood, Henry Boyden, 93

Bloody Angle, 341

Bloomfield, Alpheus S., 94

Blow, Henry Taylor, 832

Blue Springs, Tenn.: skirmish at, 264

Blunt, James G., 471

Blyth, Jonathan, 478

Board of Home Missions, 815

Board of War: (U.S.) proceedings of (1862), 896

"Boat Signals. U.S. Sloop-of-War Marion. Gulf Blockading Squadron," 505

Bolivar Heights, Md.: abandonment of Federal supplies at, 351; skirmish at, 990

Bonds; *see* Confederate States Government

Bonham, Milledge Luke, 66; as Governor of South Carolina, 718

Booth, Edwin: photograph of, 1064

Booth, John Wilkes: letter of, 413; escape of, 95; death of, 947; identification of body of, 615; comments on, 658; photograph of, 413, 1064; mentioned, 650

Booth, Junius Brutus, and family, **95**

Booth, Lionel F., 96

Booth, Mrs. Lionel F., **96**

Border, District of the: (U.S. Army) 290

Border Regiment; *see* Texas troops

Boston, Mass., 823, 844, 1058
Boteler, Alexander, 116, 475
Botts, John M., 101
Bounties (U.S.) enlistment, 20, 115, 203, 237, 355, 746, 847, 1016; subscriptions for, 590
Bounty brokers, 746
Bourland, James A., **97**
Bourne, William Oland, 98
Bouttê Station, La.: skirmish at, 137
Bowen, Nicholas, 41
Bower, Clark, 204
Bowling Green, Ky.: topographical sketch of, 820
Boyce, Charles H., **99**
Boyce, James Petigru, **100**
Boyd, Belle, 101
Boyd, Crosby Noyes, **101**
Boyers, Jacob, 795
Boyle, Francis A., 899
Boyle, Jeremiah T., 113
Boyle, William, **102**
Bradbury, William H., **103**
Bradford, J. O., 907
Bradford, Joshua Taylor, **104**
Bragg, Braxton, **105**; correspondence of, 66, 730, 846, 870, 973; plan of attack on Franklin, Tenn., 870; problems with war correspondents, 761; reports on Battle of Chickamauga, 870; capture of Col. John T. Wilder, 888; generalship of, 143; engraved portrait of, 1034; invasion of Kentucky, 473, 605, 703, 782
Branch, Lawrence O'Bryan, 532
Brandy Station, Va., 711, 958, 1009

Brannigan, Felix, **106**
Brashear City, La., 17
Brayman, Mason, **107**
Brazil; *see* Bahia Harbor
Breckinridge, John Cabell: correspondence of, 411, 532, 973, 1021; movements in Virginia and Maryland, 681
Breckinridge, Joseph Cabell, 108
Breckinridge, William Campbell Preston, 108
Breckinridge family, **108**
"Breckenridge & Union," 134
Breese, Samuel Livingston, 183, 739
Brent, Joseph Lancaster, **109**
"Brevet Major General David McMurtrie Gregg," 377
Brewer, David L., **110**
Brewster, Benjamin, 546
Brewster, William R., 711
"A Brief Reminiscence of the First Inauguration of Abraham Lincoln," 1032
Briggs, E. B., **111**
Brincklé, John Rumsey, **112**
Brisbin, James S., 979
Bristoe Station, Va., Battle of, 419, 554
Bristow, Benjamin Helm, **113**
Brock House Hospital, Richmond, Va., 200
Bromwell, Henry Pelham Holmes, **114**
Bronson, Theodore B., **115**
Brooke, Samuel, 85
Brooklyn (U.S.S.), 293; at Battle of Mobile Bay, 92
Brooklyn Navy Yard, 451
Brooks, S. P., 321
Brooks, William Elizabeth, **116**
Brophy, John P., 101
Brown, Campbell, 143

Brown, Edgar F., **117**

Brown, J. Thompson, 870

Brown, John, 226, 438, 940

Brown, Joseph B., 471

Brown, Joseph Emerson,
118; letters to
as Governor of Georgia,
234, 594

Brown, Lewis Kirk, **119**

Brown, S. H., 478

Brown, Thomas J., **120**

Browne, F. W., 86

Browne, George W., **121**

Browne, John Mills, **122**

Browne, William M., 608

Browning, Silas W., **123**

Browning, Moore and Com-
pany (slave traders), 168

Brownlow, William Gannaway,
101, **124**

Brownson, Orestes Augustus,
125

Brownsville, Tex.: skirmish
near, 347

Bruce, L. D., 113

Bryan, Thomas Barbour, **126**

Bryan, Wilhelmus Bogart, **127**

Buchanan, David, 361

Buchanan, James: correspondence of, 268, 507; Cabinet
crisis of December 1860,
1001; defends action on
Fort Moultrie, 87

Buckner, James F., 128

Buckner, Simon B.: letter of,
563; portrait of, 192

Bucks County, Pa., 1053

Budd, W. N., 128

Buell, C. C.: essay by, 411

Buell, Don Carlos: correspondence of, 215, 387, 571,
782, 850; occupies Nash-
ville, 782; removal and
reinstatement of, 782;
generalship, 759, 996;

resignation, 575, 782

Buena Vista Artillery (U.S.
Army), 539

Buford, Charles, **128**

Buford, John: letter of, 913;
reaction to death of, 436

Buford, Louis M., 128

Bull Run, Battle of; *see*
First Manassas, Battle of

Bulloch, James D., 454, 608

Bullock, Irvine S., **129**

Bull's Bay, S.C.: Federal
expedition to, 373

Bunker Hill, W. Va.:
skirmish at, 419

Buntline, Ned; *see* Judson,
Edward Zane Carroll

Burbank, Sidney, 130

Burbank—Van Voorhis family,
130

Burbridge, Stephen G.:
generalship of, 491

Burch, Samuel, **131**

Burials: agreement for
interment of bodies of
Federal soldiers, 809

Burke's Station, Va.: sketch of,
758

Burlingame, Anson, **132**

Burlingame, Edward L., 132

"The Burning of Columbia,"
497

Burnside, Ambrose Everett:
expedition to North
Carolina, 71, 84,
183, 227, 264,
354, 388, 425, 429,
523, 586, 606, 675,
686, 694, 789, 796,
822, 940; correspondence
of, 326, 346, 403, 437,
466, 571, 825, 850, 992;
character of, 417; pub-
lished photograph of, 938;
sketch of, 758; generalship

of, 417, 420, 495; relationship with Gens. H. W. Halleck, G. B. McClellan, and W. S. Rosecrans, 523; mentioned, 566, 622, 996; *see also* Fredericksburg Campaign; Knoxville Campaign
Burt, Andrew Sheridan, 133
Burt, Elizabeth Johnston Reynolds, 133
Burwell, William MacCreary, 134
Bush, T. J., 782
Butler, Benjamin Franklin, 135; correspondence of, 91, 896, 931; preparation for expedition against New Orleans, La., 304; capture of New Orleans, 1001; as military governor of New Orleans, 234, 242, 545, 694; Confederate reaction to policies of, 596; Petersburg Campaign, 211, 1036; Fort Fisher expedition, 157, 311, 346; advance on Richmond, Va., 365; service of black troops under command of, 436; meeting with President Lincoln, 626; generalship of, 306, 495, 641, 737, 822; investigation of, 482; mentioned, 369, 858
Butler, Charles, 136
Butler, Robert Ormond, 137
Butler, W. P., 138
Butterfield, Daniel, 139; correspondence of, 671, 847; mentioned, 33, 103

Caddo Parish, La., 520
Cadwalader, George, 467

Cadwallader, Sylvanus, 78, 140
Cain, James, 598
Cairo (U.S.S.): sinking of, 832
Cairo, Military District of: headquarters records, 364
Cairo, Ill.: fortifications at, 76
Caldwell, John Curtis, 629
Calhoun, John A., 789
California troops: First Infantry Regiment, 396; Second Infantry Regiment, 182; mentioned, 435
Calkins, Hiram, 78
Cameron, Simon, 141-42; correspondence of, 21, 167, 319, 524, 571, 679, 756, 825, 847, 896, 913, 1064; reviewing troops, 819
Camp Benton, Mo.: view of, 136
Camp Blair, Mich., 696
Camp Chase, Ohio: military training at, 204; political prisoners at, 961; prisoners of war at, 239, 563
Camp Curtin, Pa., 592
Camp Dennison, Ohio, 107
Camp Distribution, Md., 282
Camp Douglas, Ill.: prisoners of war at, 128, 368, 952, 1031
Camp followers, 605
Camp Ford, Tex., 179
Camp Hamilton, Va., 260
Camp Hunt, Va., 1012
Camp Jim Walker, Va., 705
Camp life: (C.S. Army) 23, 27, 85, 159, 365, 383, 386, 412, 419, 452-53, 472-73, 488, 554, 567, 598, 614, 637, 894, 901, 1014, 1021, 1058; (U.S. Army) 20, 36, 61, 63, 94, 99, 103, 106, 133, 140, 148, 179, 184-85, 188, 195, 264, 274, 279, 284, 297, 299, 309, 311, 314, 317-18, 325,

331, 335, 351-53, 355, 357,
359-60, 391, 396-97, 410,
415-16, 421-22, 426-27, 429,
434, 436, 439, 442, 449, 455,
462, 476, 478, 481, 483, 491,
495, 500, 522, 526, 529, 534,
539, 542, 544, 558, 578, 586,
592, 605, 618, 640-41,
645-46, 650, 654, 659,
666-67, 680, 685, 687,
702-703, 705, 709, 717, 736,
741, 746, 748, 758-60, 766,
772, 776, 782, 793-94, 803-
805, 816, 844, 855, 869, 886,
888, 892, 903, 907, 938, 946,
975-76, 982, 1000, 1009,
1022, 1026-27, 1029-30,
1038, 1042, 1053, 1063
Camp Lincoln, Va., 998
Camp Meigs, 257
Camp Morton, Ind.: prisoners of
war at, 239
Camp Oglethorpe; *see*
Oglethorpe Military Prison
Camp Peoria, Ill., 146
Camp Russell, Va., 382
Camp Stone, Md., 579
Camp Sutton, Va., 172
Camp Utley, Wis., 579
"The Campaign of Wilson's
Cavalry Corps Through
Alabama and Georgia," 526
Campbell, George Washington,
143
Campbell, Given, **144**
Campbell, John Allen, 820
Campbell, John Archibald, 189,
221, 411
Campbell County, Ky., 925
Campbell's Station, Tenn.:
engagement at, 264
Canada: Confederate agents in,
954; planned Confederate
clandestine activities in,
306; alleged Confederate

forces in, 747
Canadian Peace Commission,
370
Canandaigua (U.S.S.), 764
Canby, Edward Richard Sprigg:
letter of, 957; military
governor of New Orleans,
14, 41, 263; generalship of,
641, 659
Cannon, E. G. (Mrs.), 145
Cannon, William R., **145**
Canton Zouaves, 519
Cape Girardeau, Mo., 852
Cape Hatteras, N.C.: landing of
Federal troops at, 586;
military affairs at, 601
Caperton, Allen Taylor, 303
Capron, Albert B., 146
Capron, Horace, **146**
Capron, Horace, Jr.: death of,
146
Cardwell, Charles W., **147**
Carlisle, J. Mandeville, 564
Carlton, Caleb Henry, **148**
Carman, Ezra Ayers, **149**
Carmer, Charles R., 654
Carnegie, Andrew, **150**
Carolinas Campaign, 20, 43,
195, 300, 439, 483, 497, 552,
558, 618, 631, 709, 729, 733,
803, 805, 851, 886, 1000,
1055
Carondelet (U.S.S.), 565
Carpenter, S. M., 78
Carr, Eugene A., 850
Carrington–McDowell families,
151
Carrion Crow Bayou, La.:
skirmish at, 491
Carroll, Samuel Sprigg, 399
Carroll, William H., 409
Carrollton, La.: Federal camps
at, 17
Carruthers, George North, **152**
Carson, Caroline Petigru, 714

Columbus, Ga.: skirmish at, 636; capture of, 352
Columbus, Ky.: defense of, 308
Colvin, Hervey A., **186**
Combs, Leslie, 571
Commerce, 5, 132, 263, 380, 565, 672, 747, 778; *see also* Cotton
Commissary Department: (U.S. Army) 253, 607-608, 618, 959, 1005; *see also* Quartermaster Department; U.S. Army—Commissary Department; U.S. Army—Quarter-master's Department; Supplies
Commissions: (C.S. Army) 485, 489, 656, 828; (U.S. Army) 81, 167, 184, 208, 269, 288, 310, 314, 346, 355, 371, 410, 416, 423, 428, 433, 438, 527, 578-79, 590, 631, 661, 682, 835, 863, 866, 884, 895, 903-904, 934, 946, 1029, 1061; (U.S. Navy) 122, 148, 505, 611; *see also* Officers
Communications; *see* Signal communications; Telegrams
Compendium of the War of the Rebellion (1909), 162
"Complete Map of the March of the lst Brigade 1st Cavalry Divn. Dept. of Cumberland on the Stoneman Expedition Through Tenn., Va., N.C., S.C., Geo., & Ala.," 1046
"Complete Record of the Names of all the Soldiers and Officers . . . in the Naval Service of the United States," 609
Comstock, Cyrus Ballou, **187**; correspondence of, 820
Conant, Abram F., **188**
Conemaugh (U.S.S.), 858

Conestoga (U.S.S.), 784
Confederate States Army:
organization of, 27, 66, 143, 189, 358, 386, 540, 594, 614, 769, 789, 856, 973, 1021; composition of, 242; suffering in, 412, 872; faith in ultimate victory of, 586; illiteracy in, 586; *see also* various State troops; Artillery; Cavalry; Infantry; Casualties; Officers
Confederate States Congress: acts and resolutions of, 189; criticism of, 320; addressed by President Davis, 411; representatives, 38, 250, 273, 334, 628, 778, 950; senators, 47, 303, 484
Confederate States Government: organization of, 808; public dissatisfaction with, 134; cabinet meetings, 596; proclamations, 189; oaths of allegiance to, 485; leadership in, 778; flight and imprisonment of officials in, 350, 356; official correspondence and papers, 189, 461, 900; studies of, 220; *see also* Justice, Navy, Post Office, State, Treasury , and War Departments, and names of members of the Confederate cabinet
Confederate States Navy: enlistments, 23, 566; midshipmen, 157; training of cadets, 412; tactics employed by, 129; health in, 200; Maryland sailors in, 875; operations along the Georgia coast, 566; list of warships on western waters, 734; ships' logs, 189; re-

ports, 189, 232, register of commissioned and warrant officers, 535; miscellaneous affairs of, 596

Confederate States of America, 189-92; Constitution of, 189; poem eulogizing, 110; life in, 526, 781; public morale in, 56, 672, 714, 719, 950, 1014; martial spirit in, 215, 242, 507; confidence of people in, 956; political affairs in, 125, 392, 714, 798, 808, 901, 912; economic conditions in, 36, 123, 148, 207, 317, 351, 462, 476, 555, 599, 719; travel in, 761

Confederate States of America— Army of Northern Virginia, 193

Confederate States of America— Army of the Tennessee, 194

Confederate States of America Commercial Agency, 454

Confederate States Provisional Government, 900

Conger, Lewis, 189

Congleton, James A., 195

Congress (U.S.S.): destruction of, 842; *see also Monitor-Merrimac* affair

Congressional Assassination Investigation Committee: report of, 528; *see also* Lincoln assassination

Conkling, Roscoe, 196

Conley, Isaiah, 197

Connecticut, 198; wartime activities of shipbuilders and merchants in, 694; recruiting in, 112

Connecticut Infantry, 199

Connecticut troops: (artillery) 1st Regiment Heavy Artillery, 16; 2d Regiment

Heavy Artillery, 715; 2d Battery Light Artillery, 357; (infantry) 5th, 618, 923, 1013; 7th, 36; 12th, 198, 641; 13th, 641, 892; 17th, 199; 19th, 715; 25th, 685; 28th, 17; 29th, 590; miscellaneous returns and records, 892, 923

Connolly, James A., 114

Conrad, Daniel B., **200**

Conrad, Joseph, 845

Conscription: (C.S. Army) 171, 197, 242, 452, 520, 729, 755, 856, 883, 977, 1023; of foreign citizens, 977; effect of in Georgia, 901; examination of conscripts, 670; certificates of exemption, 138, 303, 567; (U.S. Army) 36, 140, 169, 214, 387, 522, 558, 717, 850, 913; conscription of blacks, 360; legislation concerning in New York, 756; response to in New York and Michigan, 124; resistance to, 641; profiteering from, 36; applications for exemption, 665; exemption certificates, 665; securing of substitutes, 140

"Consolidated Report of Cavalry Serving in the Military District of the Mississippi," 1037

Constellation (U.S.S.), 92

Continental (U.S.S.), 587

Contrabands: sketches of, 758; *see also* Blacks; Slavery

Convalescents; *see* Hospitals; Medical care; Medical Department

Cook, George P., **201**

Cook, M. Leroy, 114

313

Cook, T. M., 78
Cook, William, 1019
Cooke, John Esten, 202
Coon, A. F., 208
Coon, David, 203
Cooper, Samuel, 21, 66, 181, 789
Cooper, Thomas B., 220
Cope, John, 204
Cope, Samuel, 204
Copeland, Elizabeth: certificate
    of loyalty to U.S. Govern-
    ment, 278
Corbin, Henry Clark, 205
Corcoran, Michael: petition for
    exchange of, 430
Corduroy bridges and roads:
    photographs of, 938
Corinth, Miss., Battle of, 68
Corinth, Miss., Siege of, 1020
Corinth Campaigns, 66, 94,
    104-105, 159, 274, 300, 367,
    378, 392, 455, 473, 539, 552,
    554, 575, 782, 804, 847, 850,
    908, 942, 953, 973, 1026
Cornell University: copies of
    documents at, 40
Cornwell, John J., 373
Cotton, Charles Stanhope, 206
Cotton, Josiah Dexter, 207
Cotton: Federal seizure and sale
    of, 343, 482, 591; speculation
    in by Federal officers, 804;
    demands for, 75, 358
Couch, Darius N., 895, 913
Counterfeiting; see Paper
    currency
Court of St. James; see Great
    Britain; Adams, Charles
    Francis; State Department
Courts-martial: (U.S. Army) 62,
    205, 396, 410, 526, 552, 664,
    735, 738, 813, 820, 921,
    1038; (U.S. Navy) 561, 635,
    832, 1028; see also Porter,
    Fitz-John; Selfridge,

Thomas O.
Covington, Ky.: defenses of, 511,
    534
Covode, George H., 208
Covode, Jacob, 208
Covode, John, 208
Cox, George K., 1060
Cox, Jacob Dolson, 209, 820
Cox, John D., 845
Cox, Oliver, 210
Cox, Thomas C., 629
Coyle, John, 954
Coyle, John F., 620
Cramer, N. J., 864
Crane, Charles H., 471
Crany Island, Va.: defense of,
    743
Craven, John Joseph, 211
Craven, Thomas T., 254
Craven County, N.C., 1055
Crawford, Mr., 945
Crawford, Martin J., 718
Crawford, Samuel Wylie, 212;
    generalship of, 99, 173
Crawford, William, 38
Crawfordsville, Ind., 985
Creamer, David, 213
Crehore, Charles Frederic, 962
Cresswell, John Angel James,
    214
Crittenden, George Bibb, 350
Crittenden, John Jordan, 215,
    996
Crittenden, Thomas Leonidas,
    996
Crittenden Compromise, 215
Crittenden Union Zouaves of
    Louisville, Ky., 405
Croffut, William Augustus,
    216
Crook, George: capture of, 294
Cross Lanes, W. Va., 533
Crossly, Sylvanus, 217
The Cruise of the Kearsarge
    (1888), 1041

Tidball, John Caldwell, 939
Todd, Oliphant Monroe, 942
Torrey, Charles Oscar, 946
Van Cise, Edwin A., 972
Waddel, John Newton, 978
Ward, James Thomas, 989
Warren, Gouverneur
  Kemble, 735
Welles, Gideon, 1006
Welton, Alfred, 453
Wheeler, John Hill, 1014
Whitten, John, 1020
Wilder, William Frank,
  1026
Wiley, Harvey Washington,
  1027
Wilkes, Charles, 1028
Willard, Joseph C., 1029
Willey, Henry Stevens,
  1030
Wilson, Lawrence, 1038
Wood, James Rodney, 695
Woodwell, Charles H., 1055
Worthington, Colonel, 847
"Diary of a Woman During the
  Siege of Vicksburg," 555
Dick, Franklin A., 245
Dickinson, Anna Elizabeth, 246
Dictator (U.S.S.): trial voyage of,
  784; conditions on, 413
Diet: (C.S. Army) 23, 567, 901,
  1021; (U.S. Army) 63, 103,
  123, 188, 297, 314, 317, 522,
  618, 631, 666, 685, 687, 702,
  746, 758, 772, 938, 946, 958,
  1009, 1027, 1030; (U.S.
  Navy) 686
Dinwiddie Courthouse, Va., 102
Diplomacy; *see* Foreign affairs;
  Benjamin, Judah P.;
  Hunter, R. M. T.; Seward,
  William H.; Fessenden,
  William Pitt
Discharge certificates: (C.S.
  Army) 189, 447, 563, 567,

827; (U.S. Army) 42, 49, 184,
  295, 311, 355, 416, 441, 509,
  512, 519, 527, 559, 585, 590,
  625, 805, 818, 884, 887, 946,
  962, 983, 988, 1013; (U.S.
  Navy) 183, 606, 635
Discharges: references to, 115,
  519, 768; orders concerning,
  768; petition for, 474
Discipline: (C.S. Army) 453,
  473, 614, 733, 743-44, 859,
  894, 1015, 1023; (U.S. Army)
  20, 38, 63, 91, 94, 99, 123,
  133, 148, 185, 214, 249,
  299-300, 317, 351, 355, 359,
  367, 391, 410, 422, 426, 436,
  442, 449, 460, 462, 478, 480,
  500, 523, 526, 535, 542, 631,
  640-41, 687, 699, 703, 715,
  717, 746, 748, 758-59, 766,
  773, 782, 803-804, 816, 825,
  850, 855, 869, 888, 892, 896,
  915, 921, 942, 958, 972,
  979-80, 982, 1000, 1009,
  1016, 1022, 1026-27,
  1037-38, 1055, 1063; (U.S.
  Navy) 183, 365, 373, 561,
  565, 606, 635, 784-85, 796,
  811, 822
Disease: (C.S. Army) 23, 232,
  383, 386, 413, 473, 567,
  598-99, 637, 733, 743, 901,
  991, 1014-15, 1021, 1023,
  1058; (U.S. Army) 36, 185,
  188, 207, 249, 297, 299, 311,
  314, 351, 353, 355, 359-60,
  378, 391, 410, 422, 426-27,
  429, 434, 442, 469, 478, 500,
  523, 526, 534, 539, 542, 544,
  558, 578, 586, 605, 618, 631,
  640-41, 666, 685, 687, 699,
  702-703, 715, 717, 736, 741,
  758-59, 766, 772, 781-82,
  804, 816, 855, 869, 888, 892,
  938, 942, 946, 958, 962, 972,

975, 998, 1000, 1009, 1016, 1022, 1026-27, 1030, 1055, 1063; (U.S. Navy) 451, 565; *see also* Hospitals; Medical care; Yellow fever; Physicians and surgeons; Gangrene

District of Columbia; *see* Washington, D.C.

District of Columbia Association of Ex-Union Prisoners of War, 28

Dix, Dorothea Lynde, 101

Dix, John Adams, 247, 387, 472, 524, 571, 621, 850, 896, 913, 921

Dixon, Archibald, 247

Dixon, B. F., 347

Dock, George, 248

Dock, Mira Lloyd, 248

Dodge, Grenville M., 850

Dodge, Theodore Ayrault, 249

Dolan, Philip, 844

Donaldson, Edward, 536

Donaldson, J. L., 660

Donaldsonville, La.: burning of, 874

Donelson, Andrew Jackson, 250

Donelson, Daniel: murder of, 250

Donelson, John Samuel: death of, 250

Don Eureka (U.S.S.), 388

Doolittle, James Rood, 251, 832

Door, E. P., 154

Dorchester, Mass., 472

Dorman, Orloff M., 252

Dornblaser, Benjamin, 253

Dorsenberry, Samuel, 305

Dorsett, Edward Lee, 254

Doubleday, Abner, 56; photograph of, 286

Doubleday & Company, 255

Douglas, E. M., 475

Douglas, John Hancock, 256

Douglas, Lewis, 1054

Douglas Hospital, Washington, D.C., 69

Douglass, Charles, 257

Douglass, Frederick, 257

Dove, Benjamin M., 232

Down, M. A., 258

Downey, George Darius, 259

Downing, Samuel, 260

Draft; *see* Conscription

Draft riots; *see* New York draft riots

Dragon (U.S.S.), 388

Drake, Andrew J., 784

Drake, Charles D., 820

Drake, J. C., 700

Drake, James H., 261

Dranesville, Va.: skirmish at, 717, 748, 884, 1058

Draper, John William, 262

Draper, S. C., 1048

Draper, William B., 263

Draper, William Franklin, 264

Drayton, A. L., 265

Drayton, Thomas Fenwick, 1034

Drayton Brigade, 1034

Drennan, Daniel O., 266

Drewry's Bluff, Va., Battle of, 376, 411

Drug addiction, 784

Drunkenness: problems with, 133, 773, 921, 1016, 1038

Drury, H. M., 138

Duane, James C.: published photograph of, 938

Duane, Richard B., 21

Dudley, Thomas H., 454

Duke, James W., 128

Dungan, William W., 267

Dunlap, Henry C., 928

Dunlop, James, 268

Du Pont, Samuel Francis: correspondence of, 3, 354, 373, 673, 764, 784, 848, 913,

1057; defends action in
attack on Charleston, S.C.,
173
Durant & Hornor, 545
D'Utassy, Frederick G.: trial of,
440
Dwight, A. W., 237
Dwight, Wilder, 366
Dwight, William, 671
Dwyer, Ransom O., 269
Dyer, Alexander Brydie, **270**
Dyer, Frederick H., 162

E. B. Hale (U.S.S.), 907
Eads, James Buchanan, **271**,
784
Early, Jubal Anderson, **272**;
correspondence of, 287, 443;
description of, 894; captured
report on command of, 846;
defeat of, 413; *see also*
Early's Washington raid
Early's Washington raid, 2, 25,
330, 385, 526, 681, 853, 869;
Federal response to, 385,
903; comments on, 786
Earnshaw, William, 864
Easby–Smith families, **273**
East Gulf Blockading Squadron,
451
East Tennessee; *see* Tennessee
East Tennessee Cavalry: (C.S.
Army) 239
Eastern Shore (Maryland):
Union sentiment in, 214
Echo (privateer), 863
Economist (blockade runner),
498
Economy; *see* Inflation; Finance;
Taxes; Treasury
Department
Edings, J. E., 1034
Edisto Island, S.C.: Confederate
soldiers captured on, 968
Edwards Ferry, Va., 706

Eells, Samuel Henry, 274
Eldredge, Charles Augustus,
275
Elliott, John B., 1060
Ellis & Allan Company, **276**
Ellsesser, Jacob L., 386
Elseffer, Charles, 277
Elseffer, Harry S., and family,
277
Elseffer, Louis, 277
Eltham's Landing, Va.: engage-
ment at, 870
Emancipation, 214, 342, 691,
812, 924, 979, 1006;
response of Federal soldiers
to, 1009
Emancipation Proclamation,
126, 169; response of
Federal soldiers to, 687,
1055; public reaction to, 78
Emerson, Bart, 278
Emmons, George D., 570
Emory, William Hemsley: correspondence of, 846;
generalship of, 495
Empire City (U.S. transport),
121
Engineer Brigade: (U.S. Army)
437
Engineers: (C.S. Army) 452-53;
(U.S. Army) 351, 416, 437,
452, 702, 729, 758, 779, 783,
938, 1061; equipment of,
452; reports and sketches
of, 187; (U.S. Navy) 30,
166, 224, 267, 277, 451,
559, 570, 1003; (civilian)
587, 1059
England; *see* Great Britain
Enlistments: (C.S. Army) 358,
386, 598, 614, 778, 868, 894;
(U.S. Army) 22, 94, 115,
188, 300, 426, 481, 552-53,
618, 666, 687, 694, 703,
746, 803-804, 979, 1009,

1016, 1026, 1030, 1053, 1060; certificates of, 590, 884; orders concerning, 768; legislation concerning in New York, 756

Enslow, Charles Calvin, 279

Entertainment: (C.S. Army) 473, 614, 637, 894, 1021; (U.S. Army) 103, 309, 335, 359, 429, 434, 439, 442, 478, 522, 526, 544, 551, 631, 640-41, 667, 680, 699, 741, 746, 748, 758, 778, 782, 793, 886, 888, 938, 972, 1016, 1026, 1063; (U.S. Navy) 784

Ericsson, John, 280, 739

Espionage; *see* Allen, E. J.; Greenhow, Rose O'Neal

Essex (U.S.S.), 158; photograph of, 725

Este, David Kirkpatrick, 281

Este, William Miller, 282

Europe: public attitude toward the American Civil War, 722; economic effects of the war on, 722

European Squadron, 92, 802

Eustis, George, 283, 454

Evans, Augusta Jane, 220

Evans, Clement Anselm, 272

Evans, George, 257

Evans, Lawrence T., 284

Evans, Thomas, 284

Evarts, William Maxwell, 285

Evening Courier, 792

The Eve of Conflict (1934), 632

Everett, Edward, 91, 286, 1042

Ewell, B. S., 287

Ewell, Leczinska, 287

Ewell, Richard Stoddert, 143, 287, 532, 1021

Ewing, Andrew, 997

Ewing, Charles, 288

Ewing, George Washington, 289

Ewing, Hugh Boyle, 290

Ewing, Thomas, **290-91**

Ewing, Thomas, Jr.: papers of, 290; correspondence of, 288; popular support for, 820

Ewing, Virginia Larwill, 288

Excelsior Brigade, 348; reinforcements for, 861; *see also* New York troops, 73d Infantry Regiment; Sickles, Daniel Edgar

"An Ex-Confederate on the Late Rebellion," 761

"Exhibition of Left-Hand Penmanship," 98

"Extract From Field Notes of the Civil War: The Selma Campaign," 636

Fair Oaks, Battle of, 428, 496; report on, 1023; song commemorating, 781; *see also* Peninsular Campaign

Fairfax County, Va.: refugees from, 465; attitude of noncombatants in, 744

Fairfax Courthouse, Va.: Confederate camp near, 744; mentioned, 433, 719

Fairfax Theological Seminary: photograph of, 715

Fairy (U.S.S.), 254

Falling Waters, W. Va.: skirmish at, 99

Falls Church, Va., 1003

Falmouth, Va.: occupation of, 612; mentioned, 323, 348, 445, 893

Farinholt, Benjamin L., 151

Farnsworth, Elon John: death of, 727

Farnsworth, John Franklin, 727

"Farnsworth's Charge and Death," 698

Farquhar, John F., 423
Farragut, David Glasgow, 292-93; correspondence of, 154, 166, 206, 262, 784, 800, 858, 913; attacks on Fort Jackson and Fort St. Philip, 800; in New Orleans 624; passing batteries at Port Hudson, 244; bombards Vicksburg, 800, 874; interviews with, 1003; information on, 739; photograph of, 996

Farragut and Mobile Bay— Personal Reminiscences, 996

Farrow, William, 963
Faulkner, C. J., 475
Fauquier Artillery: (C.S. Army) 870
Fauquier County, Va.: refugees from, 465
Faxon, William, 422
Fay, John, 294
Fay, Logan, 295
Fayetteville, Va., 160, 497
Feamster family, 296
Federal Writers Project, WPA, 970
Fell, Jennie M., 53
Fell, Jesse W., 297
Fell, Joseph Gove, 298
Fell, Thomas W., 438
Fenton, Lewis R., 299
Ferguson, John Newton, 300
Ferguson, Samuel W., 158
Fernandina (U.S.S.), 121
Fernandina, Fla.: Federal occupation of, 421; need for chaplain at, 815
Ferree, Newton and Joel, 301
Ferrero, Edward, 913, 1036
Ferriday, Calvin, 160
Fessenden, William Pitt, 302, 722, 896

Field, Christopher I., 176
Field, S., 303
Field hospitals; *see* Hospitals
Fifty Years in Camp and Field: Diary of Major-General Ethan Allen Hitchcock (1909), 216
"Fighting McCooks," 575
Fillebrown, Thomas Scott, 304
Fillmore, Millard, 571, 714
Finance: Confederate plans and efforts to finance the war, 778, 856, 951; Confederate plans to disrupt northern financial markets, 833; U.S. Government plans and efforts to finance the war, 169, 302, 424, 847; *see also* Taxes; Treasury Department; Paper currency
Finnell, Jonathan W., 215
First Manassas, Battle of, 39, 156, 174, 200, 272, 330, 351, 383, 411, 552, 575, 579, 598, 671, 735, 789, 797, 850, 890, 894, 913, 1058; troop movements preceding the battle, 398, 411, 414; Confederate and Federal strategy in, 619; reaction to the battle in Washington, 1014; sketch of battlefield, 598, 1058; map of battlefield, 143; observations on, 798; mentioned, 510, 1003; *see also* First Manassas Campaign
First Manassas Campaign, 23, 66, 143, 411, 428, 567, 901; deaths in, 23; effect on northern attitudes toward the war, 1026
Firum, William, et al., 305
Fish, Hamilton, 306
Fisher, B. F., 2

Fisher, George Purnell, 307

Fisher's Hill, Va., Battle of, 500, 715

Fishing Creek: engagement at, 239

Fisk, Clinton Bowen, 308

Fisk, Wilbur, 309

Fitch, George, 981

Five Forks, Va., Battle of, 162, 315, 710; map of, 162

"The Flag and the Cross, a History of the United States Christian Commission," 363

Flagler, Daniel Webster, 310

Flags: (Confederate) proposed designs for, 1007; sketches of, 599; claims of designer, 873

Fleetwood, Christian Abraham, 311, 1054

Fleming, Charles, 654

Flint, Henry M., 78

Flogging, 38

Florence, S.C.: Confederate stockade prison at, 345; Federal prisoners of war at, 764

Florida (C.S.S.), 265, 566, 858; in France, 643; at Mobile Bay, 881; capture of, 65

Florida (U.S.S.), 365

Florida: ordinance of secession, 830; Federal operations along coast of, 493, 686; campaigns in, 24, 123, 152, 252; expedition to, 422

Flotillas: (U.S. Navy) names of ships in, 1006

Floyd, Charles R., 566

Floyd, John Buchanan: order of, 413; generalship of, 754

Floyd, Richard S., 566

Floyd family, 566

Floyd–McAdoo families, 312

Foard, Andrew J.: medical director in the Army of the Tennessee, 194; photograph of, 194

Folly Island, S.C.: records of U.S. Commissary Department at, 959

Foote, Andrew Hull, 313, 416, 739, 784, 896, 913

Foote, Henry S., 807

Foote, Lemuel Thomas, 314

Foote, S. E., 422

Foote, Solomon: photograph of, 541

"For the Union," 902

Foraging expeditions: (C.S. Army) 929; (U.S. Army) 20, 63, 140, 174, 249, 274, 284, 299-300, 309, 314, 335, 351, 355, 357, 360, 439, 462, 480, 483, 491, 500, 523, 539, 542, 558, 605, 618, 631, 636, 641, 685, 687, 703, 715, 736, 741, 746, 748, 804-805, 816, 869, 878, 884, 886, 888, 903, 938, 970, 978, 1009, 1029; orders concerning, 768; (U.S. Navy) 565

Forbes, Archibald, 315

Forbes, Robert B., 986

Forbes family, 316

Force, Manning Ferguson, 317, 318, 366, 534

Force, Peter, 318

Ford, Antonia, 1029

Ford, Clement R., 995

Ford, R. A., 995

Ford, Thomas, 524

Foreign affairs: (C.S. Government) diplomatic correspondence and papers, 241, 608, 833; special agents and emissaries, 283,

347, 443, 506, 719, 807, 954; recognition of the Confederacy, 807; plans for sending secret dispatches, 807; *see also* State Department; Benjamin, Judah P. (U.S. Government) relations with Great Britain, 5-6, 642, 747, 836; relations with Chile, 662; appointment of U.S. consul in China, 11; appointment of U.S. Minister to Austria, 132; letters and instructions to U.S. consul at Havana, Cuba, 858; instructions to Charles Francis Adams, 5, 836; letters and reports of James S. Pike, 722; miscellaneous correspondence and papers, 229, 235, 564, 583, 693, 825, 858; *see also* Seward, William H.

Forney, John Horace: campaigns in Arkansas, 894; description of, 894

Forney, John Wien, 319, 1064

Forrest, French, **320**

Forrest, Nathan Bedford, 401, 409, 730

Forscky, J., **321**

Forsyth, George A., 846

Forsyth, James W., 846

Fort Barrancas, Fla., 17, 108

Fort Beauregard, S.C.: capture of, 493, 561, 736, 784; engraved view of bombardment of, 1034

Fort Blakely, Ala.: capture of, 804

Fort Caswell, N.C., 23, 70

Fort Clark, N.C.: capture of, 135, 425, 561, 686

Fort Darling, Va.: sketch of, 784

Fort Davidson, Mo., 290

Fort Delaware Prison Times, **322**

Fort Delaware Military Prison: life at, 239, 386, 400, 411, 499, 599, 899, 922; aid to Confederate soldiers at, 524; mentioned, 322

Fort Donelson Campaign, 57, 113, 300, 313, 318, 552, 575, 804, 942, 991, 1026; capture of Fort, 387, 563, 975; casualties at, 57

Fort Fisher, N.C.: General Butler's expedition against, 70, 135, 157, 311, 346, 365, 575, 686, 734; General Terry's expedition against, 70, 173, 187, 365, 422, 575, 686-87, 734, 784, 920; Confederate defense of, 649; sketch of, 784; performance of U.S.S. *New Ironsides* in attack on, 750; powder ship attack on, 832

Fort Gaines, Ala.: Siege of, 41; capture of, 14, 206; occupation of, 279

Fort Gray, New Mexico Territory, 396

Fort Gregg, S.C.: attacks on, 513, 796, 867

Fort Hamilton, N.Y., 112

Fort Hatteras, N.C.: capture of, 135, 426, 561, 686

Fort Henry, Tenn.: campaign against, 113; capture of, 416; U.S. Post Office at, 603

Fort Hindman (Arkansas Post) expedition, 63, 175, 290, 339, 491, 554, 565, 648, 760, 850, 979

Fort Jackson, La.: plan of, 13; Farragut's order of battle

against, 800; attack on, 73; Confederate defense of, 649; mutiny of Confederate garrison, 734; capture of, 641, 686, 874

Fort Jefferson, Fla., 587

Fort Lafayette Military Prison: prisoners of war at, 584; letters of prisoners at, 827

Fort McAllister, Ga.: Federal attack on, 84, 784

Fort McHenry, Md., 50, 383, 499, 525

Fort Macon, N.C.: attack on, 523

Fort Magruder: attack on, 870

Fort Mahan, 821

Fort March, Va., 958

Fort Monroe, Va. (Fortress), 12, 50, 211, 582, 650; Jefferson Davis imprisoned at, 524; mentioned, 247, 251, 413, 524, 827

Fort Morgan, Ala.: Federal occupation of, 279, 1003

Fort Moultrie, S.C.: affairs in 1861, 926; Federal attacks on, 493, 513, 796, 867; mentioned, 87

Fort Pemberton, Miss.: engagement at, 630

Fort Pickens, Fla.: letters written from, 108; affairs in 1861, 336, 1006, 1057; as Federal prison, 234; mentioned, 412

Fort Pillow, Tenn., 97

Fort Powell, Ala.: Federal occupation of, 279

Fort Pulaski, Ga.: Siege of, 422, 591, 680, 736, 765, 822, 847; capture of, 493, 736; sketch of Federal batteries during siege, 422

Fort St. Johns, La.: black

soldiers at, 671

Fort St. Philip, La.: Federal capture of, 73, 641, 686, 800, 874; mutiny of the Confederate garrison at, 734; treatment of Confederate soldiers confined at, 234

Fort Sanders, Tenn.: action at, 264

Fort Saratoga, D.C., 821

Fort Stevens, D.C., 2

Fort Sumter, S.C.: Confederate bombardment and capture of, 4, 21, 212, 394, 562, 528, 796, 798, 926, 1017; effect of Confederate attack on public opinion in the North, 219, 1030; reports of the affair based on interviews with the participants, 955; engraved view of Confederate bombardment, 1034; Federal attacks on, 84, 183, 306, 373, 376, 493, 513, 561, 763-64, 796, 867; mentioned, 87, 238, 718

Fort Totten, D.C., 821

Fort Wagner, S.C.: Federal operations against, 36, 84, 183, 422, 493, 513, 763-64, 796, 867; performance of black troops against, 1054

Fort Walker, S.C.: Federal capture of, 493, 561, 736, 784; engraved view of Federal bombardment of, 1034

Fort Warren, Mass., 287, 400; letters of prisoners of war at, 827, 1058; visits to prisoners at, 581; photographs of prisoners at, 1034

Fort Washington, N.C., 1055

Fort Wayne, Ind., 289

Fort Whipple, Va.: Federal soldiers held at, 915

"A Forthcoming Secret History of the Confederacy," 761

Fortifications, 289, 646, 779, 821, 1023, 1054

Foster, John Gray, 346, 535, 844

Foulke, William Dudley, 323

Foute, Samuel L., 952

Fowler, Joseph Smith, 324

Fox, Gustavus Vasa, 91, 251, 306, 316, 354, 413, 739, 750, 784, 796, 847, 896, 1051

Fox, Virginia Woodbury, 1051

France: neutrality of, 624; popular reaction to the American Civil War, 75; consul in New Orleans, La., 624; Confederate agents and activities in, 189, 506; Confederate warships in, 643; activities in Mexico, 728; visit of warships from, 853

Frank, Jacob J., 325

Frankfort, Ky.: General Morgan's raid on, 405; mentioned, 408

Franklin, Henry D., 1053

Franklin, William Buel, 326; correspondence of, 913, 921; generalship of, 496

Franklin, La.: skirmish near, 412

Franklin, Tenn., Battle of, 845; Confederate plan of attack on, 870; mentioned, 61, 669

Franklin and Nashville Campaign, 94, 159, 631, 789, 820, 839, 843, 1000, 1021; General Hood's report on, 1021; postwar account of, 820

Franklin Repository and Transcript, 917

Fraser, P., 327

Fray, George W., 676

Frazier, William, 507

Frederick, Md., 725

Fredericksburg, Va., Battle of, 445, 578, 671, 831, 992; Confederate report on Battle of, 1023; defense of, 532; Federal occupation of, 612, 699, 783; wartime life in, 612; military operations near, 612; mentioned, 111, 540

Fredericksburg Campaign, 18, 116, 249, 264, 309, 323, 335, 352, 386, 391, 419, 424, 429, 437, 442, 452, 466, 502, 522-23, 526, 604, 687, 699, 727, 729, 772, 859, 894, 913, 938, 1009, 1021, 1038; narrative of, 41; photograph of bridges used in, 938

Freedmen: camps for, 600; treatment by Union soldiers, 140, 600, 815; disease among, 600

Freedmen's village, D.C., 40

Freeman, Douglas Southall, 328

Frémont, John Charles, 329; command of, 685; correspondence of, 42, 91, 132, 215, 348, 784, 825, 896; character of, 417; generalship of, 99, 417, 878; photograph of, 132; mentioned, 308

French, Benjamin Brown, 330

French, Samuel G., 1021

French Brigade: (C.S. Army) 624

Fritsch, Friedrich Otto, Baron
  Von, 331
Frogmen, 999
Frontier, Army of the, 820
Frontier garrisons, 349
Frost, Edward, 332, 594, 960
Frost, Edwin P., 332
Frost, F. H., 332
Fuller, Joseph Pryor, 333
Funerals: (U.S. Army) 605
Furloughs: (U.S. Army) 148,
  237, 309, 500, 523, 526,
  604, 640, 758, 799, 904,
  1021, 1038
Furman, Greene Chandler, 334

Gaines Mill, Va., Battle of,
  589; Confederate report
  on, 1023; mentioned, 930
Gainesville, Va.: sketch of, 758
Galatea (U.S.S.), 673
Galena (U.S.S.), 783-84
Galveston, Tex.: defense of,
  566; occupation of, 63;
  treatment of noncomba-
  tants in, 63
Galwey, Thomas Francis, 335
Gamble, William, 864
Gambling, 1016
Gangrene, 599
Gantt, Thomas A., 466
Gardner, Francis R. and
  George, 336
Gardner, Franklin, 158, 584
Garesche, Julius P., 337
Garfield, James Abram, 338,
  401, 847-48, 979
Garfield, Lucretia Rudolph,
  339
Garnett, Alexander, 489
Garrett, Edward J., 567
Garrett, Flora, 567
Garrett, Henry A., 174
Garrett, Robert, and family,
  340
Garrett, William R., 870
"Gath," 947; *see also* Townsend,
  George Alfred
Gauley, W. Va.: skirmish at,
  467
General in Chief: (U.S. Army)
  387; *see also* Halleck,
  Henry W.
"General James Longstreet
  and the Civil War," 810
"General McClellan's Dream,"
  792
General Parkhill (blockade
  runner): capture of, 358
*General Washington and
  General Jackson, on Negro
  Soldiers* (1863), 1034
*The General Who Marched
  to Hell* (1951), 627
Generalship: (C.S. Army) 143,
  287, 349, 356, 392, 596,
  598, 613, 619, 637, 687,
  754, 778, 812, 989, 1014,
  1021; (U.S. Army) 40, 63,
  99, 208, 306, 317, 326,
  331, 342, 349, 351-52,
  359, 378, 390-91, 396-97,
  417, 491, 495-96, 500, 539,
  554, 579, 591, 618, 631,
  671, 685, 687, 699, 702,
  717, 725, 748, 751, 759,
  761, 782, 793, 804, 816,
  825, 847, 850-51, 869, 886,
  896, 903-904, 913, 938,
  946, 949, 953, 972, 979-80,
  989, 992, 1000, 1002,
  1009, 1011, 1016, 1030,
  1037, 1042, 1055, 1063
George, Harold C., 341
Georgia (C.S.S.), 643
Georgia: campaigns in, 103,
  114, 116, 123, 392, 410,
  427, 462, 493, 526, 680,

1060, 1063; military affairs in, 34, 955, 1034; coastal fortifications and operations, 113, 513, 599, 1034; social and economic effects of war in, 312, 566, 978; map of (incomplete), 1046; *see also* Atlanta Campaign

Georgia troops: (infantry) 8th, 1058; 14th, 386; 15th, 901; 20th, 333; 60th, 165

Germany: Confederate special emissary to, 443; Confederate efforts to secure loan from German merchants, 932

Getty, George Washington, 346

Gettysburg, Battle of, 9, 106, 130, 236, 272, 556, 758, 898; Confederate report on, 1023; pamphlets and articles concerning, 590, 777; maps of, 162, 913; sketch of, 249; *see also* Gettysburg Campaign

Gettysburg, Pa.: attitude of inhabitants toward the war, 857

Gettysburg Address: comments on, 11, 83, 786, 1035

Gettysburg Campaign, 4, 9, 20, 41, 51, 106, 130, 162, 174, 181, 212, 229, 246, 249, 331, 335, 352, 377, 386, 391, 419, 437, 442, 452-53, 466, 500, 522, 526, 558, 575, 618, 646, 699, 727, 758, 793, 857, 869, 894, 937-38, 991, 1009, 1016, 1030, 1038; preparations for in Maryland, 773; movement and issue of

supplies during, 93, 351; Confederate report on, 1023; retrieval of U.S. Government property after, 93

Gettysburg National Cemetery: dedication of, 1035; *see also* Gettysburg Address

Ghent, William James, 342

Gherardi, Bancroft, 343

Gibbes, Lewis Reeves, 344

Gibbon, John, 81, 193

Gibbs, James G., 497

Gibbs family, 566

Gibson, S. J., 345

Gibson, William, 373

Gibson–Getty–McClure families, 346

Giddings, George H., 347

Giddings, Joshua Reed, 348

Gilbert, C. C., 349

Gilbert, Cass, 349

Gillett, Philip, 350

Gillett, Simon Palmer, 350

Gillette, James Jenkins, 351

Gillmore, Quincy Adams: correspondence of, 764, 847; generalship of, 495, 591, 736

Gilpin, E. N., 352

Gilpin, Samuel J. B. V., 352

Gist, Branford P., 353

Gist, George W., 353

Gist, Richard J., 353

Gist, Robert C.: as postmaster at Memphis, Tenn., 603

Gist family, 353

Glen, Samuel R., 78

Glide (U.S.S.): burning of, 565

Gloucester Point, Va., 700

Godfrey, Washington Hobbs, 999

Gold: Confederate plan for disrupting northern financial markets through purchase of, 833

Goldsboro, N.C.: skirmish near, 1055; Federal occupation of, 300; mentioned, 965

Goldsborough, Louis Malesherbes, 316, 354, 606, 673, 796

Goodnow, James Harrison, 355

Goodwyn, D. E., 991

Gordon, John Brown: correspondence of, 443; movements of, 681; signature of, 192-93

Gordon (Confederate privateer), 218

Gorgas, Josiah: correspondence of, 409, 1021; diary, 356

Gorgas, William Crawford, 356

Gorman, Willis Arnold: correspondence of, 706, 847, 1036; charges against, 1036

Gould, William J., 357

Gourdin, Henry, 358

Gourdin & Shackleford Company, 358

Gove, Jesse Augustus, 359

Gove family, 359

Graham, Charles K., 893

Graham, Henry, 360

Graham, R. H., 361

Grand Army of the Republic: records of, 362

Grand Gulf, Miss., Battle of, 565; burning of, 874

Grant, James, 363

Grant, Julia Dent, 878

Grant, Marcus, 188

Grant, Ulysses Simpson, 364; as commander of the Army of the Potomac, 436; correspondence of, 42, 82, 140, 143, 262, 377, 532, 546, 573, 580, 768, 820, 846, 850, 852, 913, 996, 1037; campaigns in Kentucky and Tennessee, 878; conflict with General McClernand, 953; meeting with Mrs. W. W. Lord, 555; generalship and character of, 390, 725, 878; photographs of, 363, 395, 541; sketch of, 758; staff of, 140; comments on, 871, 878; attitude of soldiers toward, 341; clippings on, 266; receives thanks of Congress, 140; mentioned, 33, 187, 291, 459, 565

Grant—Warren—Sheridan controversy, 315

Grattan, John W., 365

Gray, Horace, 366

Great Britain: reaction to the American Civil War, 5, 75, 444; concern over treatment of British citizens in the war zone, 747; reaction to Confederate privateers in European waters, 642; Confederate agents, emissaries, and secessionists in, 189, 642; activities of U. S. diplomats in, 642; Confederate diplomatic activities in, 506, 608; Confederate warships and privateers in, 642; correspondence and instructions of Charles Francis Adams concerning, 836; negotiations between U. S. and British

Hahn, Michael, 384
Hale, James, 78
Hale, Oscar A., 652
Hall, Albert, 975
Hall, Angelo, 385
Hall, Chloe Angeline
  Stickney: biography of,
  385
Hall, David, 975
Hall, George Washington, 386
Hall, Joseph, 975
Halleck, Henry Wager, 387;
  advance on Corinth, 104,
  552; appointment as
  general in chief, 117;
  correspondence of, 42, 81,
  428, 430, 467, 571, 820,
  846, 848, 850, 1059; men-
  tioned, 169, 308, 455, 622
Hallock, Isaac, 388
Halpine, Charles Graham,
  78, 389
Halyburton, James D., 872
Hamilton, Charles Smith, 390
Hamilton, James A., 41
Hamilton, John, 391
Hamilton, Robert, 1054
Hamilton, Schuyler, 467
Hamilton, William, 391
Hamlet, William, 41
Hamlin, Hannibal: engraved
  portrait of, 1034
Hammond, James Henry, 392
Hammond, John H., 847, 850
Hammond, Paul F., 392
Hammond, William A., 913;
  trial of, 440
Hammond Gazette, 393
Hammond General Hospital,
  393, 499
Hampstead County, Ark., 1015
Hampton, Sally S., 394
Hampton, Wade: correspon-
  dence of, 66, 1021; auto-

graph of, 192; portrait of,
  533; photograph of, 599;
  mentioned, 138, 991
Hampton Legion, 383; organi-
  zation and composition of,
  991
Hampton Roads, Va., 156, 223;
  naval affairs at, 606, 750
Hampton Roads Peace Confer-
  ence, 411, 901
Hancock, Winfield Scott, 395;
  correspondence of, 466-67,
  532, 629; photograph of,
  286
Hand, George O., 396
Hanna, Mark, 397
Hanna–McCormick families,
  397
Hanno, C. B., 398
Hanover Courthouse, Va.,
  Battle of, 495
Hanscone, S. R., 78
Hanson, George A., 399
Hanson, Roger Weightman,
  400
Hanson, Virginia, 400
Hard, A. D., 401
Hard, Hanson, 401
Hardee, William Joseph, 66,
  402
Hardie, James Allen, 403,
  660, 847-48
Hardie, R. E., 404
Harewood Hospital, Washing-
  ton, D.C., 69
Harlan, James, 864
Harlan, John Marshall, 405
Harlee, W. W., 21
Harman, W., 25
Harmen, Amsel: trial of, 813
Harpers Ferry, W. Va.: John
  Brown's raid on, 86, 940;
  Federal occupation of, 748;
  Confederate capture of,

200, 859; mentioned, 487,
572, 689-90, 990
Harralson, Philip Hodnett, 406
Harries, Jane Cecelia, 805
Harriet Lane (C.S.S.), 858
Harrington, John, 478
Harrington, Purnell Frederick,
407
Harris, Charles A., 408
Harris, Ira, 430
Harris, Isham Green, 143,
409, 593, 723
Harris, John, 750
Harris, W. A., 1034
Harrisburg, Pa., 646
Harrison, Albert M., 412
Harrison, Benjamin, 410
Harrison, Burton Norvell, 411;
correspondence of, 372;
imprisonment of, 70
Harrison, Ellen Reily, 412
Harrison, James O., 412
Harrison, James O., Jr., 412
Harrison, Jilson: death of, 412
Harrison, N., 754
Hart, Charles C., 413
Hartford (U.S.S.), 73, 292, 874;
sketch of, 996
Hartford, Conn., 1013
Hartranft, John Frederick, 177
Hartsuff, George Lucas: gen-
eralship of, 495; photo-
graph of, 7
Hartsville, Tenn., Battle of,
405
Hartwell, Alfred Stedman, 508
Hartz, Edward L., 414;
photograph of, 809
Harvey, Charles Henry, 415
Harwood, Andrew Allen, 313,
416, 660, 788
Harwood family, 416
Hastings, John, 944
Hatch, John Porter, 417-18

Hatch, L. M., 21
Hatcher's Run, Va., Battle of,
25, 550
Hatton, John William Ford,
419
Haupt, Herman, 420
Haupt, Lewis Muhlenberg, 420
Havana, Cuba: U.S. consul
general at, 858; Con-
federate blockade runners
at, 858
Hawkins' Zouaves, 502
Hawks, Esther Hill, 421
Hawks, J. Milton, 421
Hawley, Harriet Foote, 422
Hawley, Joseph Roswell, 173,
422
Hay, Eugene Gano, 423
Hay, John, 424; biography of,
243; correspondence of,
315, 546, 825
Hay, Thomas R., 810
Hayden, Levi, 425
Hayden, Nathaniel, 426
Hayes, Charles M., 864
Hayes, Rutherford Birchard,
1060
Hayne, Isaac, 212
Hays, Alexander: death of, 341
Hays, Harry Thompson, 272
Hazen, William Babcock: cor-
respondence of, 847; photo-
graph of, 541
Health; *see* Medical care;
Medical Department
Heath, Charles Wesley, 427
Heintzelman, Samuel Peter,
428; correspondence of,
304, 571, 895; generalship
of, 40, 496
Heisler, Henry C., 429
Helena, Ark., 600, 760
Helm, Charles J., 189
Henry, J. F., 128

Hephorn, Leonard F., 660

Herndon, William Henry, 430

Hertz, Emanuel, 431

Hesseltine, Frank S., 907

Heth, Henry: generalship of, 754

Hewitt, Edward L., 432

Heyliger, Lewis, 189

Hickey, Andrew, 433

Hickey, Frederick, 433

Hickey, Myron, 433

Hickey family, 433

Hickory Rifles: (C.S. Army) 250

Higgins, Edward, 734

Hill, Daniel Harvey, 66, 192, 913

Hill, Edward, 421

Hill, H. L., 366

Hill, L. J., 421

Hill, Sara Jane Full, 434

Hill, Sylvester, 421

Hill, Warren, 421

Hills, A. C., 435

Hills, Alfred C., 78

Hills, William G., 436

Hill's Point, Va., 346

Hilton Head, S.C.: capture and occupation of, 211, 561, 736; mentioned, 422, 474, 591, 645, 1052

Hine, Orrin E., 437

History of the American Civil War (1867-70), 262

"History of the Great Rebellion and Civil War," 327

Hitchcock, Ethan Allen, 438; memoir, 216; correspondence of, 216, 438

Hitchcock, Henry, 439; diary and correspondence of, 457

Hitt, Robert Roberts, 440

Hodges, James, 441

Hoffman, Wickham, 306

Holcombe, James P., 306

Holford, Lyman C., 442

Hollenbach, John F., 392

Holman, C., 864

Holman, Silas A., 962

Holmes, George Frederick, 443

Holmes, Oliver Wendell, 444

Holmes, Oliver Wendell, Jr., 445

Holmes, Theophilus H., 498

Holt, Joseph, 446

Holt, Samuel E., 447

Holy Springs, Miss.: skirmish at, 843

Homsher, Charles Wesley, 448

Hood, Charles Crook, 449

Hood, John Bell: correspondence of, 66, 789, 1021; reports of, 870, 1021; song about, 265; tactics of, 205

Hood's Texas Brigade, 265

Hooff, John, 991

Hooker, Joseph, 450; correspondence of, 81, 246, 403, 428, 671, 727, 913, 921, 979, 1036; General Butterfield's remarks on, 139; generalship of, 397, 420; photograph of, 938

Hooper, Samuel, 41

Hoover, J. W., 864

Horner, Gustavus Richard Brown, 451

Horner, Mabel Carlton, 148

Horses: stealing of, 261; appraisal for military use, 138

Hoskins, Henry C., 244

Hoskinson, Riley M., 208

Hospital ships: (U.S. Navy) 626, 685, 725; outfitting of, 725; remarks on, 965

Hospitals: (C.S. Army) 200; care in, 383, 386; (U.S. Army) 69,

129th, 103; 145th, 787; organization and strength of, 953; aid to families of, 469; 100-day volunteers, 787

Imboden, John Daniel, 468; movements of, 681

Impressions of Lincoln and the Civil War (1952), 164

In Camp and Battle With the Washington Artillery (1885), 692

Index (London, England), 454

"Index to Volumes, First Series of the Official War Records," 1025

Indiana: planned secessionist uprising in, 833

Indiana troops: (cavalry) 3d, 352; 5th, 448; 11th, 741; (infantry) 6th, 427; 7th, 44; 9th, 453, 527; 10th, 503; 12th, 355; 17th, 416; 18th, 480; 30th, 527; 70th, 410; 134th, 625; 137th, 1027; disposition and training of, 423

Indianapolis, Ind., 782

Indianola (U.S.S.): capture of, 109; photograph of, 725

Indians: as U.S. soldiers, 61, 1016; problems with western Indians, 156; skirmishes between U.S. soldiers and Apache Indians, 396; expedition against the Navajo Indians, 153; miscellaneous affairs of, 289

Indians, Infants, and Infantry; Andrew and Elizabeth Burt on the Frontier (1960), 133

Inflation, 23, 32, 36, 78, 94, 148, 314, 317, 375, 378, 380, 434, 480, 523, 599, 612, 672, 705, 716, 724, 733, 786, 808, 816, 912, 978, 1004

Ingalls, Rufus, 41

Ingersoll, Robert Green, **469**

Inglis, Carrie, 470

Inglis, John Auchinloss, **470**

Inglis, William: death of, 470

Inman, Mrs., 165

"Inquiries Upon Hospital Gangrene," 599

Inside Lincoln's Army (1964), 699

Inspector general: (U.S. Army) 346, 403

"Instructions for Officers on Outpost and Patrol Duty," 622

Instructions Upon Neutral and Belligerent Rights (1864), 535

Intelligence reports: (C.S. Army) 973; (U.S. Army) 33, 42, 403, 535, 573, 846, 850; (U.S. Navy) 561, 784; *see also* Allen, E. J.; Pinkerton, Allan

Interior Department: (U.S.) 970

Internal Revenue Department: (U.S.) 577; *see also* Treasury Department

Invalid Corps, 36, 442

Iowa Sanitary Association, 1047

Iowa troops: (cavalry) 1st, 460; 3d, 352; (infantry) 2d, 300; 3d, 908; 5th, 1020; 27th, 946; 28th, 474; 35th, 909; 36th, 630; 41st, 972; 46th, 277

Iredell Blues, 23

Irish Bend, La., Battle of, 892

Ironclads: conditions aboard, 350; special reports on, 229; advantages and disadvantages of, 822; compared with monitors, 784; improvement of, 425; *see also* Ships; Shipbuilding

Irvine, James A., 952

Irwin, Albert: capture of, 471

Irwin, Bernard John Dowling, 471

Irwinville, Ga., 144

Isaac Smith (U.S.S.): capture of, 968

Island No. 10: print showing Federal bombardment of, 725; capture of, 434, 979

Iuka, Miss., Battle of, 455, 1020

Ives, Cora, 472

Ives, Joseph Christmas, 472

Ives, Leonard, 472

Ives, Malcolm, 78

Ives, Ned, 472

Izard, Ralph, 1021

Jackman, John S., 473

Jackson, Henry Rootes, 55

Jackson, John T., 44

Jackson, Theodore, 474

Jackson, Thomas Jonathan, 475; correspondence of, 443, 452-53, 540, 913; description of, 894, 990; death of, 452; portrait and photographs of, 533, 599, 938; mentioned, 848

Jackson, Miss.: skirmishes near, 39; Siege of, 382, 473, 476, 805, 975; Battle of, 68, 1020; Federal occupation of, 39

Jacksonville, Fla.: skirmishes near, 252; expedition against, 879; Federal occupation of, 421; events in, 24

James, Army of the, 998

James River, Va.: Federal camps along, 435, 998; map

of lower part of, 9; naval operations on, 354, 365, 535, 842, 1028; skirmishes between Federal warships and Confederate batteries, 121, 842; reconnaissance expeditions on, 251

Jameson, Robert Edwin, 476

Jamestown, Va., 12

Jamison, David F., 21

Jamison, John, 305

Jeff Davis (C.S.S.), 313

Jenckes, Thomas Allen, 477

Jenkins, Thornton A., 611

Jewett, Dexter, 478

Jewett, George O., 478

Johnson, Andrew, 479; correspondence of, 546; supposed involvement in Lincoln assassination, 43; photograph of, 541

Johnson, E. E., 480

Johnson, John Augustine, 481

Johnson, John M., 593

Johnson, Reverdy, 482, 546, 896

Johnson, Richard W., 850

Johnson, W. C., 483

Johnson, Waldo Porter, 484

Johnson, William, 3

Johnson's Ferry, Ky.: skirmish at, 405

Johnson's Island Military Prison, 911, 952; names of Confederate officers held at, 175; life at, 453, 563, 637, 716; plan of escape from, 833; mentioned, 306

Johnston, Albert Sidney, 485; comments on, 939; petition for removal of, 334; correspondence of, 409; sketch of, 672

Johnston, Georgianna, 486

Johnston, James Steptoe, 488

Johnston, Joseph Eggleston, 487; correspondence of, 66, 143, 272, 287, 443, 475, 557, 730, 789, 870, 872, 997, 1021; relationship with President Davis, 596, 1021; problems with officials in Richmond, 1021; return of troops commanded by, 272; removal from command in defense of Atlanta, 1021; surrender of, 266, 729; sketch of, 672; description of, 894; photographs of, 533, 599

Johnston, Lydia, 1021

Johnston, Mercer Green, 488

Johnston, Randolph, 590

Johnston, William Preston, 489; correspondence of, 744; commissions of, 485; health of, 489

Jones, Catesby ap R., 492

Jones, Charles Dehaven, 490

Jones, David R.: description of, 894

Jones, John Griffith, 491

Jones, Joseph, 599, 864

Jones, Roger, 492

Jones, Roland, 520

Jones, Samuel, 493, 838

Jones, Simon, 992

Jones, Thomas Goode, 494

Jones, William Edmonson, 365, 532, 913

Jones Landing, Va., 590

Jonesboro, Ga., Battle of, 148

Jordan, Thomas, 66, 467, 789

Joslyn, Mary E., 869

"A Journal of My Life and Experience as a Soldier," 360

Journal of the U.S. Cavalry Association, 352

Journalists, 602, 632, 947; *see* *also* War correspondents

Judge Advocate General: (U.S. Army) 103, 446, 961; (U.S. Navy) 166

Judiciary Square Hospital, Washington, D.C., 119

Judson, Edward Zane Carroll, 1064

Justice Department, U.S. Government, 189

Kane, Thomas L., 319

Kansas: impact of the war on, 156; clippings concerning the war in, 984

Kansas, Department of: (U.S. Army) 661

Kansas troops: (cavalry) 16th, 661; (infantry) 11th, 290

Kasson, John A., 603

Kaufman, Jessie, 331

Kautz, August Valentine, 495; generalship of, 496

Kearny, Philip, 496; correspondence of, 428; sketch of, 938

Kearsarge (U.S.S.): battle with C.S.S. *Alabama*, 71, 224, 1041; log of, 1041; photographs of officers on, 1041; prize money from *Alabama*, 224; mentioned, 52

Keatinge, Harriette C., 497

Keeney, Mrs. George, 498

Keidel, Herman F., 499

Keidel family, 499

Keifer, Joseph Warren, 500

Keim, William High: headquarters letterbook, 501; photograph of, 501

Keim family, 501

Kelaher, James, 502

Kellenberger, Peter B., 503

Keller, Louis, 504

Kelley, Benjamin Franklin: capture of, 294

Kellogg, Edward Nealy and Edward Stanley, 505

Kellogg, Elisha S.: photograph of, 715

Kellogg, Spencer: death of, 438

Kelton, John C., 820

Kemper, D. E. C., 334

Kemper, James L., 789

Kemper, Tip: court-martial of, 334

Kendall, Charles, 254

Kenly, John R., 326

Kennard, Harriet M., 1045

Kennedy, J., 815

Kennedy, Joseph M.: promotion of, 862

Kenner, Duncan Farrar, 506, 719

Kenner, Richard P., 260

Kennesaw Mountain, Ga., Battle of, 148, 195, 300; Federal strategy in, 518; intercepted Confederate messages in, 573; report on, 610; casualties in, 610; mentioned, 1060

Kent, R. A., 253

Kentucky: neutrality of, 409, 593; campaigns in, 46, 48, 103, 114, 146, 188, 195, 226, 231, 355, 402, 405, 410, 427, 429, 473, 490-91, 500, 575, 640, 680, 702-703, 759, 816, 929, 975, 1027, 1060, 1063; skirmishes in, 186, 188, 239, 405, 495, 952, 1000; guerrilla warfare in, 128; Federal recruitment in, 409; Unionists in, 886, 929, 941; see also Magoffin, Beriah; Kirby-Smith, Edmund; Bragg, Braxton

Kentucky troops: C.S. Army (infantry) 1st, 489; 9th, 473; Kentucky Battalion, 797; U.S. Army (cavalry) 1st, 759; 2d, 578, 759; 3d, 563; 8th, 113; 9th, 108; (infantry) 2d, 489, 925; 3d, 928; 10th, 405; 16th, 1000; 17th, 353; 25th, 113; Home Guards, 405

Keorper, Jacob, 607

Keorper, Katharina, 607

Ketchum, Hiram, 571

Key West, Fla.: fortifications at, 686; mentioned, 451

Keyes, Erasmus Darwin: correspondence of, 101, 913, 921; headquarters papers of, 921; photograph of, 286

Kilpatrick, Hugh Judson: remarks on, 871

Kilpatrick–Dahlgren raid on Richmond, 436, 554, 644, 695, 699

King, Adam E., 45

King, Horatio, 507

King, Rufus, 921, 1002

King, Sue Petigru, 714

Kinsley, Edward W., 508

Kinston, N.C., Battle of, 155, 803; skirmish near, 1055

Kintigh, John E., 509

Kirby-Smith, Edmund, 510; correspondence of, 467; invasion of Kentucky, 392, 631, 703; activities in Arkansas, 246; report on operations in Louisiana, 365; clippings on, 266

Kirk, John W., 511

Kirkley, Joseph William, 512

Kloeppel, H. Henry, 513

Knights of the Crimson Cross, 584

Knights of the Golden Circle, 306; arrest of members of,

650

Knox, Dudley Wright, 514
Knox, James Suydam, 515
Knox, Rose Bell, 516
Knox, Thomas W., 78, 850
Knoxville, Tenn., Siege of, 239, 631, 1000, 1037; relief of, 605, 850; attitude of non-combatants in, 1000; mentioned, 312, 684
Knoxville Campaign, 9, 264, 495, 523, 566, 886, 996, 1037
Kock, Charles, 517
Kyle, W. J., 963

"La Concordia," 617
Lacy, Captain, 713
Lafayette (U.S.S.): outfitting of, 565; visits of Federal officers aboard, 565
Lagow, Clark B.: generalship of, 878
La Grange, Ga.: life in during the war, 716; mentioned, 469
La Grange, Tenn.: Federal occupation of, 978; mentioned, 140, 433, 610, 639
Lair, John A., 518
Laird, George F., 519
Lally, Michael, 520
Lamar, Lucius Q. C., 189, 955
Lancaster (U.S.S.): description of, 170; sinking of, 565
Land: purchased by Federal soldiers, 36
Lander, Frederick West, 521
Landis, Aaron, 522
Landis, Allen, 522
Lane, Jackson, 1060
Lane, John Q., 845
Langdon, Bassett, 925
Larned, Daniel Read, 523

"The Last Campaign—A Cavalryman's Journal," 352
Lathers, Richard, 524
Latrobe, Osmun, 525
Latta, James William, 526
Lauman, Jacob G., 850
Laundress, 682
Laurel Hill, Va.: sketch of, 758
Lawrence, Arthur, 684
Lawrence, William R., 669
Lawrence, Kans., 379
Lawrenceburg, Ky., 408
Lawton, Alexander Robert, 532
Lawton, E. A., 21
Lawton, Henry Ware, 527
Lawton, Sarah A., 532
Lawyers, 281, 285
Leale, Charles Augustus, 528
Leavenworth, Kans.: black refugees in, 897
Leavitt, Joshua, 529
Le Duc, William, 41, 845
Lee, Bradley D.: photograph of, 715
Lee, Edmund Jennings (Mrs.), 530
Lee, H. I., 530
Lee, Mary Custis, 537
Lee, Mary Lorrain Greenhow, 531
Lee, Robert Edward, 532-33; correspondence of, 43, 66, 143, 151, 212, 265, 287, 411, 443, 475, 487, 537, 657, 778, 913-14, 980, 1021; orders and reports of, 365, 413; surrender of, 140, 193, 532, 1040; notes and comments on, 82, 939; attitude of southerners toward, 214; clippings on, 266; photographs of, 533, 599; sketch of, 672; resignation from U.S. Army, 532;

memorabilia, 9, 533

Lee, Robert W., 534

Lee, Samuel Phillips, 535-36; correspondence of, 251, 316, 467, 606, 739; leadership of, 725; photograph of, 365; mentioned, 425

Lee, Stephen Dill, 845, 894

Lee, William Henry Fitzhugh, 584

Lee family, 537

"Lee and the Confederacy," 902

Lee Artillery; see Williamsburg Light Artillery

Lee's Lieutenants (1942-44): research notes, manuscript, and galley proof for, 328

Leesburg, Va.: Confederate troops in, 39

Leggett, Mortimer Dormer, 538, 850

Lehigh (U.S.S.), 92

Lenthall, John, 1050

Lester, Joseph, 539

Letcher, John, 118, 540, 912

Letters of John Hay (1908): notes for, 243

Levy, Diana Franklin, 541

Levy, Phebe, 716

Levy, S. Yates, 716

Lewis, Henry, 907

Lewis, Lothrop Lincoln, 542

Lewis, W., 991

Lewis, William Delaware, 543

Lexington (U.S.S.): photograph of, 725

Libby, Frederick Joseph, 544

Libby Prison: conditions and treatment of Federal prisoners in, 148, 184, 697, 884, 898, 1020; names of Federal officers held at, 175, 697; Confederate clerk in, 554; names of Confederate officers held at after the fall

of Richmond, 372; mentioned, 731

Liberal Republicans, 370

Libertytown, Md.: attitude and morale of noncombatants at, 989

Librarian of Congress, 475

Libraries: established for Federal convalescents, 935

"Life of Gen. I. I. Stevens," 903

Limongi, Felix, 545

Lincoln, Abraham, 546-48; correspondence of, 21, 96, 101, 167, 266, 291, 340, 387, 430, 438, 456, 571, 580, 610, 768, 792, 820, 825, 846, 850, 896, 913, 958, 980; first inauguration of, 350, 1032; interviews and meetings with, 117, 169, 461, 990, 1042; political and military appointments by, 91, 141, 416; Cabinet affairs, 58, 87, 90, 169, 340, 347, 622, 685, 1051; reviewing and visiting troops, 50, 311, 335, 354, 365, 819, 853; under fire at Fort Stevens, 2; intervenes in the execution of a deserter, 704; alters instructions to Charles F. Adams, 836; thoughts on blacks and slavery, 331, 458; discussion with General Butler on the postwar disposition of black soldiers, 626; election of 1864, 366, 462; second inauguration of, 330; notes and comments of personal secretaries (John Hay and John G. Nicolay), 424, 674; miscellaneous writings and observations on, 40, 79, 266, 342, 369, 431, 632, 653,

703, 878

Loper, R. F.: biographical sketch· of, 694; profiteering on ship leases, 694

Lord, John B., 680

Lord, W. W., 555

Loring, William W., 973

Lossing, Benjamin: correspondence of, 245, 985; reports on interviews with Federal soldiers who participated in the Fort Sumter affair, 955

Loudoun Valley Campaign, 869

Louisiana: campaigns in, 32, 41, 48, 78, 82, 91, 135, 152, 339, 360, 365, 426, 491, 558, 641, 671, 685, 748, 892; photograph of State House, 725; burning of State House, 685; State constitution, 384; ordinance of secession, 830; economic conditions in, 32; smuggling in, 672; conscription in, 190; war governors, 10, 384, 557, 624, 1008; see also Banks, Nathaniel P.; Butler, Benjamin F.; New Orleans, La.; Red River Campaigns

Louisiana troops: (artillery) 1st Lousiana, 656; Washington Artillery, 447; (infantry) 1st, 607; 3d, 738; 9th, 931; 19th, 159; Planter's Life Guard, 545; militia, 789

Louisville, Ky.: troops from, 405; fortification of, 703; mentioned, 936, 1047

Louisville (U.S.S.): photograph of, 725

Love, John James Hervey, 556

Lovell, Mansfield, 557, 719

Low−Mills families, 558

Lowe, John, 559

Lowe, Thaddeus S. C., 18

Lowndes, Thomas Pinckney: reminiscences of, 560

Lowndes, William, 560

Loyal Eastern Virginia Volunteers; see Virginia troops

Loyalists; see Unionists

Lucas, Simon, 332

Luce, Stephen Bleecker, 316, 561

Luce, William: capture of, 416

Lucy (blockade runner): capture of, 889

Ludwig, Edwin F., 562

Luella, 852

Lunsford, William D., 598

Lurton, Horace Harmon, 563

Lynchburg, Va., 191, 510

Lynchburg Artillery: at the Battle of Williamsburg, 870

Lyon, Nathaniel, 349

Lyons, Richard Bickerton Pemell, 1st Earl, 564

Lyons, Thomas, 565

McAdoo, John D., 566

McAdoo, William Gibbs, 566

McAdoo, William Gibbs, Jr., 566

McBride, Alexander: trial of, 813

McCabe, Flora Morgan, 567

McCabe, J. P., 837

McCall, George Archibald, 589, 590, 819

McCalla, Helen Varnum Hill, 568

McCarter, Mr., 569

Macartney, F. A., 214

McCleery, Robert W., 570

McClellan, George Brinton, 571; correspondence of, 18, 41-42, 76, 81, 173, 326, 428, 438, 482, 521, 524, 546, 784, 850, 872, 895-96, 913, 966,

McMichael, J. C., **589**
McNeil, John, 233
McNeill, Jesse, 294
Macomb, Ann Minerva, 783
Macomb, John N., 783
Macon, Ga.: General Stone-
man's raid on, 146;
Federal capture and
occupation of, 352, 636;
Federal prisoners of war
at, 84
McPherson, B. R., 592
McPherson, Edward, **590**
McPherson, George E., 592
McPherson, James Birdseye,
591; orders of, 768;
generalship and character
of, 380; death of, 64, 850
McPherson, Theodore H. N.,
592
McRae, Colin John, 454
McReynolds, A. T., 326
Macy, S. W., 863
Magoffin, Beriah, 409, 593,
723
Magrath, Andrew Gordon, 21,
594
Magruder, John Bankhead:
campaigns in Arkansas,
894; description of, 894;
comments on, 939
Mahan, Alfred Thayer, 595
Mahan, Dennis H., 877
Mahaska (U.S.S.), 432
Mail: military mail during
Atlanta Campaign, 603;
captured Confederate
mail, 603;
contraband mail, 472
Maine troops: (artillery) 2d
Battery, 69; (infantry) 1st,
542; 3d, 544; 5th, 806;
13th, 907; 16th, 671, 992;
18th, 991; 19th, 835; 20th,
162

*Major Robert Anderson and
Fort Sumter* (1911), 21
Mallet, John W., 220
Mallory, Stephen Russell, **596**;
correspondence of, 492,
870; official report for
1864, 232; statements con-
cerning ship purchases,
222
Malvern (U.S.S.), 177, 365,
597, 860
Malvern Hill, Va., Battle of,
148, 419, 428, 482, 488,
495, 578, 859
Manassas Campaign; *see* First
Manassas Campaign;
Second Manassas Cam-
paign
Manchester Guardian, 103
Mangum, Academus, 598
Mangum, Addeson M., 598
Mangum, Learned H., 598
Mangum, Willie Person, 598
Mangum, Willie Person, Jr.,
598
Manhattan (U.S.S.), 822
Manigault, Alfred: photograph
of, 599; death of, 599
Manigault, Charles, 599
Manigault, Gabriel E.: corre-
spondence of, 599; ex-
change of, 599
Manigault, Louis, **599**
Mann, Ambrose Dudley, 189,
454, 608
Mann, Maria R., 600
Mann, Mary Tyler Peabody,
600
Mansfield, Joseph King Fenno,
524, **601**, 847, 913
Mansfield, La.; *see* Sabine
Cross Roads
"Map of the Seat of War Show-
ing the Battles of July
18th, 21st, and Oct. 21st,

1861," 979

Mapmaking, 33

Maps and sketches: battles and skirmishes, 42, 143, 148, 162, 351, 453, 460-61, 466, 473, 503, 551-52, 598, 622, 710, 800, 865, 913, 1046, 1058; forts and fortifications, 422, 438, 533, 535, 784, 821, 888, 960; geographical areas, 9, 146, 266, 410, 460, 467, 490, 500, 505, 552, 599, 751, 781, 979; towns and cities, 168, 461, 490, 500, 715; military camps and facilities, 270, 622, 938; military hospitals and service organizations, 393, 965, 969; naval vessels and ordnance, 860, 996; flags, 599; officers, 938; bridges, 938; miscellaneous, 14, 162, 187, 290, 335, 338, 373, 377, 428, 467, 546, 582, 590, 693, 735, 758, 798, 820, 825, 850, 896, 938, 947, 1028

Marble, Manton Malone, **602**

Marblehead (U.S.S.), 673; service in the Peninsular Campaign, 764

"March From Mississippi Into Kentucky," 405

March to the sea; *see* Savannah Campaign; Sherman, William Tecumseh

Marches: (C.S. Army) 159, 383, 386, 419, 452, 473, 488, 525, 554, 859, 1021; (U.S. Army) 20, 61, 63, 99, 103, 155, 185, 188, 195, 249, 300, 318, 331, 352-53, 355, 357, 359-60, 391, 405, 410, 415, 426, 429, 436, 439, 449, 462, 476, 478, 483, 491, 500, 522-23, 526, 539, 542, 558, 578, 592, 605, 618, 640-41, 666-67, 680, 685, 687, 703, 709, 715, 717, 741, 746, 748, 758-60, 766, 776, 782, 803-805, 816, 869, 884, 886, 903, 921, 942, 946, 972, 982, 1000, 1009, 1022, 1029, 1038, 1063

Marching With Sherman (1927), 457

Marcy, Randolph Barnes, 326, 403, 571, 861, 921

Mare Island, Calif., 832

Marietta, Ga.: skirmish at, 148; mentioned, 312, 503; *see also* Kenesaw Mountain, Battle of

Marion (U.S. Sloop), 505

"The Mark of the Scalpel," 615

Markland, Absalom H., **603**

Marsh, Hayard: photograph of, 1041

Marshall, Charles, 287

Marshall, Daniel W., **604**

Marshall, Henry, 334

Marshall, John Wesley, **605**

Marshall, Tex., 411, 769

Marston, John, **606**

Mart, Charles, **607**

Martin, James A., 467

Martin, P. C., 608

Martinsburg, W. Va.: burning of public buildings in, 859

Marvin, John, 179

Mary Sanford (U.S.S.): log of, 373

Maryland: campaigns in, 35, 78, 135, 426, 438, 551, 681, 748, 855, 869, 943,

Meade, Major: death of, 532

Meade, George Gordon: correspondence of, 18, 41, 78, 81, 413, 466, 546, 571, 846, 913, 980, 1035; confidential agents to, 33; generalship of, 203; photographs of, 938, 1040

Meade, William, **619**

Meagher, Thomas Francis, **620**, 913, 992

Mearns, Edgar Alexander, **621**

Mechanicsville, Va., Battle of, 12, 148, 495, 589

Medal of Honor: awarded for service at Mobile Bay, 707; black recipients of, 311

Medical care: (C.S. Army) 23, 44, 168, 200, 332, 453, 473, 525, 598-99, 619, 716, 733, 837, 872, 982, 987, 1021; (U.S. Army) 12, 20, 23, 37, 54, 69, 80, 98, 119, 123, 187, 203, 207, 211, 237, 259, 309, 351, 353, 359-60, 363, 365, 391-92, 410, 421-22, 426, 434, 442, 455, 460, 471, 476, 478, 499, 529, 544, 551, 558, 578, 590, 617, 626, 640-41, 650, 667, 671, 685, 687, 702-703, 709, 711, 715, 717, 725, 741, 748, 759, 766, 772-73, 781-82, 804, 826, 869, 879-80, 938, 946, 953, 962, 965, 972, 978, 982, 1009, 1016, 1019, 1022, 1030, 1055, 1060, 1063; (U.S. Navy) 3, 451, 606, 635, 725

Medical Department: (C.S. Army) administration of, 599; report to the surgeon

general in, 979; pay of soldiers detained in, 870; medical examiners in, 190; contracts and supplies, 168; (U.S. Army) organization and administration of, 348, 578, 725, 962; relations with the Christian Sanitary Commission, 578; correspondence concerning appointments in, 824; confusion and mismanagement in, 578; the acquisition and distribution of supplies in, 80, 256, 650, 685; miscellaneous invoices and receipts, 906; *see also* Physicians and surgeons

Medill, W. H., 397

Meigs, John Rodgers: report on the death of, 622

Meigs, Montgomery Cunningham, **622**; correspondence of, 41, 783-84, 847, 913; military contract, 271

Meigs, Return Jonathan, **623**

Méjan, Eugene, **624**

Memminger, Christopher Gustavus, 77, 100, 189, 212, 222, 392, 608, 778, 913, 955

Memoirs of General William T. Sherman (1875): draft of, 850

"Memoranda of Events That Transpired at Jacksonville, Florida, & in Its Vicinity," 252

Memphis, Tenn.: conditions in, 250; plans for defense of, 507; fortifications at, 598; U.S. Post Office at,

603; U.S. hospitals at, 52,
471, 725; mentioned,
390, 402, 507
Mercedita (U.S.S.), 388, 411
Meredith, William D., 625
Meridian Campaign, 441, 733,
850, 953
Merriam, J. W., 507
Merrill, John H., 266
Merrimac (C.S.S.): construction
of, 304; armor and ord-
nance on, 1006; battle
with U.S.S. *Monitor*, 156,
374, 608; Federal plan of
attack on, 304; scuttling
of, 354; comments on, 686;
mentioned, 1057; *see also*
Monitor-Merrimac affair
Merrimac (U.S.S), 844
Merritt, Wesley, 193, 315, 846
Mervine, William, 832
Merwin, James Burtis, 626
Methodist Episcopal Church:
confiscation of church
property, 43; conflicting
claims for property, 864
Mexican Pacific Coal and Iron
Mining and Land Com-
pany, 728
Mexico: Confederate agents in,
189, 347, 719; release of
Confederate funds to, 77;
claim for *Oriente*, 222;
French activity in, 728;
Confederate expatriates
in, 614
Michigan (U.S. steamer):
Confederate plan to seize,
306, 833
Michigan, University of: copies
of manuscripts at, 886
Michigan troops: (artillery)
Battery F, 1st Regiment
Light Artillery, 631;

(cavalry) 2d, 299; 3d, 266,
433; 5th, 433; (engineers)
1st Regiment Engineers
and Mechanics, 188; (in-
fantry) 2d, 729; 7th, 680;
12th, 274; 18th, 186; 23d,
886
Michler, Nathaniel: photograph of, 938
Middleburg, Tenn.: skirmish
near, 274
Middleburg, Va.: skirmish at,
162
Middletown, Va., 415
Miers, Earl Schenck, 627, 967
Milan, 624
Miles, Nelson Appleton, 629
Miles, William Porcher, 628,
789, 955
Miles–Cameron families, 629
Military passes, 111, 140, 161,
176, 196, 210, 232-33, 258,
260-61, 311, 314, 348,
350, 371-72, 411, 421, 447,
486, 498, 507, 525, 578,
599, 603-604, 620, 633-
34, 638, 682, 689-90, 761,
774, 799, 844, 890, 913,
921, 934, 963, 994, 1012,
1029, 1042, 1047
Military telegraph, 150, 175,
178, 655, 659, 774, 793,
819, 846; *see also* "Semo-
phoric Telegraphic
Signals"; Telegrams
Military training; *see* Training
Militia: Louisiana, 789; New
York, 654, 801, 814;
Pennsylvania, 646; New
Jersey, 887
Milledgeville, Ga., 312
Miller, Allen Woods, 630
Miller, Frederick L.: photograph of, 1041

Miller, Marshall Mortimer, 631

Miller, William, 332

Millikens Bend, La.: engagement at, 152; mentioned, 760

Millwood plantation, Va., 619

Milroy, Robert Huston: correspondence of, 850; Confederate operations against, 532

Milton, George Fort, 632

Mine Run, Va.: skirmish at, 419

Mine Run Campaign, 130, 335, 500, 526, 699, 758, 793; reports on, 272

Mines; *see* Arms and ammunition; Torpedoes

Minnesota (U.S.S.), 156, 365, 822; torpedo attack on, 365; sketch of, 365

Minnesota troops: (infantry) lst, 579; 3d, 579

Minor, Marietta, 633

Minor, Mary, 633

Minor, Smith, 634

Missionary Ridge, Battle of, 80, 105, 450, 503, 578, 703, 850, 878, 925; *see also* Chattanooga Campaign

Mississippi (C.S.S.), 649

Mississippi (U.S.S.): log from, 535, 832; destruction of, 244

Mississippi: campaigns in, 39, 44, 46, 48, 63, 78, 82, 91, 116, 123, 152, 300, 382, 433, 491, 613, 630, 637, 671, 702, 730, 805, 946, 953, 975, 982; *see also* Corinth Campaigns; Meridian Campaign; Vicksburg Campaign; and individual battles and skirmishes. Union supply depots in, 591; Union hospitals in, 946; effects of the war in, 174, 250, 978; Confederate troop movements in, 27, 402, 1034

Mississippi, Department of the: (U.S. Army) 387

Mississippi, Division of the: (U.S. Army) 187, 729, 1061

Mississippi River: Confederate fortifications along, 723; Union troop movements on, 14, 41, 175, 804; military operations along, 32, 63, 306, 686, 734, 760, 784, 800, 972

Mississippi Squadron: (U.S. Navy) 251, 313, 686, 832

Mississippi troops: (infantry) 17th, 404

Missouri (C.S.S.): accounts concerning, 189

Missouri: campaigns in, 91, 367, 434, 480, 598, 1060; Federal policy in, 820; political and military situation in, 245, 685, 820; recruitment and military organization in, 349, 1049; Confederate sympathizers in, 300; guerrilla warfare in, 128, 434, 1060; war governors, 484, 769; impact of the war on, 156

Missouri, Department of: (U.S. Army) official correspondence and dispatches, 387, 438, 820; headquarters letterbook, 178

Missouri, Kansas, and

Arkansas, Department of: (U.S. Army) 178

Missouri troops: C.S. Army (cavalry) 1st, 525. U.S. Army (cavalry) 1st, 1049; 12th, 843; (infantry) 3d, 290, 760; 10th, 455; 11th, 488; 13th, 39; 17th, 404; 30th, 63; 33d, 733; list of regiments, 34; organization and service of the 12th Cavalry Regiment, 843; organization and disposition, 949; discipline among, 744

Missroon, John S., 673, 784

Mitchell, Benjamin, 635

Mitchell, Charles D., 636

Mitchell, James B., 637

Mitchell, James S., 638

Mitchell, Marcellus, 639

Mitchell, Ormsby M., 173

Mitchell, T. F., 85

Mitchell, William M., 85

Mobile, Ala.: defenses of, 220, 481, 856; Siege of, 14, 804, 946; treatment of noncombatants in, 63; mentioned, 987

Mobile and Girard Railroad: account of, 55

Mobile Bay, Battle of, 92, 200, 206, 279, 292, 343, 505, 707, 804; naval skirmishes in, 933; Federal blockade of, 566, 800, 881, 907, 1003; escape of C.S.S. *Florida* from, 265

Mobile Campaign, 63, 152, 187, 206, 357

Mobile County, Ala.: list of taxable property and tax rates in, 995

"A Modern Soldier of Fortune," 331

Moler, Nelia, 22

Money; *see* Paper currency

Monitor (U.S.S.): remarks on, 558, 1057

Monitor class vessels: construction and performance of, 306; comparative evaluation with ironclads, 784; living conditions on, 1003; use and utility of, 750, 1006

Monitor-Merrimac affair, 156, 223, 374, 601, 739, 842

Monongahela (U.S.S.), 407; photograph of, 802

Monongalia County, W. Va.: arrest and prosecution of Confederate sympathizers in, 795

Monroe, John J., 624

Monroe County, W. Va.: military situation in, 754

Montague, R. S., 995

Montauk (U.S.S.), 1057

Montevallo, Ala.: skirmish at, 636

Montgomery, James H., 640

Montgomery, R. H., 783

Montgomery, William Reading: generalship of, 496

Montgomery family, 641

Montgomery, Ala.: Federal capture and occupation of, 352, 636; mentioned, 628, 856, 1045

Moore, D. P., 323

Moore, R., 323

Moore, Samuel P., 599, 870

Moore, Thomas Overton, 624

Morale: (C S. Army) 18, 23, 27, 44, 85, 143, 159, 220, 367, 412, 419, 452-53, 473,

554-55, 567, 598, 619, 637,
703, 729, 736, 741, 743,
859, 901, 956, 1021, 1023,
1058; (U.S. Army) 20, 36,
63, 99, 103, 114, 155, 175,
188, 248, 264, 300, 309,
314, 351, 355, 359, 366,
391, 396-97, 422-23, 426,
434-35, 439, 442, 462, 480,
491, 495, 500, 508, 522-23,
529, 539, 551-52, 558, 579,
592, 605, 618, 659, 666,
680, 685, 687, 699, 703,
705, 717, 741, 748, 758-60,
765-66, 773, 782, 804-805,
816, 825, 844, 855, 869,
878-79, 884, 892, 896, 903,
938, 946, 958, 972, 975,
992, 1000, 1009, 1022,
1027, 1037, 1055, 1060,
1063; (U.S. Navy) 796
Morality, 183, 544, 758, 1016,
1027, 1063
Moran, Benjamin, **642-43**
Moran, Frank E., **644**
Mordecai, Alfred, **645**
Mordecai, Alfred, II, 645
Mordecai, Ellen, 645
More, E. J., **646**
Morehead City, N.C., 258
Morell, George W., 913
Moreno, Francisco, 538, **647**
Morgan, Edwin D., 546
Morgan, George Washington,
648, 979
Morgan, James Morris, **649**
Morgan, John H., 567
Morgan, John Hunt: skirmishes
with Federal troops, 449,
741; escapes trap near
Lawrenceburg, Ky., 408;
raid on Columbia, Ky.,
703; pursuit of in Ken-
tucky, 405; pursuit and

capture in Ohio, 495, 523,
683
Morgan, Margaret A., 567
Morgan, Thomas J., 86
Morgan, William C., 567
Morley, Edward Williams, **650**
Morning Globe, 1016
Moro Creek, Ark.: skirmish at,
630
Morrell, Charles W., **651**
Morrill, Justin Smith, **652**
Morris, George P., 814
Morris, J. L., 27
Morris, Martha Elizabeth
Wright, **653**
Morris–Popham families, **654**
Morris Island, S.C.: Federal
operations on, 493, 1034;
mentioned, 1017, 1054
Morse, Charles N., 656
Morse, Samuel Finley Breese,
655
Morse family, **656**
Morton, Oliver P., 413
Morton, Richard, 1021
Mosby, John Singleton, 192,
657, 872
Mosby's Rangers, 657, 943; *see
also* Partisan Rangers
Moscow, Ky., 114
Moss, Helen Palmer Hess, **658**
Motley, John L., 444
Mott, Gershom, 861
Mound City, Ill.: photograph of
commandant's house at,
725
Mountain Department: (U.S.
Army) 329, 348
Muir, Susan H., 470
Munfordville, Ky., Battle of,
741, 888
Munson, Myron A., 650
Murfreesboro, Tenn., Battle of,
239, 400, 605, 637, 640,

816, 906; secessionist sentiment in, 864

Murrell's Inlet, S.C.: sketch of, 373; expedition to, 373

Musicians: (C.S. Army) 159, 733; (U.S. Army) 49, 746

Muster rolls: (C.S. Army) 189, 296, 531, 677; (U.S. Army) 42, 146, 162, 198, 266, 355, 371, 396, 410, 422, 429, 578, 585, 609, 633, 663, 884, 891-92

"My Experience in the Quantrill Raid," 379

"My Father Led General J. E. B. Stuart to Gettysburg," 857

"My Pursuit of Gen. John H. Morgan's Troops," 405

"My Reminiscences of the War," 537

"My Service in the 1st U.S. Colored Cavalry," 86

Myer, Albert James, **659-60**

Myer, Elizabeth Shriver, 857

Myers, Abraham C., 789

Myers, T. Bailey, 395

Nahant (U.S.S.), 867

Nantucket (U.S.S.), 65, 561

Nashville (C.S.S.), 649, 995; sinking of, 84

Nashville, Tenn.: Siege of, 751; Federal occupation of, 751, 782, 878, 1027, 1063; Union sentiment in, 603; fortifications surrounding, 605; military post office established at, 603; attitude of noncombatants in, 904; mentioned, 982

Nashville, Tenn., Battle of, 838, 888

Nashville Campaign; *see*

Franklin and Nashville Campaign

Nassau: contraband trade with, 822; list of Confederate vessels at, 858

Natchez, Miss., 813

National Freedmen's Relief Association: official correspondence and records of, 421

National Tribune, 1001

Navajo expedition, 153

Naval Brigade, 375, 418

Naval Duties and Discipline With the Policy and Principles of Naval Organization (1865), 785

Naval Historical Foundation collections, 65, 71, 84, 92, 109, 122, 155, 157-58, 163, 183, 200, 206, 230, 254, 267, 293, 304, 334, 350, 359, 365, 373, 407, 418, 451, 505, 514, 535, 559, 561, 570, 595, 597, 606, 611, 649, 673, 686, 707, 712, 725, 737, 739, 742, 750, 763, 770, 784-85, 796, 800, 802, 822, 832-34, 858, 860, 867, 876, 881, 905, 920, 927, 933, 968, 996, 1003, 1039, 1041, 1045, 1050, 1056-57

Navy; *see* Confederate States Navy; U. S. Navy

The Navy in Congress (1865), 832

Neely, McGinley M., **661**

Negroes; *see* Black soldiers; Blacks; Slavery

Nellis, Joseph: death of, 590

Nellis, William, 590

Nelson, Thomas Henry, **662**

Nelson, William, 215; death of,

640, 782, 925

Netherlands: diplomatic relations with the United States, 722

Neutral rights, 132, 535; *see also* Benjamin, Judah P.

Nevin, Wilberforce, 816

New Bern, N.C., Battle of, 523, 575, 675, 796

New Bern, N.C.: Federal capture and occupation of, 425, 478, 586, 709, 803; blacks in, 478; U.S. Christian Commission delegates in, 965; mentioned, 467

New England Soldiers Relief Association, 461

New Hampshire troops: (infantry) 4th, 421; 9th, 421

New Iberia, La.: skirmish at, 491

New Ironsides (U.S.S.): construction and performance of, 71, 750; service of, 750; torpedo attacks on, 796, 867

New Jersey Infantry—7th Regiment, 663

New Jersey troops: (cavalry) 1st, 943; 3d, 921; (infantry) 5th, 887; 7th, 591, 663; 13th, 149, 556; 24th, 887; 25th, 687; 30th, 504; (militia) 4th, 887

New Madrid, Mo.: Federal capture of, 434

New Market, Va., Battle of, 422

New Mexico Territory: secessionists efforts in, 417; California Column in, 396; Federal operations in, 396

New Mexico troops: (infantry) 1st, 153

New Orleans, La.: Confederate plans for defense of, 719; fortifications at, 734; sketch of fortifications at, 438; foreign volunteer organizations in, 624; mayor of, 624; French consul at, 135, 624; German consul at, 517; Spanish consul at, 135; law firms in, 545; Federal preparations for expedition against, 304; capture of, 30, 73, 292, 1001, 1006; occupation of, 135, 242, 566, 641, 672, 686, 716, 734, 874; conditions during the Federal occupation, 14, 41, 63, 305, 318, 426, 535, 702, 716, 804; corruption in, 535, 557; escape from, 672; Federal camps near, 124, 481; Federal Treasury agents in, 169; inquiry on the fall of, 557; vessels stranded in, 694; quarantine of vessels bound for, 858; establishment of U.S. Post Office at, 603; mentioned, 278, 360, 972; *see also* Butler, Benjamin F.; Fort Jackson; Fort St. Philip

New Providence, Bahama Islands, 524

New York: adjutant general in, 756; quartermaster general in, 580; enlistments and recruiting in, 115, 756, 791; 6th Military District of, 115

New York—5th Cavalry, 664

New York City: anti-draft riots

672

Nicholson, Sommerville, 673

Nicolay, John George, 674; correspondence of, 546; notes on military appointments, 416

Niles, Peter H., 675

Noble, John Willock, 676

Nolan, B. P., 1021

Noncombatants (southern): attitude and morale of, 20, 84, 300, 309, 317, 352, 355, 396, 426, 429, 439, 452, 460, 473, 478, 488, 500, 531, 539, 575, 586, 599, 601, 618, 641, 650, 666, 686, 694, 714, 736-37, 743-44, 748, 751, 759, 764, 786, 816, 847, 857, 869, 904, 949, 975, 978, 989; treatment by Federal soldiers, 53, 140, 148, 174, 239, 274, 279, 309, 399, 468, 500, 587, 610, 631, 636, 641, 747, 847, 892, 970, 979, 1009, 1037; suffering of, 44, 453, 462, 465, 468, 555, 591, 612, 614, 636, 705, 714, 745, 850, 921, 978, 980, 1021, 1023; effect of war on, 411, 523, 555, 558, 1014, 1029; arrest of, 989; displacement of, 888; murder of, 913; Federal policy toward, 583

Norfolk, Va.: fortifications at, 994; Federal capture and occupation of, 50, 601; political prisoners at, 524; mentioned, 801, 1024

Norfolk Navy Yard: destruction of, 686

Norristown, Pa., 646

North Anna River: Battle of, 526; map of, 820; skirmishes along, 187

North Atlantic Blockading Squadron, 251, 535, 687, 796

North Carolina: campaigns in, 71, 78, 84, 116, 135, 183, 187, 226-27, 264, 311, 354, 376, 388, 410, 425, 478, 488, 508, 586, 675, 844, 1044, 1046; enlistments and training in, 598; conscription in, 755, 977; war governors, 118, 1044; map of (incomplete), 1046; coastal defenses of, 535, 1044; taxes in, 118; Unionist activities in, 197; prohibition in, 118; blockade of coast of, 156

North Carolina, University of: copies of manuscripts at, 560, 596

North Carolina Infantry—11th Regiment, 677

North Carolina troops: (infantry) 4th, 23; 11th, 677; 32d, 899; 44th, 554; General Branch's brigade, 532; 2d North Carolina Battalion, 873

North Reading, Mass.: volunteers from, 609

"The North Western Confederacy," 669

Northern Virginia, Army of: organization of, 33; service of, 554; official correspondence, orders, returns, and reports of, 272; pursuit of in the Antietam Campaign, 572; condition of on the eve of the Appomattox Campaign, 411; surrender of, 193, 1040

Northumberland County, Va.:
arming of citizens in, 995

Northwest Territory: possible
loss of to the Confederacy,
417

Norwich (U.S.S.), 592

Notre Dame, University of:
copies of manuscripts at,
125, 291, 851

Nott, Charles C., 179

Nott, J. C., 987

Nottoway Station, Va.: sketch
of, 758

Nourse, Joseph E., 834

Noyes, Edward F., 1060

Noyes, Isaac R., 678

Nurses: (U.S. Army) 1, 54, 80,
101, 227, 422, 682, 915

Nye, James Warren, 679, 832

Oaths, loyalty, 88, 180, 283;
poem about, 757

Octorara (U.S.S.), 822

Officers: (C.S. Army) need for,
789; appointment and pro-
motion of, 202, 344, 383,
392, 452, 532, 562, 769,
778, 789, 973, 1021; election of, 27; quality of, 220;
(U.S. Army) appointment
of, 142, 169, 329, 355, 450,
523, 554, 582, 685, 706,
720, 799, 804, 825, 847,
850, 861, 864, 884, 904,
921, 953, 979, 992-93,
1004, 1030; promotion of,
81, 264, 921, 979; attitude
toward recruits, 758;
attitude toward the Con-
federacy, 348; rank dis-
putes among, 41, 91, 114,
264, 315, 331, 422, 460,
495-96, 523, 552, 685, 729,

850, 921, 953, 1036; evaluation and criticism of,
124, 169, 326, 348; dis-
missal of, 804; lists of,
311, 337, 466, 512, 575,
590-91, 1038; photographs
of, 152, 350; (U.S. Navy)
assignment of, 1006; rank
disputes among, 822; lists
of, 561, 764, 996, 1006

*Officers of the Western Gulf
Blockading Squadron*, 996

*Official Army Register, for
1861*, 337

Official war records: index for,
1025

Ogden, Robert Curtis, 680

Oglesby, R. J., 784

Oglethorpe Military Prison,
197

Ohio: quartermaster general,
847; adjutant general, 847;
recruits from, 847; training camps in, 339; General
Morgan's raid into, 683;
defense of, 941; plan for
secessionist uprising in,
833; war governor, 941

Ohio, Army of the, 338;
organizational chart for,
603

Ohio, Department of the: telegraph book for, 175

Ohio, Fourth Military District,
683

Ohio Historical Society: copies
of documents at, 970

Ohio National Guard, 301

Ohio River: Federal gunboats
on, 784

Ohio troops: (artillery) 1st
Light Artillery, 94; 2d
Heavy Artillery, 888;
(cavalry) 2d, 156; (in-

680

212, 973; disappointment
with at Vicksburg, 555
Pembroke, 986
Pendergast, Garrett J., 606
Pendleton, Edward, **709**
Pendleton, William Nelson,
193
Penguin (U.S.S.), 422
Peninsular Campaign, 18, 23,
33, 41, 106, 148, 184, 249,
326, 377, 383, 386, 397,
412, 419, 428, 435, 438,
452-53, 466, 488, 495-96,
544, 571-72, 578, 589, 602,
604, 659, 686-87, 695, 729,
735, 764, 776, 784, 842,
859, 884, 894, 912, 921,
938, 953, 991, 998, 1021,
1036; list of U.S. vessels
used in, 694; suffering in,
412; mentioned, 790
Pennsylvania: public attitude
toward the war, 786; war-
time travel in, 786;
recruiting in, 112; aid to
volunteers and their
dependents, 590
*Pennsylvania Magazine of
History and Biography*,
786
Pennsylvania Militia, 646
Pennsylvania Reserves; *see*
Pennsylvania troops
Pennsylvania troops: (artillery)
1st Reserves, 854; (cavalry)
2d Reserves, 391; 9th, 61;
15th, 1046; (infantry) 2d
Reserves, 819; 5th Re-
serves, 589; 5th, 236; 6th
Reserves, 855; 7th, 590;
8th, 590; 9th Reserves,
884; 17th, 1016; 19th,
1016; 21st, 1016; 38th,
386; 48th, 429; 49th, 25;

56th, 913; 74th, 983; 78th,
944; 79th, 816; 82d, 676;
83d, 25; 84th, 638; 91st,
944; 101st, 197; 103d, 345;
106th, 944; 107th, 576,
592; 110th, 543; 111th,
361; 116th, 522; 118th,
162; 119th, 526; 125th,
676; 139th, 341; 141st,
298; 191st, 391; 196th,
368; Collis' Independent
Company Zouaves de
Afrique, 185; organization
of, 884; comments on, 904;
see also McCall, George A.
Pensacola, Fla., 156; defense
of, 856; fortifications at,
412; Spanish vice consul
at, 583; mentioned, 647
Pensacola Bay, Fla.: Federal
ships fail to enter, 737
Pensions: (U.S. Government)
120, 775; forms for, 224;
correspondence concerning,
682; certificates, 405, 676;
agent, 775; records of, 805,
895, 946, 1009
Peoria, Ill., 469
Perham, Aurestus S., **710**
Perkins, Edward Thomas, **711**
Perkins, George Hamilton, **712**
Perkins, Henry Welles, **713**
Perkins, Newton W., 641
Perrine, C. O., 781
Perryville, Battle of, 128, 605,
703, 782, 816, 886
Perryville, Ky., 745
*Personal Memoirs of P. H.
Sheridan* (1888): draft of,
846
Petersburg, Siege of, 16, 66,
112, 182, 203, 311, 335,
352, 376-77, 391, 395, 405,
419, 422, 429, 436, 466,

522, 542, 598, 638, 645, 651, 697, 709, 715, 736, 758, 930, 979, 1016, 1034, 1036, 1054; Federal ordnance in, 638; notes on, 1023; sketch of mine explosion, 758; map of, 162; sketch of, 85; mentioned, 880; *see also* Petersburg Campaign

Petersburg Campaign, 7, 25, 112, 135, 162, 187, 231, 309, 377, 429, 453, 495, 500, 523, 526, 542, 576, 602, 699, 746, 758, 778, 793, 869, 903, 938, 953, 969, 1037

Petigru, James Louis, **714**

Pettigrew, James Johnston: career of, 212

Pettigrew, S., 212

Pettus, John J., 973

Peyton, Henry E., 657

Phelps, Ethel L., 715

Phelps, John Wolcott: Confederate reaction to policies of, 596

Phelps, Samuel L., 784

Phelps, Winthrop Henry, **715**

Philadelphia (U.S.S.), 230

Philadelphia: plan for defense of, 34; British Minister at, 747; mentioned, 866, 1054

Philadelphia Inquirer, 501

Philadelphia Navy Yard, 451, 513

Philadelphia Press, 659, 1064

Phillips, Eugenia Yates Levy, **716**

Phillips, Philip, **716**

Phillips, Stephen, 366

Photographers, 998

Photographs and portraits: miscellaneous, 7, 18, 98, 192, 290, 359, 363, 377, 411, 490, 551, 980, 996, 1028

Physicians and surgeons: (C.S. Army) 137, 168, 190, 194, 453, 599, 670, 837, 870; register of surgeons in the Army of Tennessee, 194; (U.S. Army) 29, 52, 61, 74, 104, 207, 211, 226, 248, 274, 356, 387, 401, 421, 435, 471, 476, 518, 528, 544, 556, 578, 615, 711, 740, 766, 824, 854, 906, 940, 962; treatment as prisoners of war, 387, 401; (U.S. Navy) 3, 52, 122, 451, 611, 725; (private) 226, 465, 615, 740, 940

Pickard, Alonzo C., **717**

Pickard, F. A., 717

Pickens, Francis Wilkinson, 21, 212, 409, 628, 718, 856, 955, 1021

Pickens–Bonham, **718**

Pickering, Charles W., 373

Picket boats: contract for, 1050

Pickett, George Edward: report on Battle of Williamsburg, 870; attack on New Berne, N.C., 803; health of, 754; headquarters staff of, 754

Pickett, John Thomas, **719**; correspondence of, 189; paroled, 161

Pickett, Theodore, 161,

Pierce, Franklin, **720**

Pierpont, Francis Harrison, **721**

Piers, Frank, 944

Pike, Frederick Augustus, 832

Pike, James Shepherd, **722**

Pillow, Gideon Johnson, 409, **723**

Pilot Knob, Battle of, 290

Pine Bluff, Ark.: list of Unionists from, 734

Pinkerton, Allan; see Allen, E. J.

Pinkerton's National Detective Agency, 724

Pinkney, Ninian, 725

Pinola (U.S.S.), 822

Pittsburg Landing, 534, 759; *see also* Shiloh, Battle of

Planter (blockade runner): Federal capture of, 842

Planter's Life Guard, 545

Pleasant Grove, La.; *see* Sabine Cross Roads

Pleasants, Archibald, 726

Pleasonton, Alfred, 727; headquarters papers of, 921

Plumb, Edward Lee, 728

Plundering, 532, 566, 614, 618, 729, 768, 1023

Plymouth, N.C.: skirmish near, 197; capture of Federal garrison at, 345

Pocahontas (U.S.S.), 595

Pocotaligo, S.C.: Battle of, 422; engagement at, 599; mentioned, 277

Poe, Orlando, 729

Poems, 110, 265, 341, 360, 386, 442, 757, 767, 805, 909, 1009, 1034

Point Lookout, Md., 392

Point Lookout Military Prison, 333, 499, 899; life at, 899

Polignac, Prince Camille Armand Jules Marie de, 778

Political Conspiracies Preceding the Rebellion (1882), 21

"Political Experiences of Major General Jacob Dolson Cox," 209

Polk, Leonidas, 730; correspondence of, 66, 409, 997, 1021; return of troops commanded by, 409; engraved portrait of, 1034

Pollard, A. A., 503

Polsley, John J., 731

Pomeroy, Samuel Clark, 246

Pontiac (U.S.S.), 561

Pontoon Brigade, 937

Pontoons: procurement of, 437; sketch of, 938

Pontoosuc (U.S.S.), 70

Poole, Edmund Leicester, 732

Pope, H. H., 433

Pope, John: correspondence of, 820; generalship of, 99, 417, 420; character of, 417

Port Gibson, Miss., Battle of, 68, 491

Port Hudson, La.: Battle of, 1003; Siege of, 360; guard duty at, 371; attacked by Admiral Farragut, 244; mentioned, 607; *see also* Port Hudson Campaign

Port Hudson Campaign, 17, 32, 123, 641, 725, 748, 892, 973

Port Republic, Va., Battle of, 731

Port Royal (U.S.S.), 343

Port Royal, S.C.: Federal blockade of, 92; engraved view of bombardment of, 1034; mentioned, 301, 591, 849, 1010

Port Royal expedition, 182, 421, 493, 561, 736, 849; comments on, 680

Porter, Albert Quincy, 733

Porter, David Dixon, 734; correspondence of, 42, 177, 183, 573, 737, 750, 796,

832, 850; Adm. Samuel P. Lee's opinion of, 251; photographs of, 365, 739; mentioned, 535, 565

Porter, Fitz-John, 735; correspondence of, 18, 91, 466, 820, 848, 913; court-martial of, 62, 317, 422, 467; postwar reinvestigation of, 346

Porter, Horace, 736

Porter family, 737

Portland, Maine, 792

Portsmouth, Va.: abandonment of, 1006

Post Office Department, 189

Postmaster General, 507

Poston, William K., 128

Potomac (U.S.S.), 70

Potomac, Army of the: organization, 41, 309, 438, 461, 729; performance of, 729; reports on, 1034; headquarters papers of, 571

Potomac River: fortifications on, 592; Federal raids along, 229; planned operations on, 201

Potomac River flotilla, 1028

Potomska (U.S.S.), 905

Potter, Edward E., 467

Potter, Henry L., 861

Potter, William F., 738

Powel, Mary Edith, 739

Powell, C. Percy, 967

Powell, J. E., 460

Powell, John F., 740

Powhatan (U.S.S.), 737

Prairie Grove, Battle of, 290

Pratt, Nicholas, 742

Pratt, Richard Henry, 741

Pratt, William Veazie, 742

Preble, George H.: attempt to prevent C.S.S. *Florida*

from entering Mobile Bay, 881; correspondence of, 375, 418; dismissal and reinstatement of, 881; information on, 739

Preble, Henry, 34

"Precis of the Military History of B. J. D. Irwin," 471

Prentice, Fowler, 688

Prentice, George D., 997

Prentiss, Benjamin Mayberry, 291

Presidential campaign of 1864, 366, 462, 571, 847; results among Vermont troops, 652; miscellaneous figures on votes cast by soldiers, 768

Preston, John Thomas Lewis, **743**

Preston, William, 454

Preston family of Virginia, 744

Price, Benjamin, 348

Price, Sterling: strength of, 613; Federal maneuvers against, 367, 480; correspondence of, 730; generalship of, 613; criticism of, 411

Prince, Lt. Colonel, 266

Princeton (U.S.S.): construction of, 280

Princeton University, 974

Prisoners of war: (Confederate) 24, 57, 63, 85, 128, 156, 168, 234, 239, 259, 279, 322, 333, 357, 367, 383, 386, 400, 441, 460, 470, 499-500, 525, 532, 539, 552, 558, 563, 581, 584, 586, 618, 640-41, 646, 650, 667, 677, 699, 772, 782, 793, 803, 805, 811, 886, 899, 903, 911, 946, 989, 1058, 1063; life and treat-

Putnam, George H., 558

Quaker City (U.S.S.), 158
Quantrill, William Clarke,
    379, 460
Quartermaster Department:
    (C.S. Army) supply reports,
    accounts, receipts, and
    requisitions, 23, 27, 159,
    168, 189, 222, 234, 276,
    409, 452, 472, 498, 532,
    567, 613, 637, 645, 769,
    789, 859, 973, 1021, 1023,
    1058; early requisitions
    for supplies, 732; supply
    shortages, 383, 1023; theft
    from supply depots, 733;
    certificates of appraisal
    and seizure, 138, 176;
    (U.S. Army) quarter-
    masters and assistant
    quartermasters, 41, 93,
    178, 414, 580, 622, 888;
    official correspondence,
    accounts, reports, requisi-
    tions, invoices, and re-
    ceipts, 41, 162, 199, 591,
    622, 666, 717, 963, 1034;
    fraud in, 622; depots in
    Mississippi, 591; movement
    and distribution of supplies
    during campaigns, 150,
    204, 240, 351, 713; *see
    also* Commissary Depart-
    ment; Subsistence Depart-
    ment; Sutlers
Quartermaster General: (U.S.
    Army) 622
Quartermaster General of New
    York, 580
Quincy, L. M., 366
Quincy, Samuel Miller, 748
Quincy–Wendell–Upham–
    Holmes families, 748

R. E. Lee (1934-35): source
    material, manuscript, and
    galley for, 328
R. Hoe & Company, 749
Radford, William, 750
"Raid by Morgan's Men on
    Frankfort, Kentucky," 405
Railroads: Baltimore and Ohio,
    340; Mobile and Girard,
    55; sabotage of, 566; de-
    fense of, 552, 590, 735;
    production of rails for
    southern lines, 1006; con-
    struction and management
    of Federal military rail-
    roads, 67, 420, 1061; fees
    charged to Federal soldiers
    for transportation on, 67;
    see also Haupt, Herman
Raleigh, N.C.: capture and
    occupation of, 43, 300; U.S.
    Christian Commission
    delegates at, 965; men-
    tioned, 713
Ramsay, George D., 601
Ramseur, Stephen D., 681
Ramsey, Margaret Lawrence,
    751
Randall, James Garfield and
    Ruth P., 752
Randolph, George Wythe, 409,
    753
Randolph, William B., 754
Rankin, David, 43
Ransom, Robert, 755
Ransom, Thomas Greenfield,
    326
Rapidan River, Va.: operations
    along, 335, 352-53, 377,
    386, 391, 419, 500, 618,
    711, 1021
Rappahannock (C.S.S.), 643,
    802
Rappahannock Bridge, Va.:

Cumberland Township, Pa., 590

Religion: as practiced by Federal soldiers, 314, 386, 578, 715, 717, 864, 878, 888, 913; attitude of southern clergy, 778

Remey, George Collier, 763

Remey family, 764

"Reminiscence of the War Between the States" (Harralson), 406

Reminiscences; see Diaries

"Reminiscences of the Civil War" (Hill), 434

"Reminiscences of the Civil War" (Kautz), 495

"Reminiscences of the Civil War" (Wilder), 1026

Remsen, Tredwell W., 765

Report of General Robert E. Lee (1864), 365

Report of Lieutenant General U. S. Grant (1865): draft of, 850

Report of the Adjutant and Inspector General of South Carolina (1863), 1034

Report of the Chief of the Department of the Military of South Carolina (1862), 1034

Report of the Congressional Committee on the Operations of the Army of the Potomac (1863), 1034

Report of the Secretary of the Navy (1864), 232

Report on the Organization and Campaigns of the Army of the Potomac (McClellan), 571

Reports on battles and skirmishes: (C.S. Army) 365, 452, 1034; (U.S. Army) 41-42, 162, 290, 326, 338, 364, 377, 422, 428, 438, 466, 571, 806, 825

Republicanism; see Liberal Republicans

Resaca, Battle of, 195, 300, 578, 610, 1038; casualties in, 610; Federal strategy in, 518; see also Atlanta Campaign

Reserve Corps: (U.S. Army) 69, 696, 835

Resignations: (U.S. Army) 532, 552, 645, 660, 735, 953, 1000

"Résumé of Regiment Activities During 1863," 715

Rettew, Sallie, 12

Returns, miscellaneous: (C.S. Army) 174, 189, 272, 296, 409, 452, 724, 875, 956, 1021; (U.S. Army) 42, 146, 162, 282, 364, 405, 422, 428, 438, 466, 546, 571, 711, 806, 820, 825, 892, 896, 913, 923, 1037; (U.S. Navy) 784

The Reveille, 1009

Revenue Cutter Service (U.S.), 881

Revere, Edward Hutchinson Robbins, 766

Revere, Paul Joseph, 766

Revere family, 766

Reynolds, Alexander Welch, 174, 767

Reynolds, Charles, 768

Reynolds, John Fulton: correspondence of, 326, 913; memoir, 770; photograph of, 286

Reynolds, Joseph, 450

Reynolds, Thomas Caute, 411,

484, 769

Reynolds, William, 764, **770**

Rhett, Robert Barnwell: correspondence of, 1021; sketch of, 90

Rhode Island troops: (artillery) 1st Light Artillery, 604; (infantry) 10th, 8

Rhodes, Gussie, 397

Rhodes, James Ford, **771**

Rice, David A., **772**

Richardson, Charles H., **773**

Richardson, George W., 991

Richardson, Hamlet F., 35

Richmond, Lewis, **774**

Richmond, Ky., Battle of, 392, 631

Richmond, Va.: defenses of, 18, 143, 778; Confederate troops in, 220; political affairs in, 484, 596, 616; intelligence on military situation in, 242; prisoners of war in, 84, 351, 579, 697, 764, 979; public morale in, 484, 645; wartime life in, 214, 383, 472, 566, 596, 614, 778; business affairs in, 380; hospitals in, 383, 979; physicians in, 168; description of (1865), 330; map of, 461; sketch of, 168; Siege of, 214, 614; evacuation of, 734; capture and occupation of, 214, 365, 495, 515, 614, 616, 651, 732, 734; burning of, 287, 614; reaction to Lincoln assassination in, 651; miscellaneous events in, 356, 411; mentioned, 540, 554, 619, 644-45, 695, 697, 699, 716, 724, 769, 870, 872,

945, 950, 994, 1021

Richmond-Fayette Artillery, 870

Richmond Whig, 753

Rienzi: notes on, 672

Rifling machines, 749

Riggs, George W., 775

Riggs family, **775**

Rigolets, La.: naval skirmish at, 438

Riley, H., 944

Rinaldo (H.M.S.), 608

Ringgold, Cadwalader, 800

Rinson, Thomas, 864

Ripley, Josiah W., **776**

Ripley, Roswell Sabine, 66, 212

Rittenhouse, Benjamin F., **777**

Rivanna River, Va., 532

Rives, A. J., 532

Rives, Alfred S., 532, 778

Rives, William Cabell, **778**, 912, 1042

Roanoke (U.S.S.), 304, 606

Roanoke Island, N.C., Battle of, 264, 425, 523, 575, 586

Roanoke Island expedition; *see* Burnside, Ambrose Everett

Roanoke River, N.C.: naval engagement in, 785

Robert, Henry Martyn, **779**

Robert J. Lowry and Company, **780**

Roberts, Junius B., 781

Roberts family, **781**

Robertson, Beverly Holcombe, 488

Robinson, James S., 847

Robinson, Peter B., 570

Rock Island, Ill., 128

Rock Island Military Prison, 333

Rockbridge, Va., 507

Rockwell, Almon Ferdinand,

St. Louis Arsenal, 245
St. Louis District, 290
Salem Church, Va., Battle of, 1023
Salisbury, N.C.: Union prisoners of war at, 697; mentioned, 1033
Saloons: as refreshment and rest stations for new Federal recruits, 969
Saltpeter: manufacture of, 220
Sampson, Thomas, 524
San Antonio Express, 347
San Antonio, Tex., 418
San Francisco, Calif.: voyage to, 170; mentioned, 403
Sanborn, Fred G., **806**
Sanders, George Nicholas, **807-808**
Sanders, G. N. (Mrs.), 807
Sanders, William Price: generalship of, 495
Sands, Frank T., **809**
Sandy Valley Campaign, 338
Sanford, Joseph P., 673
Sangamon (U.S.S.), 788
Sanger, Donald Bridgman, **810**
Santee (U.S.S.), **811**
Saratoga (U.S.S.), 65
Sargent, D. M., 1042
Sargent, George Washington: murder of, 813
Sargent, John Osborne, **812**
Sargent, Winthrop, **813**
Sassacus (U.S.S.): engagement with C.S.S. *Albemarle*, 785
Saugus (U.S.S.), 183
Saul, T. S. F.: describes the death of Thomas J. Jackson, 475
Saunders, M. W.: photograph of, 365
Savage, John, **814**
Savannah, Ga., Siege of, 439, 518; prisoners of war at, 84, 764; mentioned, 951; *see also* Savannah Campaign
Savannah, Tenn., 981
Savannah Campaign, 15, 20, 68, 80, 114, 195, 300, 439, 441, 518, 552, 618, 768, 805, 851; *see also* Sherman, William T.
Saxton, Rufus, **815**; mentioned, 1010
Sayler's Creek, Va., Battle of, 112, 147, 500, 903
Sayre, Francis Bowes, **816**
Schaumburg, Orleana Christy (Mrs. Charles W.), **817**
Schaumburg family, **817**
Schele, Mr.: appointed special emissary to Germany, 443
Schenck, Robert C., 847
Schenectady, N.Y., 1050
Schlossen, Peter, **818**
Schnell, Joseph, **819**
Schofield, John McAllister, **820**; correspondence of, 850; service in the Carolinas Campaign, 365, 483, 709
Schonborn, Harry F., **821**
Schoonmaker, Cornelius Marius, **822**
Schoonmaker, Marius, **822**
Schouler, William, **823**
Schuckers, Jacob William, **824**
Schurz, Carl, **825**; correspondence of, 850, 895; photograph of, 541
Schuyler, Louisa Lee, **826**
Sciota (U.S.S.), 536
Scott, John White, **827**
Scott, Melvin, 147
Scott, T. Parker, 827

Scott, Thomas A., 387, 896

Scott, Winfield: correspondence and orders of, 21, 41, 81, 201, 413, 521, 626, 714, 847; relationship with General McClellan, 1042; generalship of, 40, 496; photograph of, 490; remarks on, 1042

Scranton, Pa., 959

Seabrook, Edward M., 828

Searcher, Victor, 829

Secesh (blockade runner): capture of, 763

Secession, 19, 58, 82, 125, 189, 251, 273, 283, 289, 350, 358, 366, 394, 414, 434, 562, 569, 612, 614, 714, 798, 808, 900-901, 912; ordinances of, 830

Secession conventions, 830

Secessionists: in the North, 200, 300, 833, 1011; in West Virginia, 305

Secessionville, S.C., Battle of, 422, 736, 903

Second Manassas, Battle of, 272, 825, 848, 944, 1023; observations on, 798; map of, 148; *see also* Second Manassas Campaign

Second Manassas Campaign, 42, 44, 99, 116, 249, 325, 335, 351, 417, 428-29, 442, 452, 465, 488, 699, 729, 735, 783, 859, 884, 894, 913, 938, 991, 1029, 1038

Secret Service (U.S. Army), 33; *see also* Allen, E. J.

Secretary of State: (C.S.) *see* Benjamin, Judah P.; (U.S.) *see* Seward, William H.

Secretary of the Navy: (C.S.) *see* Mallory, Stephen R.;

(U.S.) *see* Welles, Gideon

Secretary of the Treasury: (C.S.) *see* Trenholm, George A.; (U.S.) *see* Chase, Salmon P.

Secretary of War: (C.S.) *see* Benjamin, Judah P.; Randolph, George W.; Seddon, James A.; Walker, Leroy Pope; (U.S.) *see* Stanton, Edwin M.

Seddon, James A., 222, 372, 718, 778, 870

Sedgwick, John: photographs of, 286, 550; death of, 341

Sedgwick, Thomas D., 925

Seeley, Francis Webb, 831

Selfridge, Thomas Oliver, 832

Selfridge, Thomas Oliver, Jr., 832, 833

Selma, Ala.: Confederate arsenal at, 181; Wilson raid to, 352, 526, 1037; skirmish at, 636

Selma Campaign, 636

Selma plantation, Va., 465

Sellers, David Foote, 834

Semmes, Paul J.: sketch of, 758

Semmes, Raphael, 189, 192

"Semophoric Telegraphic Signals," 788

"The Seven Days Fighting About Richmond," 453

Seven Days' Battles, 659; *see also* individual battle names

Seven Pines, Va., Battle of, 23, 428, 488, 496

Seventh Louisiana Infantry of African Descent; *see* Black troops, 64th U.S. Colored Infantry

Sewall, Frederick Drummer,

835

Sewall, Joseph, 835

Seward, William Henry, 836; diplomatic instructions, 5, 662; correspondence of, 42, 132, 285, 290, 546, 606, 737, 739, 825, 913, 995; meetings with Secretary Chase, 169; remarks concerning, 1042; photographs of, 490, 541

Seymour, Horatio, 177, 546

Shackleford, W. C., 837

Shaffer, H. C., 25

Shafter, Harriet Grimes, 838

Shafter, William Rufus, 838-39

Shaler, Alexander, 840

Shaler, William, 841

Shaler's brigade, 840

Shankland, William F., 842

Sharpsburg, Battle of, 488, 578, 766, 859; see also Antietam, Battle of

Shaver, W. T., 843

Shaw, Lemuel, 844

Shaw, Mrs. Lemuel, 844

Shawmut (U.S.S.), 559

Shawsheen (U.S.S.): sketch of sinking of, 365

Shellenberger, John K., 845

Shenandoah (C.S.S.): purchase and service of, 222; list of officers on and prize vessels, 129

Shenandoah Valley: early troop movements and skirmishes in, 619; effects of war in, 383, 488, 786; mentioned, 532

Shenandoah Valley Campaigns: (1862) 20, 42, 99, 185, 229, 284, 325, 335, 351, 417, 419, 438, 452, 475, 618, 748, 790, 825, 913, 979;

(1863) 23, 25, 173, 272, 309, 415, 436, 500, 526, 542, 558, 588, 641, 681, 715, 846, 869, 903, 921; (1864) 25, 173

Shepherdstown, W. Va., 530

Shepley, George Foster: as military governor of New Orleans, 545; investigation of, 482

Sheridan, Edward, 694

Sheridan, Philip Henry, 846; correspondence of, 266, 413, 820; generalship of, 641; relieves Gen. G. K. Warren of command, 710; Shenandoah Valley Campaign of 1864, 25, 173; notes on Rienzi, 672

Sherman, Eleanor Boyle, 288

Sherman, Ellen Ewing, 850

Sherman, John, 847-48, 850

Sherman, Thomas West, 849; letter of, 913; generalship of, 306, 591, 736; Port Royal expedition, 182

Sherman, William Tecumseh, 850-51; personal and official correspondence, 21, 42, 89, 91, 148, 262, 287-88, 290, 377, 467, 714, 768, 820, 846, 913; messages received during the Vicksburg Campaign, 573; material concerning the Savannah and Carolinas Campaigns, 15, 68, 483, 497; meeting with Montgomery C. Meigs, 622; generalship of, 725; published remarks on, 266, 475; miscellaneous orders, reports, and correspondence of, 291, 768, 851,

951; photograph of, 599;
certificates commemorating
his role in the battles of
Shiloh and Atlanta, 850;
mentioned, 291, 565, 603,
733, 760, 1000, 1047
Sherman brigade, 847
Shields, J. E., 852
Shields, James, 937
Shiloh, Battle of, 113, 128,
215, 277, 318, 438, 534,
552, 759, 847, 904, 908;
certificate commemorating
Sherman's role in, 850;
poem commemorating, 865;
maps of, 865, 985; *see also*
Shiloh Campaign
Shiloh Campaign, 66, 94, 103,
105, 113, 274, 300, 317,
338, 367, 378, 392, 434,
473, 741, 759, 782, 804,
847, 850-51, 942
Shiner, Michael, 853
Ship Island, Miss.: camp life
and fortifications on, 17,
686; treatment of prisoners
of war on, 234, 716
Shipbuilding, 280, 316, 694,
822, 876, 927, 1006, 1050;
see also Ericsson, John;
Forbes, Robert B.
Shippen, Edward, 854
Shippen family, 854
Ships: contracts for, 271; purchase and repair of, 463,
606, 614, 635, 694, 796;
stations of, 1006; move-
ments of, 1051; notes on,
876; photographs of, 725;
see also Hospital ships;
Ironclads; Monitors; Picket
boats; Transports; Torpedo
boats; Warships; Flotillas;
Squadrons; and names of

individual vessels
Ships' logs; *see* Logbooks
Shock, William H., 166
Shockley, L. S., 630
Shortelle, James Edward, and
family, 855
Shorter, John Gill, 856
Shover, Felicia Lee, 402
Shreveport, La., 769
Shriver, S. C., 857
Shriver, William H., 857
Shufeldt, Robert Wilson, 858
Shuler, M., 859
Shumaker, L. M., 560
Sicard, Montgomery, 860
Sickles, Daniel Edgar, 861;
correspondence of, 78, 913;
photograph of, 286
"The Seige [*sic*] of Charleston,"
493
Sigel, Franz, 862; correspon-
dence of, 42, 326, 825, 895;
generalship of, 99; men-
tioned, 461, 532, 926
Signal communications: (C.S.
Army) 535; (U.S. Army)
573, 659, 660, 664; *see
also* U.S. Army Signal
Corps; U.S. Army Signal
Corps Museum. (U.S. Navy)
505, 535, 788, 858
"Signal Detachment," 661
Simmons, James Fowler, 863
Simpson, James H., 534
Simpson, Matthew, 864
Sisson, Lewis E., 865
Skelton, Maria, 202
Sketches; *see* Maps and
sketches
Slack, Hedgeman, 731
Slave hunters, 84
Slave traders, 168
Slavery: notes and observations
on, 84, 125, 168, 283, 370,

Sparta, Tenn.: map of, 820
Spaulding family, 886
Spears, Stewart, 887
Speed, James, 546
Spence, James, 608
Spencer family, 888
Sperry, Charles Stillman, 889
Spies: (Confederate) 314, 535,
    618, 716, 816, 827, 848,
    892, 1029; (Federal) 20,
    487, 724, 763, 816, 846,
    861
Spiria (U.S.S.), 52
*The Spirit of Washington: or
    McClellan's Vision* (1862),
    660
Spofford, Ainsworth Rand, 890
Spooner, John Coit, 891
Spotsylvania, Va., Battle of:
    map of, 820; *see also* Spot-
    sylvania Campaign
Spotsylvania Campaign, 25,
    112, 187, 231, 309,
    335, 341, 352, 386, 419,
    429, 436, 453, 500, 522-
    23, 526, 667, 699, 715, 746,
    758, 793, 806, 869, 899,
    938, 1023, 1037
Sprague, Homer Baxter, 892
Sprague, John T., 10
Sprague, John W., 847
Spring Hill, Battle of; *see*
    Thompson's Station,
    Tenn., Battle of
Squadrons: (U.S. Navy) 1006;
    see also North Atlantic
    Blockading Squadron;
    South Atlantic Blockading
    Squadron; Gulf Blockading
    Squadron; East Gulf Block-
    ading Squadron; West
    Gulf Blockading Squadron;
    European Squadron
Squier, Ephraim George, 893

Squires, Charles W., 894
Stafforce, John, 478
Stafford Courthouse, Va., 397
Stahel, Julius, 895; correspon-
    dence of, 825; generalship
    of, 727
Stanford University: copies
    of documents at, 416, 839
Stanley, David S., 845, 847
Stanton, Edwin McMasters,
    896; correspondence of,
    18, 21, 42, 262, 319, 326,
    416, 428, 438, 524, 546,
    571, 580, 582, 691, 714,
    820, 846, 913, 966; re-
    marks on the problems of
    blacks, 331; meetings with
    Salmon P. Chase, 169;
    role in Benjamin F.
    Butler's expedition against
    New Orleans, 1001;
    comments on, 695; notes
    on military appointments,
    416; asked to pardon a
    deserter, 704; photograph
    of, 541; mentioned, 291,
    622, 1047
Stanton, Elizabeth Cady, 897
Stanton, Henry B., 897
Starr, George H., 898
Starrville, Tex., 630
Stars and Bars; *see* Flags
The State (Columbia, S. C.),
    497
State Department: (Con-
    federate) orders and dis-
    patches from, 283;
    diplomatic agents, 189,
    506, 807, 954; relations
    with Great Britain, 77,
    608, 614, 642; negotiations
    with Mexico, 77, 614;
    secret service fund, 454;
    see also Benjamin, Judah

ship of, 1030
Stragglers, 768
Strait, N. A., **910**
Strang, Edward J., 437
Strategy: (C.S. Army) 143,
409, 452, 532, 789, 900,
1021; (U.S. Army) 34, 51,
169, 387, 438, 496, 847-48,
850, 861, 877, 896, 1051
Stribling, Cornelius K.:
correspondence of, 673,
796; information on, 739
Stribling, Robert M., 870
Strong, Alexander, 911
Strong, William E., 850
Strong, Hayward & Company,
911
Stuart, Alexander Hugh
Holmes, **912**
Stuart, David, 850
Stuart, George Hay, **913**
Stuart, James Ewell Brown,
914; correspondence
of, 657; service in the
Gettysburg Campaign, 4,
857; effect of death of,
116, 436; engraved
portrait of, 1034;
mentioned, 174, 202, 619
Stuart, Milton, 305
Stull, Lydia J., **915**
Sturgeon, Robert, **916**
Sturges Rifles, 33
Sturgis, Samuel Davis, **917**
Subsistence Department: (U.S.
Army) 72; *see also*
Quartermaster Depart-
ment; Commissary Depart-
ment
Substitutes: (C.S. Army) provi-
sions for, 303; exemption
certificate, 841;
(U.S. Army) exemption
certificate, 507

Suffolk, Va.: Siege of,
903; fortifications at,
717, 869; mentioned, 574
Sullivan, Jeremiah Cutler, 469
Sullivan, John T., **918**
Sumner, Charles: correspondence of, 21, 96, 366, 413,
546, 582, 825, 896, 913;
photograph of, 541
Sumner, Edwin Vose, 571
Sumter (C.S.S.), 189
Sumter (C.S. privateer), 293
Sunnyside, Miss., 488
Supplies: (U.S. Army) procurement, transportation,
distribution, and accounts
of, 24, 41, 94, 150, 331,
340, 351, 405, 414, 420,
422-23, 436-38, 442,
461, 480, 552, 605, 641,
667, 717, 766, 799, 804,
821, 847, 877, 888, 913,
979, 982, 993, 1004, 1037-
38, 1049; illegal trade in,
978; (U.S. Navy) 606, 811,
907; *see also* Quarter-
master Department; Com-
missary Department;
Subsistence Department
Surgeons; *see* Physicians
and surgeons
Surratt, John H.: trial
of, 307
Surratt, Mary Eugenia
Jenkins, **919**; execution of,
403
Susquehanna (U.S.S.), **920**
Susquehanna, Department of
the, 1061
Sutherland, Doctor, 781
Sutherland, Edwin W.:
planned defection of, 158
Sutlers: (U.S. Army) 618, 620,
671, 847, 878, 1009,

Tennessee Cavalry, 239;
(infantry) 5th, 563; 8th,
116; list of regiments, 409.
U.S. Army (infantry) 1st
East Tennessee Regiment,
155; 2d East Tennessee
Regiment, 155

Terry, Alfred Howe: correspondence of, 796, 820; Fort
Fisher expedition, 173,
187; service in the
Carolinas Campaign, 483

Texas (C.S.S.), 222

Texas: campaigns in, 702;
secession movement in,
414; popular support for
the war in, 566; blockade
of, 566; impact of the war
on, 566; military affairs
in, 953

Texas troops: (cavalry)
Waller's Cavalry Battalion,
931; (infantry) 21st Border
Regiment, 97; Hood's
Brigade, 265; promise
of additional regiments,
532

Thatcher, Henry Knox, 933

Thibodeaux, La.: Federal
troops at, 137

Thomas, Calvin H., 934

Thomas, George Henry, 467,
751, 820, 850, 870

Thomas, John E., 275

Thomas, Joseph Conable, 935

Thomas, Lorenzo, 21, 42, 428,
846-47, 850, 861, 936

Thomas, William, 813

Thomas Freeborn (U.S.S.), 59;
engagement at Aquia
Creek, Va., 796

Thompson, Ambrose W., 937

Thompson, Gilbert, 938

Thompson, Jacob, 189, 306,
789, 833

Thompson, M. Jeff, 460

Thompson, W., 47

Thompson's Station, Tenn.,
Battle of, 61

"Through the Carolinas to
Goldsboro, N.C.," 483

Thurman, J. B., 852

Tidball, John Caldwell, 939

Tidd, Charles Plummer, 940

Tilghman, Lloyd, 409

Tod, David, 580, 850, 941

Todd, Oliphant Monroe, 942

Tompkins, Aaron B., 943

Toner, Joseph Meredith, 944

Toombs, Robert Augustus, 945;
correspondence of, 134;
generalship of, 901

Topographic engineers;
see Engineers

Tories; *see* Unionists

Toronto, Canada, 587, 954

Torpedo boats, 365; construction of, 1050; salvage of,
933

Torpedoes, 163, 365, 514,
612, 796, 803; design
and manufacture of, 614,
1034, 1050; use of, 163,
365, 822; effectiveness of,
357; *see also* Arms and
ammunition

Torrey, Charles Oscar, 946

Totopotomoy Creek, Va.:
skirmishes along, 187, 526;
map of, 820

Totten, Joseph G., 779

Tower, Zealous B., 387

Townsend, Edward D., 820

Townsend, George Alfred, 947

Townsend, Martin I., 574

Tradewell, James D., 332

The Tragic Years (1960), 627

Training: (C.S. Army) 411, 472,

488, 614, 637, 1021; training camps established, 498; (U.S. Army) 20, 22, 97, 99, 106, 195, 203, 264, 300, 317, 351, 359-60, 423, 436, 442, 449, 455, 462, 478, 500, 519, 526, 553, 578-79, 618, 631, 640-41, 650, 654, 666, 685, 687, 703, 729, 741, 748, 758, 776, 782, 803-804, 825, 844, 869, 921, 938, 972, 976, 981, 1000, 1009, 1026, 1030, 1055; instruction manuals, 622, 781; (U.S. Navy) 407, 606, 635, 822, 1039

Traitors, 158

Trans-Mississippi Department, 222, 498, 759

Transports: names of Federal transports, 175; Confederate attacks on, 760; troop movements on, 4, 121, 844

Travel: in the war zone, 672, 724, 789-90, 1014

Treadway, Allen Towner, 948

Treasury Department: (C.S. Government) miscellaneous records and accounts, 55, 189, 276, 332, 392, 482, 719, 778, 951, 995; bonds, certificates, and related items, 88, 100, 110, 191, 196; loans and loan certificates, 88, 662, 918, 932; (U.S. Government) miscellaneous affairs of, 169, 228, 302, 577, 897

Treat, Samuel, 949

Tredway, Thomas Thweatt, 950

Trenholm, George Alfred, 951

Trent affair, 33, 75, 283, 608, 1028

Trescott, William H., 189

Trevilian Raid, 436, 869

Trevilian Station, Va.: engagement at, 599

Trigg, Connally F., 952

Trigg, E. C., 952

Trimble, Isaac Ridgeway, 272

Tripp, W. D., 478

Troop movements: (C.S. Army) 23, 27, 312, 358, 383, 402, 409, 411, 452, 472-73, 567, 594, 598, 612, 724, 769, 973, 991, 1034; (U.S. Army) 4, 24, 32, 67, 94, 106, 121, 169, 215, 249, 274, 289, 312, 340, 351-53, 387, 420, 426-27, 461, 500, 526, 552, 630, 685, 697, 761, 799, 804, 816, 825, 834, 844, 848, 857, 888, 978, 989, 1037, 1051

Trumbull, Lyman, 953; correspondence of, 546; photograph of, 541

Tucker, John C., 582

Tucker, John R., 872

Tucker, Nathaniel Beverley, 954

Tullahoma, Tenn., 870

Tullahoma Campaign, 105, 159, 605, 736, 846

Turner, Josiah, 598

Turner, Justin G., 955

Turner, Thomas, 306

Tupper, Captain, 510

Tyler, John, 956

Tyler, R., 717

Tyler, Robert O., 466

Tyler (U.S.S.), 784

Unadilla (U.S.S.), 158

Underwood, John Curtiss, 957

Underwriter (U.S.S.): Confederate attack on, 200

"Under the Blue Pennant, or Notes of a Naval Officer," 365

Unidentified manuscripts collection, 958

Union Defense Committee, 285

Union Defense Committee of New York, 461

Union League Defense Committee, 306

"Union Volunteer Refreshment Saloon," 969

Unionists (southern), 15, 20, 99, 155, 197, 260, 409, 566, 618, 714, 729, 734, 736, 886, 903, 946, 949, 957, 1000, 1027

U.S. Army—Commissary Department miscellany, 959; see also Commissary Department

U.S. Army—Engineers, 960; see also Engineers

U.S. Army—Judge Advocate General miscellany, 961

U.S. Army—Medical Department, 962; see also Medical care; Medical Department; Physicians and surgeons

U.S. Army: organization and administration of, 41, 99, 150, 264, 301, 309, 335, 391, 409, 438, 450, 461, 466, 480, 495, 500, 523, 552, 554, 571, 591, 603, 660, 666, 702, 715, 724, 727, 758, 804, 816, 820, 825, 847, 850, 866, 869, 937, 949, 972, 979, 990, 1022, 1030, 1049, 1055; miscellaneous correspondence, orders, records, and reports, 42, 146, 148, 162, 290, 311, 314, 318, 326, 338, 346, 371, 377, 422, 437-38, 466-67, 495, 546, 552, 571, 578, 591, 603, 661, 664, 673, 711, 729, 735, 805, 820, 835, 839, 895, 903, 910, 913, 921, 934, 1029, 1049, 1061; regulars, 4th U.S. Artillery, 831; 11th U.S. Infantry, 1016, 1049; plan for increasing manpower in, 660; crime and corruption in, 20, 103, 351, 699, 813, 1016; certificates of service in, 277, 504, 787; problems anticipated in the disbanding of volunteer units, 11

U.S. Army—Quartermaster's Department, 963-64; see also Quartermaster Department

U.S. Army—Signal Corps, 573, 675; organization and performance of, 659; list of signals used by, 664; instructions on the use of signals, 660; annual report for 1863, 659; miscellaneous photographs, 660; Signal Corps museum, 660; see also Fisher, B. F.

U.S. Army Register; see Official Army Register

U.S. Christian Commission, 80, 259, 363, 935, 965

U.S. Coast Survey, 1, 34

U.S. Congress: Representatives, 89, 114, 196, 208, 214-15, 237, 275, 348, 381, 401, 477, 590, 652, 861, 904, 992-93; Senators, 167, 251, 430, 482, 832, 847-48, 863-64, 953, 979, 1036; minutes of the Senate Finance Committee, 8

U.S. Constitution: notes on, 372

U.S. finance miscellany, **966**

U.S. Government: official papers and proclamations, 546; certificates of loyalty to, 260; postwar claims against, 587

U.S. Lincoln Sesquicentennial Commission, **967**

U.S. Marine Corps: training and service in, 874; plan to transfer the Corps to the U.S. Army, 750; mentioned, 156, 336

U.S. Marine Hospital, Key West, Fla., 451

U.S. Military Academy, West Point, N.Y.: life and discipline at, 14, 89

U.S. Naval Academy, 407; examination of candidates, 451; letters of Civil War cadets, 1039; photographs of (Annapolis), 505

U.S. Navy, **968**; official correspondence, letterbooks, orders, reports, and records, 183, 189, 232, 267, 313, 354, 373, 407, 505, 535, 606, 635, 673, 725, 734, 742, 750, 764, 784, 796, 822, 832; officers in, 739; southern officers in, 595; battles and battle reports, 784, 1006; medical records of sailors, 451; miscellaneous affairs, 461, 611, 737, 968; *see also* Naval Brigade; Squadrons; and names of individual officers, officials, ships, and battles

U.S. Navy Yard: Philadelphia, Pa., 451, 513; Portsmouth, Va., 1006; Washington, D.C., 654, 725, 853, 1003

U.S. Post Office: appointments and irregularities in, 603; special agents and operations in captured territory, 603

U.S. Sanitary Commission, **969**; official correspondence and papers of, 685; officials in, 256, 650, 685; nurses and agents of, 600, 915; miscellaneous affairs of, 74, 256, 476, 600, 602, 650, 653, 864, 935; conflict with the Army Medical Department, 578; mentioned, 246, 309, 458, 871

U.S. Work Projects Administration, **970**

United States Army and Navy Journal, 173

Upperville, Va.: skirmish at, 377

Usher, John Palmer, **971**

Vallandigham, Clement Laird, 571

Van Cise, Edwin A., **972**

Van Dorn, Earl, 66, 272, 613, **973**

Van Dyke, Richard Smith, **974**

Van Horn, Arthur, **975**

Van Horn, Mary, 975

Van Norman, C. R., **976**

Van Vliet, Stewart, 847

Vance, Robert B., **977**

Vance, Zebulon Baird, 118, 594, 755

Vanderbilt (U.S.S.), 687

Varnell's Station, Ga.: sketch of fortifications at, 888

Varney, John H., 671
Vermont: recruiting service in, 112
Vermont troops: (cavalry) 1st, 698; (infantry) 2d, 309, 773; 6th, 652; 16th, 1030; 17th, 1030
Veteran Reserve Corps, 69, 696
Veterans: (C.S. Army) treatment of, 721, 745, 888; (U.S. Army) aid for, 98; (U.S. Navy) disabled, 3
Vevay Reveille Enterprise (1946), 427
Vichy, France, 918
Vicksburg, Miss.: Farragut's bombardment of, 473, 686, 800, 874; Confederate garrison at, 464, 555; Siege of, 91, 187, 288, 292, 473, 539, 555, 868, 975; Battle of, 68; fall of, 53, 464, 555; treatment of noncombatants in, 63; suffering in, 53; *see also* Vicksburg Campaign
Vicksburg Campaign, 63, 68, 159, 175, 231, 264, 274, 279, 288, 290, 317, 355, 367, 378, 434, 455, 473, 491, 552, 573, 630, 702, 725, 734, 760, 804-805, 827, 850-51, 973, 1020-21, 1026, 1037; *see also* Yazoo Pass expedition; Champion's Hill, Battle of; Jackson, Battle of; Grant, Ulysses S.; Sherman, William T.
Vidalia, La.: treatment of noncombatants in, 63
Viele, Egbert, 524
Vienna, Austria, 444
Views, 1034
Villepigue, John B., 973
Vindicator (U.S.S.): design and performance of, 832
Virginia: ordinance of secession, 830; war governors, 118, 540, 721, 912; popular support for the war in, 537, 786, 956, 991; military affairs in, 420, 496, 612, 754, 1014; suppression of Loyalist sentiment in, 989; indifference toward invasion, 596; fortifications in, 535, 991, 1021; depredations in, 16, 43, 442, 465, 574, 619; impact of the war in, 85, 419; wartime travel in, 786; map of (incomplete), 1046; campaigns in, 35, 44, 78, 82, 102, 112, 135, 174, 184, 200, 202, 215, 226, 229, 296, 311, 371, 376, 426, 436, 438, 442, 452, 496, 500, 522, 551-52, 571, 576, 681, 717, 748, 806, 855, 869, 938, 943, 1014, 1022, 1046; *see also* names of individual battles and campaigns
Virginia, Union Department of, 41
Virginia, University of: copies of documents at, 444, 453
Virginia troops: C.S. Army (artillery) 20th Heavy Artillery, 147; (cavalry) 1st, 261; 2d, 837; 12th, 499, 923; 14th, 296; (infantry) 2d, 200; 8th, 532; 9th, 743; 21st, 827; 24th, 567, 614; 33d, 859; 40th, 995; 58th, 588; morale among, 956. U.S. Army (infantry) 1st Loyal Eastern Virginia Volunteers, 903
Vliet, Stewart Van, 571

Volunteers; *see* individual State troops
Voorhees, Daniel W., 571

Wabash (U.S.S.), 92, 561, 905, 927
Wachusett (U.S.S.), 65, 788
Waddel, John Newton, 978
Wade, Benjamin Franklin, 167, 979, 980
Wade, Henry, 979
Wade, James F., 979
Wadsworth, Craig W., 980
Wadsworth, James, 980
Wadsworth, James Samuel, 980, 1002
Wadsworth, James W., 980
Wagoners, 772
Walke, Henry, 565
Walker, Alexander, 234
Walker, Andrew J., 981
Walker, C. P., 208
Walker, Edward T., 567
Walker, Francis, 41
Walker, H. P., 718
Walker, James, 982
Walker, James A., 872
Walker, Leroy Pope: correspondence of, 66, 82, 189, 718, 955; as C.S. Secretary of War, 596
Walker, Nicholas, 983
Walker, Robert John, 984
Walker, William, 981
Walker, William S., 211
Wallace, Lewis, 546, 985
Wallach, Richard, 986
Waller, Edward, 931
Walthall, Edward C., 105, 708
Walton, John T., 987
Wanamaker, Winfield S., 988
War correspondents, 78, 140, 610, 761-62, 850, 1002
War Department: (C.S.

Government) official correspondence and records, 189, 411, 753, 1021; (U.S. Government) official correspondence and reports, 896, 1037; orders and circulars, 768; annual report of the Secretary of War, 896; administration of, 141
"War Statistics," 31
Ward, Charles, 990
Ward, James H., 59
Ward, James Pegram, 991
Ward, James Thomas, 989
Ward, John, 990
Ward, William N., 991
Ward, William N., Jr., 991
Ward, William Thomas, 103
Ward family of Richmond County, Va., **991**
Waring, George E., 34
Waring, George S., 685
Warm Springs, Ga.: refugees at, 672
Warren, Gouverneur Kemble: correspondence of, 913, 998; military record of, 710; photographs of, 739, 938
Warren County, Miss.: report on destitute families in, 591
Warrenton, Miss., 536
Warrenton, Va., 572
Warships: life on, 170, 592; *see also* names of individual vessels
Washburn, Cadwallader Colden, 850, 870
Washburn, Israel, **992**
Washburne, Elihu Benjamin, 140, 546, **993**
Washington, J. E. McPherson: life of, 560
Washington, John A., 994
Washington, Lawrence, 994

West, Robert M., 854
West, Military Division of
the (C.S. Army), 789
West Gulf Blockading
Squadron, 13, 30, 293,
407; *see also* Blockade
West India Squadron, 832,
1028; *see also* Blockade
West Liberty, Ky.: skirmish at,
215
West Tennessee, Military
District of, 364
West Virginia: campaigns in,
44, 175, 200, 296, 335,
519, 521-22, 729, 925, 975,
1014, 1060; war governor
in, 721; Union sentiment
in, 348; secessionists in,
305
Western Department (C.S.
Army), 409
Western Sanitary Commission,
80
Western Sanitary Fair,
Cincinnati, Ohio, 969
Westervelt, H. C., **1011**
West Virginia troops: U.S.
Army (cavalry), 7th, 731
Wetmore, Henry S., 254
Whaley, Daniel, **1012**
Wharton, John A., 1021
Wharton, T. J., 708
What We Did at Gettysburg
(1863), 826
Wheeler, Charles Scully, 1014
Wheeler, Henry, **1013**
Wheeler, John Hill, **1014**
Wheeler, Joseph, 789
Wheeler, Woodbury, 1014
Wheeling, W. Va.: Confederate
sympathizers at, 795;
mentioned, 329, 348, 721
Whelan, William, 3
Wherry, William M., 820

Whipple, Amiel Weeks: photo-
graph of, 913
Whipple, Henry B., 571
White, B. F., **1015**
White, John Chester, **1016**,
1054
White, Julius, 913
White Hall, N.C.: skirmish
near, 1055
White House Landing, Va.,
700
White Oak Swamp, Battle of,
428, 589, 1023; *see also*
Peninsular Campaign
White River, Ark.: Federal
expedition on, 804
White River Station, Ark.:
Federal camp at, 725
Whiteley, L. A., 78
Whitesides, Edward G., 845
Whiting, Jasper S., 489, **1017**
Whiting, William, 366
Whiting, William D., 373
Whiting, William Henry, **1018**
Whitman, George W., 1019
Whitman, Walt, 119, **1019**
Whitney, D. H., 864
Whitten, John, **1020**
Whittier, Charles W., 445
"Who Began the War, and
What Was the Cause of
It?" 411
Wickham, Williams C., 912
Wigfall, F. Halsey, 1021
Wigfall, Louis Trezevant, 265,
532, 730, **1021**
Wigfall, Charlotte, 1021
Wight, Frederick H., **1022**
Wilcox, Cadmus Marcellus,
1023; report on the Battle
of Williamsburg, 870
Wilcox, John Alexander: corre-
spondence of, 1023; death
of, 250

documents at, 1019

Yancey, William L., 189

Yankee (U.S.S.), 254

Yazoo Pass expedition, 455, 491, 539, 565, 630, 725, 760, 832

Yazoo River: list of Confederate warships on, 734

Yellow fever: plan for infecting Federal troops with, 719; *see also* Disease

Yoder, Jacob, 1063

Yoder, Moses F., 1063

Yoder, Noah W., 1063

Yoder, Samuel S., 1063

York River, Va.: skirmishes along, 842

Yorktown, Va.: report on General Keyes' command at, 921; mentioned, 397

Yorktown, Va., Siege of, 106, 184, 359, 404, 496, 578; map of, 162; photograph of batteries at, 938

Young, John Russell, 1064

Zollicoffer, Felix Kirk, 996

Zook, Samuel K.: photograph of, 286

Zouaves de Afrique; *see* Collis' Independent Company